Toeus

Doug Keenan

Financial Futures: Practical Applications For Financial Institutions

Carroll R. Melton Ph.D.
and
Terry Vance Pukula

Reston Publishing Company, Inc.
A Prentice-Hall Company
Reston, VA

Library of Congress Cataloging in Publication Data
Melton, Carroll, R.
      Financial futures.
      1. Hedging (Finance)   I. Pukula, Terry Vance.
II. Title.
HG6024.A3M44   1984   332.64 '4   84-1971
ISBN 0-8359-2019-4

Comtrend® is a registered trademark of ADP-Comtrend.

IBM PC® is a registered trademark of International Business Machines Corp.

Apple® is a registered trademark of Apple Computer, Inc.

TABLE OF CONTENTS

PREFACE

We wrote this book to fill a vacuum in the available published material on financial futures. In the course of several years of speaking with thousands of bankers and savings and loan executives, both in their offices and at seminars, conferences and conventions, we repeatedly encountered three comments: all of the material published on hedging was too simple; it showed only "perfect" hedges; and it was not related well to actual banking practice. Nearly everyone we spoke with about financial futures hedging wanted to know how to develop a hedging strategy to fit his operation and how to implement such a strategy once it was developed. Many of these executives had read several books on futures but still had not found out what they wanted to know. We hope that this book will fill the need for a practical guide to the futures market for banks and savings and loan associations.

Our emphasis is on the practical applications of financial futures. We have tried to steer the banker-reader through a complex market without getting bogged down in institutional detail. Theoretical explanations of how the market "should" work and why it works the way it does are relegated to academics, who never have real money on the line. We explain the jargon of the market as we go along; there is a lot of jargon, but operating in the futures market is impossible without it. We also have added a dash of humor here and there to make the book more readable.

We would like to express appreciation to our associate, Joyce Sarnotsky-Barnett, for many helpful comments before, during, and after the writing.

Carroll R. Melton, Ph.D.
Terry Vance Pukula

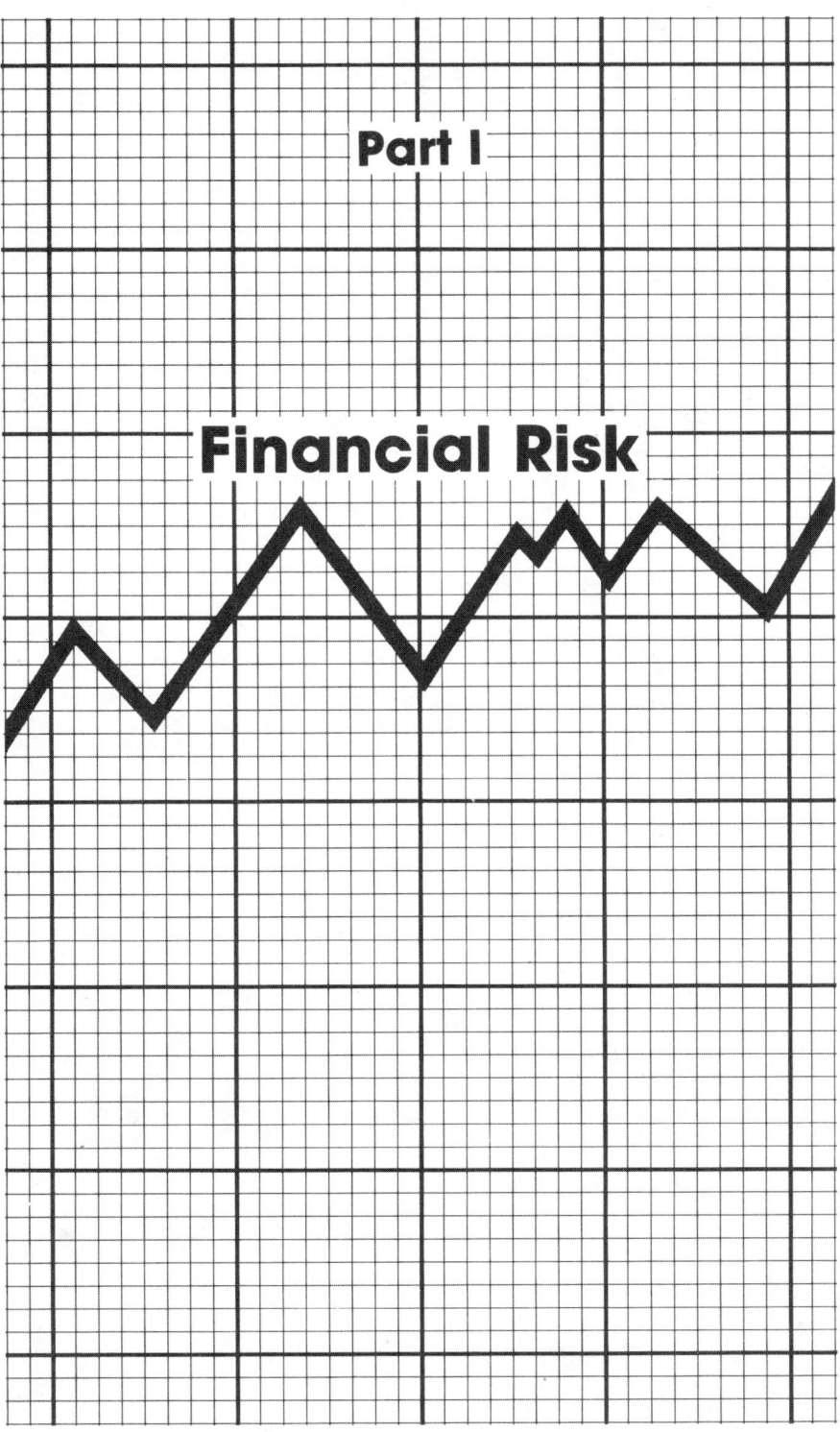

Part I

Financial Risk

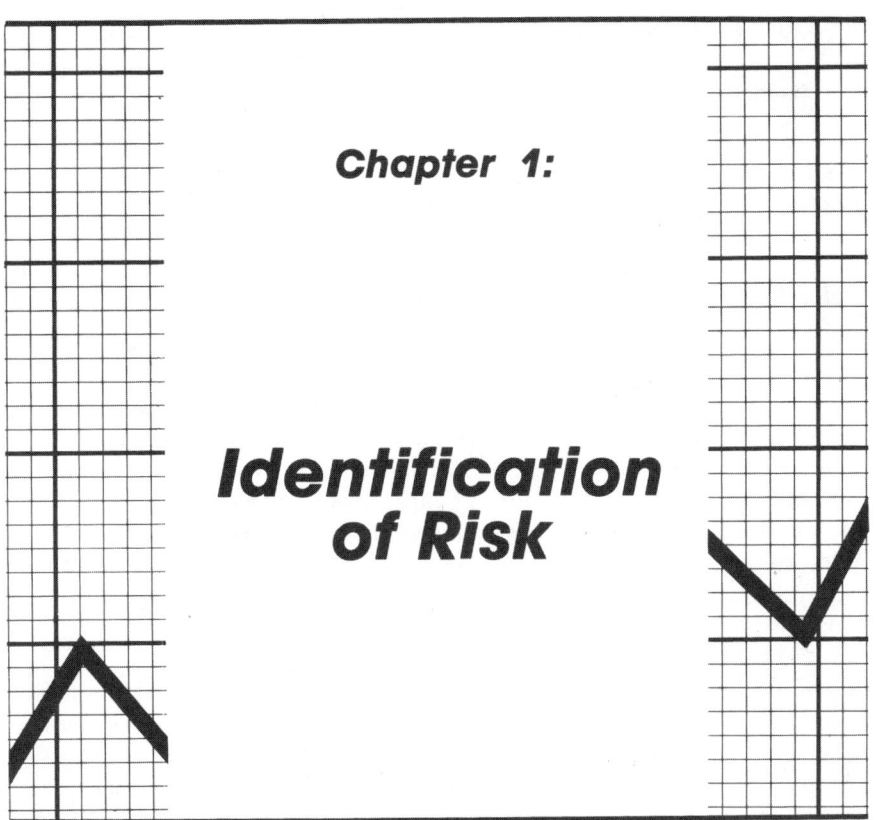

Chapter 1:

Identification of Risk

THE DICTIONARY defines risk as the chance of injury, damage or loss. Since no one likes injuries, damages or losses, people try to eliminate risk. For the last two or three hundred years the most popular way to do so has been to buy insurance. It must be noted that buying insurance does not eliminate the risk—insurance is paying someone else to assume the risk. While all risks can be insured in the conventional sense, the cost may be enormous. An adage in the insurance business is that there are no unacceptable risks; there are inappropriate premiums.

TYPES OF RISKS

Since this book is about how to control the risk faced by financial institutions, it seems like a good idea to define further just what risks we are talking about. For an institution such as a bank or savings association there are four specific types of risk:

1. General business risk
2. Default risk
3. Price risk
4. Liquidity risk

Our concentration is on the latter two types of risk. It may be useful to explore briefly the first two types in order to illustrate the differences among all four.

GENERAL BUSINESS RISK

Some risks faced by financial institutions are no different from the risks faced by any other business. There is always a chance of a natural disaster such as a flood, tornado, or earthquake, which can destroy a bank just as easily as a restaurant. (Architects beware: making a bank look as solid as the Rock of Gibraltar doesn't necessarily make it earthquake proof.) These kinds of risk generally can be insured with casualty insurers at a moderate cost. Other types of risk such as theft, embezzlement, or fraud can also be insured easily.

There are, however, some types of general business risk that cannot be insured easily or cheaply. Even Lloyd's of London is not likely to write a policy insuring a bank or a savings association or a department store against a lack of customers. They might, but it probably would be cheaper to hire the customers than to pay the premium on the policy. The popular wisdom on this subject is that the firm's capital is the insurance against this risk; not a cheerful thought but true nevertheless.

So much for risk type number one. The story improves as we go down the list.

DEFAULT RISK (CREDIT RISK)

From a theoretical point of view default risk is not very interesting. But since theorists don't run financial institutions, we will spend a moment on this important topic. Default risk is easy to define—the borrower may not pay up on time or ever—but difficult to measure and sometimes difficult to insure. There is no absolute measurement of default risk. The accepted methodology is to measure relative default risk. The reference standard against which all default risk is judged in the United States (and probably the world) is the zero default risk on U. S. government debt. (This is an interesting anomaly of modern economies—the government issues debt payable in money, and the government defines money and has a monopoly on its creation. All in all it's the ultimate "sweetheart" deal.)

In some instances default risk can be insured in the conventional way. The most common example is mortgage insurance in which the borrower buys an insurance policy that protects the lender. On other types of loans this insurance is not generally available, in which case the lender relies on underwriting experience. The standard control procedure is simply to refuse to make loans when the borrowers do not measure up.

For the investor holding publicly traded securities there is no insurance against default either. The bond rating agencies do undertake to gauge the likelihood of default by a complicated lettering scale, and they have high prestige in the financial community. Bond ratings are just that, though—ratings. None of the default risk is eliminated by a particular rating. Investors are simply notified as to the rater's best judgment of the relative degree of risk after which investors must make their own decisions.

Using the financial futures market may tend to decrease credit risk. Rapidly rising interest rates may increase the likelihood of default by a borrower. If the lender hedges his interest rate risk, increases in market rates need not be reflected in the rate paid by the borrower, thereby lowering the possibility of default.

PRICE RISK

Price or capital value risk accompanies any fixed-rate debt security. If interest rates change, the capital value of the security changes in order to reflect the current yield available in the marketplace. The amount of the price change depends on how much interest rates change and on the remaining term to maturity of the security. For a perpetual debt instrument with no maturity date, the change in price will fully reflect the change in rate. A $1000 face value perpetual bond with a coupon of 10 percent pays $100 interest each year. If rates increase to 12 percent the value of this bond declines to $833; interest rates have risen 20 percent and bond prices have declined 16.7 percent. If rates fall to 8 percent the bond is worth $1250; rates fell 20 percent and bond prices rose 25 percent. The asymmetrical relationship between changes in capital value and interest rates raises some interesting points about the degree of price risk on a portfolio of securities. We will come back to this point in detail in later chapters.

This relationship becomes more asymmetrical as the maturity of the debt decreases from infinity. The shorter the maturity of an issue the smaller will be the effect of a given interest rate change on the capital value of the security. For example, a 10 percent Treasury note with a maturity of one year will decline in value by only $20 per $1000 of face value if interest rates climb to 12 percent. If rates fall to eight percent, the price of the note will increase by $24 per $1000 of face value. Thus for a one year note a 20 percent increase in rates causes a two percent decline in value, and a 20 percent drop in rates causes a 2.4 percent increase in price.

As Figure 1.1 illustrates, the relationship between interest rate changes and price changes is amplified as the maturity of the security approaches infinity. Obviously the price risk on long-term debt is substantially higher than it is on short-term debt. Since this book is about how to manage risk, it is tempting to conclude that the easiest way to do so is to hold only short-term securities. Tempting as that is, there are more efficient ways to manage price risk than by holding strictly short-term portfolios.

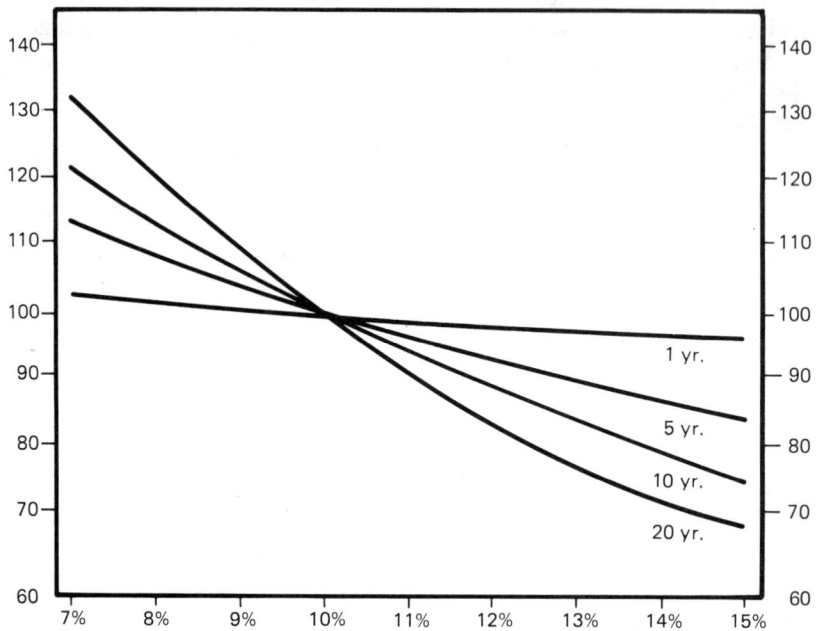

Figure 1.1. Yield-Price-Maturity Relationships on Debt Instruments With a 10 Percent Coupon

LIQUIDITY RISK

The primary liquidity risk for a depository financial institution is that it will not be able to raise cash to meet withdrawals. On an emergency basis, such as existed in the 1930s, this problem is solved by the willingness of the Federal Reserve System to go to almost any lengths, including chartering airplanes, to supply cash whenever and wherever needed to avoid a panic run on a bank or savings and loan association.

A far more serious liquidity risk now is that retail time deposits, which constitute a substantial source of funds to banks and savings associations, will dry up. If the liquidity crunches of 1966 and 1969 did not prove that depositors would switch their savings away from depository institutions if interest rates rose, the astronomical growth of money market funds from 1979 to 1982 certainly did.

For an institution facing liquidity risk there are three possible responses: (1) attempt to prevent the withdrawal; (2) find replacement funds; (3) sell assets to raise cash. None is easy and none has particularly favorable consequences for the institution.

Attempting to prevent withdrawals generally has taken the form of "early withdrawal" interest penalties on certificates of deposit. Interest penalties that have been allowed by regulation have proven to be inadequate at discouraging early redemption since the depositor has never been forced to bear any price risk on his fixed-rate fixed-term security. Principal remains intact and the interest rate is reduced upon redemption. At various times in the past the penalty has been so miniscule that even a small rise in open market rates has made it profitable to cash in CDs and search for higher yields.

Finding replacement funds for one certificate of deposit redeemed early is not the major problem. Finding replacement funds for large numbers of redemptions is a serious problem that has bankrupted more than one institution. It is generally acknowledged that wholesale withdrawals can be replaced easily only with wholesale sources of new funds: large CDs ($100,000 +), commercial paper, Eurodollars, or outright borrowing from some other financial institution. The unpleasant aspect of all these sources is that they are almost always more expensive than the funds that were withdrawn.

The third response to withdrawals is to sell assets to raise cash. This shrinks the size of the institution and reduces its leverage ratio. This is generally resisted by the management of the institution. If rates have risen, the value of most of the institution's assets will have declined as well. In this case, the effect is magnified: the institution shrinks and may experience a loss on the sale of assets, unless it has hedged its fixed-rate assets. In the extreme case, or even less than extreme case, liquidity risk and price risk compound each other. It seems that interest rates are both the sine qua non and the bane of a banker's existence.

_____ ASSET RISK

The primary risks associated with the majority of assets held by banks and savings associations are default risk and credit risk. At the risk of redundancy, financial futures hedging may reduce the likelihood of default risk but will not control it directly. Price risk can be directly controlled by using the futures market. In fact, controlling price or capital value risk is a primary reason for financial institutions to be involved in the futures market. The futures market may also be used for yield enhancement as well as protecting asset values.

Unlike futures contracts, bank assets are not homogeneous products and do not, therefore, have identical types or degrees of capital value risk associated with them. It should be clear from the previous section that the degree of capital value risk varies directly with the maturity of the asset—the longer the maturity, the higher the degree of price change as interest rates change. In the good old days of stable interest rates, long-term bonds were thought to be an excellent investment. They paid a higher return over a much longer period and provided secure incomes for widows, orphans, and pensioners. The price-rate relationship was still the same, only in those days interest rates didn't change by very much, very often.

It is worth noting that the good old days were not 30 years ago. In 1977 the rate on 10-year Treasury bonds varied between 7.21 percent and 7.69 percent, less than one-half percent variation in an entire year. By 1981 rates were changing by more than that amount in one week! It is also worth noting that the interest rates on securities all across the maturity spectrum tended to move in the same direction at about the same time by about the same amount. That is no longer true either. It is not unusual now for Treasury bill rates to fall while bond rates increase and vice versa. In order to control asset risk it is first necessary to get a grip on the magnitude of the risk on particular assets since they definitely do differ. The next three sections of the chapter explore the degree of price risk on particular assets held by banks and savings associations.

COMMERCIAL LOANS

The majority of commercial loans made by banks are tied to the "prime" rate. The prime rate generally reflects the bank's cost of raising funds. If the prime rate is changed, the rate on most outstanding business loans is changed accordingly. If the rate on outstanding loans is not increased

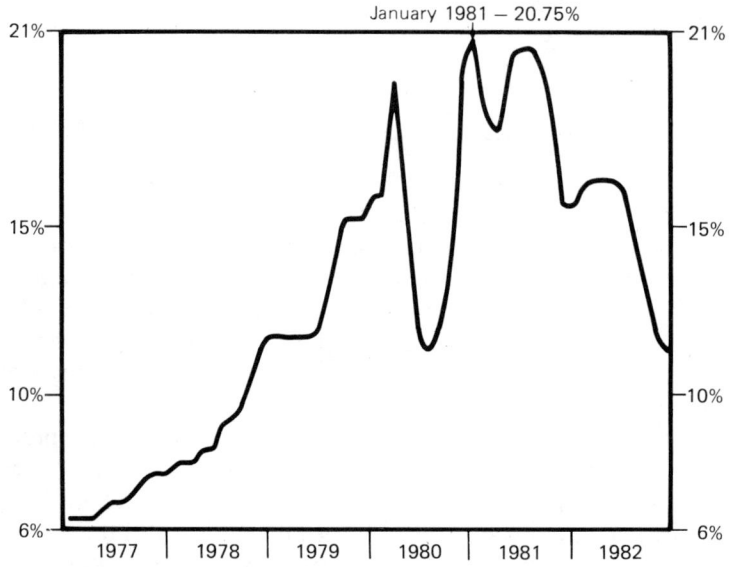

Figure 1.2 Prime Rate, 1977–82
Source: Board of Governors of the Federal Reserve System.

when prime increases, perhaps to avoid bankrupting the borrower who might then default, bank earnings may decline. In a period when prime doesn't change very often or by very much, this is not a serious problem. In short, if rates are stable the risk to the bank is at a minimum.

As the accompanying Figure 1.2 shows, the prime rate has not been at all stable from the mid-1970s onward. In 1976 the prime rate changed only eight times; in 1977 only six changes occurred. In both 1978 and 1979 there were 15 changes in the prime rate. As the chart shows, 1980 was the roller coaster year for bank prime. There were 39 changes in the rate throughout the year. Only slightly less hectic was 1981, when the rate changed 26 times.

The most unfortunate aspect of this extreme volatility is that it only seems to occur when interest rates are at a very high level. In 1977 and 1978 when the prime rate changed only eight times, the average for both years was 6.8 percent and varied only in the range of 6.25 percent and 7.75 percent. In 1980 prime averaged 15.3 percent but varied in the range of 11.0 percent to 21.5 percent. At interest rates this high the default risk of the borrower is higher; price risk of the loan is higher when the rate volatility is this large. Controlling this risk can be difficult to be sure, but not controlling it can be fatal.

RESIDENTIAL MORTGAGES

Residential mortgages were once thought to be one of the best possible assets to hold, both by banks and by savings associations. The rate on mortgage loans was traditionally higher than the long-term bond rate; the loan was secured by real estate appraised at 25 percent or even 100 percent higher than the loan amount; the increased default risk on any high ratio loans could be insured privately or guaranteed by the government; the loan amortized at a steady known rate; and the "pride of ownership" gave the borrower the incentive to maintain and even upgrade the collateral. Even though mortgages had stated maturities that placed them in the long-term segment of the capital market, the high mobility of Americans pushed the effective holding period of mortgages down to about six years as more people moved, sold the house, and prepaid the mortgage.

How did such a wonderful asset turn into the gigantic albatross around the neck of so many savings associations by 1980? Undoubtedly, the steady rise in interest rates that began in 1977 is the answer. Beginning in April of that year the rate on conventional residential mortgages began an upward climb that continued through November 1981. As Figure 1.3 shows, the mortgage interest rate began its rise from 8.9 percent and increased steadily throughout the end of 1981, standing at 15.9 percent by the end of the year. Simultaneously, the rapid turnover of mortgages ground to a halt, perhaps because of the sharp increase in rates. Many mortgagors, whenever possible, cancelled plans to move in order to hold onto their existing mortgages at eight percent or nine percent, thinking that they would never have the opportunity to obtain credit at that price again. Holders of mortgages watched the market value of their portfolios decline with every uptick in rates. While the futures market for Government National Mortgage Association (GNMA) certificates held the solution to the problem of those sinking fixed-rate loans, no legal authority existed for using the futures market as a life preserver.

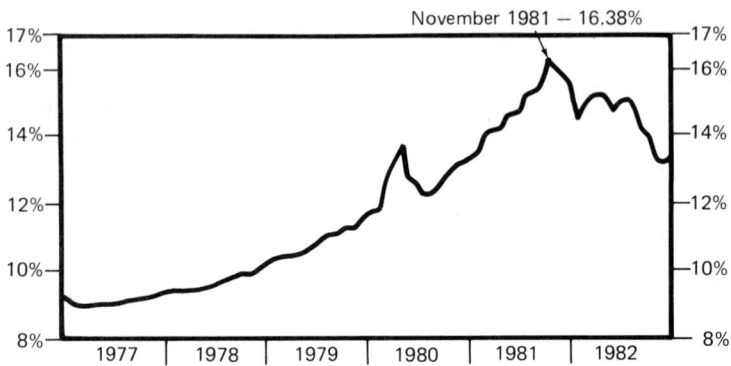

Figure 1.3 Mortgage Rate, 1977–82
Source: Federal Home Loan Bank Board

Table 1.1 indicates the magnitude of the problem faced by the holder of a 30-year mortgage of $50,000 at nine percent. The lender who had made such a loan at the beginning of 1977 would have received repayments of $715 by the end of 1978, but the market value of the loan would have declined by $3978, with no way to prevent it.

TABLE 1.1
Market Value of a 30-year Mortgage of $50,000 at 9%

Market Rate	Market Value
9%	$50,000
10	45,884
11	42,245
12	39,112
13	36,369
14	33,954
15	31,817
16	29,917
17	28,219

The much heralded variable rate loan in effect at the time would have held its market value only through the end of 1978—beyond that point market rate increases outpaced the authority to hike the mortgage rate. By the beginning of 1980 when the market rate was 11.87 percent, the rate on the outstanding variable rate mortgage could have been 10.5 percent, leaving a decline in market value of $6667. This is better than the $9880 loss that would have occurred on a similar fixed-rate loan, but it is still nothing to cheer about.

Clearly, the ability to change the rate on outstanding mortgages results in an unambiguous reduction in price risk on those assets. It does not, however, eliminate the risk. The currently allowable adjustable rate mortgage is not perfect either. While it can be made to adjust to market rates every month, doing so raises the strong possibility of substituting increased credit risk for the reduction in price risk. Prudent use of the financial futures market does not make that same substitution.

INVESTMENT SECURITIES

If the variation in mortgage rates can be considered erratic, the variation in Treasury rates over the five years 1977–1981 must be called chaotic. From the beginning of 1977 through the end of 1981 the rate on 91-day

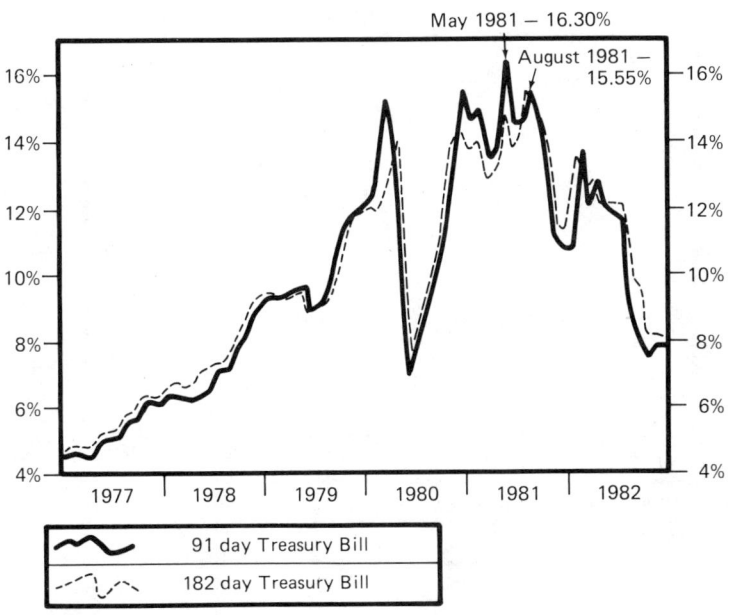

Figure 1.4 Rates on both 91-day and 182-day U. S. Treasury bills
Source: Board of Governors of the Federal Reserve System

Treasury bills varied between 4.6 percent and 16.3 percent; 182-day bills between 4.8 percent and 15.5 percent; three-year notes between 6.2 percent and 16.2 percent; 10-year notes between 7.2 percent and 15.3 percent.

More important than the extreme range of rates is their volatility. Figure 1.4 shows the pattern of rates on 91-day and 182-day Treasury bills. In the 60-month period shown here, although the rate trend was upward most of the time, rates changed direction 14 times in the case of 91-day bills and 22 times in the case of 182-day bills! The direction of rate changes on three-year notes reversed 19 times; on 10-year notes, 20 times. (See Figure 1.5.)

Any financial institution holding an investment portfolio composed of a variety of Treasury securities would have experienced wide swings in the value of that portfolio during those five years.

While all securities and loans are held in order to add income, the primary reason that banks and savings associations hold short-term, easily marketable Treasury securities is to maintain a liquidity reserve position. Wide swings in the value of such a reserve fund reduce its usefulness. If the

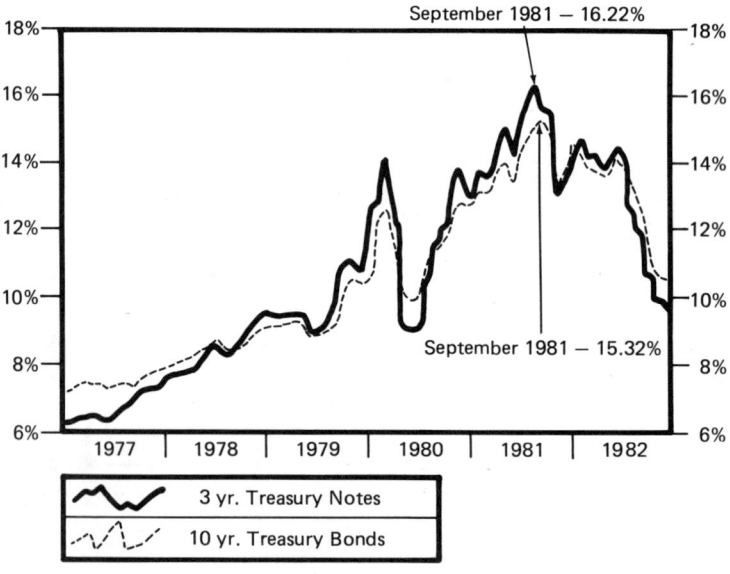

Figure 1.5 Rates on both three-year U. S. Treasury notes and 10-year U. S. Treasury bonds

Source: Board of Governors of the Federal Reserve System

need arises to liquidate this portfolio, and its value has declined due to interest rate increases, it will not adequately provide the liquidity reserve desired or perhaps required by law or regulation.

Fluctuation in the value of these securities is beyond the control of any individual institution. However, controlling the *impact* of these fluctuations is not beyond the institution's capability.

LIABILITY RISKS

The primary risk that accompanies the liabilities of the insured depository financial institutions is liquidity risk. Price risk in the conventional sense of fluctuating capital value does not occur since the principal of deposit liabilities is not allowed to fluctuate with market rates. This does not mean that market interest rates have no effect on the liquidity risk of liabilities; they most assuredly do.

In the first part of the chapter we defined liquidity risk as the chance that a deposit will be withdrawn prior to maturity or will not be renewed when it matures. Even though this risk differs for every single account, the risk of the entire liability portfolio is somewhat predictable. It is not reasonable to assume that withdrawals will occur for no reason at all. For consumer oriented institutions, some withdrawals may be totally predictable such as the holiday season in December and the tax season in April. Other withdrawals may be traced to unique individual circumstances of the depositor such as death, unemployment or illness. Not all institutions are affected by this seasonality of deposit flows. Withdrawals which are seasonal can be anticipated and a controlled response can be planned. Random withdrawals cannot be anticipated or controlled by any particular management strategy.

What is of interest then are large scale withdrawals from savings accounts and redemption of certificates of deposit. The most immediately obvious explanation is that higher yields are available elsewhere. This has probably always been true. The determining factors have been that in the past few years higher yields have been available without the depositor having to assume higher default risk or meet higher minimum balance requirements. To some extent Treasury securities put the ball in motion, but the money market funds have made the big score. Their high yields, instant liquidity, and high grade investments proved to be unstoppable.

When an institution is faced with this problem, the response choices are to find replacement deposits, borrow to meet withdrawals, or sell assets. All three choices usually result in lower profits for the institution. There is also the choice of doing nothing and becoming insolvent.

Perhaps the most demoralizing aspect of this process is if the replacement funds come from the institution's own depositors. Account switching from passbook and lower cost certificates of deposit to high-cost money market certificates and small saver certificates has had a greater impact on the cost of funds for depository institutions than have overall higher rates of interest. Consider, for example, the first money market certificates (MMC). They were issued at 7.45 percent in June 1978. When they matured in December 1978, if they had been renewed at the then-current rate of 9.65 percent, the cost of those funds would have increased by 220 basis points due to the rise in rates. However, if a passbook account which paid 5.25 percent had been shifted to an MMC at that time, the cost of those funds would have jumped by 440 basis points, or twice as much. This situation continued almost uninterrupted from 1978 through 1983 as the proliferation of new accounts cannibalized passbook savings accounts.

Borrowing to cover withdrawals may be a short-term solution, but the very high cost is a decided drawback against its use as a permanent one. This can be seen clearly from Figure 1.6 which charts the rate on passbook accounts and the federal funds rate, taken as the best indicator of short-term borrowing costs for financial institutions. From mid–1977 onward the cost of borrowing vastly exceeded the cost of deposits that could have or would have been easily withdrawn. Other easily accesible sources of borrowed funds, such as Federal Reserve Bank discounts or Federal Home Loan Bank ad-

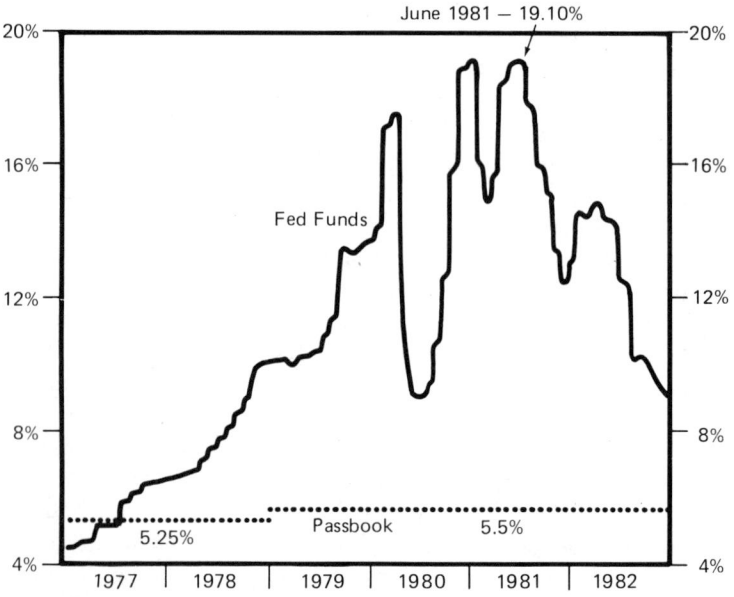

Figure 1.6 Rate on Fed Funds and Passbook Rate, 1977–82
Source: Board of Governors of the Federal Reserve System

vances, while not shown on the chart, would have been equally as expensive over this period.

Selling assets to raise cash is a much more viable option for banks than for savings associations. It is considerably easier to sell short-term government securities or commercial loans tied to a floating prime rate than to sell long-term fixed-rate mortgages at par. In either case it can take time and involve some expense which may even exceed the cost of other alternatives.

Thus, we come full circle to finding replacement funds, since it is the most viable long-run solution to large scale withdrawals and the one most frequently used. Borrowing is normally a very short-run stopgap measure, while selling assets to cover withdrawals is essentially a last step. Finding replacement deposits may be difficult or easy, but in either case it is sure to be expensive. Moreover, a change in the composition of its deposit base, whether voluntarily or involuntarily induced, exposes the institution to a different liability risk profile.

While that may seem to be a radical thought, it is easily understandable by looking behind the deposit to the deposit holder. The typical event is a withdrawal of a passbook account or small certificate of deposit and its replacement by a money market certificate or a jumbo CD. It is possible that the same depositor will be involved in the swap, but it is by no means universally true. Thus, the investment strategy and interest rate sensitivity of the new deposit holder is substituted for that of the former deposit holder. This changes the institution's risk exposure in the following ways.

The holders of passbooks and small CDs are almost exclusively individuals or households whose motive for holding savings accounts traditionally has been liquidity—savings for a rainy day or for an emergency. Admittedly, in recent years many depositors have become increasingly yield sensitive, but the liquidity aspect still appears to be uppermost—witness the check writing features nearly universal among money market funds.

Holders of jumbo CDs, while not insensitive to liquidity, are generally more sophisticated investors, even if they are individuals, which is not common. Jumbo holders typically are other financial institutions or corporations which have cash flows that are reasonably predictable. Purchasing a CD is a convenient way to earn high interest on excess funds for a fixed period of time without assuming any price risk on the investment. There is a high likelihood that corporate CD holders in particular will not rollover their CDs at maturity, since the money placed in the account is only temporarily not needed. The likelihood of nonrenewal by a financial institution at any one rollover date is only somewhat lower since such deposits are typically viewed as an investment security, just as Treasury securities are. A decision to reallocate the investment or liquidity portfolio could result in nonrenewal of a CD. The less frequently the institution reevaluates its portfolio, the lower the likelihood of withdrawal. Corporate CD holders are also price sensitive—not all withdrawals by corporate depositors are based on portfolio reallocation decisions.

What is important, though, is that there is practically no inducement that can be offered to persuade the larger CD holder to renew once the decision has been made to withdraw. Corporate holders may have some other use for the money, and financial institutions either need the cash immediately or have made a fundamental portfolio restructuring decision which does not include holding that particular security any longer. If such is the case, offering a higher yield will not always work with these CD holders, although it might well work with an individual deposit holder.

The increased yield sensitivity of individual depositors has now made offering a higher rate an option, albeit an expensive one for banks and savings associations, and its use has had widespread ramifications. Substituting a money market certificate at 10 percent for a passbook at 5.5 percent has deterred absolute cash withdrawals. However, such a response by the depository institution also increases the yield sensitivity of the depositor, creating a situation from which there can be no retreat. As soon as a similar investment appears at a rate of 12 percent which the bank or savings association cannot or will not match, the deposit may disappear. This leaves the institution where it began—looking for replacement funds. If this occurs on a large scale, the options are reduced to two: borrowing or selling assets.

The crucial element to this entire problem is that unanticipated withdrawals are what cause problems for depository institutions. If withdrawals are anticipated, they can be managed with greater ease and flexibility; or, if liquidity risk can be insured in some way, the effects of unanticipated withdrawals can be ameliorated.

To state the obvious, the key to a profitable operation is to maintain a positive or more positive spread between earnings on assets and the cost of liabilities. As we have seen, this has become difficult by conventional methods from the late 1970s onwards. Fluctuating interest rates, deposit runoffs, and account switching have made liability management almost a mythical goal in the minds of many. Nothing could be further from the truth.

Even wildly fluctuating interest rates can be managed. The way to do so, quite simply, is to give the risk to someone else. In some ways financial institutions are already able to do that. A savings association, for example, holds a large portion of its assets in very long-term mortgages. If the rates it pays on deposits fall, it will widen its spread if it holds onto the mortgages. However, this is a one-sided proposition which has caused difficulty for a number of associations when interest rates have risen rather than fallen. The financial futures market, on the other hand, is designed to allow traders to make money whether interest rates go up or down; but most especially for financial institutions the opportunity exists to benefit when rates go up. A jump in interest rates means that the institution's cost of funds will increase. Although earnings on assets may increase, they probably will not do so as quickly as the cost of funds; consequently, profits will be squeezed in the short run. Financial futures hedging allows the bank or savings association to earn profits on financial futures when interest rates rise, thereby offsetting the spread compression on its actual balance sheet. Many institutions are asset sensitive so that profits are squeezed when rates fall. This situation can also be hedged with financial futures. A hedging plan that is properly designed and managed can achieve an offset of 70 percent to 90 percent, and occasionally more, of this profit squeeze.

At the beginning of this book we said that the goal of financial institutions which use the futures market is to transfer some of their interest rate risk to someone else. So far we have discussed risk in general, as well as specific risk associated with specific financial assets and liabilities. We have not talked about how to measure that risk. In order to do so we now widen our approach to encompass the entire balance sheet. While that complicates things somewhat, it is necessitated by the lack of an absolute measure of risk. The only risk measurement technique available is a relative one. Recall that Standard and Poor and Moody's rate bonds on the basis of their credit risk relative to the credit risk on Treasury bonds, which is assumed to be zero. A bond rate AA is riskier than one rated AAA and less risky than one rated BBB, but it cannot be quantified into a numerical index. Suppose Treasury bonds are given a risk index rating of 0. A AAA bond is not necessarily given a 1 and a AA bond given a 2 and so forth. The AAA bond could just as easily be 43 on the index and the AA bond could be 187. As crazy as that sounds, it is just as accurate as any other risk index rating, which is to say not accurate at all since there is no established scale.

In the case of a financial institution, a risk rating is even more of an enigma since there are several kinds of risk inherent in its balance sheet. However, a technique exists for measuring the relative interest rate risk of the institution's total balance sheet. We discuss this technique in Chapter 2, as well as its importance to efficient use of the financial futures market.

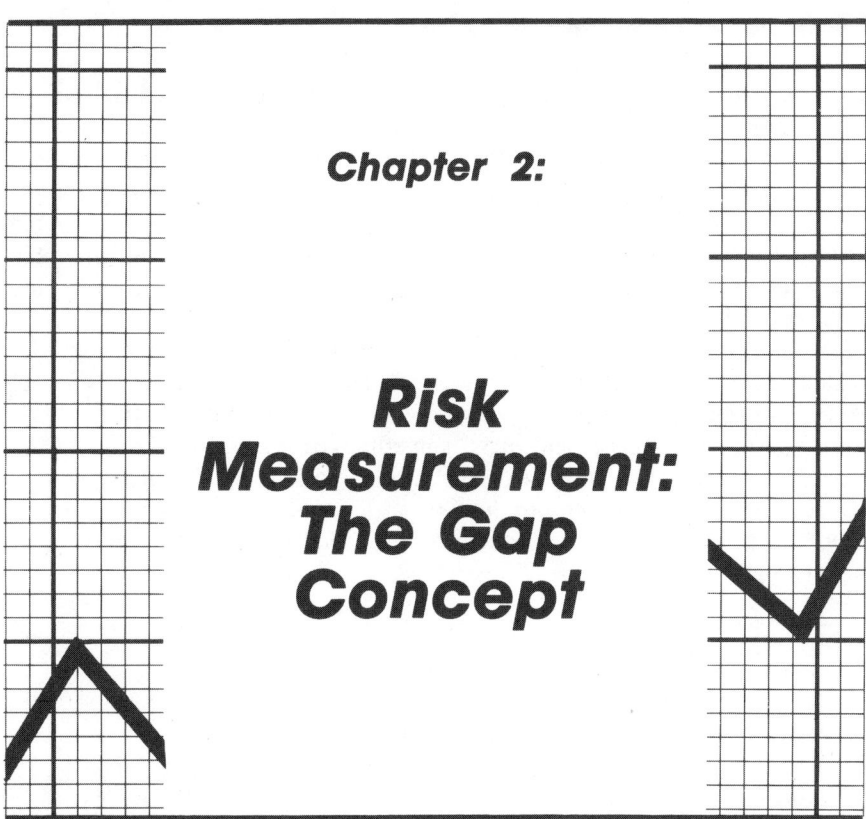

Chapter 2:

Risk Measurement: The Gap Concept

IN ORDER to take effective action to reduce its risk, whether in the cash or futures markets, an institution must know what its overall risk really is, how much it is, and of what type.

So far we have discussed several types of risk, particularly asset risk and liability risk. As we have seen, each asset or liability has its own risk associated with it. When all the assets and liabilities are assembled onto the balance sheet, the combination creates a somewhat different picture. The various risks combine either to offset one another or to create further risk by the imbalances among them. The net effect of these imbalances is the cumulative risk to which the institution is exposed, otherwise known as its *gap*.

GAPS—ANALYSIS AND TYPES

Managing this cumulative risk is known as Asset-Liability Management or Funds Management. This function, usually handled weekly or biweekly by a committee, has become the single most important management group and function within a bank. Financial futures is its latest and potentially most useful tool.

Measuring this overall risk is called "gap analysis" and involves a detailed study of the institution's balance sheet. *This is the single most important concept to be grasped by the reader in order to utilize fully hedging strategies developed in subsequent chapters.* Embarking upon a hedging plan which ignores gap analysis could very well increase the institution's risk rather than reduce it.

Under quiet market conditions the mismatch of assets and liabilities could be tolerable for a time without jeopardizing the profitability or survival of the institution. However, in today's world of extreme rate volatility, this is not the case. Shifts in the yield curve, sometimes over a period of seven years, as well as rate level fluctuations which are as volatile as nitroglycerine (see Figure 2.1) affect the bottom line of an institution so quickly and so noticeably that Funds Management has propelled itself to the forefront of modern bank management.

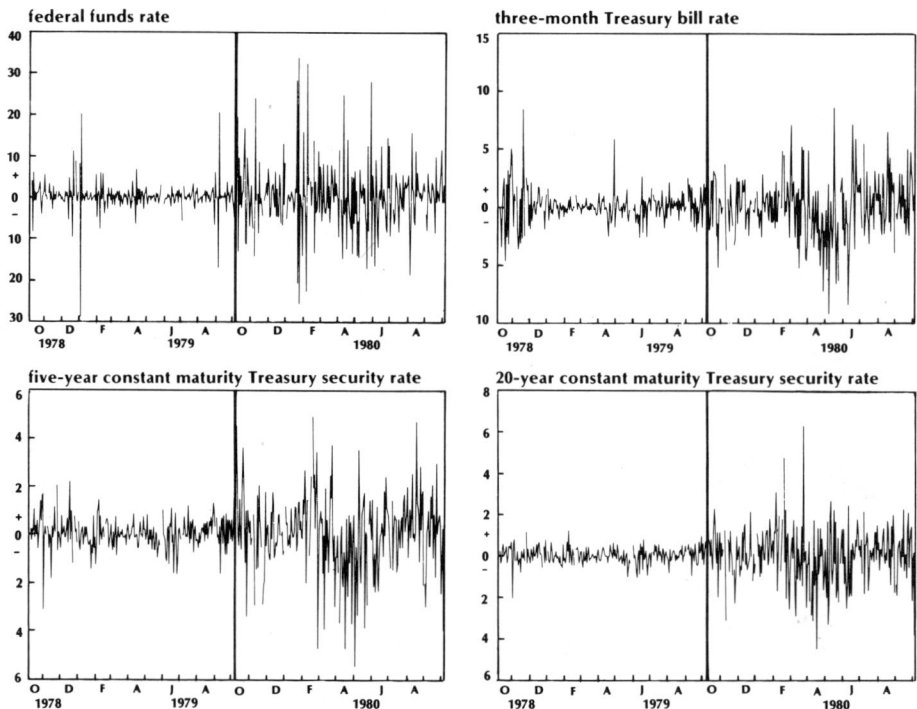

Figure 2.1 Daily Percentage Changes in Selected Interest Rates
Source: Federal Reserve Bank of Chicago

GAP ANALYSIS

Isolating and quantifying the maturity imbalance of assets and liabilities is also known as Interest Rate Sensitivity Analysis. This subject is complex and sometimes difficult to grasp but vital to the preservation of stable interest margins. This will become evident as we proceed.

The concept is basically a simple one. A gap or maturity risk exists whenever the maturity of an asset differs from the maturity of a corresponding liability. For example, a bank might have a one-year fixed-rate loan funded by six-month money market certificates. Since after six months it will have to pay whatever the prevailing rate for 6-month MMCs will be in order to retain the money market certificates used to fund the loan, it has a gap. It is exposed to interest rate risk.

This is, of course, a simple example and has not been quantified to show the dollar amounts of assets and liabilities. A typical institution has numerous assets and liabilities of varying size and maturity. What complicates gap analysis for some is that the analysis is accomplished by observing the imbalance of assets and liabilities by segregating them into various time frames of maturities (e.g., 30 days, 90 days, etc.), thus creating a new terminology based upon the time at which interest rate risk is incurred. The new terms using time and maturity as new and different ways of describing risk often confuse the uninitiated. This may impede an understanding or proficient use of the technique.

One key term in asset and liability management is "reset." This means that an asset's or liability's yield is repriced (i.e., reset) to the current market yield. This rate change is the vulnerability which is the core issue of interest rate sensitivity and gap management.

Also, we will only be interested in assets and liabilities that are subject to a rate change within a specific period of time (the period of reset). These are called Rate Sensitive Assets (RSA) and Rate Sensitive Liabilities (RSL), respectively. The gap concept could than be rephrased as a formula:

$$GAP = RSA - RSL$$

Let us now proceed with the gap analysis step by step.

First, identify the specific nature of the portfolio by dividing the rate sensitive assets and liabilities into categories of time frames when resets will occur. This will result in a matrix of various dollar amounts or assets and liabilities versus gap periods. Second, calculate the gap for each time frame category by subtracting the dollar amounts or rate sensitive liabilities from rate sensitive assets. The result is the gap.

Example: A bank has $10 million of six-month loans that it funds out of $20 million of three-month deposits. Its gap position looks like the following:

		60	**90**	**120**	**180**	**Period (days)**
Asset	Loans	–	–	–	10	
Liability	3 mo. dep.	–	20	–	20	
GAP		0	(20)	0	(10)	

At 60 days there is no gap since there is no rate change (no reset).

At 90 days the deposit rate is reset so there is a gap.

$$0 \text{ mil.} - \$20 \text{ mil.} = -\$20 \text{ mil.}$$

At 120 days there is no reset, therefore, no gap.

At 180 days both rates are reset and there is a gap.

$$\$10 \text{ mil.} - \$20 \text{ mil.} = -\$10 \text{ mil.}$$

A more realistic example would look something like the spread sheet in Table 2.1.

Notice the term "cumulative gap" in Table 2.1. This is merely the running total of all gaps and gives the net gap for the institution. This overall gap is sometimes used as a rough approximation of the interest rate sensitivity of the institution. When multiplied by a hypothetical (i.e., forecast) change in interest rates, it can give a general idea of the impact this will have on the institution's earnings. Since we know that in reality rates do not change equally for all assets and liabilities, it is more accurate and useful to examine this rate sensitivity using different rate changes for each maturity gap.

Depending on the size of the institution, this process should be done each quarter in the case of $100 million institutions to as frequently as weekly in multibillion dollar organizations. Probably the most useful frequency for monitoring the gap for a medium-sized institution would be monthly, however the use of computers might make weekly observation possible. Also, the volatility of rates is another determinant of how often you should do a gap analysis. In periods of less volatile rates quarterly re-evaluations may suffice for even the largest institutions.

At this point most financial officers are probably saying to themselves, "This is a lot of work. How am I going to do this on a timely basis?" Take heart, there are quite a number of asset/liability management computer software packages and timesharing services available, and the number is growing rapidly. They vary considerably in sophistication and ease of use. Many are being implemented on microcomputers that you can set right on your desk. So now that there are no excuses, let's continue.

TABLE 2.1
Periodic and Cumulative GAP Analysis

Period (days)	O/N	30	60	90	180	360	360 +
Rate Sensitive Assets							
Fed Funds Sold	11,207	---	---	---	---	---	---
Treasuries & Agencies	---	1,851	1,543	1,388	3,623	7,021	30,362
Muncipals	---	505	432	396	757	1,514	27,620
Banker's Acceptances	---	---	---	---	---	---	1,098
Commercial Loans*	19,250	5,193	4,155	3,462	8,309	13,502	34,366
Installment Loans	16,024	3,459	2,767	2,306	5,535	8,994	7,094
Mortgages	20,037	1,384	1,730	1,038	3,805	7,265	19,392
Total	66,518	12,392	10,627	8,590	22,029	38,296	119,932
Rate Sensitive Liabilities							
Fed Funds Purchased	4,649	---	---	---	---	---	---
Repos	2,942	---	---	---	---	---	---
NOW Accounts							2,901
Savings Accounts							36,533
All Savers						11,756	3,919
IRAS	7,563	---	---	---	---	---	11,345
MMCs	---	15,505	14,471	13,437	42,379	---	12,404
Large CDs	---	5,122	4,482	3,202	9,899	4,249	19,576
Total	15,154	20,627	18,953	16,639	52,278	16,005	86,678
GAP	51,364	−8,235	−8,326	−8,049	−30,249	22,291	33,254
CUMULATIVE GAP	51,364	43,129	34,803	26,754	−3,495	18,796	52,050

*includes prime rate loans

TYPES OF GAPS

Gaps, otherwise known as "mismatches," come in basically four categories: (1) positive and negative; (2) voluntary and involuntary; (3) temporary or permanent; and (4) contractual or effective.

Positive and Negative Gaps

As we have seen, when rate sensitive liabilities are subtracted from rate sensitive assets, the resulting gap can be positive, negative, or zero. A positive number denotes a positive gap; the institution is vulnerable to falling rates as assets reprice faster than liabilities. A negative gap indicates that the institution is exposed to rising rates as liabilities reprice faster than assets. A zero gap, which is the goal of many institutions, takes out the rate risk component and focuses attention on margins, or spreads, which can be controlled to a greater extent and gives rise to the term "spread banking."

One point to be considered is that not all gaps are undesirable. In fact, institutions have purposely produced gaps in order to profit from interest rate moves they have foreseen. With today's rate volatility, however, the risk that rates will move in an unexpected direction and to a greater extent than anticipated has fostered the growth of asset/liability management to eliminate gaps, as well as an increased reliance on spread banking for profits.

Voluntary and Involuntary Gaps

As we have just noted, not all mismatches are undesirable or unintentional. These "voluntary" gaps are designed to benefit the institution based on resets which will provide lower cost or a greater spread for the transaction should rates move as forecast. They are deliberate maturity disparities between assets and liabilities resulting from specific lending and funding commitments. However, involuntary gaps, mismatches which occur unintentionally from a combination of actions of the institution and its customers, can affect earnings negatively. The bank or savings and loan association may, but should not, be unaware of their existence.

An example of a voluntary mismatch is a bank that makes a loan of $10 million to a corporation at 15 percent for one year and knows that it is going to fund it with $10 million of six-month CDs at 13.5 percent, creating a 180-day negative gap of $10 million. This is a voluntary gap, since the asset/liability committee is expecting rates to drop and expects to refund the loan six months hence at a lower rate.

As an example of an involuntary mismatch, suppose the same bank has a corporate customer who takes down $10 million of its line of credit on a temporary basis at one percent over prime, resulting in a rate of 16 percent. Also, the bank has an inflow of $10 million of six-month money market certificates at 13 percent, thereby creating a 180-day negative gap of $10 million, exposing the institution to risk if interest rates rise.

When viewed together on the balance sheet, the institution's situation looks as follows:

Period (days)	O/N	180	360
Assets			
Corp. loan @ 15%	0	0	10
Credit line @ 16%	10	0	0
Liabilities			
CDs @ 13.5%	0	10	0
MMCs @ 13%	0	10	0
NET	+ 10	− 20	+ 10
GAP	+ 10	− 20	+ 10
CUMULATIVE GAP	+ 10	− 10	0

As you can see, these transactions tend to offset one another cumulatively, but one may want to hedge the bank's involuntary exposure at the 180-day mark as the involuntary mismatch doubles the amount of risk the institution is willing to take during that time period. This in why monitoring each time sector is more important than watching an institution's cumulative gap.

Therefore, when embarking upon a hedging program, the asset/liability committee must differentiate between these two types of gaps and decide, based on its forecast of rates, which gaps it wishes to keep. If it is unsure of rate direction or has a policy of spread banking, it should aim toward matching assets and liabilities with a combination of cash and futures to reduce the gaps to zero.

Temporary and Permanent Gaps

Mismatches often occur only for relatively short periods of time, either voluntarily or involuntarily. The "temporary" gaps can be managed by the asset/liability committee in various ways and to varying extents, probably a combination of hedging most of the risk while taking some of it. (See Chapter 13 for a more detailed discussion of this strategy.)

As an example of a temporary gap, a liability manager may book a deposit because the rate is attractive, but then may find the bank does not have a continuous use for this source of funds. This creates a gap. Since the funds are only temporary, the bank wouldn't want to change any terms on its outstanding loans. The bank is exposing itself to some risk, but that is part of the business of financial intermediation.

Long lasting or "permanent" mismatches have put some institutions on the list of endangered species. In recent years volatility in short-term rates has been so great and lasted for so long that many organizations have found it difficult to withstand. They have experienced a long period of lending at lower rates and at substantially longer maturities than those of its marketable liabilities. Take, for example, savings and loan associations that have been funding 25- and 30-year mortgages with an average yield of nine percent with six-month money market certificates sometimes paying as much as 16 percent. With rates remaining at record levels for a record length of time, they are faced with a permanent gap. Obviously, they must employ new measures for new situations if they are to remain in business.

Futures provide a cost-effective and flexible tool to reduce the effects of such a situation, as we will see, as well as allowing an institution the ability to create a voluntary, but hedged, mismatch to gain a marketing advantage by being able to offer lower rates than its competition.

Contractual v. Effective Gap

Some individuals have advocated a modified concept of gap analysis based on adjusting for the difference by maturities and weighting them to reflect a greater impact on the resetting of longer term instruments, as well as adjusting for relative volatilities of various instruments against some benchmark rate. This alternative technique has been named "the effective gap." It adds several layers of complexity to gap analysis. While its benefit remains questionable in the short term, it may be useful in long-term analysis.

If you want to delve more deeply into the different philosophies of gap definition and are prepared to do some analytical statistical research for verification, this may be of interest to you. However, as the scope of this book is practical application of existing tools, we believe the previous definition of gap, otherwise known as "contractual gap," is sufficient for our purposes.

In later chapters we will develop strategies to use the information gathered from gap analysis to aid in hedging your overall gap or specific parts of your interest rate risk exposure.

HEDGING THE GAP—MACRO VS. MICRO

Once an interest rate sensitivity analysis of an institution has been done and its gaps identified, a hedging program can then be pursued.

The first decision to be made concerning the hedging program is whether to hedge the overall gap or to hedge certain component assets or liabilities which constitute the largest exposure to interest rate risk.

There exists a spurious controversy between accountants and regulators over whether it is more advantageous for an institution to engage in a hedging program in which the overall asset and liability position is net hedged (known as a "macro" hedge), or one which views and hedges sectors individually (known as a "micro" hedge).

This debate between macro and micro hedging brings some important issues to light, the primary one being which system actually reduces a given institution's interest rate risk. This may at first seem baffling, since the whole purpose of a hedging program is to reduce this type of risk. The controversy arises from the possibility that one of these programs may actually create new risks in an unforeseen manner that could dramatically affect the institution's earnings, especially when it believes it is protected.

THE MICRO CASE

The proponents of micro hedging claim that macro hedging ignores the underlying characteristics of the assets and liabilities being hedged and does not take into account the differing behavior of various financial instruments with similar maturities. They believe that because of this a macro hedger may construct a hedge which may not respond to certain shifts in the yield curve in the same manner or degree as that of its portfolio, resulting in a loss on the futures position not commensurate with the gain on the cash side of the transaction. Similarly, in a hedge of the overall gap, because a specific exposed rate may not be identified, the hedge may be on the wrong way for that sector. If that sector were to move disproportionately, it might actually create a new rate risk for the institution.

THE MACRO CASE

The proponents of macro hedging (generally the regulators) claim that micro hedging, by focusing on specific asset or liability hedges, may alter the cumulative gap of the institution, sometimes to the extent that it then has a greater overall exposure to rate risk.

The micro hedgers (generally accountants) counter this with the argument that micro hedging allows the user to define more clearly his risk and to offset it with better strategies that have a higher statistical correlation with market performance, thereby reducing overall risk.

Since this is a practical book on the applications of hedging programs, let's put this into perspective. Technically, each side can show examples to illustrate its point. However, either a blend of the two viewpoints or one strategy employed with cognizance of its potential pitfalls makes an effective plan with which to move forward.

The decision depends primarily on the size of the institution. In general, macro hedgers tend to be small while micro hedgers tend to be large. This is primarily due to the fact that larger banks and savings and loans have greater access to secondary cash markets and have a greater number of alternatives with which to hedge, as well as the fact that futures contract sizes are of a magnitude ($1 million) that makes hedging of small individual sectors difficult if not impossible for a small institution.

A composite approach combining the best of both strategies seems the most practical way to proceed. From the sensitivity analysis, with gaps known for each time sector, the asset/liability manager will then need to determine the effects of various interest rate scenarios upon the institution's earnings. Then, depending on the size or policy preference of the institution, one may proceed with a micro hedging program which employs a hedge that consists of various instruments appropriate to the risk at each maturity, or a macro hedging program which is initially checked and continually monitored for changes in the institution's overall exposure.

CASH v. FUTURES

Before we proceed into a detailed look at the futures market and the strategies for its practical application in a hedging program, some discussion should be given to its merits as the most appropriate vehicle compared to alternatives for offsetting interest rate risk.

CASH

First, the asset/liability committee should see what can be accomplished using the cash markets. To the extent possible, it should try to reduce as much of the institution's gap as possible by reducing or increasing maturities of CDs, altering the amount of fixed and variable rate loans, and moving into and out of longer term investments.

Much of what one would like to do to match-fund an institution by these methods is limited by what instruments are available, the amounts, and the time it takes to find and implement the necessary transaction. Also, maintaining good customer relations may present a constraint on this process. It may not always be possible, or advisable, to pass the risk on to the customer, especially in a deregulated environment where competition has increased and customers are generally more sophisticated about risk.

FUTURES

The alternative is futures or options or a combination of both. Unlike altering customer terms on loans and deposits or purchasing and selling various government securities and Fed funds, futures are uniform, flexible, fast, anonymous, and generally less costly.

In contrast to a forward contract that a securities dealer may offer, futures contracts are transferable. Since they are standardized contracts of uniform size, they are quite fungible to many different users with different purposes.

The primary advantage of using futures in a hedging program is that they are flexible. That is, one may buy or sell them in a matter of seconds and use them in various combinations and quantities in numerous risk-averting strategies.

Furthermore, the futures markets are very efficient markets, offering tighter bid/ask spreads than the cash markets. This is due to the large number of participants in the market with opposing motivations and rationales, as well as the enormous liquidity available. Bottom line: this means getting in and out fast at better prices than in alternative markets.

The depth of the futures markets is evidenced by recent volume and open interest figures which have been growing steadily each year. Daily trading volumes in T-bond and T-bill futures, the most popular contracts, average $8 billion and $15 billion, respectively. This is five to eight times greater than the volume of trading in the underlying cash markets for these government securities.

Also, the futures market offers numerous contracts from which to choose throughout the maturity spectrum in either government or non-government securities. This makes for nearly one-stop shopping, so to speak. For example, there are futures on Eurodollar time deposits, bank CDs, 90-day T-bills, one-year T-bills, 7–10-year Treasury notes, 12-year GNMAs and 20-year T-bonds, with more contracts being created to fill out the possibilities. This large choice of instruments allows a financial hedger to match the volatility and price movement characteristics of his hedges to track his portfolio with a high degree of correlation.

By using the appropriate contracts most situations can be hedged. Because of the futures market's flexibility one can quickly respond to changing conditions, allowing the institution to adapt to unforeseen events rapidly. This alone may mean the difference between life and death for quite a few institutions throughout the country.

Another useful feature of futures contracts is their low credit risk. Due to the clearing corporation system, described in a later chapter, there is very low risk of default; the degree of default risk on futures contracts approaches that of the government securities market itself.

The last and probably least obvious advantage of the futures market is the competitive edge that it can give an institution. It can allow an institution to offset risk in many cases where there is no other alternative risk avoidance mechanism. A bank or savings and loan could offer a fixed-rate loan or mortgage since its interest rate risk is avoided by the use of the futures market. A fixed-rate loan or mortgage can be a distinct competitive advantage for the institution, especially if all other institutions in the marketplace are offering only variable rate loans.

Futures sound great, yet it is important to note that there are some potential thorns on these roses. The main one is a possible negative cash flow from the hedger to the futures market in meeting "margin calls." During extremely volatile market conditions this could be of considerable consequence to the hedging institution. We will discuss this in greater detail in later chapters, as well as outline practical guidelines to minimize this effect on one's hedging program.

The other alternative to the cash markets is options on futures. An option, being a right and not an obligation to buy or sell a futures contract, potentially offers many of the advantages of hedging with futures while eliminating margin calls.

But, as we all know, you don't get something for nothing. There is a premium to be paid for the limited risk of options. Using options in a hedging program could increase the cost of the hedge compared to using futures outright.

However, for some small institutions this could be a very practical alternative. Also, options open up the possibility of new portfolio management techniques for large financial institutions. Yields on a portfolio could be increased significantly by an options writing program.

A more detailed discussion of options follows in a later chapter. At the time this book was written, the practical application of options in a hedging program was quite limited due to the existence of only options on T-bond futures. This is not to say that options will not become a viable hedging tool—the options market can be expected to grow as financial futures did.

In summary, futures are the most cost-effective and flexible vehicle for offsetting interest rate risk exposure for financial institutions. Let's now look in detail at the often confusing and often misunderstood futures market. Since we are concerned with the bottom line, we'll start with the financial requirements and implications of futures market activity.

Part II

The Futures Market

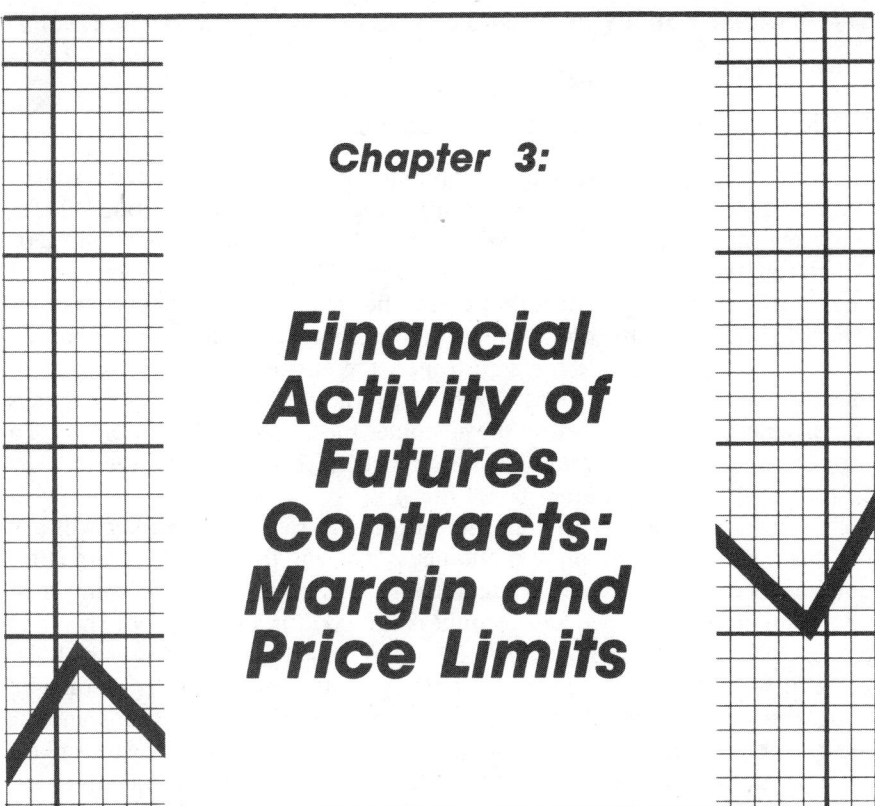

Chapter 3:

Financial Activity of Futures Contracts: Margin and Price Limits

MARGIN FOR futures contracts is a performance bond insuring compliance with the contract terms. It is not a down payment and does not represent any ownership interest in the underlying securities or commodities. Margin on stocks does represent a down payment and partial ownership. The distinction between margin in these two markets is that in the stock market the broker lends the customer the difference between the purchase price and the down payment. In the futures market this does not happen. In the stock market the securities are the collateral for the broker loan. If the value of securities falls below the amount of the loan, a margin call occurs; that is, the loan must be partially repaid to maintain the adequacy of the collateral. Margin calls in the futures market are completely different and are discussed in detail in Chapter 20.

MARGIN MONEY

Every exchange sets a margin requirement for every contract that is traded on the exchange. The size of margin requirements varies from $300 for some agricultural contracts to $2000 for most financial instrument contracts. All margin requirements are subject to change. The margin requirement must be met by the brokerage firm that clears the trade through the exchange. If the trade is made for the brokerage firm, it uses its own money for the margin, while if the trade is made for a customer, the customer's money is used to meet the margin requirement. (Technically the clearing member is always responsible for margin whether the customer meets his obligation or not. To protect itself from this liability the brokerage house will reverse the customer's position if margin is not met.)

Before opening an account and beginning trading the broker will ask the customer for an amount of money sufficient to meet the margin requirements for the volume of trading that is anticipated. The nearly universal minimum amount to open any account is $10,000 for a speculator. This may be deposited in cash or high-grade liquid securities—usually Treasury bills. For a financial institution this will not always be the case as it will generally be on a wire transfer arrangement and will wire the appropriate funds and/or securities as needed. Once a margin account is opened, trading may take place and continue as long as the amount of money in the account is equal to or exceeds the required margin amounts. This is the simple part of margin accounts and requirements. Before turning to the more complex part we must take a quick look at daily price limits which influence much of the activity in margin accounts.

DAILY PRICE LIMITS

For every futures contract traded there is a maximum amount by which the price is allowed to change in any one day. "Change" here means the change from the previous day's settlement or closing price. The daily price limit is set by the exchange and, like everything else, is itself subject to change.

The daily price limits for financial instrument contracts are shown in the contract specifications in Chapter 6. As an example, the price limit for U. S. Treasury Bonds is 64/32ds. If Tuesday's settlement price was 63–10, then on Wednesday no trades in that contract can be executed at a price above 65–10 or below 61–10. The daily price limit is independent of the opening price for the day. In this example if trading opened at 64–16—up 48/32ds—the upper limit would still be 65–10. During the trading session if the bid price reached 65–10 and no sell offers were forthcoming, trading would stop until someone offered to sell at 65–10 or below. Trading would also stop at the lower limit if no one bid 61–10 or more. If either situation occurs, the market is said to be locked at the limit or simply a "locked limit" market. The upper or lower limit then becomes the settlement price and new limits are established for the next day. Locked limit days are not unusual in agricultural commodities but are infrequent in financial instrument contracts.

MORE ON MARGIN

The amount of required margin is not only different for different contracts, it is different for the same contract at different times. As Chapter 6 will point out, there are two different margin requirements: initial margin and maintenance margin. Initial margin is the amount required at the time the trade is initiated. After the first day the maintenance margin is the amount required to be maintained on deposit with the exchange.

The amount of money in a margin account will vary every day due to the daily mark-to-market system used on futures exchanges. Simply stated, if the market price of a contract goes against your position, you have lost money that day even though the contract may not mature for months. Gains or losses are not accrued as in other markets but are recognized on a cash basis every day. If prices have declined during the day, traders who have short positions have made money and have the amount of the gains added to their margin account. Similarly, traders who have long positions have lost money and have the amount of the loss deducted from their margin account. This transfer of funds happens every trading day that the position is open.

The maintenance margin requirement is the minimum amount required to be in the account after any losses for the day have been deducted. If the initial margin is $2000 and the maintenance margin is $1500, a loss of $400 on the first day will not require the trader to deposit additional margin. As long as the net losses over the life of a trader's position do not add up to more than the difference between the initial and maintenance margin requirements, additional margin is not required.

Suppose, however, that on the first day the market moves against the trader's position by $700. This leaves $1300 in the account, which is $200 less than the required maintenance margin. Exchange rules require that if a margin account falls below the maintenance level, the account must be brought back to the initial margin level. Therefore, an additional $700 must be deposited to maintain the position.

If the trader is accumulating money on his position, any amount above the initial margin requirement may be withdrawn. This is usually done by wire transfer and only for relatively large amounts. Excess margin of $400 is usually left in an account, as it may be needed the next day if the market moves the other way.

Margin accounts are handled on a consolidated basis for each clearing member and for each customer. This can be quite useful for the hedger who has simultaneous positions in more than one contract. If the total amount in the margin account exceeds the required maintenance level for all positions, no additional margin is required. A loss on one position may be offset by a gain on other positions. For example, a bank opens short positions of 20 T-bill contracts and 40 T-bond contracts on the same day; required initial margin for all 60 contracts is $120,000 ($40,000 on the bills and $80,000 on the bonds) and maintenance margin is $90,000 ($30,000 on the bills and $60,000 on the bonds). If bill prices rose by 40 basis points, the margin against the short T-bill position would be deficient by $10,000 (40 basis points × $25/basis point × 20 contracts = $20,000 loss). If bond prices didn't change, the total margin account would still be $100,000 at the end of day 2, greater than the consolidated maintenance margin requirement of $90,000. No additional margin money need be deposited.

If markets become extremely volatile and trade with expanded price limits, the exchanges may increase the size of the initial and maintenance margin requirements for new and outstanding contracts. Depending on market conditions these increases may be double, triple, or quadruple the normal margin requirements. For example, if margins are doubled, a trader with $1800 in his account with a position previously requiring $2000 initial/$1500 maintenance margin would be required to add $2200 in order to bring the margin up to the new initial level ($4000). When variation margin is relaxed, the usual rules apply, and the trader would have these excess funds at his disposal.

DAILY PRICE LIMITS AND MARGIN REQUIREMENTS

For financial instrument futures the size of the maintenance margin requirement is generally equal to the maximum gain or loss that would result if the price changed by the daily price limit. For example, multiply the limit move by the price per tick; e.g., one basis point for T-bills or CDs is $25—60 basis points is $1500, the amount of the maintenance margin.

The relationship between daily price limits and the maintenance margin is not coincidental. The rationale behind price limits is to maintain the financial integrity of each market participant. A sudden surge, or drop, in prices sparked by events external to the futures market or to the cash market for the underlying securities would be slowed or checked by price limits. Sufficient flexibility exists—limits may be doubled or tripled as per exchange rules—that the influence of a large shift in fundamental conditions will enable the futures market to respond adequately. If a large drop or jump in price occurs for only one day, a trader will only lose in any one day what he has already put up as margin. If there were a high probability that a trader would lose in one day considerably more than the initial margin deposit, the futures market would be much less attractive. On the other hand, a trader wishing to hold onto a short position in the face of rapidly rising prices will have to add funds continuously for the privilege of doing so. He may decide after a few days that this strategy will not work and decide to give it up. Effective as it is, this can be an expensive way to learn how to trade futures.

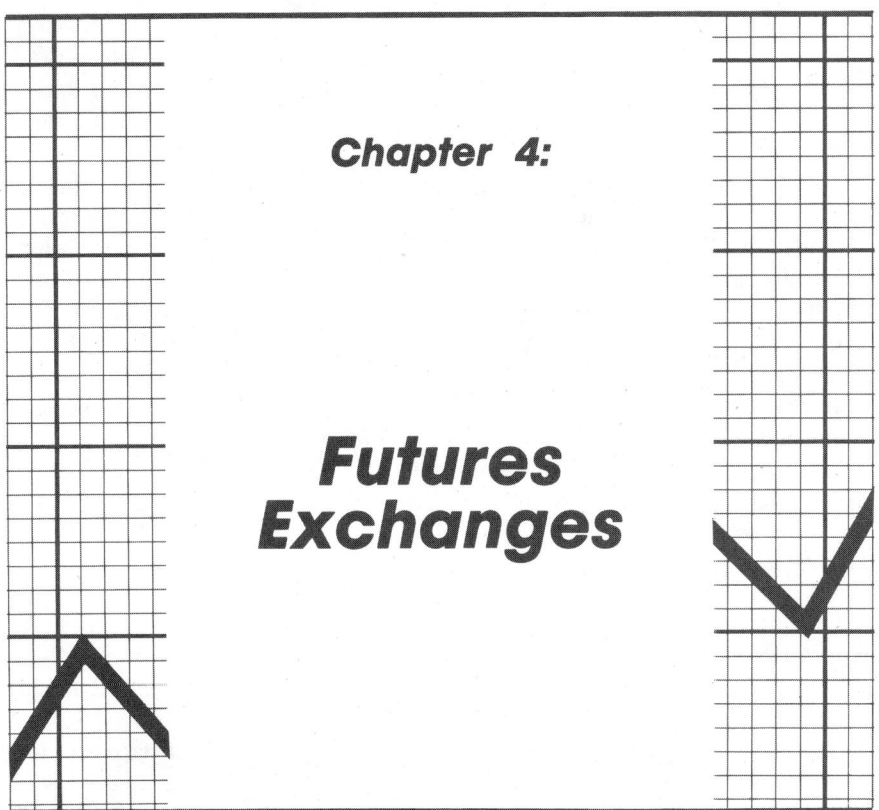

Chapter 4:

Futures Exchanges

FUTURES EXCHANGES, like most organizations, are comprised of people; the major difference is that in the case of futures exchanges, the people are the organization. The members of the exchange are the owners and managers of it. All exchanges have professional staffs who handle the accounting, research, legal, and other functions, but the members control the structure of the exchange. This is accomplished through a board of directors and a system of committees made up of individual members.

EXCHANGE MEMBERS

Membership, or ownership of a seat on an exchange, entitles the member to execute trades on the floor either for the member's own account or for customers. Most exchanges have several membership classes. A general or full membership entitles the owner to trade any of the contracts listed on the exchange. Other categories of membership entitle the member to trade only certain contracts. This is most typical of financial contracts where a certain type of seat enables the member to trade all financial contracts and no grains, livestock, or metals. Even more limited memberships allow trading in only one or two financial contracts.

Most of the exchanges have several hundred or even several thousand members, and a large number of memberships or seats are usually controlled by the large brokerage houses—Merrill Lynch, E.F. Hutton, etc. These houses may own two or three dozen seats and have that many traders on the floor all the time. The advantage of doing so is that they can then simultaneously execute trades for customers in all of the commodities traded on the exchange. The remainder of the seats on the exchange are owned by individual private entrepreneurs. Of course, an individual can only be in one place at a time and therefore only trade one commodity at a time; most of the individual traders specialize in trading only one commodity. Thus, the limited membership classes do not really impose much of a handicap on the traders.

THE CLEARING CORPORATION

Standing behind the exchange, and providing the financial muscle for continued operation of the exchange, is the clearing corporation. All exchanges have clearing corporations, which have three functions: reconciling or clearing trades between members, insuring contract compliance, and acting as an intermediary in the event of a delivery. In the fast-paced trading in the pits tens of thousands of contracts are traded among hundreds of members each day. All trades are recorded on small cards in shorthand unique to the exchange. The clearing corporation keeps track of trades and prices and reconciles all transactions overnight. Anyone who visits the floor of an exchange can see how easy it would be to record a trade incorrectly—the clearing corporation detects these errors.

The clearing corporation also insures compliance with the provision of the contracts traded. Most notably, this involves enforcing the margin requirements. In the process of clearing all trades, the clearing corporation determines the net gain or loss on margin accounts for all traders every day. The clearing corporation deals directly only with a few of the largest exchange members, who are also clearing members. The clearing members of the exchange are the owners of the clearing corporation and put up the capital to maintain its and the exchange's operation and solvency. Non-clearing members clear all their trades through one of the clearing members and then maintain a separate accounting system for customer accounts.

The clearing corporation and the clearing members are the backbone of the financial structure of any commodity futures exchange. Under the daily mark-to-market system all traders, either members or customers, are entitled to profits when their futures positions make money. The clearing corporation, backed up by the clearing members, insures the integrity of the system. Should a trader fail to put up additional margin when required, it is the clearing member who must make good on the margin deficiency to the clearing corporation. A clearing member thus has considerable capital at risk. In order to be a clearing member a firm must keep several million dollars in cash available as a reserve against such possibilities, somewhat like a financial institution.

Clearing member firms are generally financially stronger because they have stiffer financial requirements imposed upon them by the exchange. Commodity brokerage firms, like all firms, can fail because they are overextended on the amount of capital they have. Fortunately, few firms do fail, partly due to exchange rules and partly due to government regulation of commodity exchanges. However, the size of a member firm or the fact that it is not a clearing member is not an indication of its ability to execute trades efficiently.

 **FUTURES REGULATION**

The government agency which regulates the futures industry is the Commodity Futures Trading Commission (CFTC). The CFTC must approve all contracts that are proposed for trading by any futures exchange. The CFTC also has the authority to suspend trading in any contract, can force the exchange to increase margin requirements, and can bar individuals or firms from trading futures contracts. All persons involved in the futures business who deal with the public for profit must register with the CFTC by filing extensive public disclosure statements concerning themselves personally and their firms. This applies to futures commission merchants (brokerage firms), floor traders associated with a firm, brokers or account executives, commodity trading advisors, and commodity pool operators. Registration statements are public information and should be made available to any customer who asks for it.

At the beginning of 1983 there were 11 commodity futures exchanges registered with the CFTC. These were: Chicago Board of Trade, Chicago Mercantile Exchange, New York Futures Exchange, Kansas City Board of Trade, Commodity Exchange (New York), Coffee, Sugar and Cocoa Exchange (New York), New York Cotton Exchange, MidAmerica Commodity Exchange (Chicago), Minneapolis Grain Exchange, New Orleans Commodity Exchange, and New York Mercantile Exchange.

Of these, only the Chicago Board of Trade and the Chicago Mercantile Exchange (actually the International Monetary Market Division) are of real importance to financial institutions since they handle the vast majority of all financial instrument contracts with which banks or savings and loan associations are likely to be hedging interest rate risk. Financial instrument contracts are traded on other exchanges, but most of the action is in Chicago.

Between these two exchanges there is little difference in terms of liquidity which primarily determines the ability to hedge interest rate risk. The fundamental difference between the Board of Trade and the IMM is in the type of contracts traded. (Particular contract specifications are shown in

Chapter 6.) Since financial futures were introduced, the Board of Trade has tended to specialize in contracts for longer maturity instruments (GNMAs, Treasury bonds, Treasury notes) while the IMM has concentrated on contracts for short-term instruments (Treasury bills, bank CDs, Eurodollar CDs). This division of the market is not written in stone—indeed the Board of Trade has traded contracts for commercial paper and bank CDs. The success of a contract depends on the willingness of the locals to make markets in that contract as well as the participation of commercial interests. The preferences of traders on these two exchanges have been revealed fairly well. One would expect that in the future new contracts at the short end of the yield curve will prosper on the IMM and the long end will continue to be dominated by the Chicago Board of Trade. The significance of this for hedgers is that you want to hedge in the most liquid and most active futures market and you should know which exchanges provide this for your particular application.

Chapter 5:

Risk Takers and Risk Averters: How the Market Works

IN ORDER for a bank to use the futures markets to reduce risk effectively there must be an opposite party in the market who is willing to assume that risk. These people are known as speculators. There is nothing evil about speculators. Without speculators in the market there would be no one to whom financial institutions could transfer risk.

SPECULATORS: THE RISK TAKERS

In general, a speculator in the futures market is a person who takes a position in a contract for a commodity which is not used in his normal business. An example is a physician who trades cattle futures and does not also own a cattle ranch. A physician who owns a cattle ranch is probably a hedger if he trades cattle futures; if he trades silver he is probably speculating.

A speculator's objective is to profit from a change in the price of futures—no more, no less. It does not matter whether the price goes up or down; it is still possible to make profits trading futures. It's also possible to make losses. What attracts speculators to the market is the possibility of making huge gains on a tiny investment. The enormous leverage of futures contracts can produce astronomical rates of return if the speculator picks the direction of a price change correctly. The example below illustrates how this works:

> Example: A speculator buys five Treasury bill contracts at 90.00 and pays $10,000 in margin. The next day the price of the contracts increases to 90.60, the maximum increase allowed in one day. The speculator's profit is $7500. The annualized rate of return on the $10,000 initial investment is 27,000 percent.

If the speculator in the example had sold five contracts and the price fell to 89.40 (a limit move), the annualized rate of return would also have been 27,000 percent. A rate of return this high can be expected on high leverage investments. The leverage on T-bill futures is 500 to one—a $1 million T-bill can be controlled for only $2000. For Treasury bonds the leverage ratio is only 50 to one but the maximum annual rate of return is 36,000 percent due to higher daily price limits. For Eurodollar futures the annualized rate of return could be 45,000 percent.

The reason speculators are not all multi-trillionaires is that picking a limit move like the one shown in the example is very difficult. They do not happen very often and the chance of catching one exactly when it occurs is small. Still, the possibility of making such a fantastic return is what draws speculators into the market. On the average they do not make rates of return that run into thousands of percents. Most speculators lose money in the long run—only 15 percent of speculative accounts make a profit over the long haul. However, if you hit one, the return can be fabulous.

HEDGERS: THE RISK AVERTERS

The opposite of speculators are, of course, hedgers. In the financial contracts hedgers are banks, savings and loan associations, corporations, security dealers, pension funds, or other types of financial institutions which buy, sell, or hold the financial instruments underlying the contracts. Hedge transactions are those which mirror a transaction in the cash market. (These transactions are explored extensively in Part III, Strategies for Financial Institutions.) The purpose of mentioning hedgers here is to demonstrate the necessity of having both types of traders involved in the market. Without hedgers in the market the speculators could only trade with each other. For trading to continue, the speculators would have to be about evenly split between bulls and bears, which is not very likely.

A closer look at the actual mechanics of futures trading should make this clear.

ACTIVITY IN THE PIT

Anyone visiting a commodity exchange for the first time is liable to think it is chaos personified, but stepping into the pit dispels that impression immediately. In any trading pit the players can be divided into two main groups: floor brokers and "locals." Floor brokers are those traders who execute public orders that flow through brokerage houses. Some brokers work exclusively for one house and others execute trades for more than one brokerage firm. The "locals", so called because they trade only on one exchange, are trading only for themselves, buying and selling with their own capital.

In a typical trading session the locals are constantly making a market by shouting bids and offers for contracts. Occasionally, a local will trade with a local. Usually, though, trading activity centers around the floor brokers, who have public orders. Brokers maintain a "deck" of orders. In the deck are all the buy and sell orders that have been sent to the floor and are waiting to be executed. The broker maintains the orders in sequence by price. If the broker hears a bid price corresponding to a sell order he is holding, he hits the bid and fills the order. "Market" orders, which are orders to buy or sell immediately at the current market price, are filled right away. "Price" orders or "stop" orders may be held for some time by the broker until the market price moves to the price on the order.

Only the broker holding the deck knows what the prices are for public orders. The locals bid or offer prices they believe to be reasonable. What is believed to be a reasonable price is determined by the trader's opinion as to whether prices will rise or fall. This opinion could be right or wrong, of course. What makes the futures market a dynamic market is that the locals will very quickly change their opinions if they are wrong. If a large number of locals are selling in anticipation of falling prices, and a large number of buy orders come into the pit at the market price and higher, the locals will quickly switch directions. Usually the entire trading pit will switch directions in a short period of time. There is a great deal of "herd instinct" in the pits, mainly as a result of the open outcry system whereby everybody is vocally indicating some market preference and can see some of the actions that others are taking.

It is important for a hedger to realize that the locals do not randomly make bids and offers, nor do they all just buy and sell all day hoping to have a profit at the end of the day. Some traders, known as "scalpers," do buy and sell a few contracts at a time all day long. Since futures prices do move up and down by at least a few ticks all day, scalpers can make money by moving with the flow of the market. They are taking small profits on each trade, but making it up on the volume. This is not an extremely lucrative strategy, but then neither is it a high-risk one.

Another category of locals is "day" traders. A day trader is anyone who trades during the day but closes out all of his positions before the market closes. His horizon is to hold onto a position for a few hours; unlike a scalper, whose horizon is a few minutes. Day trading is a risk-limiting strategy, as it generally limits the trader's risk exposure to price moves within the established daily limits. Since he does not hold a position overnight, he is not affected by developments outside the market trading hours.

Yet another type of trader is known as "spread" trader. In a spread transaction one contract is sold at the same time a different contract is bought. An example of a spread would be to sell March bills and buy June bills. One could also sell March bonds and buy June notes; there are thousands of possible spread combinations. In spread trading the objective is to profit from price changes of different magnitudes when rates move according to one's forecast. For example, if rates rise one might expect the T-bill spread mentioned above to be profitable, as the price of the March contract would decrease by a greater amount than the June contract. Some consider spread trading to be safer than other types of trades. That is not always the case, however, since many times economic conditions can cause relationships between rates to respond differently in direction or magnitude than might otherwise be expected. This may create more risk than if a trader were simply long or short. Spreading is a highly sophisticated technique which is definitely not recommended for amateurs.

INTERACTION BETWEEN HEDGERS AND SPECULATORS

The connection between hedgers and speculators—the transfer of risk—is accomplished by the order flow in the trading pits. The floor brokers who execute public orders are the middlemen between hedgers and speculators. Hedge positions are executed by the floor brokers with the local traders. Every bid shouted by a local represents an offer to assume price risk from someone. The importance of having a large group of local traders actively shouting bids cannot be overemphasized. Hedge orders come from a wide variety of players, all of whom have different underlying positions in the cash market and different hedge objectives and strategies. In order to accommodate all of the hedgers who will want to use a particular contract, there must be a sizable group of speculators on the opposite side.

Moreover, it is important that a large number of these speculators be actively trading on the floor. Some speculative transactions do come from the public and are handled by floor brokers along with hedge transactions. These orders add additional liquidity to the market and are written orders held in a broker's deck to be executed at the appropriate time or price. Locals add a dynamic to the market as they can change their bid or offer in seconds if it is not hit right away. This quick adaptive response to order flow changes the depth and "tone" of the market momentarily and affects a hedger's ability to execute a trade at a given price. The floor broker cannot change a customer's order if no corresponding trade is offered.

The larger the number of locals and outside speculators trading a particular contract the easier it will be for the floor broker to execute a public order for a hedger. Easier, that is, in the sense of immediate execution at the desired price. This will invariably result in more efficient hedges as you are more able to enter or exit the market at your desired price. If you are a hedger you ought to love speculators in the market, the more the better. You can't have too many people standing by ready to take your risk away with both hands.

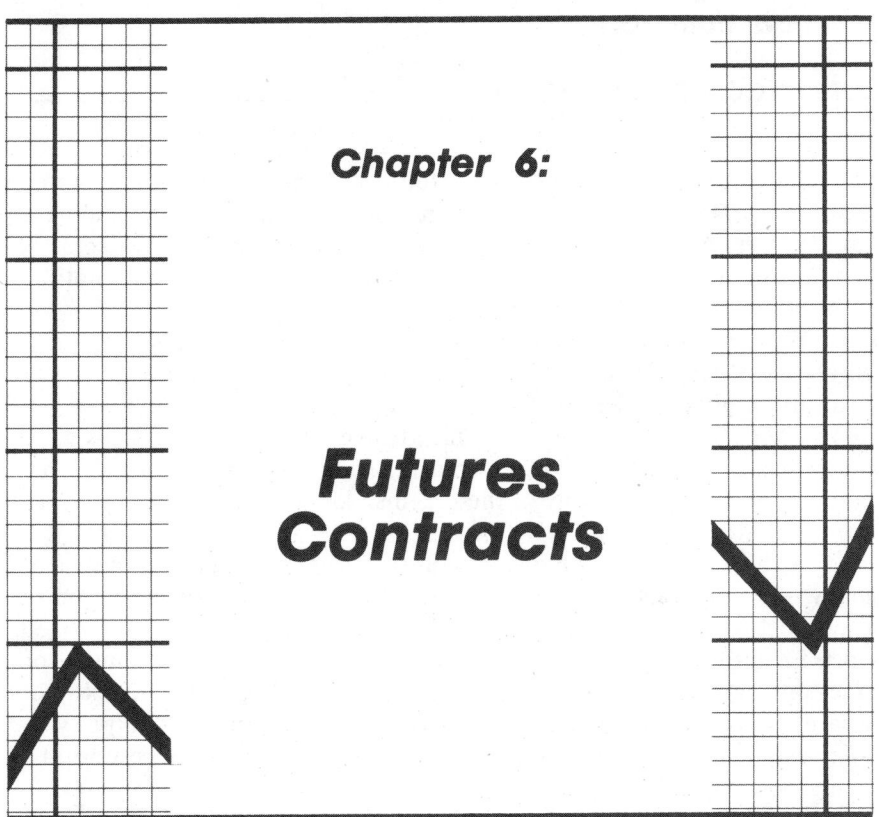

Chapter 6:

Futures Contracts

A CONSIDERABLE amount of confusion exists among those not familiar with the market about just what a futures contract is. In its simplest dimension, a futures contract is a binding agreement to buy or sell something in the future. The "something" which is to be bought or sold could be soybeans, Treasury bills, plywood, cattle, GNMAs, or any of four dozen agricultural commodities, metals, currencies, or financial instruments. It may seem odd that there are futures contracts for such widely different things as wheat, Treasury bills, and heating oil, yet there is a common link. All commodities for which futures contracts are traded have the following thing in common: There is a large, actively traded market in these commodities with a high degree of price risk over time. Since futures markets are designed to shift risk, only those markets which entail high risk and high volume need apply for a futures contract.

FUTURES CONTRACTS DEFINED _____

One distinguishing feature of a futures contract is that it is a binding agreement. This separates futures from options, which are not binding on both parties. A person with a futures contract is obligated to take some action in the future—a person with an option contract may or may not take some future action, as he chooses.

We can add a further dimension to the definition by saying that a futures contract is a binding agreement which is standardized as to the quantity of goods to be bought or sold, the minimum acceptable grade of goods, and the date and place at which delivery is to be made. This added dimension distinguishes a futures contract from a forward contract, which is not standardized as to any of these terms. All terms of forward contracts are negotiated.

A third dimension of futures contracts that distinguishes them from many other contracts is that they are liquid. If you buy a contract on the Chicago Board of Trade, you can sell it almost any time the exchange is open for trading. Contracts are not fully negotiable—you can't buy a contract on the Chicago Board of Trade and then sell it on the Kansas City Board of Trade. Neither can you sell it on the street corner so don't buy one there either; it would be as genuine as the Renoir your worthless son-in-law bought on the sidewalk in Paris.

The unique feature of a futures contract is that the counter party is always known and is always the same. No matter what kind of contract is bought or sold, or to whom, the other party is always the clearing corporation (explained below.) Obviously, on the floor of the exchange a trader who wants to sell must find a trader who wants to buy the same contract. Once they agree on a price and record the transaction, no further communication between the two traders is required. One trader has agreed to make delivery of (sell) the standardized quantity and quality of the commodity at a certain time and place. The other trader has agreed to take delivery of (buy) the same quantity and quality at the same time and place. They have not agreed to buy and sell to each other. Rather, they have agreed to sell the commodities to or buy the commodities from the exchange itself through an entity known as the clearing corporation. Once the initial floor trade is made and recorded each of the traders then has a binding agreement with this buffering corporation.

This arrangement makes a number of things possible, especially the continued operation of the exchange. All traders either on or off the floor only have to deal ultimately with one party that is well known to everyone. This assures financial stability to the whole process. Even though defaults are rare, the existence of a large corporation standing ready to take financial responsibility keeps the whole thing honest.

The other advantage to having the clearing corporation as the counter party to all contracts is that contracts are then easily negotiable. Imagine how complicated the system would be if the two original traders had to find each other again in order to get out of their contract. Nearly impossible would be an accurate description. With the clearing corporation arrangement a trader who has bought a contract for soybeans but does not really want 5000 bushels on his front lawn in September can reverse that contract by selling a soybean contract for September delivery. At that point he has an agreement with the clearing corporation to buy 5000 bushels of soybeans from it and to sell 5000 bushels to it at the same time. The trader's net position with the clearing corporation is zero. The original agreement to buy has been cancelled by the offsetting agreement to sell.

TRADING PERIODS AND THE DELIVERY PROCESS

Trading Periods

Contracts are originated for a specific delivery time in the future and are so denoted in the market, hence the name futures. A contract for delivery of a $100,000 Treasury bond in June 1983 is referred to as the June '83 bond contract, or more succinctly, a June '83 bond. Delivery months are spaced three months apart. Trading may occur any day the exchange is open and may continue from the first day the contract is available until the last day of trading as spelled out in the contract specifications. The first day of trading is when the contract is listed by the exchange and may be as much as 42 months prior to maturity. For example, trading of the December '86 CD contract could begin on July 1, 1983. Even though the contract is listed for trading it may not be traded that day—actual trading begins when two want to take a position in that contract.

During the trading period of a particular contract the volume of trading will vary considerably. The number of transactions is called "volume," while the number of outstanding contracts at the close of every trading day is known as the "open interest." Each open contract indicates that one person has bought and one person has sold so there are twice as many traders with positions as indicated by this number. At the beginning of a contract's life and at maturity the open interest is zero—in between it can be anywhere from one to 50,000 or more. In financial instrument futures open interest is usually very low— a few hundred— until six or seven months prior to maturity, at which point it tends to balloon. High open interest, say 20,000 to 30,000 contracts, is indicative of an active and liquid market which makes it easier to buy or sell on demand.

The volume of trading that occurs each day is reported in the same one-sided fashion—a volume of 500 contracts indicates that 500 contracts were bought and 500 contracts were sold. Daily trading volume, except on the first day a contract is listed, is almost always different from the open interest, because some traders may buy a contract and hold onto that position for quite a long time. If this occurs it will still be an open contract, but there is no further trading. Thus, it is quite possibile to have an open interest of 10,000 contracts but trading volume of zero, although such an extreme difference is unlikely. On the opposite side, many traders will open and close positions several times in one day, leaving the net open interest unchanged but increasing the trading volume. The relationships of price to volume and open interest are often used by many traders as indicators to future price activity.

The last day of trading is specified in the contract and is some particular day during the delivery month. For the Bank CD contracts traded on the International Monetary Market, the last trading day is the second Tuesday of the month. If an open contract has not been offset by an opposite trade before the last day of trading, delivery against the futures contract is then required; but this may be made even before that, as early as the beginning of the delivery month, depending on various factors.

Delivery Process

The delivery period and the delivery process are completely spelled out in the contract specifications. The delivery period may be either a single day in the month or a sequence of days in the month, depending largely on the transportability of the commodity. Transfer of Treasury bills, which is done by computer, is much easier and faster than transferring a carload of cattle, so the delivery period for cattle is longer than for Treasury bills.

While delivery is rare there are detailed procedures for doing it. Although the clearing corporation is the counter party to all contracts, if there is a delivery the clearing corporation acts only as an intermediary. If there is one seller (short) who wants to deliver, there must also be one buyer (long) remaining to take delivery. If this occurs, the short notifies the clearing corporation of intent to deliver and the clearing corporation then notifies the long that delivery will occur. If there is more than one trader who intends to deliver, shorts and longs are matched or assigned by the clearing corporation according to a chronological preference order determined by the clearing corporation, *except in the case of options on futures which occurs in random order.* All deliveries take place through the exchange's designated agents. When delivery occurs, payment in full in cash or wire transfer must be made directly to the short by the long.

FINANCIAL INSTRUMENT FUTURES: A DETAILED LOOK

Since this book is written for financial institutions who probably are not going to be trading agricultural commodities, we won't bother with the details of contract specifications for sugar or feeder cattle. The contract terms of financial futures are quite important to efficient decision making in the hedging process. In this section we describe the debt instrument contracts that were actively traded on commodity exchanges in late 1983.

GNMA FUTURES

Futures contracts on Government National Mortgage Association certificates (GNMAs or Ginnie Maes) are the oldest financial instrument futures contracts. Trading in GNMA futures began on the Chicago Board of Trade on October 20, 1975. The original GNMA contract called for delivery not of actual GNMA certificates but of a Collateralized Depository Receipt or CDR. The CDR is an ersatz security used only as a delivery instrument against the GNMA futures contract. On September 12, 1978 a new GNMA futures contract was introduced which called for delivery of actual GNMAs; it was subsequently phased out. The contract terms for the GNMA contract are given in Table 6.1.

TABLE 6.1
GNMA Futures Contract Terms

Exchange	Chicago Board of Trade
Contract Size	$100,000
Deliverable Grade	Modified pass-through mortage-backed certificates guaranteed by GNMA, with coupons or an equivalent principal balance based on an 8% coupon yielding 7.96% at par, 30 year maturity, assumed totally prepaid in 12th year.
Delivery Method	Collateralized Depository Receipt from CBOT approved originator
Price Quotation	Percent of par
Minimum Fluctuation	1/32d of 1% ($31.25)
Price Limit	64/32ds ($2000) above or below previous day's settlement price*
Initial Margin	$2000*
Maintenance Margin	$1500*
Trading Hours	8:00 a.m. to 2:00 p.m. Chicago time
Months Traded	March, June, September, December
	*subject to change

While the GNMA contract is based on an eight percent coupon, any other coupon can be delivered against the contract, provided that the principal balance is adjusted to conform to the eight percent standard coupon. Conversion factors are published by the exchange for determining the equivalent principal balance. The conversion factors are also used to determine hedge ratios for GNMAs, a topic covered in Chapter 14.

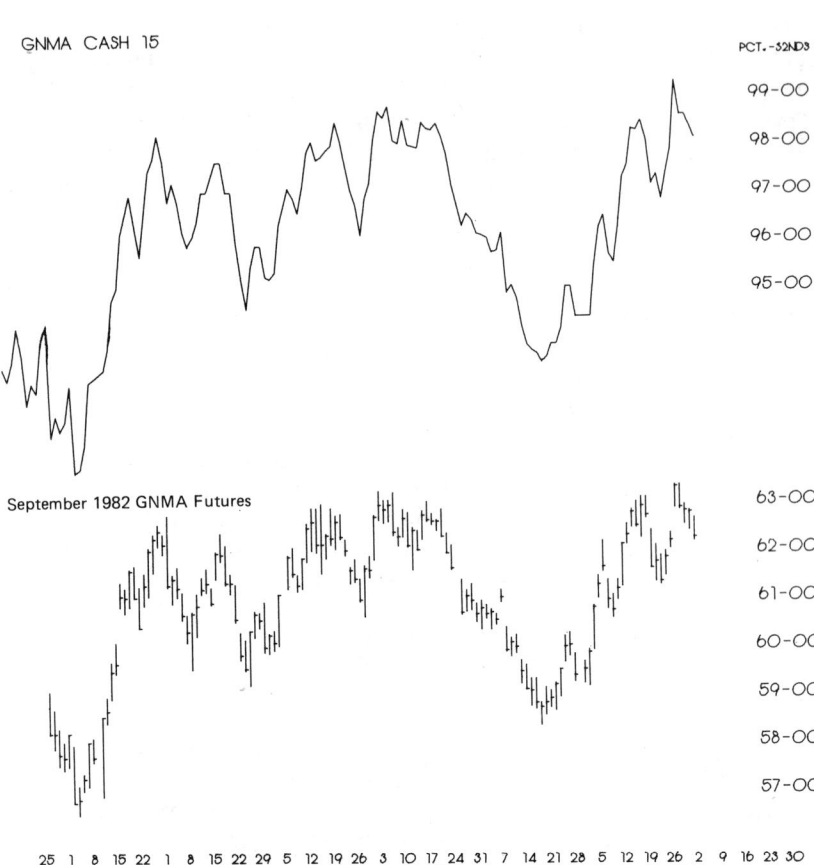

GINNIE MAE
CBT   SEPTEMBER 82
with GNMA cash 15

GNMA CASH 15

PCT.-52NDS

99-OO

98-OO

97-OO

96-OO

95-OO

September 1982 GNMA Futures

63-OO

62-OO

61-OO

60-OO

59-OO

58-OO

57-OO

25 1 8 15 22 1 8 15 22 29 5 12 19 26 3 10 17 24 31 7 14 21 28 5 12 19 26 2 9 16 23 30 6
   FEB   MAR   APR   MAY   JUN   JUL

**Figure 6.1 Fluctuating GNMA Futures
Relationship Between Ginny Mae Futures
and Cash Ginnie Maes**

Courtesy Datalab Corp.

What is of interest at the moment is that the ability to deliver coupons other than eight percent means that the price of GNMA futures will reflect the current price of cash market GNMAs. For example, if new GNMAs are being produced at 15 percent, the price of an eight percent coupon would be 62-12. A GNMA futures contract would also be priced in the same price range. If rates on new GNMAs fell to 14 percent, the price of the eight percent coupon would rise to 66-10, a change of 3-30 or $3937.50 for a $100,000 GNMA. The price of the futures contract should rise by a similar amount. As Figure 6.1 indicates, the price of a GNMA futures fluctuates in a fashion similar to the cash market price of GNMAs. This close correlation increases the hedging efficiency of the GNMA contract. Figure 6.2 below shows the trading volume in GNMA futures, indicating it is a liquid market, which enhances its usefulness to a hedger since positions can be taken or reversed easily.

U. S. TREASURY BILL FUTURES

Contracts for future delivery of U.S. Treasury bills are available for trading on the New York Futures Exchange, the Commodity Exchange of

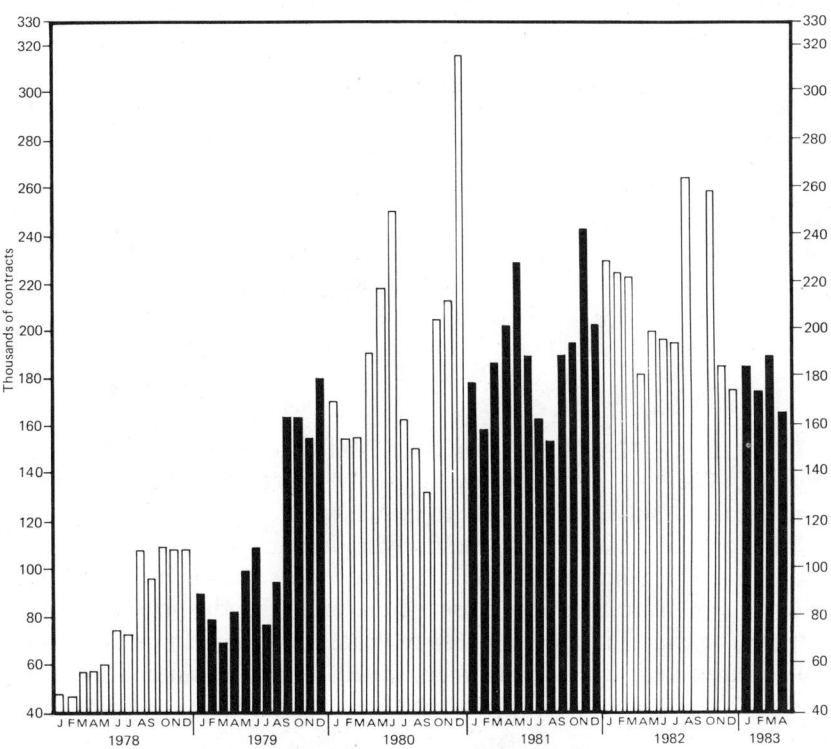

Figure 6.2. Volume of Trading of GNMA (CDR) Futures

New York, the International Monetary Market of the Chicago Mercentile Exchange, and the Mid-America Commodity Exchange. In reality, the only active market for T-bill futures is the International Monetary Market, known on the street as the IMM or the "Merc." Trading in the IMM's 90-day T-bill contract began on January 6, 1976. A 1-year T-bill contract was listed on September 11, 1978, but failed to generate sufficient market interest to remain a viable contract. Trading in the 90-day bill contract has continued to be active. The specifications for the 90-day Treasury bill contract are given in Table 6.2.

TABLE 6.2
90-day Treasury Bill Futures Contract

Exchange	IMM Division of Chicago Mercantile Exchange
Contract size	$1,000,000
Deliverable Grade	U. S. Treasury bill with 90, 91, or 92 days to maturity
Delivery Method	Federal Reserve wire transfer
Price Quotation	Index—100 minus discount yield
Minimum Fluctuation	.01% (1 basis point = $25)
Price Limit	.60% (60 basis points = $1500) above or below previous day's settlement price)*
Initial Margin	$2000*
Maintenance Margin	$1500*
Trading Hours	8:00 a.m. to 2:00 p.m. Chicago time
Months Traded	March, June, September, December
	*subject to change

Unlike the GNMA futures contract, T-bills have no delivery conversion factors. The delivery procedure is simply to transfer $1 million face value of Treasury bills with 91 days to maturity.

The short-term nature of the underlying instrument makes the T-bill contract extremely responsive to market interest rates. As Figure 6.3 shows, the price of T-bill futures is very closely correlated with the price of T-bills at auction. The chart in Figure 6.4 also indicates that the volume of trading in T-bill futures has increased commensurately with the volatility in rates.

TREASURY BILLS
IMM DECEMBER 83
WITH CURRENT 90 DAY T-BILLS

PTS OF 100 PCT.

Cash

Futures

92.20
92.00
91.80
91.60
91.40
91.20
91.00
90.80
90.60
90.40
90.20
90.00
89.80
89.60
89.40

4 11 18 25   2 9 16 23 30   6 13 20 27   4 11 18 25   1 8 15 22 29   5 12 19 26   3 10 17 24 31
APR   MAY   JUN   JUL   AUG   SEP

Figure 6.3. Relationship Between T-bill Futures and Cash T-bills at Auction

Courtesy Datalab Corp.

Beginning in the late 1970s the average variation in the auction rate on new bills began to rise, and the volume of T-bill contracts traded began to rise as well. This is to be expected since futures contracts become more viable when market risk increases.

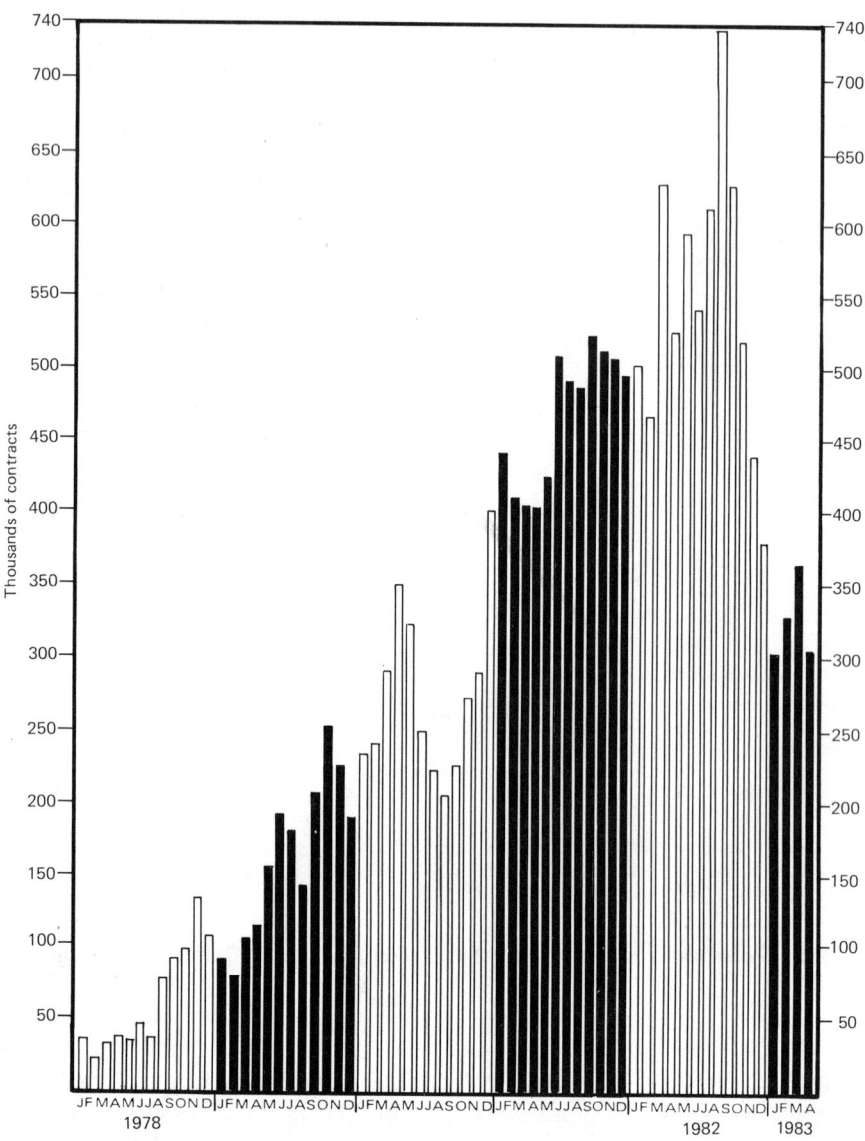

Figure 6.4. Volume of Trading of Treasury Bill Futures

U. S. TREASURY BOND FUTURES

Even though Treasury bonds have been around for years, the development of a Treasury bond futures contract only became a realistic possibility in the mid–1970s. Prior to that time there was no active secondary market in long-term Treasury bonds. Subscribers to Treasury issues held them to maturity because of their yield advantage and zero default risk—holders of long-term bonds were not interested in liquidity. In the mid-1970s the income potential of actually trading long bonds became apparent as interest rates began to vary in ever-larger ranges. A small rate change could mean a larger change in the price of a 30-year bond than in that of a three-month bill. The development of an active secondary market in long bonds was the prerequisite for the U.S. Treasury bond futures contract which had its debut on August 22, 1977 at the Chicago Board of Trade. The contract specifications for Treasury bond futures are listed in Table 6.3.

TABLE 6.3
U. S. Treasury Bond Futures Contract Terms

Exchange	Chicago Board of Trade
Contract Size	$100,000
Deliverable Grade	U. S. Treasury bonds either maturing or not callable for at least 15 years from delivery day. Contract calls for 8% coupon, $100,000 face value; other coupons deliverable on an adjusted basis provided they meet maturity standard.
Delivery Method	Percent of par
Minimum Fluctuation	1/32d of 1% ($31.25)
Price Limit	64/32ds ($2000) above or below previous day's settlement price*
Initial Margin	$2000*
Maintenance Margin	$1500*
Trading Hours	8:00 a.m. to 2:00 p.m. Chicago time
Months Traded	March, June, September, December
	*subject to change

The price relationship between T-bond futures and cash market bonds is similar to that in the GNMA market for the same reason. Bond futures based on the eight percent coupon trade well under par when the current rate on Treasury bonds is well over eight percent. The major difference between the two markets is that deliverable GNMAs are newly originated certificates, while deliverable Treasury bonds may have been outstanding for as long as 25 years. Thus, the supply of deliverable instruments is well known, since outstanding Treasury bonds are identifiable while GNMAs are not. For this reason the price of bond futures tends to parallel the price of the cheapest deliverable bond available in the market. Obviously, a short who wanted to deliver would pick the cheapest one out of his portfolio or the cheapest one he could buy in the market. The cheapest deliverable bond changes as bond prices change in the cash market. However, as Figure 6.5 shows, the relationship between bond futures and cash bonds is a close one.

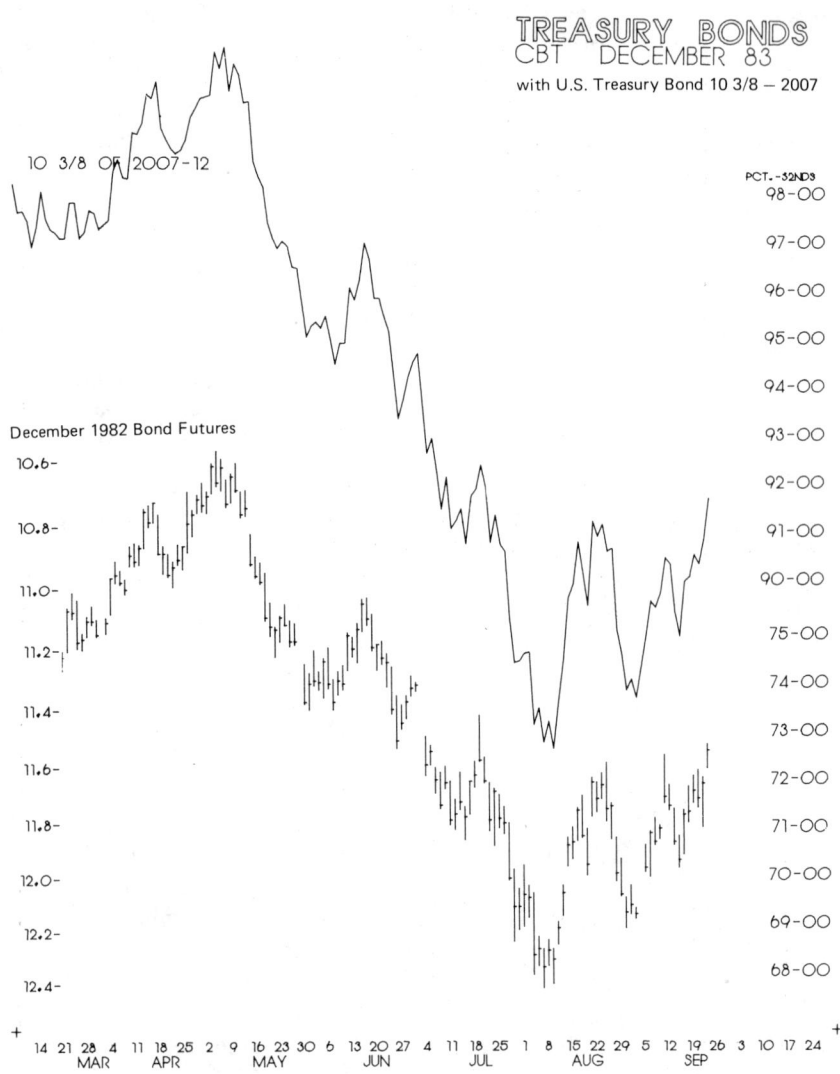

Figure 6.5 Relationship Between Bond Futures and Cash Bonds

Courtesy Datalab Corp.

The volume of trading in bond futures is nothing short of incredible. The bond contract is the largest single futures contract traded anywhere in the world and accounts for about 25 percent of the daily trading volume at the Chicago Board of Trade. The major growth in trading volume (see Figure 6.6) began in late 1979 when interest rates began to gyrate and climbed steadily upward through 1982. Average daily trading volume in mid-1982 was 60,000 contracts per day.

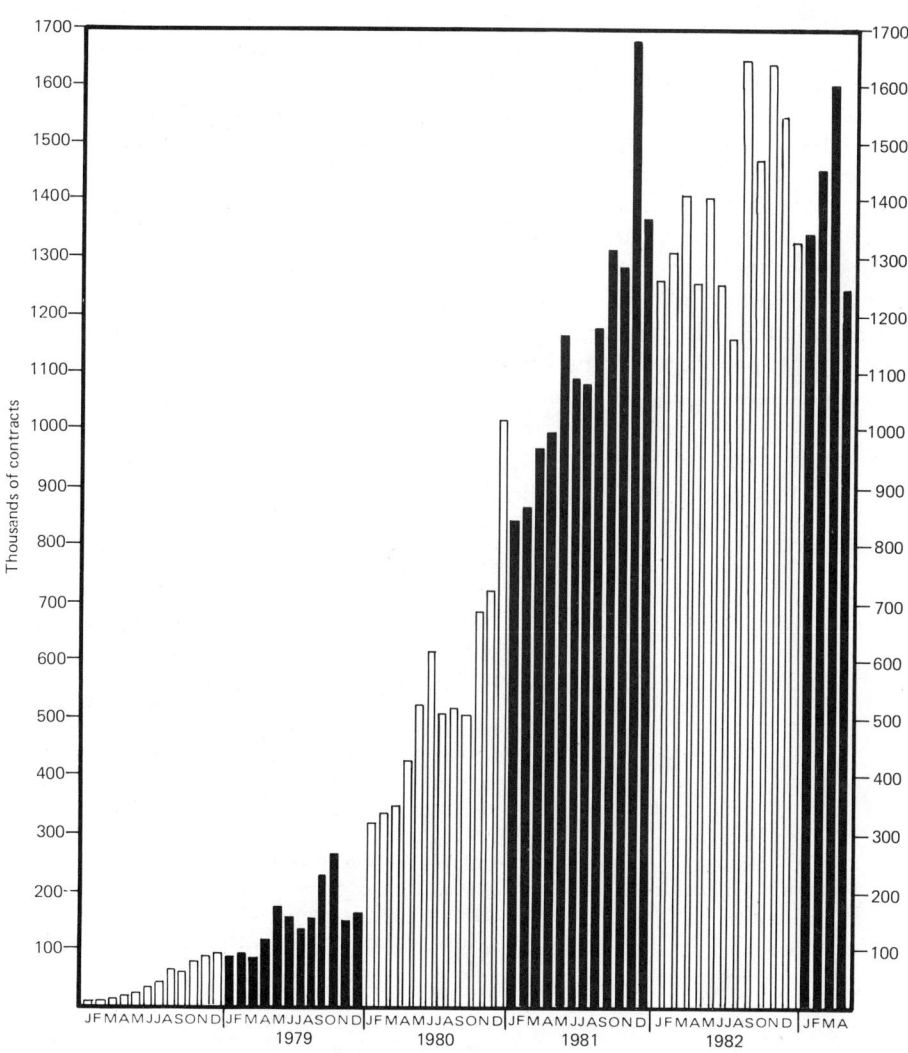

Figure 6.6. Volume of Trading of Treasury Bond Futures

BANK CD FUTURES

Trading in futures contracts for bank certificates of deposit began at the New York Futures Exchange on July 9, 1981 and was followed by contracts at the Chicago Board of Trade on July 22, 1981 and the IMM on July 29, 1981. The contract on the IMM quickly became the dominant one of the three—by July 1982 open interest in the IMM contract was 15,000, the Board of Trade reported open interest of around 1500 contracts, and the NYFE did not publish any open interest in bank CDs.

The development of the bank CD futures contract represents a new direction for the financial futures market in that it was the first contract for a purely private debt instrument. The background of the CD contract is not materially different from that of the other financial futures—increased interest rate variability from the late 1970s onward. There is, of course, a large and active secondary market in bank CDs. Trading CDs involves a degree of price risk similar to that inherent in the Treasury market. The need for a separate futures contract based on a short-term debt instrument arises from the poor correlation between CD rates and T-bill rates. The best substitute for a bank CD, in terms of yield and term, is commercial paper. The rate on T-bills frequently moves opposite to the rate on CDs, whereas commercial paper closely tracks the new-issue CD rate. Treasury bills also have fixed maturities, while both commercial paper and CDs are negotiable

TABLE 6.4
Three-Month Domestic CD Futures Contract Terms

Exchange	International Monetary Market (Chicago Mercantile Exchange)
Contract Size	$1,000,000
Deliverable Grade	"No Name" CDs; deliverable banks announced 2 business days before 15th of delivery month. CDs must mature 2½ to 3½ months after delivery. CDs must have no more than 185 days accrued interest. Variable rate and discount CDs deliverable if and when yields are equivalent to "no name" list.
Delivery Method	
Price Quotation	Index—add-on interest
Minimum Fluctuation	.01% (1 basis point = $25)
Price Limit	.80% (80 basis points = $2000) above or below previous day's settlement price*
Initial Margin	$2000*
Maintenance Margin	$1500*
Trading Hours	7:30 a.m. to 2:00 p.m. Chicago Time
Months Traded	March, June, September, December
Last Trading Day	Last business day before last day of month
	*subject to change

have fixed maturities, while both commercial paper and CDs are negotiable as to term. The bank CD futures contract provides a more efficient method of transferring risk in the short-term private debt market. Specifications for the IMM three month Domestic CD contract are given in Table 6.4.

The specifications of the CD futures contract are closely aligned with standard practices in the secondary market. The CDs issued by the largest banks are interchangeable in the secondary market, provided they have the same yield and maturity. CDs issued by these large banks are sold on a "no name" basis—the buyer doesn't know the specific bank until the CD is delivered. The futures market relies on this practice to make the contract delivery procedure work. At the IMM the exchange polls the secondary CD dealers to determine the list of "no name" CDs currently traded which meet

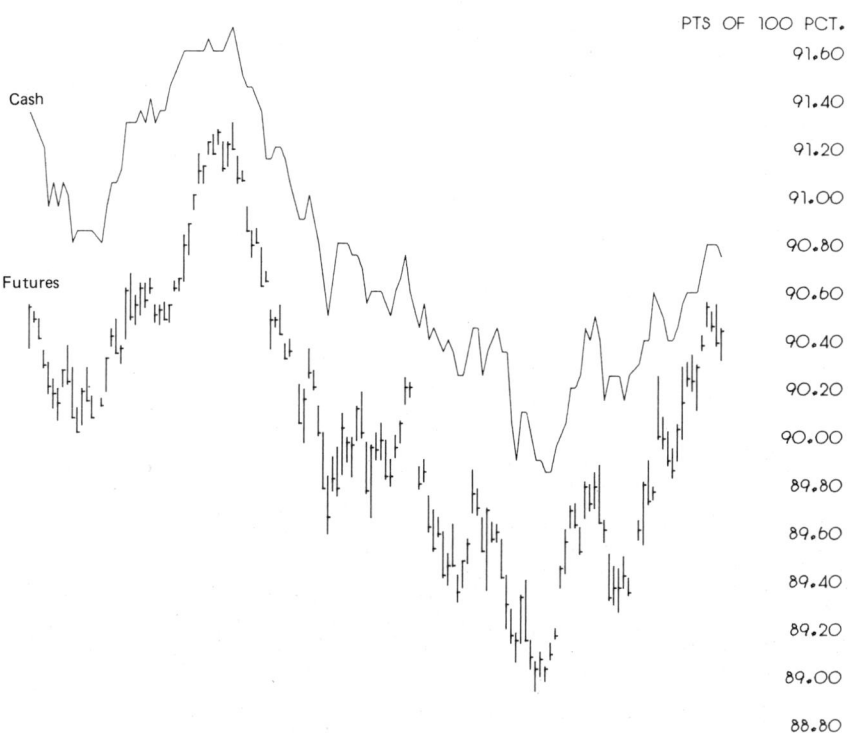

Figure 6.7 Cash Market CD Rates and CD Futures

Courtesy Datalab Corp.

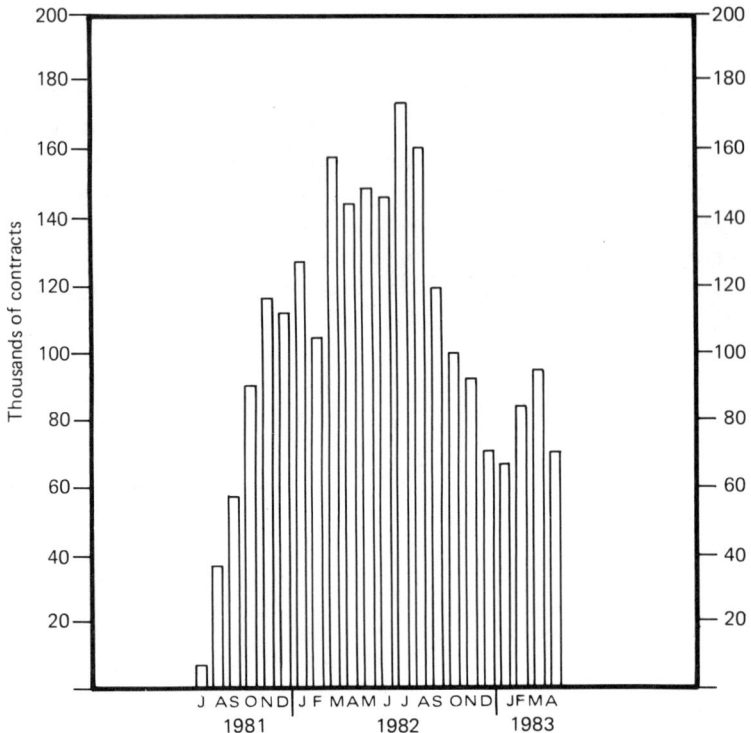

Figure 6.8. Volume of Trading of Certificate of Deposit Futures
Source: International Monetary Market

the contract specifications and then publishes a list prior to the delivery period. Deliverable grade CDs comprise on the average 10 percent of the entire CD market of about $120 billion.

The charts in Figures 6.7 and 6.8 indicate the relationship between cash market CD rates and CD futures and the trading volume in CD futures, respectively. As the charts show, the CD futures market is an active one that closely tracks the cash market in CDs. Close correlation between any futures contract and the cash market instrument underlying it means the futures contract may serve as an efficient hedging vehicle.

EURODOLLAR TIME DEPOSIT FUTURES

The only other actively traded futures contract based on a private debt security is the Eurodollar Time Deposit contract at the IMM. Trading in

Eurodollar contracts began on December 9, 1981. The Eurodollar market is a market for time deposits which are not negotiable. These deposits are bought or sold primarily by London banks or London branches of U.S. banks. The interest rate risk that exists for Eurodollar deposits is totally different from that of other debt instruments for which there are futures contracts. There is no price risk of the type found on Treasury bonds or notes since Eurodollar deposits are always very short term, typically three months. Unlike bank CDs which are also short term, there is no inventory price risk for Eurodollar deposits since there are no secondary market dealers.

The risk that banks face in dealing in Eurodollar deposits is an anticipatory funding cost risk. Eurodollar time deposits are sold by drawing down a line of credit from the buying bank. The bank which issues the line of credit (buys the time deposits) has a commitment to fund those deposits at whatever the current market rate is for some number of months or even years in the future until the entire line of credit is taken down. The existence of Eurodollar futures contracts allows the bank funding Eurodollar time deposits to hedge the interest rate on those deposits. The bank that is selling Eurodollar time deposits can also hedge its interest costs on the opposite side. (Specific strategies are dealt with in Chapters 9 and 10.)

The contract terms of the Eurodollar futures contract are shown in Table 6.5.

TABLE 6.5
90-Day Eurodollar Time Deposit Futures Contract Terms

Exchange	IMM
Contract Size	$1,000,000
Deliverable Grade	Cash settlement with clearing corporation
Delivery Method	Cash (Federal Reserve wire transfer)
Price Quotation	Index, add-on interest
Minimum Fluctuation	.01% (1 basis point = $25)
Price Limit	1.00% (100 basis points = $2500) above or below previous day's settlement price*
Initial Margin	$2000*
Maintenance Margin	$1500*
Trading Hours	7:30 a.m. to 2:00 p.m. Chicago time
Months Traded	March, June, September, December
Last Trading Day	2d London business day before 3d Wednesday of delivery month
	*subject to change

U.S. TREASURY NOTES

The newest financial futures contract is the U.S. Treasury note contract first traded on the Chicago Board of Trade on May 3, 1982. Note contracts had previously been traded on several exchanges but had disappeared as active instruments prior to the introduction of the newest Board of Trade contract. The Treasury note contract stands between the very short-term Treasury bill and CD contracts and the long-term GNMA and Treasury bond contracts. Development of an intermediate term futures contract reflects to a large extent the maturity shift in the cash bond market. Beginning in 1981 corporate treasurers and the U.S. Treasury began to offer significantly more intermediate-term bonds instead of long-term bonds; new seven and 10-year Treasury issues jumped 52 percent in 1981, and 51 percent of all new corporate bonds were in the five-to 12-year maturity range. In large part this shift was due to the increased rate volatility following the Federal Reserve's new monetary policy of October 1979. Switching from long-term bonds to intermediate-term notes significantly reduces price risk of both holders and issuers of fixed-income securities. This shift in the cash market makes a futures contract based on medium-term Treasuries a viable possibility, particularly since the supply of new notes which are deliverable against the contract has been increased and will presumably remain a significant Treasury financing instrument.

The contract terms of the Treasury Note contract are given in Table 6.6.

TABLE 6.6
U.S. Treasury Note Futures Contract Terms

Exchange	Chicago Board of Trade
Contract Size	$100,000
Deliverable Grade	U. S. Treasury Notes maturing not less than 6½ years or more than 10 years from delivery date. Standard coupon of 8%, other coupons deliverable on adjusted basis.
Delivery Method	Federal Reserve wire transfer
Price Quotation	Percent of par
Minimum Fluctuation	1/32d of 1% ($31.25)
Price Limit	64/32ds ($2000) above or below previous day's settlement price*
Initial Margin	$2000*
Maintenance Margin	$1500*
Trading Hours	8:00 a.m. to 2:00 p.m. Chicago time
Months Traded	March, June, September, December
Last Trading Day	Last business day prior to last seven business days of the delivery month
	*subject to change

The ability to deliver notes across a 3½ year maturity range injects a wrinkle into the pricing of the note contract. A seven-year note with a 12 percent coupon would conform to the eight percent standard at a price of

81-13 while a 10-year note with a 12 percent coupon would be priced at 77-02 to yield eight percent, a price difference of $4343.75 on the $100,000 contract size. The principle of delivering the cheapest possible security tends to push the futures price towards the price of 10-year notes rather than the shorter maturities, since they would be more expensive.

NEW CONTRACTS

The preceding section of this chapter discussed the contract terms for financial futures contracts that were available for trading at the time this book was written. The six contracts were not introduced all at once but over a seven year period. During that time a number of other contracts have been authorized and listed for trading. Some were subsequently withdrawn by the exchanges due to lack of adequate trading volume. In this respect, futures markets are not appreciably different from other markets—some products take off, some bomb.

However, the futures market is a dynamic one and that implies change. The form of those changes is usually the introduction of brand new contracts and the withdrawal of existing ones by the exchange. Old contracts are almost never modified to reflect a change in market conditions, a feature which seems to be endemic to the whole futures market—the same process occurs in agricultural contracts as well as in financial instruments.

The introduction of a new contract is usually a lengthy process, requiring as long as two years between inception and the first day's trading. The steps involved include research on the cash market instrument, design of the contract specifications, regulatory approval, and commencement of trading. That is, of course, an abbreviated view of the process, but the details are not of crucial importance in the context of hedging strategies for financial institutions. What is of importance is that new futures contracts must be designed to meet legitimate hedging needs in order to gain regulatory approval. "Legitimate hedging needs" is a somewhat nebulous term, but it is incumbent upon the exchange to demonstrate that a great deal of trading in the new contract will be done by hedgers rather than speculators, since one can speculate in any currently traded contract. Because of this regulatory bent new contracts tend to be introduced only for financial instruments which have a cash market that has a lot of participants, large trading volume, and high risk for trader/dealers and financial institutions. In addition to regulatory constraints, it is in the interest of the exchange to trade contracts for these types of markets. Hedgers are dealing in the underlying cash market constantly and are therefore more apt to trade futures contracts to offset their cash market risk.

Financial futures contracts have been developed because market volatility has increased. Grain markets have been volatile for centuries, but extreme volatility in debt markets is a very recent phenomenon. From 1974 onward volatility and risk in fixed-income debt instruments has increased steadily. Concurrently, the pace at which new financial futures contracts have been developed has also accelerated. The possibilities for new financial contracts are by no means exhausted, so new contracts should be forthcoming.

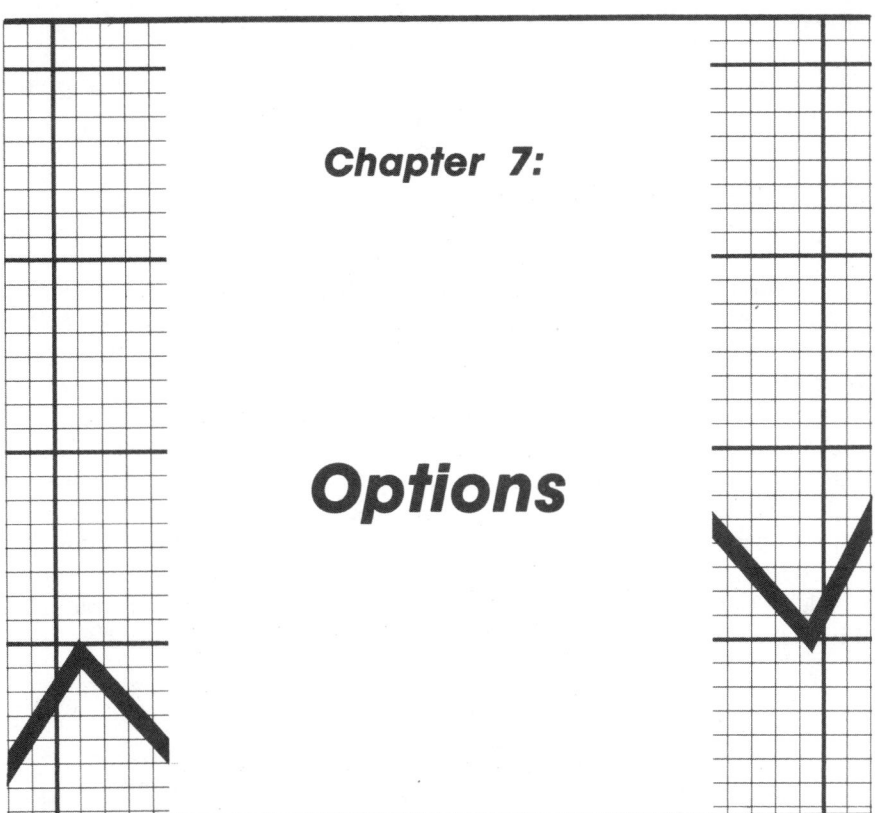

Chapter 7:

Options

THE MOST recent addition to the hedger's toolkit is options. As we mentioned earlier, they offer another way to offset interest rate risk exposure with the added feature of not requiring the hedger to forego all of the advantages that may accrue from favorable interest rate changes.

Currently, there are options on futures and options on actual securities. The greater liquidity and closer relationship between the futures market and the underlying cash market favors using options on futures as opposed to options on actuals. Therefore, we will limit our discussion to futures options.

_____ DEFINITIONS

You will find that the terminology of futures options is very similar to that of stock options with which you may already be familiar. There are some differences and characteristics unique to futures options, but they will be pointed out as we proceed.

First, an option on a futures is defined as a right to buy or sell a specific futures contract at a predetermined price at any time prior to the expiration of the option. For this right, the purchaser of the option pays a fee known as the *premium*.

PUTS AND CALLS

Therefore, an option which allows its purchaser to *buy* a futures contract at a given price, called the *strike price*, is known as a *call*. Conversely, an option which allows its purchaser to *sell* a futures contract at a given strike price is called a *put*. To *exercise* an option means to demand that the right be granted. In exercising a call, the buyer of the option, known as the "holder," exchanges his call option for a long futures position. Similarly, the holder of a put receives a short futures position upon exercising his option. The price of the futures contract received is the strike price.

Generally, strike prices will be at relatively convenient price levels near the price at which the underlying futures contract is currently trading. For example, if the current T-bond futures is a March contract and it is trading at 74-00, then the typical strike prices for the March options would be:

March	Calls	Puts
	80-00	80-00
	78-00	78-00
	76-00	76-00
	74-00	74-00
	72-00	72-00
	70-00	70-00
	68-00	68-00

Similarly, if the June futures contract is trading at 73-10, then at the same time June options have the following strike prices:

June	Calls	Puts
	80-00	80-00
	78-00	78-00
	76-00	76-00
	74-00	74-00
	72-00	72-00
	70-00	70-00
	68-00	68-00

IN AND OUT OF THE MONEY

Just like stock options, futures options are termed At-the-Money, In-the-Money, and Out-of-the-Money, depending on how far away the strike price is from the current market price of the underlying futures contract. If the strike price is very far away from current futures price levels, options may be called Deep-in-the-Money and Deep-Out-of-the-Money. The "in- & out-of-money" terms essentially arise from a determination of whether the option has *intrinsic value*; that is, for calls, if the futures price exceeds the strike price, the option has intrinsic value. For example, if the futures contract is selling at 74-00 and you hold an option with a strike price of 72-00, you could exercise the option, receive a long futures position at 72-00, and then cover that position at 74-00, making a profit of $2000. For puts, intrinsic value is the amount by which the strike price exceeds the price of the underlying futures contract. If you hold a put with a strike price of 74-00 (called a 74 put) and the futures contract is selling at 72-00, you could exercise the put and make the same $2000 profit.

These terms are precisely defined by the following examples. If March T-bond futures are trading at 74-00, a March 74 call would be termed at-the-money; it has no intrinsic value but is near the current price. A March 72 call would be an in-the-money option as it has two full points of intrinsic value. An option with no intrinsic value, such as a March 78 call, is termed out-of-the money. By the same example, a March 74 put would be at-the-money; a March 78 put would be in-the-money; and a March 72 put would be out-of-the-money. Intrinsic value is only one factor in the price of an option. We will discuss options valuation in greater detail below.

OTHER OPTIONS

To round out our options definitions we now come to *naked, covered*, and *dressed* options. These terms do not have anything to do with someone losing his shirt, or pants, but describe varying amounts of risk to the options writer. An options buyer or holder has his risk limited to the premium that he has paid. An options writer (seller), on the other hand, could have potentially unlimited risk as the option he writes might be exercised. In this case he would have a speculative futures position with all the attendant risk. A *naked option* is one which is written without any opposite position either in cash or futures bonds. A *covered option* is one which is written against an opposite position in cash bonds. For example, you write a call against 30-year Treasury bonds that you own. A *dressed option* is one written against an opposite position in T-bond futures; you write a put against a short futures position that you now have. Obviously, the last two types of options have less risk, and any institutional options writing program would generally be in this area.

PREMIUMS AND VALUATION OF OPTIONS

Determining the *premium* or price of an option is a somewhat complex task. This is due to the fact that the value of an option is based on several factors, most of which are constantly changing.

Much of the sophisticated options trading by professionals revolves around computer models that are based on various market assumptions and calculate theoretical values for options premiums. There are, however, some generalized formulae which are quite suitable for use by a hedger and which do not get too complex.

For our purposes it is sufficient to know that an options premium is essentially derived from two components: intrinsic value and time value. This can be written as follows:

$$\text{Premium} = \text{Intrinsic Value} + \text{Time Value}$$

We have already discussed intrinsic value and need now only to explore the time value component.

Basically, an option is a decaying asset of sorts; since for a given period of time, generally anywhere from one to six months, the holder has a right to a futures position at a fixed price. The value of that right diminishes as the expiration date of the option draws near. (See Figure 7.1.) A considerable part of an option's premium is composed of this value and is known as the *time value premium*. Just as ice melts, this component decays over time. When taken in conjunction with the intrinsic value, the time value and total value can be graphically represented as in Figure 7.2. (Options traders are very big on diagrams, the more complicated the better, showing almost every possible relationship. Perhaps this is because options valuation is such an abstract subject.)

Two other factors influence the value of an option: volatility of the underlying futures contract and the short-term interest rate level. Computer models that spew out theoretical premium values are dependent upon these factors. How far their initial assumptions deviate from reality will determine the usefulness of the model's predictions in the marketplace. Along with theoretical premiums, the computer models also generate numbers called *deltas* which are indicators of relative price movement for each option versus a movement in the futures price.

Deltas are important to watch, for both speculators and hedgers, as they give an indication of what to expect in the fluctuation of an option's price in a given market. For the hedger they can be very useful in determining hedge ratios. Deltas, one must remember, are only as good as the model which produced them, which is only as good as its assumptions about volatility and interest rate levels.

Volatility refers to the probability that the futures price will change by a given percentage over a year's time. Statistically, it is the standard deviation of the percent change in the futures price. In most cases you will see volatility assumptions given in terms of a percentage. (See Figure 7.2.)

A 10 percent volatility factor presumes that there is about a two-thirds probability that the futures price will not fluctuate more than 10 percent from its current price level. With T-bond futures trading at 74-00 this means futures prices over the next year are expected to remain in the 66-20 to 81-12 range. As volatility rises, uncertainty in prices pushes up the value of an option.

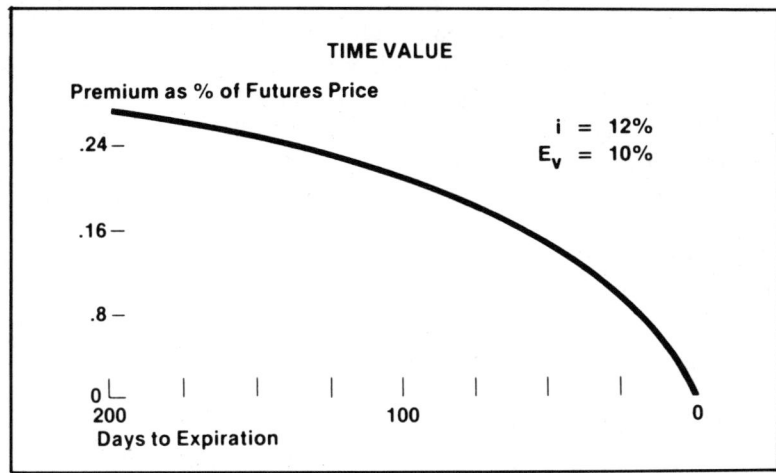

Figure 7.1 Time Value Decay Rate of a Futures Option

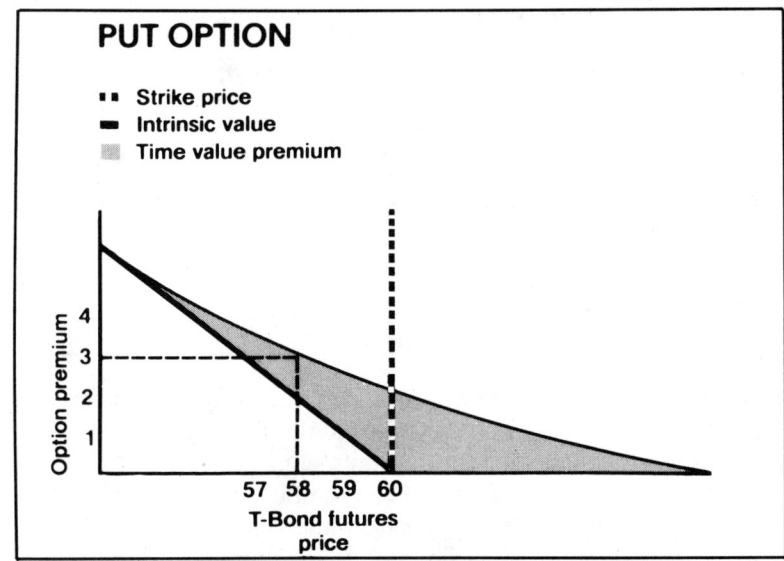

If the strike price is 60-00...when T-Bond futures are trading at 58-00 and the put option premium is 3-00 ($3,000), the option's intrinsic value is 2-00 and its time value premium is 1-00.

Figure 7.2 Options Premium Composed of Intrinsic Value and Time Value

The other factor, the short-term interest rate level, also affects the price of an option, since it reflects the cost of carry; that is, the cost of the money to purchase the option. This value is also viewed on an annual basis. Like interest rates, the cost of carry rises, and so, too, does the value of an option.

One thing should be pointed out about T-bond futures options in order to avoid confusion. T-bond futures prices are quoted in terms of 32ds of one percent of par based on an eight percent coupon. Options on T-bond futures are quoted in 64ths! This is due to the smaller price fluctuations of options relative to futures. Therefore, a move from 74-00 to 74-16 indicates a $500 move in futures while a move from 3-00 to 3-16 indicates a move of $250 in the option price.

An example of how futures options are quoted can be seen by the following addition to our previous strike price example:

March T-Bond Futures Price: 74-00

March	Calls	Puts
80-00	0-02	6-08
78-00	0-05	4-12
76-00	0-17	2-24
74-00	0-47	0-58
72-00	2-11	0-17
70-00	3-62	0-07
68-00	5-58	0-03

Time: 52 days to expiration

This indicates that it would cost $5,906.25 to purchase a March 70 call and $2,375.00 to purchase a March 76 put.

OFFSETTING AND EXERCISING OPTIONS

Since futures options are exchange traded options of standardized size and specifications, they need not be exercised to extract value from them. In a process similar to closing out a futures contract position, a futures option can be offset by a closing transaction. For example, by selling a call one can liquidate one's position of owning a call, while selling a put terminates one's ownership of a put. Sorry Charlie, you don't buy a put to offset a call.

Exercising a futures option gives you a short futures position if you own a put or a long position if you have a call. Just as most futures contracts are not held until delivery, neither are most futures options exercised. However, the percentage of options exercised may be higher than that of futures contracts delivered due to advanced strategies used in arbitrage situations.

MARGINS AND COMMISSIONS

Options, unlike futures, are not margined. When an option is purchased, the premium is totally paid. Since there is no margin of which to keep track, there is no mark-to-market system of adding funds to or deleting funds from an account based on the daily change in valuation of the option. This means no margin calls. When we discuss margin calls in a later chapter, this benefit will be more apparent.

Since options premiums are fully paid at the time of purchase, an options writer derives income when they are written. This creates the opportunity for an institution to increase the yields on its portfolio by using a covered writing program. Exchange rules do require a certain amount of margin to be placed by an options writer since the options may be exercised, which creates a futures position for which margin is required. These rules are quite complex, and since describing a detailed options writing program is not within the scope of this book, we will not discuss them.

Commissions on futures options are handled in a similar fashion to those on futures contracts. Presently, they are charged to the customer when the options position is offset or exercised, although there is some discussion in the industry about altering this practice on a firm-by-firm basis. One situation to note concerning commissions is what happens if the option is left to expire unexercised. In this case, the commission is charged to the customer at the time of expiration as if he had offset it with a closing transaction. The customer always pays a commission; there are no loopholes.

OPTIONS V. FUTURES

Futures options are currently limited in number. The Commodity Futures Trading Commission (CFTC) has only authorized a one option per exchange pilot program. For the financial hedger this means that only options on T-bond futures are available. (See Table 7.1 for specifications.) When the options program is expanded, options on bank CDs, T-bills, GNMAs, and T-notes seem inevitable and will open up various hedging opportunities.

Options hedging programs will offer some interesting differences from those employing only futures. Since options are not margined, there is a defined risk-reward relationship. For a hedger this means being able to establish a ceiling cost of hedging one's rate exposure. And, as noted earlier, there will be no unexpected negative cash flows from margin calls.

Options are similar to futures in that there is a high correlation to market rate movement, offering good hedging stability. They also have similarly low transaction costs. Since options are still in relative infancy, it is hard to compare their liquidity with that of futures except to state that, so far, they have caught on reasonably well, with good trading participation from a diverse group of speculators, arbitrageurs, dealers, and institutions. And if the history of stock options is a guide, they can be expected to enjoy as great, if not considerably greater, liquidity as that of futures.

The downside of options is their possible higher cost relative to futures. You don't get something for nothing, and in the case of options you are paying a premium for the relative safety they provide from price fluctuations and margin calls. A hedger who has the cash flow and the ability to sleep at night can probably achieve his hedging goals more cost efficiently with futures, although there will be ever-increasing room for mixed strategies involving both options and futures.

TABLE 7.1
Options on U. S. Treasury Bond Futures Specifications

Exchange	Chicago Board of Trade
Contract Size	$100,000
Deliverable Grade and Method	A holder of a call receives a long position of CBT U.S. Treasury bond futures
	A holder of a put receives a short position
Strike Price	Integral multiples of two point per T-bond futures contract, e.g., 74, 72, 70, etc.
Premium Payment	In full at the time of the option purchase
Price Quotation and Min. Fluctuation	1/64th of 1% of a T-bond futures contract ($15.625)
Price Limit*	128/64ths ($2000) above or below previous day's settlement price.
	Limits do not apply during the option's expiration month.
Exercise	The buyer may exercise the option on any business day prior to expiration by giving notice to the clearing corp. by 8:00 p.m. that day. A notice will be assigned to the seller. The clearing corp. will establish a futures position for the buyer and an opposite futures position for the seller at the strike price before the opening of trading on the following business day.

Last Day of Trading and Expiration	Options cease trading in the month prior to the futures contract delivery month at 12:00 p.m. on the first Friday preceding, by at least 5 business days, the first notice day for the corresponding T-bond futures contract.
	Unexercised options expire at 10:00 a.m. of the first Saturday following the last day of trading.
Trading Hours	8:00 a.m. to 2:00 p.m. Chicago time
Months Traded	March, June, September, December
	*subject to change

REGULATIONS AND THE FUTURE OF OPTIONS

At this point in evolution, the regulators have awakened to the wisdom of an institution offsetting its interest rate risk by using a hedging program. In fact, the Federal Home Loan Bank Board (FHLBB) even issued its regulations (see Appendix B) allowing the use of options by savings and loan associations in advance of the first day of options trading! As you will see, they were very flexible and accommodating to a wide use of strategies-employing options.

The Office of the Comptroller of the Currency (OCC) has not issued any regulations as such and is handling each bank on an individual basis. It is probably just a matter of time until they issue some guidelines probably very similar to those of the FHLBB.

As the CFTC feels more comfortable with futures options and sees that they are being traded in an orderly fashion on the exchanges, they will authorize more options contracts. This will open up the entire yield curve spectrum and will create practical opportunities for use of futures options by institutions well beyond the present limited long end sector.

Statistical analysis of stock options shows that, after a given period for introduction and education, options volume and open interest eventually will be approximately three to four times as large as those of its underlying security. Given the current enormous size of the financial futures market, this portends a truly huge and extremely liquid options market. The only obstacle to this growth may be the relative competition for learning time as the futures exchanges continually introduce new contracts, thereby creating an overload of information to absorb and work into the mix of hedging strategies.

Part III

Strategies for Financial Institutions

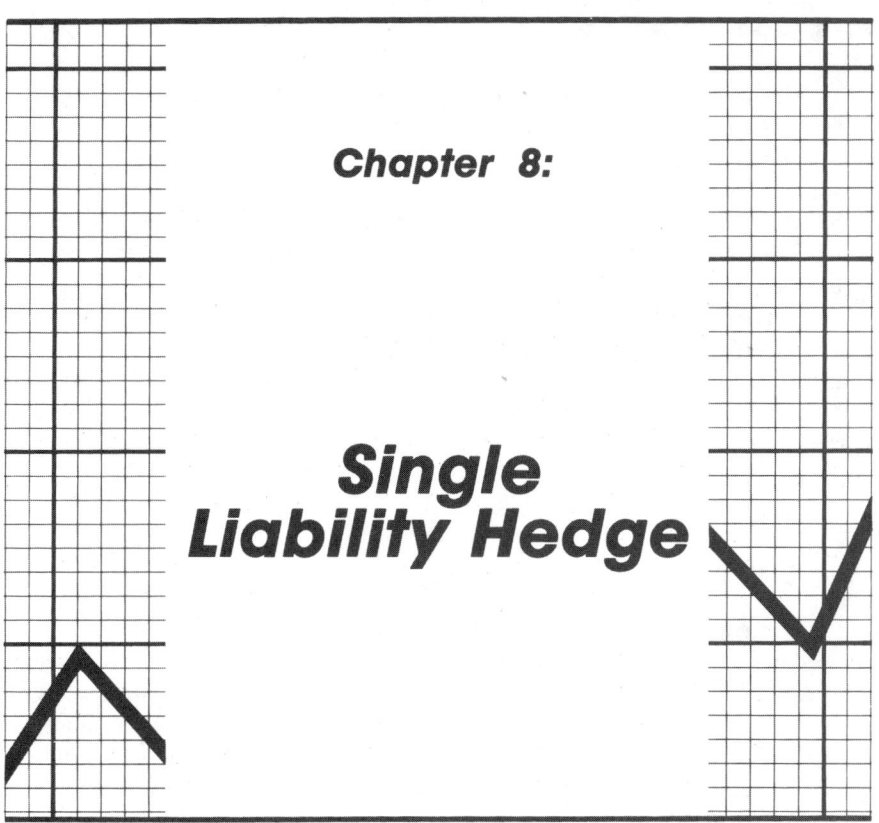

Chapter 8:

Single Liability Hedge

THE PURPOSE of liability hedging for a financial institution is to control the cost of funds. There are many ways to control the cost of funds, traditionally the most popular of which has been matching maturities of assets and liabilities. However, this has become almost impossible to do in the wake of financial deregulation. Other hedging methods, such as writing forward contracts on assets, have not only also become more difficult but in essence put the cart before the horse. A forward contract to buy or sell assets is an attempt to lock in a positive spread between assets and liabilities rather than an attempt to control liability costs. A great many things can go wrong with using forward contracts, and most problems with them cannot be solved unilaterally. There is no bail-out option on forward contracts.

Futures contracts, on the other hand, not only have a bail-out option, but are always more cost effective. There is no cost of finding an opposite party to a contract, no credit investigation costs, no contract compliance or enforcement costs incurred by the trader; and transactions costs are truly minimal. Moreover, hedging with financial futures, if done properly, directly controls liability costs.

The purpose of this chapter is to develop and illustrate strategies for hedging liability costs in the financial futures market. In order to do that, it is necessary to determine which liabilities can be hedged with futures and which cannot. This is Part One. Part Two is deciding how to hedge a particular liability. In Part Three we will develop specific liability hedging strategies, moving from the simple to the complex. The examples will show you how to structure a hedge to fit a variety of circumstances.

NOTE: Structuring hedges is a complicated task that will take some time and effort by the hedger and by the broker. Do not be dismayed if you don't grasp the full meaning or importance of everything in this chapter the first time you read it. Some of the material may require two readings, some of it may require two readings of other chapters, and some of it will require some experience with hedging. This will vary from reader to reader.

PART ONE: WHAT CAN BE HEDGED?

While it is theoretically possible to hedge any liability of a financial intermediary, it is not practical or possible to hedge any liability with financial futures contracts. The first task in designing a liability hedging strategy is to zero in on those liabilities which can be effectively hedged with financial futures. This is most easily accomplished by classifying liabilities in terms of their financial characteristics, rather than their regulatory characteristics.

For a great many bank and savings and loan executives, classification of liabilities has traditionally been done according to regulatory characteristics. This includes such classifications as deposit and nondeposit liabilities, insured and uninsured deposits, and "inside" and "outside" borrowings in the case of savings and loans. The tendency to do this has been fostered by the regulatory framework to which these institutions are subjected. The Federal Reserve System, Federal Home Loan Bank System, and state regulators have insisted for years that the regulated intermediaries use report forms which classify liabilities, as well as assets, according to the criteria which are important to the regulators, not formats which are useful to those being regulated. After many years of this experience, regulatory classifications have become imprinted on the minds of many.

In order to hedge the institution's interest rate risk effectively and efficiently, this pattern must be replaced at the outset. Insurance companies broke this regulatory choke hold many years ago by keeping two sets of books, one set to satisfy regulators and one set to indicate what is going on in the business. It is time for banks and savings and loan associations to adopt the same practice. Doing so, or just thinking as if you actually did keep two sets of books, will make hedging much easier.

Thinking now in this new mode, the most important financial characteristics of liabilities are the holding period and the interest rate, exactly what we were interested in to analyze the institution's gap. The holding period is the length of time that a liability will be on the institution's books, or the maturity, *whichever is shorter*. When a liability is initially created, the holding period is usually assumed to be equal to the maturity of the liability. If a bank opens a six-month CD for a customer, it normally assumes that account will remain on the books for six months. But initial assumptions, however reasonable, may not be fulfilled. If they are not fulfilled, the institution may experience an increase in its risk.

The holding period of a deposit liability is generally the time remaining to maturity since only the depositor has the ability to expunge such a liability. For some nondeposit liabilities the institution can, unilaterally, change the holding period. Usually this is done by repaying borrowed funds such as Fed funds, Federal Home Loan Bank advances, or by calling mortgage-backed bonds prior to maturity. Since the holding period of deposit and nondeposit liabilities can be changed in different ways, it makes sense to draw an analytical distinction between the two.

For the most part, changing the holding period of a nondeposit liability, which is at the institution's discretion, will not increase risk exposure. Changing the holding period of deposit liabilities, which is at the depositor's discretion and normally involves shortening rather than lengthening the holding period, will normally increase the institution's risk. Some of this risk can be hedged and some cannot. Before coming to grips with a hedging strategy, let's take a more detailed look at the types of risk created by deposit liabilities.

DEPOSIT LIABILITY RISK

Single categories of liabilities—MMCs, demand deposits, NOW accounts—present only two types of risk to the financial institution. The first type of risk is that the cost of retaining these deposits will increase. That is interest rate risk. The second type of risk is that they will be withdrawn. This is liquidity risk. In general, interest rate risk can be hedged in the futures market, liquidity risk cannot. It may be possible to offset cost increases due to liquidity risk, but liquidity risk cannot be hedged in the sense that a mechanism can be established for shifting that risk to someone else.

The prime distinction to be drawn here is between risk arising from market forces and risk arising from non-market forces. Price movements of futures contracts are driven almost totally by market forces. Attempting to offset risk which arises from non-market forces by hedging with futures contracts is not likely to prove beneficial. Even if it does work once in a while it's merely a matter of luck rather than some underlying relationship which can be relied upon. Hedging risk arising from market forces will work because there is an underlying, and fairly stable, relationship between the futures market and the cash markets for securities. Using that relationship to lay off risk not only is more prudent than trying a long shot to cover non-market risk, but it will promote long term stability in the institution's profit.

The abolition of regulated interest rates on deposit accounts at federally insured intermediaries, which began in 1978 and will be completed by 1985, has totally changed the risk profile on deposit liabilities. Prior to 1978 all of the risk on deposits (except for $100,000 + certificates of deposit) was regulatory risk. At any time the federal regulators could raise the cost of deposit liabilities by any amount. There existed only the weakest, and totally unpredictable, relationship between market interest rates and any such regulatory decision, thereby making that a risk which could not be externally hedged, in the futures market or in any other market. As long as the bulk of deposit liabilities was strictly regulated, financial institutions were at the mercy of the regulators with no built-in relief mechanism. The transition from totally regulated to totally unregulated rates has made hedging in the futures market a viable option for most financial institutions.

NONDEPOSIT LIABILITY RISK

The majority of the risk that an institution faces on nondeposit liabilities is interest rate risk. With the exception of very short-term loans which may be callable on demand, there is no chance that nondeposit sources of funds will be pulled out of the institution. As long as the institution retains control over these sources of funds, it will experience no liquidity risk on them.

There may be considerable interest rate risk on nondeposit liabilities, however. For a bank the typical nondeposit liabilities are Fed funds purchased, Federal Reserve Bank discounts, borrowings from foreign branches and, in the case of banking holding companies, commercial paper or notes outstanding. For a savings and loan association typical nondeposit liabilities include Federal Home Loan Bank advances, mortgage-backed bonds, and short-term borrowings from banks. Since most of these funds are borrowed short term, the institution is at risk as interest rates vary over time. Most, but not all, of this risk can be hedged.

The most obvious items that cannot be hedged are Federal Reserve Bank discounts and Federal Home Loan Bank advances. There is no close relationship between the cost of these sources of funds and market interest rates which would allow a hedging mechanism to be established that would work over an extended period of time. Administered rates, whether on deposit or nondeposit liabilities, cannot be hedged in a market which does not operate with administered rates. Other nondeposit liabilities are traded in free markets and thus are potentially hedgeable. In Part Two of this chapter we explore ways to hedge these liability costs in the futures market.

This section might be entitled "How To Hedge With Futures" since that is what this book is all about. This section deals with the selection of futures contracts with which to hedge specific liabilities and the determination of the most efficient contract to use. The selection of the most efficient contract depends entirely upon the degree of correlation between the cash and futures markets; the more closely correlated the two markets are, the more efficient the hedge will be. With the rapid expansion of the futures market since 1981 and the wider variety of contracts that are being traded, it is possible that more than one contract will be closely correlated with a particular type of liability. Even when this is true, however, there will always be a dominant contract. Even though all interest rates tend to move in the same direction and by about the same amount in the long run, in the short run there are many diverse moves that can and do occur. Hedging, even though it may continue for years, is essentially a short-run activity which requires monitoring and perhaps adjustments and fine tuning on a regular basis. Short-run deviations from a long-term trend can make or break a hedge. There is a greater likelihood of this occurring if a cross hedge is used or if a contract is used which does not have the closest correlation with the liability being hedged. Again, because of the differences between deposit and nondeposit liabilities, we will discuss them separately.

DEPOSIT LIABILITIES

At the beginning of 1983 banks and savings and loan associations were issuing the following deposit liabilities:

TABLE 8.1
Deposit Liabilities of Banks and
Savings and Loan Associations, 1983

Account	Term	Rate Base
Passbook	1 day	regulated
NOW	1 day	regulated
Demand Deposit	1 day	regulated
MMC	3 mos.	91-day T-bill
MMC	6 mos.	182-day T-bill
MMA	floating	floating
CD	floating	floating
CD ($100,000 +)	floating	floating

Only three of the eight principal categories of accounts are still regulated. These are the one-day accounts—passbook savings accounts, checking accounts, and NOW accounts. These accounts present the lowest level of individual risk since they tend to be a stable portion of the liability portfolio. During the deregulation process large shifts away from savings accounts to other market rate accounts occurred, but this process was largely completed by the end of 1982. The residual amounts in these accounts may be thought of primarily as liquidity balances—"rainy day savings"—which are not rate sensitive. Attempting to hedge these accounts by any method is not a high-percentage strategy. The bulk of the risk the institution faces on these accounts is liquidity risk, which cannot be hedged.

The remaining categories of deposits are a different story altogether. Although the institution is exposed to liquidity risk on MMCs, MMAs, and CDs, this is largely overshadowed by interest rate risk. The majority of the holders of these accounts can be persuaded to leave funds on deposit if they are offered a higher interest rate. Thus, deregulation has substituted interest rate risk for liquidity risk for most accounts at most institutions. True, some depositors will withdraw funds even if offered an interest rate five times the market rate. There's nothing that can be done to predict this; a depositor who is interest rate insensitive is simply a random occurrence. To be effective over the long haul, hedging must be concentrated on systematic rather than random risk.

Money Market Certificates

In order to hedge the systematic risk of any single deposit liability, the nature and cause of that systematic risk must first be ascertained. The most logical starting point in the search is an examination of the rate base of the account. In the case of the three- and six-month money market certificates the rate base is the auction rate on 91-day and 182-day Treasury bills, respectively. Even though these accounts will be freed from regulation, there is little reason to believe this rate base will disappear for *some* type of account; these accounts enjoy immense popularity among the public and the interest rate connection with Treasury bills is easy to understand. The interest rate at auction on Treasury bills is determined primarily by Treasury financing needs in the short term and the amount of liquidity in the financial system. The latter is partially, but not wholly, determined by the action of the Federal Reserve System. As long as MMC rates have deterministic relationships with the Treasury bill auction, the reason for changes in auction rates can be ignored for the most part. However, when MMC rates cease to have a deterministic relationship to the auction rate, the forces influencing the auction will become much more important in the design of effective hedging strategies. This would be true of any semi-regulated deposit account—if you know how the rate varies, you can design an effective hedge without knowing why the rate varies.

As the situation currently exists, MMCs have an *exact* relationship to Treasury bill rates and Treasury bill futures have a *direct* relationship to Treasury bill rates. The distinction between exact and direct is quite important. If the 91-day T-bill auction rate increases by 50 basis points, the MMC rate will increase *exactly* 50 basis points. On a week-to-week basis there is perfect correlation between the T-bill auction rate and the MMC rate, with no slippage anywhere. In the same circumstances, though, the implied rate on 90-day T-bill futures contracts may increase by more than 50 basis points, less than 50 basis points, or exactly 50 basis points. That is, there is some slippage between the auction and the futures market. The amount of slippage is variable so there is not an exact relationship between the two markets. The correlation between the two markets is high but not perfect, i.e., the correlation coefficient is not equal to one.

If MMC rates are exactly related to the T-bill auction rate and T-bill futures are directly and closely related to the T-bill market, hedging MMCs with T-bill futures will prove to be a more efficient hedging strategy than hedging with some other futures contract not directly or as closely related to the T-bill cash market. Table 8.2 shows the correlation between the implied interest rate on three short-term futures contracts and the Treasury bill cash market rate from 1979 through 1981. The highest correlation is with the T-bill futures contract. This will provide the most efficient hedge; that is, a greater percentage of interest rate risk will be offset.

TABLE 8.2
Correlation Between Treasury Bill Cash
Market And Short-Term Futures Contracts

Contract	Correlation Coefficient
T-bill	.949
Bank CDs	.915
Eurodollars	.906

Money Market Accounts

The new money market account (MMA) is a true "wild card" account. Banks or savings and loan associations which offer it are free to vary the rate they pay at will. Most institutions which were offering MMAs in early 1983 were pegging the rate to the rate on some well-known market instrument. One principal advantage of pegging the rate is a marketing ploy. The public has shown a great affinity for variable rate financial contracts, such as certificates of deposit and mortgages, which are pegged to well-known and widely reported market rates. In addition, the ability to define the rate base for the MMA allows the bank or savings association to hedge the interest rate risk of this account. (The liquidity risk cannot be hedged.) Suppose the institution offers an MMA with the following characteristics:

1. The rate is variable and equal to 80% of the average yield on outstanding 91-day Treasury bills during the preceding month.

2. The rate is adjusted monthly on the 15th of each month.

Structuring an MMA this way provides the same type of direct relationship between a deposit liability and a futures contract that exists on MMCs. In fact, from a hedging standpoint, the cash-futures market relationship on the MMA would be stronger than that on the MMC since the rate adjustment date coincides with the maturity date of the futures contract. The MMA rate is determined by price movements in the cash T-bill market over the entire month, rather than by just the auction which occurs once a week. T-bill futures prices vary every day of the month in relation to movements in the cash market. Variation in the MMA rate is thus more closely linked to the forces which drive the T-bill futures market. The correlation between futures and the MMA is increased, other things being equal.

This may strike you as being a backward way of implementing a hedging strategy. It is not. There are an infinite number of possible MMAs that could be designed; there are only a small number of futures contracts that can be used to hedge this or any other account. Given the flexibility to design your own account, why not design one which maximizes your ability to hedge its risk with a futures contract that you already know about? This is bound to increase the efficiency of any hedge you put on and thus reduce your risk.

This MMA example is only that: an example. You could just as easily design an MMA that is closely related to the bank CD futures contract or Eurodollar CD futures or Treasury bond futures. Doing so will achieve the same result of increasing the potential hedge efficiency. However, this strategy may have some drawbacks. The public may not go for it or you may not like the rate that results, especially if you tie the short-term MMA to a Treasury bond or note futures. Making this decision requires some judgment about what will be a marketable account, but you get the idea: try to make it as easy as possible to hedge a new account, within whatever marketing constraints you face.

Certificates of Deposit

Large negotiable certificates of deposit present the issuing institution with almost no liquidity risk at all. This is the one type of deposit which, because of its negotiability, is not likely to be withdrawn early. Still, the liquidity risk has been replaced by interest rate risk. Even though CD issuers theoretically can write CDs for any maturity up to 10 years, the market for these instruments is for maturities of less than six months, making the use of CDs as a permanent funding source a high-risk strategy. This is true even if rates vary only slightly; if rates are extremely volatile, as they have been since late 1979, the interest rate risk on a CD position is extremely high.

Variability in CD rates can be hedged with a variety of futures contracts. There is a high correlation between CDs and Treasury bills in the cash market, so that is a potential hedge vehicle. However, the introduction of the CD futures contract in 1981 provides the same direct cash-futures market link that existed on other deposit accounts. Following the general rule of avoiding cross hedges when direct hedges are possible, CDs should be hedged with CD futures.

NONDEPOSIT LIABILITIES

The possibilities for hedging nondeposit liabilities are limited, precisely because the number of such liabilities which can be hedged is limited. The constellation of nondeposit liabilities that can be hedged is composed of Fed funds purchased, commercial paper, mortgage-backed bonds, and bank loans in the case of savings and loan associations. The high correlation among all short-term interest rates suggests that the shortest maturity liabilities such as Fed funds, commercial paper, and bank loans could be effectively hedged with any of the short-term futures contracts, that is, Treasury bills or bank CDs. A few years ago there was a commercial paper futures contract, but it failed to generate sufficient interest to remain viable and has been withdrawn from trading. In this particular case neither of the two short-term contracts dominates the other in terms of a higher correlation with the Fed funds, commercial paper rate, or the prime rate.

Hedging mortgage-backed bonds is a somewhat complicated venture. The minimum maturity of mortgage-backed bonds is much longer than the maximum trading period of any futures contract available. Mortgage-backed bonds have maturities of at least five years, while active trading of most futures contracts is limited to about a 12-month period. Use of the futures market to hedge mortgage-backed bonds is also somewhat redundant since acquiring funds via this instrument assures the institution of what is a very long-term source of funds relative to other sources.

PART THREE: HEDGING STRATEGIES

This is the part you have been waiting for—how to do it! *The general idea behind a hedge of any kind is to make a transaction in one market which is the opposite of a transaction in another market.* That is, you sell in one market and buy in the other market. For a financial institution the transaction *looks* a little different but amounts to the same thing. If you buy funds in the cash market, you want to sell in the futures market. This will limit your risk exposure on the funds you purchase. Specifically, it will limit your risk exposure when you repurchase, or roll over, liabilities in the cash market. Unless you want to shrink the size of the institution, you will always be repurchasing or rolling over liabilities in the cash market. Whether you always will want to be hedging with futures depends on a great many things, which we will discuss shortly. For now, let's look at a simple example of how a hedge works.

STRATEGY #1: SHORT-TERM HEDGE

Suppose you issue $500,000 worth of six-month money market certificates at the maximum rate allowed, and you have guaranteed these depositors the right to renew those certificates at the maximum rate when they mature 182 days from now. You now have two contracts. The first is a contract to pay interest on $500,000 worth of MMCs for six months. The second contract is a forward contract to sell $500,000 worth of MMCs six months from now and to pay interest, *at an unknown rate*, on those MMCs for six months. There are three possible outcomes: (1) the MMC rate increases; (2) the MMC rate stays the same; (3) the MMC rate decreases. Unless you are a clairvoyant this can be a relatively high-risk position, and you are faced with taking this risk or shifting it to someone else. At some point you have to make the decision as to which of these you wish to do. Presumably, you would like to find out how to shift it.

The way that you shift the risk is to sell futures against your forward contract to sell MMCs six months hence. Since MMCs are based on Treasury bill rates, the futures contract that you would sell is the 91-day T-bill contract at the IMM. Consider the following example:

Situation 1: The MMC Rate Increases

You sell the MMCs today at an interest rate of eight percent. The price of a T-bill futures contract maturing in six months is currently 92.00, implying an interest rate of eight percent (100.00 − 92.00 = 8.00). You think that interest rates may rise over the next six months, resulting in higher interest payments for these MMCs when they renew. To hedge this risk you sell T-bill futures today at 92.00 and cover that short position in six months when the MMCs are renewed. Sounds simple enough, but does it work? It depends on what happens. Suppose that the MMCs roll over at a rate of 10 percent. The interest cost of this $500,000 liability for a holding period of six months will increase by $5,000. (For the first six months the interest cost is: $500,000 × .08 / 2 = $20,000. For the second six months the interest cost is: $500,000 × .10 / 2 = $25,000). If you make a profit of $5,000 in the futures market on your transaction, you will have offset the cost increase on the MMCs and will have successfully hedged your risk of an interest rate rise. Let's see how.

If the rate on cash market Treasury bills rises to 10 percent over the next six months, the price of T-bill futures should fall.

Not only should it fall, but it will fall because an arbitrage opportunity will be created if the futures price does not fall. The futures market is so large that arbitrage opportunities are wiped out almost instantly. In fact, the futures price will fall to a level that implies a 10 percent interest rate on T-bills. That is, the price of T-bill futures should be at 90.00 in six months (100.00 − 90.00 = 10.00). Since each basis point on a T-bill futures contract is worth $25, you will have exactly $5,000 in profit on your short sale in six months (200 basis points × $25 = $5,000).

One thing should be pointed out before proceeding. The size of the Treasury bill futures contract is $1,000,000, while the MMC position that is being hedged is only $500,000. The ratio of futures to cash is two to one. The reason for this is that the Treasury bills underlying the futures contract have a maturity of 91 days and the MMCs have maturity of 182 days. One basis point per million dollars on a six-month instrument is worth $50.00 while one basis point per million dollars on a three-month instrument is worth $25.00. Hedging a six-month cash instrument with a three-month futures contract requires that you use futures contracts equal in value to twice the amount of the cash instrument you are hedging. This insures "dollar equivalency" between the two markets. If you hedged a one-year instrument with a three-month futures contract, the proper ratio would be four to one in order to have dollar equivalency.

Situation 2: The MMC Rate Stays the Same

Suppose now that interest rates do not rise but instead remain the same in six months' time. In this case the cost of the MMC position will not increase. Also, the price of T-bill futures will not fall, so that you will have a zero profit on your futures market position. You simply break even on both the forward contract on MMCs and the futures position. You do have to pay a commission of about $50.

In both Situations 1 and 2 you broke even. You either successfully shifted the interest rate risk on your MMCs to someone else or the risk failed to materialize. In the event that rates decline *exactly the same result will occur.*

Situation 3: The MMC Rate Declines

Suppose that the rate on MMCs declines to six percent over the next six months. In this situation the price of Treasury bill futures should increase to 94.00. Since you sold short at 92.00 you will have to cover at 94.00 and will thus lose $5,000 in the futures market. Remember, however, that a successful hedge offsets a loss in one market with a gain in another market. You pay only $15,000 in interest on the MMCs for the second six-month period, thereby saving $5,000. This offsets your futures market loss.

This example deviates slightly from reality in that it postulates a *perfect* relationship between the futures market and the cash market, when in fact no such perfect relationship exists. Both the futures market and the cash market are auction markets with a large number of participants all acting independently. For all of these participants in both markets to act identically all the time would be a major miracle. Thus, even though there is high correlation between prices in both markets, they do not move in lock-step fashion. Instead of the futures price falling to 90.00 in Situation 1 it might only fall to 90.15, in which case the profit on the futures transaction would be $4,625, not the $5,000 that will be due on the MMCs. The futures price might also have fallen to 89.80 in which case the futures market profit would exceed the increased interest cost of the MMC position by $500. The closer you come to offsetting transactions in both the cash and futures market, the more efficient is your hedge. Even if the two markets do move together exactly, you will always have to consider the transactions costs involved in hedging with futures, even though they are small. Still, offsetting 98 percent of a loss in the cash market is better than offsetting zero percent of it.

So far we have looked at a hedging example only in the context of offsetting cost increases or decreases. However, it is easy to examine hedging in the context of gap analysis. Consider the first example again. In Situation 1 we rolled over the MMCs at 10 percent but were able to offset the increased interest cost with a futures market gain. The MMCs were rolled over at an effective rate of eight percent since the same amount of net interest is paid during the second six months as during the first six months. In effect, the maturity of the MMCs was extended from six months to one year, since the rate is not reset at the end of six months, thereby lengthening your gap.

Other things equal, the hedge produces a longer or more positive gap at six months since the MMCs are *not* reset. If asset yields rise, the hedge controls the cost of liabilities and increases the institution's spread. In Situation 2 nothing happens. In Situation 3 the longer gap produces some spread compression. On the surface this appears to be inappropriate. It appears inappropriate only if the purpose of liability hedging is forgotten. Liability hedging is designed to control liability costs which de facto means producing a more positive gap for the institution. If one particular hedging strategy produces an effective gap structure which is undesirable, then management should consider a different strategy. This subject, and how to decide whether or not to hedge, will be taken up in subsequent chapters.

STRATEGY #2: ROLLING HEDGE

Consider the first example again at the end of six months. The short futures position has just been covered and the MMCs rolled over at 10 percent. What about the next six months? You can just repeat the entire process by rolling your hedge forward. Only now you sell futures at 90.00. Suppose that rates do rise again and that six months later the MMCs roll over at 12 percent. The futures position is covered at, say, 88.00 resulting in another $5,000 profit to offset a further $5,000 increase in MMC interest cost. It looks like you're golden again, but closer inspection reveals that you are not. Examine Table 8.3.

TABLE 8.3
Strategy #2: Rolling Hedge

Time Period	MMC Rate	MMC Cost	Futures Profit	Net Cost	Effective Rate
1st 6 mos.	8%	$20,000	$ 0	$20,000	8%
2d 6 mos.	10%	$25,000	$5,000	$20,000	8%
3d 6 mos.	12%	$30,000	$5,000	$25,000	10%

The effective rate on the MMCs has moved up after one year to 10 percent. If rates increased by two percent over the fourth half-year, you would see the effective rate on the MMCs climb to 12 percent.

The effective maturity of the MMCs is being extended only temporarily. The institution's gap is being lengthened only temporarily. This may or may not be desirable, and brings us to a different strategy.

STRATEGY #3: LONG-TERM (STRIP) HEDGE

The next strategy that we want to look at is one which will hedge the cost of a liability for a period longer than the maturity of the liability. In Stragegy #1 we only tried to hedge the cost of MMCs for a period equal to their maturity, e.g., six months. If the cost of rolling them over continues to rise for more than six months, we will be faced with actual cost increase on liabilities *even if the hedge is perfectly efficient.*

The principle behind this hedging strategy is to extend the effective maturity of the liability as far as possible. If rates continue to rise, the risk is hedged. This strategy is usually referred to as a "strip" hedge because it involves a strip of futures contracts strung out into the future. Here's how it works:

At any one time there may be eight or nine different delivery months of a futures contract that are listed for trading on the exchange. Delivery months are normally spaced three months apart so that it is possible to trade a contract today which calls for delivery 24 or 27 months from now. (Technically the exchange could list contracts which call for delivery in 42 months but this is rarely done since there is very little interest in trading those contracts.) These *back-month contracts*, as they are called, are normally not as liquid as the nearby month, so caution must be exercised in using them to hedge.

Putting on a strip hedge involves selling a series of futures contracts with different delivery months for the same underlying commodity. Suppose that you have $10 million of three-month CDs outstanding and anticipate rolling them over at least three times; but you fear that interest rates will rise during the next 12 months so you would like to hedge the CDs. In essence, you would like to push the effective maturity of the CDs out from three months to 12 months. The only way to do that is a strip hedge of CD contracts. Suppose that it is December 1982 and the following CD contracts are available on the IMM: March 83, June 83, September 83, and December 83. Selling all of these contracts at the same time is a strip hedge and will effectively push the maturity of the hedged CDs out to 12 months.

Suppose that the rate on the CDs is nine percent when issued in December and that the prevailing market rate increases by one percent each quarter during 1983. The cost of this liability during 1983 is shown in Table 8.4.

TABLE 8.4
1983 Liability

Quarter	Interest Rate	Interest Cost	Increased Cost
I	9.0%	$ 225,000	$ 0
II	10.0%	250,000	25,000
III	11.0%	275,000	50,000
IV	12.0%	300,000	75,000
YR	10.5%	$1,050,000	$150,000

If the CD position is not hedged, the actual cost of these funds will amount to 10.5 percent over the one-year period. Using a one-period hedge that is rolled forward would result in a cost of 9.75 percent. Using the strip hedge will hold the cost at nine percent for the entire year.

Suppose that in December a flat yield curve is implied by the four CD contracts currently being traded so that the prices are as shown in Table 8.5. (This is an example only; it is unlikely that all four contracts could be sold at the same price.)

TABLE 8.5
Strip Hedge Example, 12/31/82

Contract	Price
Mar83	91.00
Jun83	91.00
Sep83	91.00
Dec83	91.00

In December 1982, a short position of 10 contracts is taken in each of the first three delivery months; e.g., March 83, June 83, and September 83. If interest rates rise, as we fear, the price of all these contracts will fall, producing profits in the futures market for the bank which it will use to offset the rising interest cost that will be experienced.

The bank is now obligated to cover part of its futures position every three months, just at the time that the CDs are renewed and the interest must be paid. We will assume, for expository purposes only at this point, that rates rise one percent each quarter and that the CD futures price declines by exactly 100 basis points at the same time. That is, we'll assume no slippage between cash and futures. This assumption is removed later on.

In March the first leg of the strip matures and is covered by the bank at a price of 90.00. It has the position shown in Table 8.6.

TABLE 8.6
$10 Million Strip Hedge Example, 3/31/83

	Sell	Position	Profit
Mar83	91.00	closed @90.00	$25,000
Jun83	91.00	open	
Sep83	91.00	open	

From Table 8.4 we know that the cost of the CDs will increase by $25,000 during the second quarter. The profit in the futures market during the first quarter offsets this cost increase. In June and September the bank also covers its respective positions. However, the profit made in the futures market increases over the year. Since the interest rate increased by one percent *each* quarter, the futures price declines 100 basis points *each* quarter. The June position is covered at a price of 89.00 resulting in a profit of $50,000—exactly equal to the cost increase that will be experienced during the third quarter. In September, futures prices will have declined by another 100 basis points so the Sep83 position is covered at 88.00, resulting in a $75,000 profit. Again, the futures profit is exactly equal to the cost increase on the CDs that will be experienced over the next quarter. The total strip hedge results are shown in Table 8.7.

TABLE 8.7
$10 Million Strip Hedge—Final Results

Contract	Sell	Buy	Profit
Mar83	91.00	90.00	$ 25,000
Jun83	91.00	89.00	50,000
Sep83	91.00	88.00	75,000
Total Profit			$150,000

The strip hedge has, in effect, extended the maturity of the $10 million in CDs out to one year from three months. The effective cost has been held at nine percent for the year. If the simple one-period hedge had been used, the cost of the CDs would have lagged the market by one quarter and would have totalled 9.75 percent for the year.

The design of this hedge, like that of all good hedges, is based on the expected holding period of the liability being hedged; the bank planned to maintain the CD position for one year only and the hedge was structured for a one-year period. If the bank had intended to hold its cash position longer than one year, a different strategy would have been necessary. Coming right up!

STRATEGY #4: ROLLING STRIP HEDGE

Our bank now has decided to retain the $10 million in CDs for at least two years rather than one year, but continues to roll them over every three months. Unfortunately, only four delivery months in CD futures contracts are being traded. Taking a short position of 10 contracts in all four months will hedge the first four renewals or resets of the outstanding CDs. The bank can hold the effective interest rate at nine percent for 15 months. It cannot, *in December 1982*, guarantee that the rate can be held at nine percent for the entire two-year period because there are no CD futures contracts available further out in time.

As time marches on, those further deferred contracts will be listed and traded. The bank only has to make use of them as they become available. This is the whole idea of a rolling strip hedge. The strip is rolled forward just like the simple short-term hedge in Strategy #1. Initially the bank shorts all four available CD delivery months: March, June, September, and December 1983. When the first short position matures in March 1983 it is covered, and another contract is added to the back of the strip. Table 8.8 shows the bank's futures position in March 1983.

Table 8.8
Rolling Strip Hedge, 3/31/83

Contract	Position
Mar83	short 10 @91.00, covered @90.00
Jun83	short 10 @91.00
Sep83	short 10 @91.00
Dec83	short 10 @91.00
Mar83	short 10 @90.00

If interest rates continue to rise by one percent each quarter, the bank's futures position will generate sufficient profits to offset cost increases on its CDs through the end of the year. By December 1984 it has the results shown in Table 8.9.

The effective annual cost of the $10 million in CDs is nine percent for 1983 and 11.5 percent for 1984. This is a considerable cost reduction for the bank over either an unhedged CD position or a hedged position using the one-year strip. The rolling strip hedge fails to hold the effective cost of the

Table 8.9
Rolling Strip Hedge, Final Results

Contract	Open Price	Close Price	Profit	CD Cost Increase*	Effective Rate#
Mar83	91.00	90.00	$ 25,000	$ 25,000	9.0%
Jun83	91.00	89.00	50,000	50,000	9.0
Sep83	91.00	88.00	75,000	75,000	9.0
Dec83	91.00	87.00	100,000	100,000	9.0
Mar84	90.00	86.00	100,000	100,000	10.0
Jun84	89.00	85.00	100,000	150,000	11.0
Sep84	88.00	84.00	100,000	175,000	12.0
Dec84	87.00	83.00	100,000	200,000	13.0

*per quarter interest cost
#annual rate

CDs at nine percent only because there aren't enough contract months being traded at the start of the hedge. If the 1984 contract months were available at the end of 1982, it would be possible to extend the effective maturity of the CD position out to two years instead of one year.

STRATEGY #5: TRUNCATED STRIP HEDGE

One possible drawback of a strip hedge or a rolling strip hedge of liabilities is that they involve shorting futures contracts considerably far out in time. These far back month contracts are not nearly so liquid as nearby months. Should a hedger wish to lift a strip hedge all at once—possibly because the market is going against the hedge or it is no longer necessary due to a portfolio shift by the institution—it may be more difficult to cover futures positions in back months. Should this occur, the efficiency of the hedge may be severely reduced. This is particularly true in the case of a large hedge. Covering 500 short contracts 12 months out is sure to affect the price much more than covering five contracts. Since these are auction markets, it must be considered by the hedger that roaring into the pit with a buy order for 500 contracts is sure to bid up the price if the typical trading volume is 20 contracts per hour. The last thing you want to do is affect the price *as a result of your order*.

An alternative strategy is to use a truncated strip. In this type of hedge an identical total number of contracts are sold, but the strip is loaded up on the nearby months rather than being spread out over the entire time that the institution is at risk on the liabilities. This is not a strategy widely used by financial institutions but it does have its advantages, the chief one being the avoidance of illiquidity in far out contracts. The main disadvantage is that the truncated strip is usually not as efficient as the normal strip because of the process of convergence (covered in Chapter 17). Also, since the strip is truncated, it does not roll forward as easily or smoothly, either.

Recall the strip hedge of CDs in Strategy #2. In this strategy the bank shorted 30 contracts at $1 million each to hedge three rollovers of $10 million in CDs. In a truncated strip hedge it still shorts 30 contracts, but they are not spread out over the year. Instead, the bank hedges the first rollover of the CDs with 10 Mar83 contracts and then loads up the remainder in Jun83 contracts. Its position is:

Contract	Position
Mar83	short 10 @91.00
Jun83	short 20 @91.00

The 10 March contracts would be covered at 90.00 and the 20 June contracts would be covered at 89.00. This results in total profits in the futures market of $125,000—$25,000 in March and $100,000 in June. This profit is then used to offset the cost increases on the CDs. Yet, at the end of the year the CDs end up having cost the bank a total of $1,050,000 or 10.5 percent. The effective cost after the hedge is $925,000, or 9.25 percent; 25 basis points more than the regular strip hedge. That 25 basis point difference is the price of dealing only in the most liquid nearby month contracts.

The important question is whether the price is too high. There really is no general rule on this, but here are some considerations. If you want to lift a hedge because interest rates level off or start down, how difficult will it be to cover positions in far deferred months? Covering 300 or 500 contracts 15 months out probably will not be very easy. If a major shift in the market occurs, that contract may go to limit bid for a day or two which may wipe out all the benefits you have previously achieved. You might also want to lift a hedge because you decide not to roll over the CDs but switch to Eurodollars or borrow from a foreign branch. You are still faced with the liquidity problem. In a nutshell, if you think it is likely that you will change your mind about your portfolio or about your hedge, the truncated strip provides more flexibility for doing so than does the standard strip hedge.

On the other hand, the truncated strip does not roll forward as smoothly. If interest rates continue to rise over a long period, each time you restart the truncated strip you do so at ever higher levels. Remember, if you start hedging when rates are at 10 percent, the best you can do is hold the cost at 10 percent—you can't push it down to eight percent.

SUMMARY

The five hedging strategies that have been developed here are just that—strategies. Developing specific hedges depends on specific liability positions, of which there are infinite combinations. All five strategies can be used to hedge any hedgeable liability. You can hedge CDs with a rolling hedge and MMCs with a truncated strip, or vice versa. You can hedge MMAs with a rolling strip and Eurodollar CDs with a short-term hedge, or vice versa. Any combination of hedging strategies can be employed by one institution. Which one you choose depends on what you hope to achieve with the hedge and what other portfolio changes you might make or might want to make at the same time. Not every strategy is appropriate for every situation. Here, then, are the major strengths and weaknesses of all five strategies, the study of which will help you select a hedging strategy for a particular situation.

Strategy #1, the short-term hedge, works only one time. Its most effective use is for hedging a liability that will be on the books only for a short period of time and is not expected to be permanent. This strategy will only cover the interest rate risk for one renewal. For a liability category that is designed to be a permanent source of funds for the institution, using this strategy will not be very effective in the pursuit of cost control. However, it is simple to put on and take off. It's a good way to start learning how to hedge; once you become a more experienced hedger this strategy will have limited use.

Strategy #2, the rolling hedge, offers protection from rising interest costs over a longer term than the simple short hedge. This strategy is appropriate mainly for two circumstances. The first use is during a period when interest rates are expected to rise for only a short period of time, say a few months, rather than over an extended period. The second use is for a liability that is expected to be held for more than one rate reset (renewal) but will not be a permanent liability, and where there is some uncertainty concerning the likelihood of renewal. If you are not 100 percent positive that it will be rolled over, employment of the rolling hedge preserves your bail-out option while offering some risk reduction. Using the rolling hedge will control the cost of the liability in both of these situations, but it is a strategy which commits the institution for only the short term.

On the other hand the strip hedge, Strategy #3, does commit the institution to a longer term hedge. Using this strategy is appropriate for hedgeable permanent liabilities; that is, those that will be on the books for a long period of time but have floating or variable rates of interest. For example, a bank which plans to permanently maintain a 90-day Eurodollar CD position as 10 percent of liabilities should consider using this strategy. But a savings and loan which plans to issue 10-year fixed-rate mortgage-backed bonds should not consider using this strategy. The advantage of this strategy is that it effectively extends the maturity of short-term liabilities when rates increase. It will not work forever, though, but is limited by the availability of futures contracts with which to hedge. Putting on a strip hedge, running it out, and then replacing it does preserve flexibility but exposes the hedger to periodic cost increases at the ends of the strips.

The periodic jump in liability costs can be avoided to some degree by using a rolling strip hedge, Strategy #4. This type of hedge offers the maximum protection from rising costs over the longest period of time. It is the closest thing to a permanent hedge, as it continues to push a liability's effective maturity way beyond its stated maturity. It is not perfect, however, since there are no futures contracts which mature in three or four years. The effective cost of a liability, even one hedged with a rolling strip, will gradually inch up if rates continue to rise over an extended period of time. However, the cost will lag the current market rate by a period of time equal to the length of the strip, typically 12 or 15 months. The chief disadvantage of a rolling strip is that the hedger *always* has a position in far deferred contract months which may present some difficulty with large positions.

The partial reduction of liquidity implied by a strip hedge or a rolling strip hedge can be avoided by the truncated strip hedge, Strategy #5. Using this strategy, it is possible to extract nearly all the benefits of a full strip without locking into a large position in far deferred contracts. The downside risk is that the truncated strip cannot be easily replaced or rolled forward. Once the truncated strip is played out, reinstituting it must occur at the higher rates prevailing at that time. It does offer good protection from rate increases for one year or less without imposing potential liquidity problems.

All five strategies can be used to hedge most types of individual liabilities. However, they are not likely to work as precisely as the examples shown here indicate. The examples shown were based on assumptions which deviate from reality. First, the examples assumed that absolutely perfect correlation exists between the futures market and the cash market; when the T-bill rate increased by 100 basis points, the implied rate on T-bill futures increased by *exactly* 100 basis points (the price declined by 1.00 on the index). *This almost never happens.* Second, the examples assumed that all futures contracts move together in lock-step; all contract prices in the strip hedges changed by the same amount. *This almost never happens either.* This does not mean that these hedging strategies will not work. Rather, it means they will not work *perfectly*.

Shown below as Tables 8.10 and 8.11 are actual hedges that might have been put on and the actual results that would have been obtained. The sales and purchases of futures contracts in the examples were made at a price midway between the day's high and low price.

In the first example a bank issues $10 million in 90-day domestic CDs on January 8, 1982 at a rate of 12.95 percent. It plans to roll these over only once so it uses a short-term hedge of CD futures. The maturity of the cash CDs does not match the maturity of the nearest contract (March 82) so the bank sells June 82 CDs instead. If it had used the March contract it would either be unhedged for a month once the March position was covered, or it would have to replace it with a June position at that time. Sounds complicated, you say. We said it wasn't perfect. On April 8th the CDs are rolled over at the then-current rate of 14.70 percent. The cost of the CD position has risen by 175 basis points; the increased interest costs on the $10 million position amount to $43,750.

To hedge the CDs the bank shorts 10 June 82 CD contracts at 85.58 on January 8th. When the CDs are rolled over on April 8th the bank covers its futures position at 84.80. The 78 basis point drop in the futures price amounts to a profit of $19,500 on the 10 contracts. After subtracting commissions and wire transfer fees, the net futures gain is $18,980. Thus, the hedge offsets 43.4 percent of the increased interest cost. This is not perfect but it's better than zero.

Table 8.10
Actual $10 million CD Hedge

Contract: IMM 90-day domestic CD
Number of Contracts: 10
Initial Margin: $20,000
Maintenance Margin: $15,000

Date	Cash Market	Futures Market
1/8/82	Issue $10 million of 90-day CDs @ 12.95%	SELL 10 Jun82 CD contracts @ 85.58
4/8/82	Renew $10 million of 90-day CDs @ 14.70%	BUY 10 Jun82 CD contracts @ 84.80
	Increased Cost: $43,750	*Profit:* $ 19,500
		Commissions − 500
		Wires − 20
		NET $ 18,980

HEDGE EFFICIENCY: $18,980 / $43,750 = 43.8%
(Recapture)

In the second example, on July 10, 1978 a savings and loan association decided to strip hedge a $5.4 million position in MMCs taken in June 1978. To do so it sold 11 March 79 T-bill contracts at 91.78 to hedge the first rollover in December 1978. Continuing the strip, it sold 11 Sep 79 bills at 91.34, and 11 Mar 80 bills at 90.93, all on July 10, 1978.

The initial MMCs were at 7.73 percent; in December they would have rolled over at 10.07 percent, in June 1979 they rolled over again at 9.81 percent, and in December 1979 they were renewed a third time at 12.33 percent. The first renewal cost the association $63,350 in additional interest over the original rate. The second renewal cost $56,235 more than the initial rate. The third renewal added $124,065 onto the original cost—a total of $243,650 more than it would have paid had the MMCs been held at the original rate of

7.73 percent. The strip hedge would have cut these costs dramatically. Examine Table 8.11.

Table 8.11
Actual Strip Hedge of MMCs by a Savings and Loan Association

Date	Contract	#	Sell	Buy	Profit (Loss)
7/10/78	Mar79	11	91.78		
7/10/78	Sep79	11	91.34		
7/10/78	Mar80	11	90.93		
1/10/79	Mar79	11		90.45	$ 36,575.00
7/10/79	Sep79	11		91.01	9,075.00
1/10/80	Mar80	11		89.02	52,252.00

TOTAL $ 98,175.00

LESS COMMISSION   1,650.00

NET PROFIT $ 96,525.00

HEDGE EFFICIENCY: $96,525 / $243,650 = 40%
(Recapture)

The efficiency of this strategy in this case was 40 percent. It is not 100 percent efficient because there isn't a perfect relationship between the two markets. Look at the first leg of the strip, the March 79 contract. It declined in price over the six-month period by 133 basis points, while the cash market rate increased by 235 basis points. The second contract declined by 89 basis points while the cash market went up by 208 basis points. The third contract declined by 191 basis points, but the cash market increased by 460 basis points. The slippage between the cash and futures markets will keep the efficiency of most strategies at something less than 100 percent. It is worth considering that margin inflows may be invested at some (T-bill, Fed funds) interest rate which will improve the efficiency of the hedge. The degree to which the efficiency will be enhanced can only be determined after the fact. In some circumstances it may be possible to compensate for this if the degree of slippage is stable and predictable. Read more about that in Chapter 13. For now consider that a 40 percent offset is better than a zero percent offset. This topic, evaluating hedge efficiency, is covered in detail in the last section of the book.

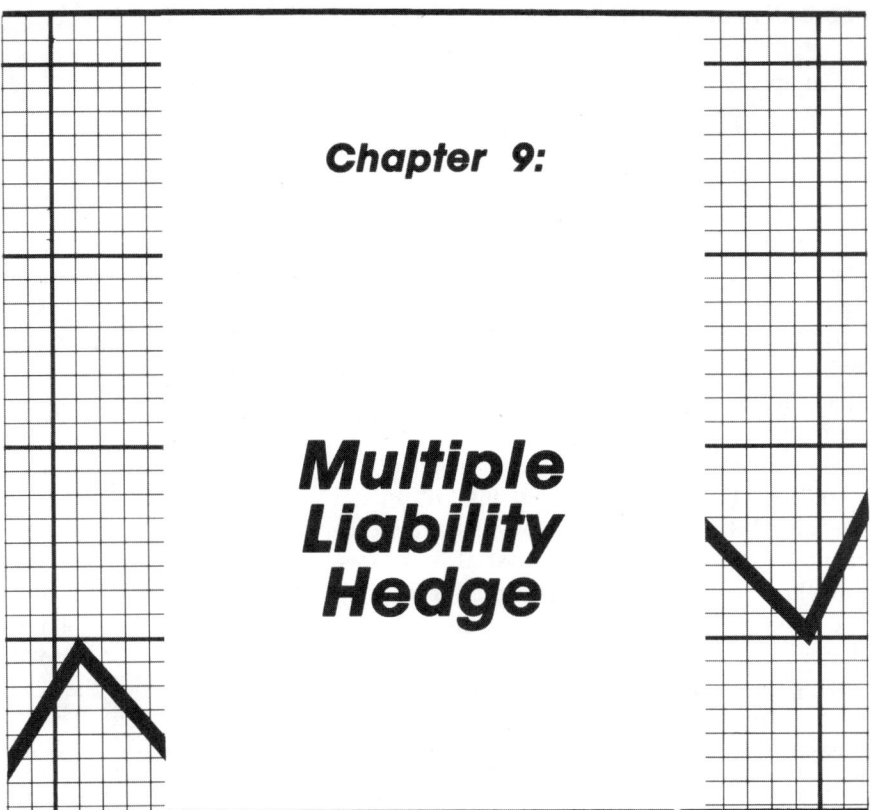

Chapter 9:

Multiple Liability Hedge

The last chapter dealt with a set of strategies which may be employed by financial institutions to hedge the interest rate risk on one particular class of liability. Using any of those strategies should enable an institution to get a greater degree of control over the cost of that particular type of liability. Various hedging strategies may be employed for different periods of time. However, using single-liability hedges will only protect the institution against a rise in the cost of that particular liability. At times, this may be the smallest part of the interest rate risk the institution faces, and hedging one specific liability may not hold down the institution's cost of funds.

This last statement may *appear* to the careful reader to be a contradiction of everything we've said up to now. Rest assured that such is not the case. The reason a single liability hedge may not hold down the cost of funds is due to account switching by the institution's customers. Customers' switching from a low-cost account to a high-cost account at any time will drive up the bank's or saving association's cost of funds. This is sometimes an easily identifiable action on the part of the customers; at other times the effect may be masked. This discussion probably sounds like an attempt to peel an artichoke—you never get to the center; but we will.

The issue at hand is to determine what is driving up the cost of funds and then to determine if the institution faces a risk that can be hedged. If the costs of all deposit liabilities go up uniformly, the institution's cost of funds will rise by roughly the same amount. If the costs of all liabilities go up uniformly and some customers switch from lower cost to higher cost liabilities *at the same time*, the institution's cost of funds will go up more than the general rise in rates. This is how the effect of account switching can be overshadowed.

Consider this example. Shown in Table 9.1 is a distribution of liabilities, their costs, and an institution's total cost of funds. At Time Period #2 the rates on all deposits have increased by 20 percent (except demand deposits), but the total cost of funds has increased by 30 percent. Only two-thirds of the total cost of funds increase is due to the general rise in rates; the remaining third is due to the shift in deposits from demand and savings deposits to the higher cost MMC and MMA. If the distribution of deposits during Time Period #1 had prevailed during the second period, the total cost of funds would have risen by only 20 percent to 6.66 percent. The increased cost of funds due to account switching cannot be conventionally hedged with the strategies developed in the preceding chapter since we have not yet identified the specific nature of the risk.

TABLE 9.1
Effect on Cost of Funds of Account Switching, Example #1

Account	Time Period #1		Time Period #2	
	% of Total	Rate	% of Total	Rate
Demand	20%	0%	18%	0%
Savings	20%	5%	10%	6.0%
MMC	25%	8%	35%	9.6%
MMA	30%	7%	32%	8.4%
Large CD	5%	9%	5%	10.8%
COST OF FUNDS		5.55%		7.19%

Account switching is tied into the entire interest rate risk inherent in the retail deposit market. When rates rise, some customers will be induced to shift funds from one type of account to another. The degree to which this occurs is not primarily a function of the *level* of interest rates but rather of the amount of the differential between rates. Look again at Table 9.1. In the first time period the spread between the MMA and regular savings accounts was 200 basis points; between the MMC and regular savings accounts the differential was 300 basis points. As all rates rose, those spreads widened to 240 basis points and 360 basis points, respectively. At this point half of the amount in regular savings accounts was switched to higher cost accounts. Some demand deposits were also switched. Tracing actual dollars from one account to another is difficult to do but may provide some useful information later. For now, let's concentrate on the resulting distribution of deposits, which provides two very useful pieces of information.

First, it indicates that some trigger point has been hit in the customer's sensitivity to yield and yield spreads. Why hadn't those customers who held savings accounts switched to MMCs before now? They could have earned 60 percent more on their money. Obviously, some other factor besides yield, such as the liquidity of a savings account and the illiquidity of the MMC, was important enough to those customers to prevent the switch. A 300 basis point differential was not sufficient to overcome these other factors, but a 360 basis point spread was large enough. Similarly, the increase in the spread relationship between the MMA and other accounts was large enough to induce a shift. The trigger point for the MMC is somewhere between a spread of 300 and 360 basis points. Just where it lies is a complex question that would require extensive econometric studies to answer. But it does exist and it is important to know that it has been hit, since hitting it changes the institution's risk exposure on deposits. This is the second useful piece of information.

Once a trigger point has been reached and deposits have switched, will they switch back if the yield spread shrinks? The answer is "probably not"; there is no evidence to support such a hypothesis. One of the main reasons is that a large (and rapidly diminishing) group of customers simply hadn't paid attention to these yield spreads. Once aware they are not likely to ignore them again. The money market funds have proven that conclusively. If the yield spread increases and customers become interest rate sensitive, the financial institution faces increased interest rate risk on its liability portfolio. In order to retain the deposits of these customers it will have to bid higher rates. If it does not, and does not wish to shrink the size of the institution, those lost deposits will have to be replaced with wholesale funds, either deposit or nondeposit. This is clearly a higher risk environment for the institution.

DOLLARS SHIFTING

Consider now tracing the actual dollars shifted. The table shows only gross shifts after the rate increase. Demand deposits decreased by two percentage points and MMAs increased by the same share. The share of MMCs increased by the same amount that savings accounts declined. It is naive to conclude that these figures represent direct dollar-for-dollar transfers. Although this cannot be proven without an extensive marketing survey, it is more reasonable to conclude that multiple types of shifting oc-curred. There are multiple spread relationships to be considered. (See Table 9.2.) All of the spreads increased by 20 percent in Time Period #2. Each dif-ferent spread potentially affects different depositor groups in different ways. It is likely that some customers who held MMAs in period one switched to MMCs in period two. Some customers who held savings accounts switched up to MMAs, replacing funds transferred to MMCs by former MMA holders. Some may have switched directly to MMCs. The diagram shown as Figure 9.1 indicates the possibilities.

TABLE 9.2
Deposit Yield Spreads (in basis points)

Spread	Time Period #1	Time Period #2
MMC-MMA	100	120
MMC-Savings	300	360
MMC-Demand	800	960
MMA-Savings	200	240
MMA-Demand	700	840
Savings-Demand	500	600

How does this help you hedge the risk of your liabilities? If all rates in-crease, and no switching occurs or is likely to occur, hedging the entire deposit liability portfolio will result in the risk reduction you want by holding down costs. If rates rise and account switching occurs or is likely to occur, you need to hedge the switchable accounts.

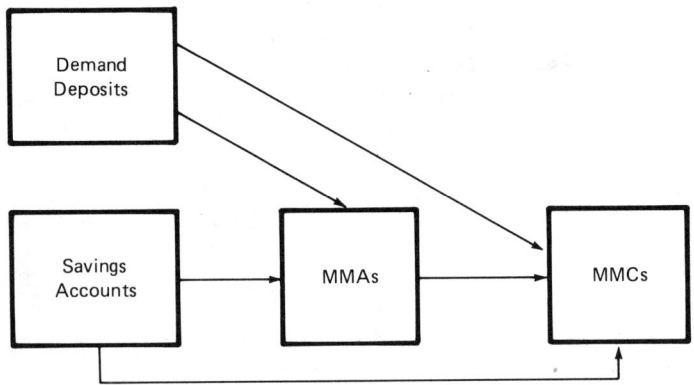

Figure 9.1. Account Switching Trace

Before reading any further make a mental note: This is the most sophisticated and complicated liability hedge that can be done. Do not try it the first time out!

THE HYBRID HEDGE

We are introducing a totally new type of hedge strategy which we call a hybrid hedge. Many brokers may not understand this concept of multiple liability hedges all in one package. The hybrid hedge is a strategy designed to temporarily avoid cost increases due to account switching within the institution. The hedge design consists of two or more different futures contracts and any multiple combination of delivery months. The size of the hedge is determined by the amount of funds that are at risk of being shifted. The futures contracts that are used are those best correlated with the accounts into which the funds will flow. In order to use this strategy you must know your depositor base and be able to make an accurate forecast of deposit shifts within your institution. The appropriate uses of this strategy are limited—it will not hedge every risk at all times. If you use it, be sure you have correctly identified the risk you are hedging.

Throughout this book we have repeatedly stressed that successful hedging with futures depends on a strong and reliable relationship between the futures contract and the cash market being hedged. This is no less true here. You may wonder (by now we hope you are far enough along to wonder about this) how in the world you can find a relationship between a group of futures contracts and a group of cash market instruments. Actually, we wondered the same thing and it took us six months to figure it out. The answer is that you don't have to find such a relationship—there's an easier way.

The problem that we are attacking is how to reduce the risk to the institution of funds floating around in the liability portfolio, a process over which you have little or no control. If the relationship between yield spread and account switching holds—and there is a lot of evidence that it does—it should be easy to identify those accounts which are likely to be switched. It's also fairly easy to zero in on the accounts into which these funds will flow. The obvious accounts that are potentially switchable are those at the lower end of the yield spectrum—demand deposits, NOW accounts, and savings accounts. The obvious accounts into which funds are likely to be transferred are those at the higher end of the yield spectrum—three- and six-month money market certificates, money market accounts, and Super

NOW accounts. Whether an account is at the "lower end" depends on the yield spread. The highest yielding account offered is not likely to experience any erosion to other accounts within the institution. Everything else is at risk; when the tide comes in all the boats rise. So it is with deposit liabilities—shifts occur all the way up the yield spread ladder. Fine, but what futures market-cash market relationship is correct?

The one that is *not* correct is the one between a futures contract and the accounts which are potentially switchable. If rates rise and funds switch out of savings accounts, the total cost of savings accounts falls. That's not a problem. If those funds shift to MMCs the *total* cost of MMCs rises, but the *average* cost of MMCs also rises because all rates have risen. That is the problem. The relationship that is correct is the one between a futures contract and the accounts which are likely to experience internal inflows.

Single liability hedges will not cover the risk of account switching, but the hybrid hedge will. Here's how: One fundamental risk faced by financial institutions that cannot be hedged with financial futures directly is what we previously referred to as regulatory risk. Administered rates cannot be successfully hedged in the futures market, which is driven by rates determined in auction markets. The interest rates on demand deposits, NOW accounts, and savings accounts are administratively set and will continue to be set that way for a few more years. If you believe what we said about that earlier, you will not try to hedge them with futures, you will be concentrating on hedging your market rate accounts—MMCs, MMAs, and CDs. If you are not speculating by overhedging, your futures positions will be scaled to the size of those balances at the time the hedge is put on. If these balances grow, you will have to increase the size of your futures position in order to retain the same hedge proportion.

Take the example shown in Table 9.1 At the beginning 25 percent of the deposits were in MMCs at an eight percent rate, but at the end they were at 9.6 percent and accounted for 35 percent of deposits. Let's make this a bit more realistic—total deposits are $100 million, so MMCs grew from $25 million to $35 million. This occurred over one six-month period. Fully hedging the MMCs implies a futures market position short 50 T-bill contracts at a price of 92.00. (We assume there's no basis shift anywhere.) In six months the $25 million of MMCs have rolled over at 9.6 percent, increasing interest costs by a total of $200,000. Covering the futures position at 90.40 fully offsets the cash loss, less commissions. What about the cost increase due to account switching? That amounts to $480,000 if the funds came from demand deposits; $217,500 if the funds came from NOW accounts; and $205,000 if they came from savings accounts. If you simply increase the size of your futures position to reflect the increased MMC balances, you will *not* offset the cost increase. Remember, you can only lock in the rate that prevails at the time the hedge is put on. In this case you would be locking in 9.6 percent on $10 million of new MMCs. You will have to eat the increase over what those funds would have cost if they had stayed put—something between $205,000 and $480,000. That's not going to be a lot of fun.

Suppose that the accounts which are potentially switchable had been hedged against a switch. There is an important distinction to be drawn here between hedging a rate increase on the original account and hedging against a shift in deposits. Hedging against a switch tries to recover the increased cost when funds flow from savings accounts to MMCs, or from MMAs to MMCs. This can only be done by scaling a hedge on the amount of funds that will be switched. *This is not easy or obvious.* Finding the size hedge to put on requires that you be able to make an accurate forecast of the amount of funds that are likely to be switched up to higher cost accounts. The accuracy of the forecast will determine how good the hedge is. Making a good forecast requires that you have detailed knowledge of the interest rate sensitivity of your customers. This information may be obtained either by survey methods or by an analysis of deposit shifts that have occurred in the past. Without such information you cannot make an accurate forecast of future shifts; the hybrid hedge would, therefore, *not* be a prudent strategy.

Here is an example of how it works. You believe, or fear, that interest rates will rise by about 200 basis points in the next six months and that as they do, half of your savings accounts will shift to MMAs. Your institution's MMA is tied directly to the CD rate so you are going to hedge them with CD contracts. The amount of savings accounts at risk is $10 million. The current CD rate is seven percent, implying a futures price of 93.00, but the MMA rate is only six percent. To hedge the switch of savings accounts, you short 10 CD contracts at 93.00. If rates rise 200 basis points, the futures position is covered at 91.00 for a profit of $50,000. The savings accounts switch to MMAs at the new cost of eight percent. If they earned 5.25 percent before, the cost increase amounts to $753.42 per day. The futures hedge profit will cover the cost increase for 66 days. If rates are expected to peak and then fall, this strategy will hold your cost increase to zero for a little more than two months and then nearly zero thereafter depending on the decline.

If rates are expected to peak and then level off, you will experience actual cost increases thereafter. In this latter case, a strip type hedge will be more efficient. That is, you sell ten CD contracts in the nearby month and ten in the next delivery month. Covering all twenty contracts will get you rate protection, in this case for about 135 days.

Previously we evaluated hedge performance by the percentage of cost increase recaptured by the hedge. In the case of hybrid hedges discussed here this method is not appropriate. Funds that are shifted from low-cost to high-cost accounts are not likely to ever shift back. The $10 million shifted into MMAs will permanently increase the institution's cost of funds. The hybrid hedge will only stave off that cost increase for some time. The number of days relief that you get from the higher cost that eventually arrives is the indicator of how well the hedge has performed.

HYBRID STRIP HEDGE

The strategy just outlined only works for one possible account switching. A general shift along the whole yield spread ladder requires a more sophisticated hedge design. Table 9.3 shows two deposit account distributions, one before the rate increase, one after. The assumption on the trace of funds is that accounts switch to the next higher yielding account. This results in a total increase in the cost of funds of 207 basis points, or $5,671.23 per day. The net effect of the shift is to move half of the two low-cost deposits into the two high-cost deposits. In order to hedge this shift a multiple liability hedge—the hybrid hedge—is called for. A total of $10 million is shifted so the total hedge size is based on $10 million of deposits. Since they are moving into two high-cost accounts, the total hedge is split between two contracts—CD contracts and T-bill contracts—since these contracts have the closest underlying relationship with the accounts into which funds are flowing. If funds are flowing into three or four accounts, the number of different types of futures contracts in the hedge is increased.

TABLE 9.3
Account Switching, Example #2

Account	Dollar Amounts (Millions)		Rate	
	Period 1	*Period 2*	*Period 1*	*Period 2*
Demand	$ 10	$ 5	0%	0%
Savings	$ 10	$ 5	5.25%	5.25%
MMA	$ 35	$ 40	6.00%	8.00%
MMC	$ 45	$ 50	7.25%	9.00%
TOTAL	$100	$100		
COST OF FUNDS			5.89%	7.96%

The reason that the hybrid hedge is used is that all interest rates, and therefore all futures prices, do not always move exactly together. This situation involves a cost increase on two separate accounts which have strong relationships with two separate futures contracts. Using both of them together creates the strongest futures-cash market relationship. For the example shown in Table 9.3, the shift that is forecast is for $5 million to shift out of both demand deposits and savings accounts and to flow into MMAs and MMCs. The total $10 million hedge size is split evenly between the two contracts used to hedge MMAs (CD futures) and MMCs (T-bill futures). If the T-bills are shorted at 92.75 and covered at 91.00, the futures profit is $21,875.00. Shorting CDs at 93.00 and covering at 91.00 yields a profit of $25,000.00. (The MMA rate is 100 basis less than the CD rate.) This will cover the increased cost of funds for only nine days. Sure, it's better than nothing but it is not very good. This is not an atypical result, suggesting immediately that hybrid hedges, when used, ought to be hybrid strip hedges.

Using a hybrid strip increases the amount of time that the cost of funds increases due to the shift can be avoided. Putting on a four contract month hybrid strip hedge would have resulted in futures profits of about $187,000, implying 33 days protection against rising costs.

On paper this sounds like a good strategy, but a number of very important questions are still left unanswered. For instance, how do you know what size hybrid strip hedge to put on? How much of those potentially switchable deposits are going to switch? If the hybrid is designed to hedge a $10 million switch and $20 million actually switches, the length of time that costs are contained is cut in half. There is no way to know this in advance unless you are a perfect forecaster. (If you are, you should be living on the Riviera instead of reading this book.) The best that can be done is to get a good idea about the interest rate sensitivity of your customer base. The best guide to that, short of hiring an economic consulting firm, is to look at your past experience. This may be done by charting the amount of deposit shifts that have occurred against the increases in yield that have occurred in the last few years. To do this you must have done the type of asset and liability analysis suggested in Chapter 2 so that you know what has actually been happening. This may seem tedious but you have to do it if you want to get the most out of hedging. If your prior experience indicates that shifts will occur only if the yield spread widens by 250 basis points, you will not want to hedge against a switch if you expect rates to increase by no more than 150 basis points. If you don't have any risk, there is no point in hedging.

SUMMARY OF HYBRID STRIP HEDGES

The hybrid strip hedge relies on good forecasts of both interest rate changes and interest sensitivity of the institution's customers. This is the primary reason not to try it right away. Once you have some experience in futures hedging and are confident of your ability to design and manage hedges efficiently you may want to try it. You may never try it, for any number of reasons, but at least you will be familiar with the concept.

One final word about the hybrid strip hedge. This hedging strategy spans a segment of the term structure of interest rates (the yield curve), rather than just one point, which is what single liability hedges do. With this type of hedge you not only must confront *basis risk—the risk that the futures market and the cash market don't move exactly together*—you must also face the risk of a rotating yield curve. A yield curve rotation means that the yield-to-maturity curve gets steeper or less steep. *This can magnify the futures market profit or loss.* In the previous example the rates on CDs and T-bills both increased and deposits shifted up from demand deposits and savings accounts, so the hybrid hedge offered some offsetting profits in the futures market. If the yield curve flattens, the deposits may shift but the futures price may not change; ergo, no profits to offset the cost increases on deposits. You may even have losses on futures positions. Figure 9.2 shows how this might occur. Yield curve 1 prevails at the beginning and curve 2 at

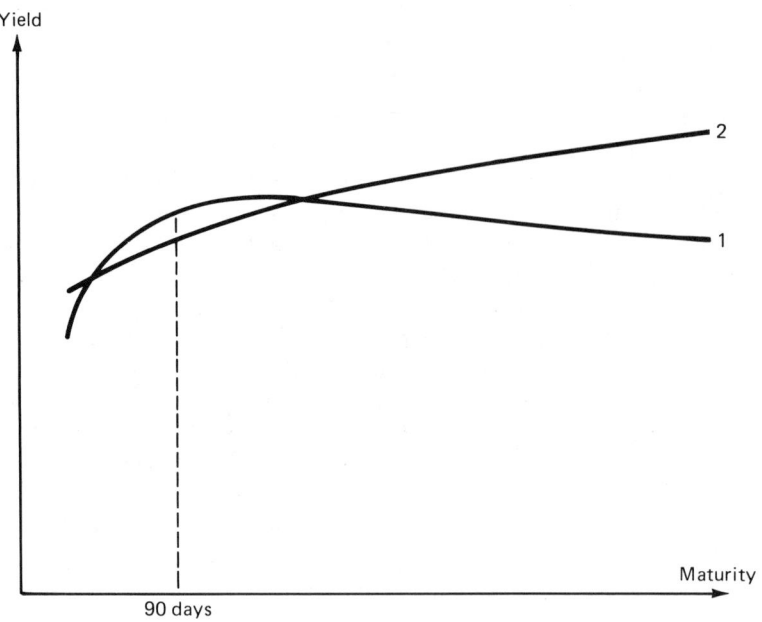

Figure 9.2. Rotating Yield Curve

the end. Most interest rates have risen on yield curve 2, but at the 90-day maturity point rates fell. A short position in T-bills and CDs would have resulted in a loss as futures prices went up! The hedged institution would have taken a double hit—cost of funds would rise as the widening yield spread induced a deposit shift, but the rotation in the yield curve would prevent a recapture in the futures market. If the yield curve is humped or negative over the maturity range of a contemplated hybrid strip hedge, there is a possibility that a yield curve rotation may occur. If you are confident of your ability to trace deposit shifts within your institution and you have plenty of experience doing this, the hybrid strip hedge may offer risk reduction not obtainable by other strategies. If you believe it may be appropriate for your liability portfolio, try it in very small amounts *only* after careful investigation and discussion with your broker and/or consultant. Even then, think about it again before going full steam ahead. We will come back to this theme of multiple hedging strategies in Chapter 11, Hedging the Overall Gap. For now, read about asset hedges in Chapter 10. You will want to try that before you try any multiple liability or gap hedges.

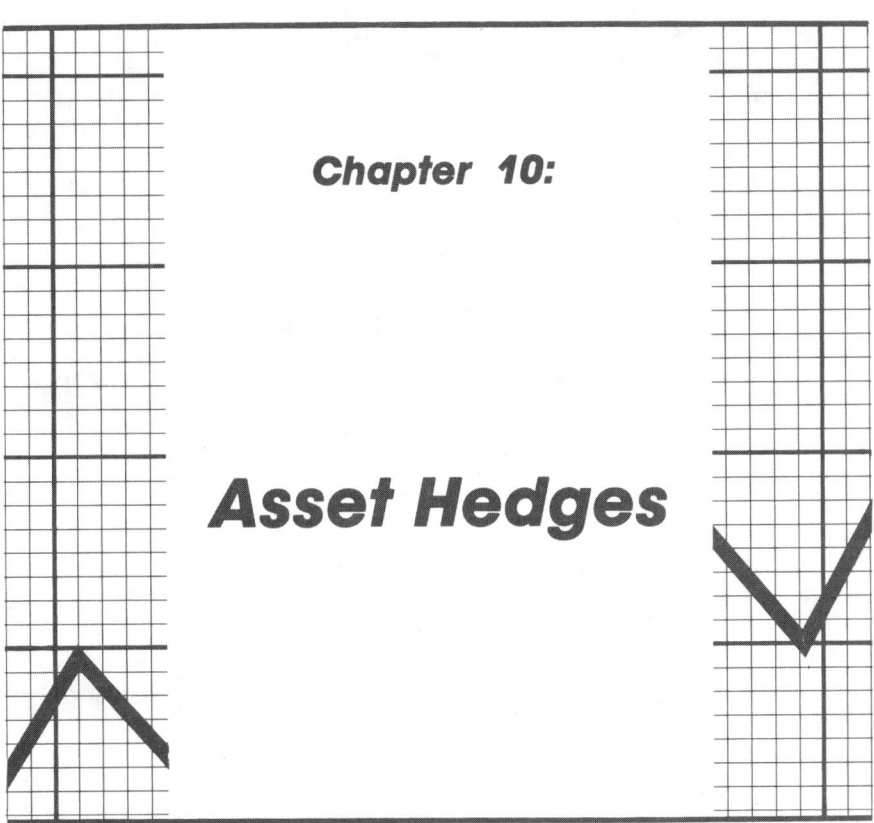

Chapter 10:

Asset Hedges

THE MAJOR risks that a financial institution faces on the asset side of its balance sheet are default risk and capital value risk. Default risk cannot be hedged in the futures market. The normal procedure for default risk management is the institution's investment policy and loan underwriting policy. If an institution makes a bad investment or a loan to a high-risk customer, the futures market cannot and will not bail it out. Price, or capital value risk, is another story altogether. Use of the futures market is an appropriate risk management strategy for this risk and is recommended in a great many circumstances.

ASSET RISKS

The specific risk of concern here is that the value of a fixed-rate asset will decline if market interest rates increase. There is a precise mathematical relationship between the price of an asset, its maturity, and the interest rate. As the term of the asset increases, the same increase in interest will produce a larger depreciation of the asset's value. Table 10.1 shows how this relationship works by indicating the market value of a $50,000 bond with a fixed rate of 10 percent when interest rates rise to 12 percent. The longer the maturity of the bond, the more the price falls.

TABLE 10.1
Price Depreciation of Fixed-Rate Bonds
When Interest Rates Rise

Maturity	Price (PV) when r = 12%	Depreciation from Par
1 year	$49,083.30	− 1.8%
3 years	45,778.94	− 8.4
10 years	43,485.53	− 13.0
20 years	42,476.86	− 15.1

Interestingly, this particular interest rate risk has not received widespread attention in the financial press. Holding bonds is actually riskier than holding mortgages, although the plight of savings and loan associations holding low-rate mortgages has been widely publicized. Compare Table 10.1 to Table 10.2, which indicates the change in value of a $50,000 mortgage made at 10 percent when the market rate rises to 12 percent.

TABLE 10.2
Price Depreciation of $50,000 Fixed-Rate Mortgage
When Interest Rates Rise

Maturity	Price (PV) when r = 12%	Depreciation from Par
1 year	$49,475.01	− 1.0%
3 years	48,574.23	− 2.9
10 years	46,054.88	− 7.9
20 years	43,821.35	− 12.4

Contrary to popular wisdom, holding mortgages is actually less risky than holding bonds of comparable maturity. The reason for this is simple: mortgages have monthly payments of interest and principal which can be reinvested at the higher rate, while bonds have only semiannual interest payments and principal repayment at maturity. Despite the high level of publicity surrounding fixed-rate mortgages, fixed-rate bonds present the holder with more risk.

Since the depreciation from par of either instrument occurs because market interest rates change, the risk of capital value loss can be hedged in the futures market. Changes in cash market interest rates will be reflected by changes in the prices of futures contracts. The interest rate risk on *any* asset can be hedged with futures if that risk arises from market forces. How they can be hedged is the subject at hand.

Identifying the proper hedging vehicle is the first step. To do this it is necessary to look at the exact risk on different types of assets held by banks and savings and loan associations. These assets may be grossly divided into three categories: investments, non-amortizing loans, and amortizing loans. Within these three categories many narrower classifications can be made. We will do that directly.

INVESTMENTS

"Investments" typically means investments in Treasury or government guaranteed securities of one or more types. We will adopt that same nomenclature. The primary subclassification of investments is by maturity—short term or long term.

Short-term investments typically held by banks and savings and loan associations include Treasury bills of all maturities, large certificates of deposit, and municipal warrants. These investments are held primarily for liquidity purposes, rather than as a profit center for the institution. These securities are short term so the capital value risk is at a minimum. Moreover, the maturity schedule of liquidity investments is usually spread out over a period of six to nine months so that some portion of the portfolio is maturing and being reinvested almost continuously. For very large institutions this may amount to as much as $10 or $20 million per day. That is, when necessary, cash can be raised in large amounts by simply not reinvesting. Liquidity risk on this portfolio is essentially eliminated by the maturity schedule. Default risk is not a consideration at all on Treasury or government guaranteed securities. Even though the price of these securities is affected by changes in market interest rates, use of the futures market to hedge this part of an institution's portfolio is not to be recommended. The institution faces no real risk, short of a total collapse of the financial system, on this portfolio. Hedging with futures, therefore, is not likely to be viewed as appropriate by the financial regulators. Note: Before you quit reading here, recall that in this instance we are only talking about the bank's or savings and loan association's own liquidity portfolio. If your institution has a trading desk and holds an inventory of short-term securities as part of its dealer operation, that is a different situation, which is covered in Chapter 12, Hedging the Trading Desk and Arbitrage.

Long-term investments held by most banks and savings and loan associations include Treasury notes and bonds, federal agency securities, and municipal bonds. The maturity on these investments runs from three to 30 years with an average portfolio maturity in the 12-to-15 year range. While this portion of the investment portfolio does provide a secondary liquidity reserve, it is also typically viewed as a source of stable earnings for the institution. The fixed interest rate on securities and the rather long average maturity generates a constant income stream which requires little management time. At least, that's the way it used to be.

Rapid escalation of all interest rates has left the long portion of most investment portfolios seriously underwater. This is an extremely complicated problem which is not easily solved. Lower than market earnings on long bonds and market rate liabilities restrict the institution's ability to dump those investments and reinvest at higher rates. The capital loss that can be sustained on a sale is limited by income available or excess net worth. The spread compression that has occurred in the past several years has left many banks and savings and loan associations with no pleasant options. Unfortunately, the problem of assets that are already underwater cannot be solved in the futures market.

Hedging with financial futures can prevent a return of this unpleasant situation in the future. By hedging against a decline in market value of long-term investment securities, the institution preserves for itself the option of reallocating its portfolio when rates rise. The option that is preserved is the option to do so at no or only a small cost in terms of reducing its capital. This option becomes more valuable to the institution the more volatile that interest rates become and the longer that the volatility persists. If complete interest rate stability returned to the financial markets, the value of hedging would fall to zero since interest rate risk would disappear.

NON-AMORTIZING LOANS

The earlier example of different interest rate risks for bonds and mortgages automatically suggests a division between loans where the principal is amortized and loans that earn interest only with a lump sum repayment of principal. Non-amortizing loans include most commercial loans and agricultural loans made by banks. These loans are not now typically made by savings and loan associations.

Loans that are not amortized present the lender with a degree of interest rate risk directly related to the time period between resets of the loan rate. Obviously, banks would prefer to reprice the loan every month if rates are rising and not reset at all if rates are falling. That, of course, is impossible to do; some time period during which the loan rate is fixed must be negotiated with the borrower. In the absence of any hedging, determination of the period during which the rate is fixed is critical to the profitability or lack of profitability of the loan. Even if you attempt to hedge this type of loan, determining the rate adjustment period and method is critical.

Most business loans made by most banks are priced on the basis of some prime rate, plus a number of points. The prime rate is set by a market mechanism commonly known as price leadership. A few very large banks in New York, Chicago or California announce a prime rate periodically and other banks follow it or not. If an announcement by one bank is not followed quickly by several more of the price leaders, it is usually withdrawn. The ability to hedge with future portfolio of loans tied into this type of market depends entirely on a tight connection between the futures market and the prime rate loan market. If the seven large market banks announce a prime rate change on the same day and the futures market ignores it, there is no possibility of an effective hedge; there must be simultaneous movement in both markets in order to offset losses in one market with gains in the other market. There is no futures contract based on bank prime. There is also no fixed relationship between the bank prime and any futures contract based on any cash market instrument.

The lack of a direct, identifiable and stable relationship between the prime rate and one futures contract does not mean that commercial and agricultural loans cannot be hedged; it just takes more work. The possibilities for crosshedges are nearly limitless. The drawback of crosshedges is that they are almost never as efficient as direct hedges. However, a hedge that is 30 percent efficient, or even 10 percent efficient, is better than no hedge at all. Any risk that is offset cannot hurt you.

The question becomes one of finding a suitable crosshedge for prime rate floating loans. In this area one thing is known with certainty—the prime rate will never fall below the negotiable CD rate. No bank would pay more for deposits than it could earn on loans funded by those deposits. An increase in the prime rate should be accompanied by a decline in the price of bank CD contracts, and vice versa. Whether that provides an effective hedging vehicle for an individual bank depends on how its prime rate is set. If the bank is a price follower and sets its prime on the basis of a consensus prime rate, the efficiency of a hedge using CD contracts will depend on the relationships between prime and the futures market. During 1982 the prime rate was cut 10 times and raised twice. The implied interest rate on December 1982 CD contracts which were traded throughout the year is plotted in Figure 10.1, along with the prime rate.

For a price leader bank the effectiveness of a prime loan-CD futures hedge depends on how closely its prime rate follows changes in its CD rate. For example, suppose that Bank of America always holds its prime rate 200 basis points over its 90-day CD rate. Those CDs are deliverable against the IMM's CD futures contract. A change in Bank of America's prime rate would be triggered by a change in its CD rate which would also effect a change in the price of CD futures. Being a price leader in both markets puts Bank of America in the unique position of being able to affect both markets at the same time. (This does *not* mean they are perfectly hedged internally—that depends on their gap.) What if your bank is not Bank of America or one of the other price leaders in both markets? *In this case hedging efficiency depends on how closely your prime rate follows the CD market.* A bank that is not a price leader is in a position to insure that its prime rate loans can be much more easily hedged in the futures market. Recall that deposit liabilities can be made very hedgeable by tying them to market rates that are tied directly into a futures contract. This same strategy can be adapted to the asset side of the balance sheet.

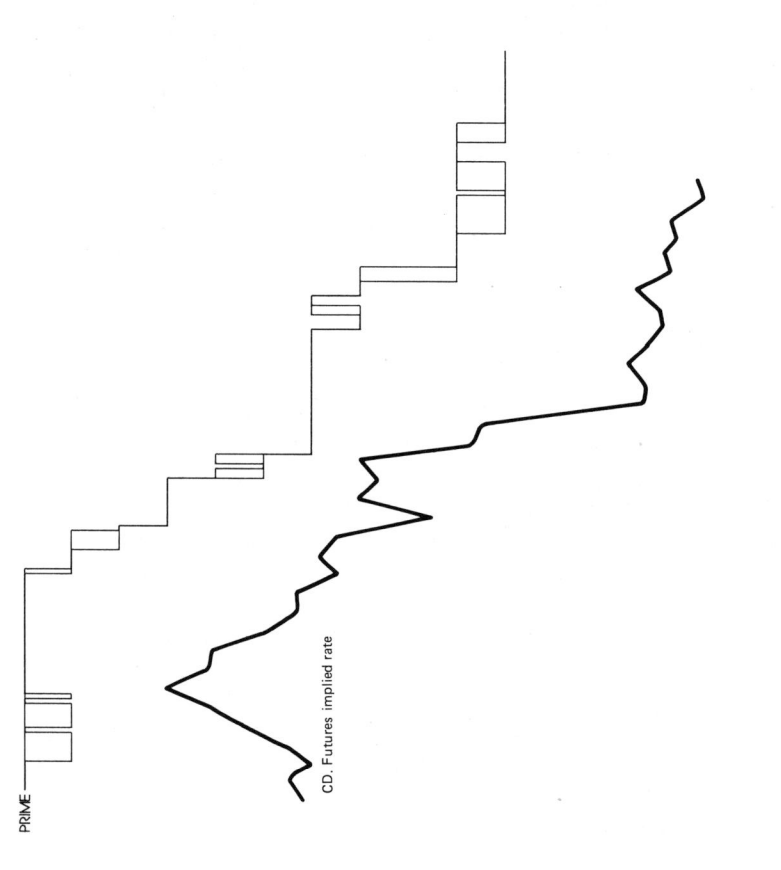

Figure 10.1. Implied Interest Rate on December 1982 CD Contracts and the Prime Rate.

116

Pricing commercial and agricultural loans against the CD rate creates a direct relationship between these assets and the CD futures contract which can be used as a hedging vehicle. This does not mean that loans *should be* priced in relation to the large bank CD rate. Rather, doing so increases a bank's ability to hedge the interest rate risk of its loans in the futures market if it does price them against the rate on an instrument underlying a futures contract. There are two immediately obvious possibilities for doing so, one direct, one indirect. The indirect method is to continue writing loan contracts which specifically tie the loan to the prime rate and then tying the bank's prime rate directly to the market rate on large CDs. The direct method is to tie the loan rate explicitly in the contract to the market rate on CDs. Writing loan contracts either way will allow the bank to make hedged fixed-rate loans without taking on the attendant interest rate risk of the unhedged traditional fixed-rate loan. The implications of this strategy are explored in the latter part of this chapter, which discusses specific strategies.

AMORTIZING LOANS

Amortizing loans such as term loans and mortgages present the lender with lower interest rate risk *a priori* since some portion of the principal is being continuously returned and can thus be reinvested at market rates. Government National Mortgage Association securities also fall into this category since they are longer term and the principal does amortize over time. This is a distinct advantage when rates are rising and something of a disadvantage when rates are falling. The interest rate risk that does exist is directly related to the rate on such loans in the secondary market.

The most fully developed secondary loan market, by far, is the resale market for mortgages. Both banks and savings and loan associations deal in this market in essentially two ways. The first is through direct inter-institution sales of mortgages and mortgage participations. The second is through the sale of mortgage pass-through securities, either privately issued by mortgage originators or those guaranteed by GNMA of the Federal Home Loan Mortgage Corporation, a subsidiary of the Federal Home Loan Bank Board. Institutions which hold pass-through securities or direct mortgage loans are receiving interest and principal which can be reinvested. The obvious hedging possibility is with the GNMA futures contract at the Chicago Board of Trade, although using that contract is not a perfect solution.

First, there is the universal problem of imperfect correlation between the futures market and the GNMA cash market. The substitution of basis risk for interest rate risk will almost always reduce the institution's overall risk, but nonetheless leaves the institution with some risk. The second, and by far larger, difficulty is that a very large fraction of all mortgages and other amortizing loans bears very little resemblance to GNMA pass-throughs. Ginnie Maes represent pools of FHA and VA guaranteed mortgage loans. On the average, such loans represent at most one-third of the total mortgage market, and a much smaller percentage of all amortizing loans held by all financial institutions. The interest rate on non-FHA or non-VA mortgages is not perfectly correlated with the rate on Ginnie Maes, and this puts two layers between the institution's assets and the futures market.

Looking at these relationships in greater detail reveals more useful information in terms of designing a hedge for these assets. The maximum allowable interest rate on FHA and VA loans is administratively determined by agencies of the federal government, making the GNMA certificate rate primarily an administered rate. The relationship between the GNMA cash market and the GNMA futures market is a close one because the futures market is based on cash market instrument. The fact that the GNMA rate is an administered rate means that the secondary relationship between conventional mortgages and other amortizing loans, and GNMA futures is a weak relationship—there is a lot of room for basis shifting.

Therefore, hedging conventional mortgages and other amortizing loans with GNMA futures actually constitutes a cross hedge. Unfortunately, there is no direct hedge which can be used. The GNMA futures contract is the only futures contract traded on any exchange which is based on a security with a self-liquidating or amortizing principal. The price of the GNMA contract behaves in a manner similar to other amortizing securities, but is not exactly the same. Its use should be viewed in the context that eliminating some of the risk is better that not eliminating any of it.

ASSET HEDGING STRATEGIES

For financial institutions asset hedging may logically be either long or short, unlike liability hedges which make sense only on the short side. Financial institutions, depository or otherwise, face interest rate risk on assets whether interest rates rise or fall. Rising rates put the institution in a loss posture on its fixed-income investment securities and falling rates create potential losses on any floating rate loans. Thus, institutions may prudently hedge against both rising and falling rates.

Cautionary note: Hedging against falling rates may be allowed for your institution only under certain conditions determined by your regulatory agency. Make sure you have regulatory authority or specific approval *before* putting on these hedges.

PROTECTING ASSET VALUE

In order to hedge assets against a rise in interest rates, the bank or savings and loan would institute a short hedge, much like the hedge used on the liability side; that is, it sells an appropriate amount of a futures contract. If rates rise, the short futures position is covered at a profit that offsets the decline in value of the hedged asset. To hedge against a rate decline a long hedge is used. The institution takes a long futures position (buys contracts) and covers at a higher price, thus offsetting decreased earnings as a result of a decline in the rate on a floating loan. This is the general idea; let's look at some specifics.

Consider first the interest rate risk of holding investment securities. If market rates go down the value of securities goes up; if rates go up the market value goes down. The institution is chiefly at risk when rates increase. This risk is hedged by a short hedge. Suppose you hold an eight percent U.S. Treasury bond with a face value of $100,000 that you bought at 100-00. If the market rate rises to 10.5 percent, this bond will be worth 77-00. At the time of purchase, or any time that it is at par, you sell one Treasury bond futures contract at 100-00. As the cash market bond depreciates to $77,000 the price of the futures contract will also decline to 77-00. Covering the futures contract results in a profit of $23,000, just equal to the depreciation of the bond you hold. At this point you may dispose of the bond at the then-current market price without experiencing a capital loss. The entire $100,000 may then be reinvested at 10.5 percent. This probably sounds too good to be true. You're right, sort of; it won't work out this way *exactly* but it will be close.

The selection of the Treasury bond contract to hedge a Treasury bond seems rather obvious. However, the process of contract selection is a bit more rigorous than it may appear. For hedging investment securities there are a variety of futures that can be used—Treasury bills, 10-year Treasury notes, and 15-year Treasury Bonds. For an institution which holds one of these same securities in its investment portfolio and wants to hedge it, the choice of a hedging instrument is almost automatic. It makes sense to hedge Treasury bonds with Treasury bond futures since as a last resort the bonds could be delivered against the contract. Treasury bills cannot be delivered against a bond contract so the price of the bond contract will not be closely correlated with cash market Treasury bill prices. Of course, these are opposite ends of the maturity spectrum, and absolutely direct hedges are available. What if no absolutely direct hedge is available? The first rule of thumb is to match maturities as closely as possible. This will result in the most efficient cross hedge since the correlation between the cash and futures market is closer for instruments of like maturity.

PROTECTING ASSET YIELD

Another strategy which may be employed to hedge assets brings the question of asset selection to center stage. One widely publicized but little implemented asset hedging strategy is the creation of a hedged fixed-rate loan. Making a fixed-rate loan in a volatile market is a high-risk strategy, so it is natural to think that the futures market would be of use since it is widely touted as the place to lay off risk. As there is no futures contract based on bank loan rates, the selection of the contract with which to hedge is critical to the success of a hedged fixed-rate loan. A quick glance at the menu of the available futures contracts turns up only two realistic possibilities: domestic CDs and Eurodollar TDs. These are the only contracts based on private securities. Unless there is some correlation between loan rates and these futures contracts, no effective hedge can be placed.

The objective of the fixed-rate loan is to protect both the bank and the customer from rising rates.

A hedged loan package works in the following way: A bank, or savings and loan association now, makes a $10 million loan to a customer for one year at a rate of 10 percent. At the end of the year the customer owes $11 million. The loan agreement specifies that the actual loan rate is variable quarterly but that the lender will hedge against rate changes during the year. The basis for changing the rate is specified in the contract. This mandates coordination between the selection of rate base and a futures contract. The goal here is to provide the customer with a fixed-rate loan but not to deprive the bank of the opportunity to earn market rates. Consider the scenario presented in Table 10.4. By making a fixed-rate loan the bank gives up $150,000 in interest earnings that it could have made on a floating-rate loan. The customer is the big winner by saving the same amount. The bank might just as well have given the customer $150,000 in cash. The alternative of floating the loan rate would produce the following interest earnings scenario for the bank:

TABLE 10.4
Fixed Rate Loans Example

Quarter	Market Rate	Interest Accrued	Gain or (Loss)
I	10.0%	$ 250,000	$ 0
II	12.0	250,000	(50,000)
III	11.5	250,000	(37,500)
IV	12.5	250,000	(62,500)
Year		$1,000,000	($150,000)

TABLE 10.5
Floating Rate Loan Example

Quarter	Market Rate	Interest Accrued
I	10.0%	$ 250,000
II	12.0	300,000
III	11.5	287,500
IV	12.5	312,500
Year	11.5	$1,150,000

The question that must be asked, and answered by the synthetic fixed-rate loan, is how to divide the $150,000 between the borrower and lender. Hedging the loan in the futures market obviates this choice to the degree that the bank recovers the lost opportunities for higher yields by profits on a futures position. That's great, but two critical issues must be decided before proceeding.

First, what futures contract should be used to hedge this type of loan? In order to create a satisfactory cash-futures correlation, the loan must be priced relative to some futures contract, the bank CD contract, for example. At this point you may be saying that this approach amounts to the tail wagging the dog. The futures market should be adaptable to the banking business, the banking business shouldn't be adapting itself to the futures market. This is not a trivial issue to be dismissed out of hand, but it does beg the question of whether a bank wants protection from interest rate risk or not. Traditional banking practice has been no match for the interest rate volatility of the early 1980s. For the bank that wants to control its interest rate risk some of those practices will have to give way to the structure of the futures market. Moreover, the admission of spread banking into the banker's toolkit makes this adaption even more reasonable. Pricing loans at some fixed mark-up over cost of funds paves the way for the type of synthetic fixed-rate loan strategy we're talking about. Tying the loan rate to a hedgeable interest rate provides the maximum protection against interest rate risk. If that's your objective, this is the best way to do it.

The second issue concerns the possibility that the customer will walk away from the loan by repaying it prior to maturity and leave the lender with a futures market position against which it has no cash market asset. If interest rates rise, the lender can bail out of this position at a profit, and the most serious consequence may be a reprimand from the bank examiners. Most customers will not walk away from a fixed-rate loan in a rising rate environment. A falling rate environment is another story altogether. Suppose that instead of the interest rate scenario shown in Table 10.5, that shown in Table 10.6 prevailed and the bank had hedged by shorting a strip of CD contracts for three, six, and nine months out. If the customer prepays after six months the bank has booked $500,000 in interest income, and each leg of the strip would have a loss of $75,000 on its futures position. This results in an effective loan rate of 8.5 percent *and* the bank is able to reinvest at only 9.0 percent. Ultimately, the earnings on that $10 million could fall to 8.75 percent. The purpose of putting together this complicated hedged loan

TABLE 10.6
Falling Rate Loan Example

Quarter	Market Rate	Interest Accrued
I	10.0%	$ 250,000
II	9.5	250,000
III	9.0	250,000
IV	8.0	250,000
Year		$1,000,000

package is to be able to offer the fixed-rate loan that customers prefer. If there is a possibility that the bank may have to endure a penalty this harsh, most bankers will not be interested in pursuing it at all. It's nice to have satisfied customers but they shouldn't, and can't, always be the winner at the bank's expense.

One solution to this dilemma is to write a prepayment penalty into the loan contract which will protect the bank in the event that interest rates decline rather than rise during the term of the loan. Again, this begs the question of what the appropriate prepayment penalty is. This question is at the frontier of knowledge in bank lending so there are no pat answers. It seems unrealistic to believe that a customer should be expected to "make the bank whole" on the entire amount of the loss; i.e., the loss on the futures position and the lost opportunity of a one-year loan at 10 percent. From the scenario in Table 10.6, the opportunity loss could be as much as $75,000 if the $10 million were reinvested at 9.0 percent for 90 days and then at 8.0 percent for the remaining 90 days. The futures market loss would be $75,000. An appropriate penalty, and one that may be acceptable to the customer, would be to set the prepayment penalty equal to any futures market loss accrued as of the date of prepayment. This enforces the original loan rate on the customer up to the time of prepayment but leaves the bank in the same reinvestment position it would have with any unhedged fixed-rate loan. Any other standard prepayment charges could also be added.

An alternate solution to the prepayment problem is simply to lift the hedge if rates start to fall. Doing this unilaterally puts the bank solely at risk if the rate decline should reverse itself. Abandoning hedges on the bank's own positions in mid-course may be perfectly acceptable under some conditions, but doing so when a complicated deal with a customer is involved is likely to be misunderstood by that customer and other customers. This argues for close consultation with the customer about the hedge and how it's working. Remember, the futures market is probably three times as mysterious to your customers as it is to you. Selling this idea is not going to be an easy task but it is not an impossible one by any means.

This brings up an additional point about hedging fixed-rate loans. If it can be done so easily, why don't borrowers just create a synthetic fixed-rate loan themselves? There are at least three excellent reasons. First, they probably have no idea that it can be done or how to do it. Second, the customer may not be large enough to handle the cash flow that may be involved in futures hedging, or the loan may not be the right size in relation to available futures contracts. Third, and probably most importantly, customers look to bankers for innovation in financial services. Providing this service is likely to bring in some new customers since your bank can offer fixed-rate loans without building an interest rate risk premium into the loan rate.

Hedging assets affords a financial institution protection from rising or falling interest rates. Certain classes of assets, such as the investment portfolio, present the institution with relatively greater risks when rates rise. To protect itself against asset depreciation when rates rise, the institution can take a short position in the futures market so that, as prices fall, the loss in the cash market is offset by profits in the futures market. The amount of the loss that can be offset depends directly on how closely the cash and futures markets are correlated.

On other classes of assets, such as loans, the greater risk occurs when interest rates fall. This may be a risk that is fully realized, such as when earnings decline on floating-rate loans; or it may be an opportunity loss if the institution can only roll over maturing loans at lower rates. Both of these situations can be hedged with a long futures position where the institution profits in the futures market when rates fall.

Another strategy is to create a synthetic fixed-rate loan by hedging a variable rate loan with a short position in the futures market. Using this strategy requires close coordination and collaboration by the institution with the borrower in order to avoid the risk exposure that may occur should a prepayment occur. However, a lender which is willing to offer a synthetic fixed-rate loan may enjoy a competitive advantage in its loan market if it can price the loan cheaply enough.

To some extent using these asset hedging strategies requires a shift in loan pricing policy by the institutional hedger. Successfully hedging interest rate risks on assets can *only* be done if there is a close relationship between the price of or rate on the asset and a financial futures contract.

For the bulk of bank or savings and loan association assets there is no directly comparable financial futures contract. There is also little likelihood that such contracts will be developed. Futures contracts call for *standardized* quality. Standardizing the quality of business loans or mortgage loans is not feasible. Without a delivery mechanism the integrity of futures contracts would collapse; without a deliverable instrument there is no delivery mechanism. In short, the futures will not and cannot adapt to the banking business.

The banking business can adapt to the futures market by pricing loans in a way that creates that cash-futures market relationship necessary for successful hedges. All that is involved is a loan pricing mechanism which ties loan rates to *some* futures contract. This is neither difficult nor imprudent. The financial institution which decides to alter its loan pricing policy, on some types of loans or all types, will assure itself of the possibility and the opportunity to shift its interest rate risk to an outside party other than its customers. This is unambiguously beneficial to the institution and to its customers. Failure to so adapt loan pricing policies means that the institution gives up the opportunity to shift most of its interest rate risk to an outside party. The institution must either bear the risk itself or shift it to its customers to the extent that is possible. A great many institutions absorbed large amounts of interest rate risk in the early 1980s and shortly thereafter disappeared. It seems foolish to repeat this pattern when it is unnecessary.

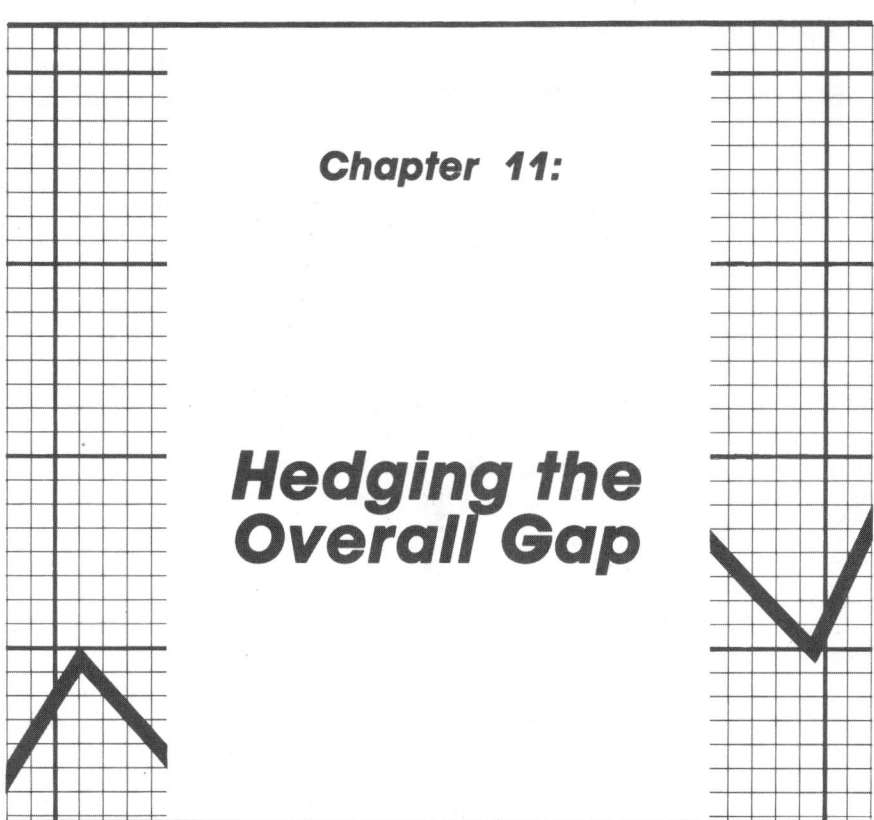

Chapter 11:

Hedging the Overall Gap

TOTAL GAP hedging has received a great deal of publicity recently, partly because gap management has become a hot topic in the financial world, and partly because regulators of financial institutions have become fascinated with gap hedging as a way to wipe out interest rate risk with one fell swoop. As appealing as that prospect is, it is far from being a practical reality. Finding such a hedging strategy which can be implemented by most depository financial institutions is *extremely* difficult. We are not ready to write off the whole idea, though. There are specific circumstances for which gap hedging is appropriate, and we discuss them in this chapter. What we would like to do is warn you that many, maybe most, advocates of gap hedging have not done their homework as well as we would like. Advocating a complicated hedging strategy is one thing, actually implementing it is something else altogether. We are concentrating on the latter.

THE GAP CONCEPT IN A HEDGING CONTEXT _____

From Chapter 2 you will recall that there are quite a variety of gaps that can be calculated. There are component gaps—those that exist at specific points in time, such as 30 days, 60 days, 90 days, etc. There is also a cumulative gap which is a summary indication of the institution's overall gap position for a certain duration of time. We are going to assume now that you understand these concepts.

In order to make some headway on gap hedging it is imperative that you look at gaps from a different angle than we did in Chapter 2. In that chapter the emphasis was on measuring the institution's overall risk by looking at its gaps. Recall that a positive gap means the institution's rate sensitive assets are greater than its rate sensitive liabilities. A negative gap means that the amount of rate sensitive assets are less than the amount of rate sensitive liabilities. This is a measure of risk in the sense that the institution's gap indicates whether it will benefit (i.e., make higher profits) from rising interest rates or falling rates in the future. An institution benefits from rising rates with a positive gap and from falling rates with a negative gap. It is the flip side of that coin that we want to look at in this chapter.

A positive gap is a bet that interest rates will rise; a negative gap is a bet that interest rates will fall. Whether the institution's management consciously makes such a prediction or bet is irrelevant. If you have a positive gap and rates rise, you win; if rates fall, you lose. It's as simple as that. The purpose of learning about gap management is to be able to see, in advance, how interest rate changes will affect the institution's performance. Being aware of the possible ramifications of an asset or liability management decision may change your decision, or it may not; but if you don't know the ramifications, you won't know what your options are.

Suppose you want to continue running a positive gap but would like to hedge your stance in case of a decline in interest rates. This obviously calls for a long position in the futures market. If rates go up the institution wins on its long gap position in the cash market but loses on its long position in the futures market. If rates decline the institution loses on its long gap position in the cash market and wins on its long futures position. In either case, the institution breaks even if the two markets are offsetting. Thus, gap hedging closes or eliminates the gap.

Two interesting questions arise at this point. Do you want to close the gap? Is this the only way to do it? Whether or not it is desirable to close the gap is a management decision. That's what they're paying you for—to decide how much risk is acceptable. The larger the gap, either negative or positive, the larger the risk. If management is convinced that rates will rise and feels that the size gap that exists does not represent an excessive risk should rates fall, then the first question is answered. There is no reason to eliminate the gap, so no hedge should be put on. This may sound trivial, but unless you have done the gap analysis you won't know whether you are improving your strategy or not.

In the event that you do wish to narrow or close your gap, hedging with financial futures may not be the best method available to you. Changing the institution's gap(s) merely means to change the amount of rate sensitive assets or liabilities. To narrow a negative gap the institution needs more rate sensitive assets and/or fewer rate sensitive liabilities. To narrow a positive gap it needs fewer rate sensitive assets and/or more rate sensitive liabilities. This is all well and good, but how do you do that?

Recall from Chapter 9, Multiple Liability Hedges, that one of the most difficult problems facing a depository financial institution is how to effect changes in its liability portfolio since depositors are mainly in control on that side of the balance sheet. The degree to which an institution is in control of the liability side is primarily a function of the size of the institution. A $10 billion bank can change the amount of its rate sensitive liabilities almost at will by issuing more or fewer $100,000 + certificates of deposit. Eurodollar CDs could be replaced with borrowings from foreign branches. A $25 million bank in all likelihood does not have these options.

Creating or expunging rate sensitive assets is somewhat less dependent upon customer preferences, but it is still a function of the size of the institution, somewhat because it depends on the amount of assets which can be unilaterally transformed by the institution and what the cost of the transformation is. It is much easier to sell $1 million of Treasury bills and invest the proceeds in Fed funds than it is to convince 20 mortgage borrowers to convert fixed-rate loans to variable-rate loans. It is also probably cheaper to sell the T-bills than the mortgages. Again, the larger institution enjoys an advantage over the smaller one in its ability to effect changes in its gaps.

An institution which wishes to reduce the interest rate risk exposure implied by its gap *and* finds itself unable, or is unwilling, to do so by adjusting its cash position may want to consider a gap hedging strategy. In our opinion these are the only circumstances for which a gap hedge is appropriate. Here's how to do it:

COMPONENT GAP HEDGE

Designing a component gap hedge requires that the institution's component gap be known. If the institution has the gaps shown in Table 11.1, it is positioned for a six-month rise in rates and then a six-month decline in rates, with rates at the end of the year equal to their level at the beginning of the year. If the institution has no opportunities to change its gap in the cash market, it could put on a long hedge against its positive gap or a short hedge against its negative gap. If its cash positions are heavily influenced by Treasury bill rates, it would take a long position in T-bill futures in the nearby delivery months and a short position in the deferred months, covering all positions as they reach maturity. This is not one position but rather two separate futures positions taken to hedge two different risks. Under no circumstances should this type of hedge ever be referred to or shown on the contract register as one position. If it were shown as one position it would constitute a spread position. Make sure you stay within regulatory limits.

TABLE 11.1
Component Gaps

Time Period	GAP
90 days	$ + 50 M
180 days	$ + 50 M
270 days	$ − 50 M
360 days	$ − 50 M

Consider now the possible outcomes. If interest rates rise for six months and then fall for six months, the hedge offsets the risk implied by the cash market gap for both periods. In fact, no matter what interest rates do during the year the cash market risk during each quarter is offset by an opposite futures position. The institution simply breaks even. The gap, and its effect on profitability, is eliminated by the hedge.

CUMULATIVE GAP HEDGE

The cumulative gap hedge is the one widely touted by regulatory authorities. The gist of the argument is that hedging the cumulative gap allows an institution to hedge the total imbalance between its assets and liabilities. This is typically discussed in the context of savings and loan associations which have enormous negative gaps—huge amounts of long-term fixed-rate mortgage loan assets and large amounts of short-term rate sensitive liabilities. A short position in the futures market is supposed to hedge that imbalance. However, we have some serious reservations about this type of hedge.

The institution which finds itself with a large negative gap with no practical way to eliminate it in the cash market must structure a *hybrid* strip hedge across its entire balance sheet, not just the liability portfolio, in order to hedge its overall cumulative gap. Nobody has yet come up with a hedge design to do this *that actually constitutes a hedge*. During a year's time—the typical cumulative gap period analyzed for hedging purposes—interest rate changes will cause ripple effects across the whole balance sheet. Unless you know where they are in advance, you cannot structure a hedge against them. Or, you could simply lock in rates for the whole year, measure the resulting cumulative gap and then structure the hedge to fit the gap. This is impossible to do—locking in rates on the entire balance sheet for a full year has not been possible since at least 1978. Taking a futures position and then trying to make the institution's cash position fit the futures position is not a hedge, even though this is the essence of a cumulative gap hedging strategy.

It may be possible to hedge one quarter's cumulative gap on a weighted basis, and then roll the hedge forward each quarter. This requires recalculating the gap and the weights for the hedge each quarter. Not only are there fewer difficulties in doing this but it corresponds to the time intervals over which bank performance is measured, i.e., quarterly. Why hedge an entire year's gap and then measure performance during each quarter? There is no intermediate indication of whether the hedge is working or not. As far as we know no one has answered these questions.

In summary, component gap hedging may be appropriate for small institutions which do not have ready access to cash markets that can be used to change their gaps, or have specific asset or liability positions which are smaller than the minimum futures contract size. Cumulative gap hedging is still a theoretical concept that has not yet been translated into a practical hedging strategy. This book is about practical applications of financial futures hedging for financial institutions.

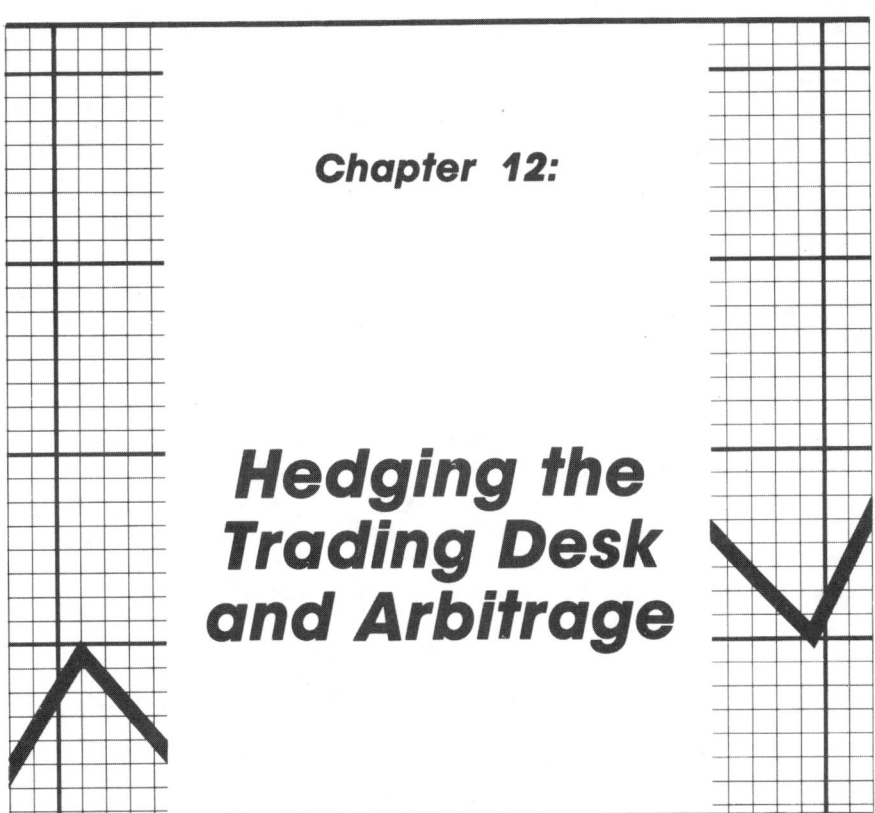

Chapter 12:

Hedging the Trading Desk and Arbitrage

ALSO OF interest, although a detailed discussion of its strategies and techniques are not within the scope of this book, is hedging the trading desk and arbitrage opportunities.

Increasingly, more banks are becoming government securities dealers. Their dealer/trading operations within the bank can also make use of financial futures to minimize their exposure to changing market conditions from time to time, and to make profits from engaging in so-called "riskless" arbitrage transactions.

Government securities dealers are currently large participants in the futures markets. They are generally very highly leveraged operations vulnerable to changes in financing rates. They have found that the depth and flexibility of these markets offers them a means of hedging their inventories, "riding" the yield curve, and locking in "bargains" through arbitrage.

A bank's trading desk, although it may not be as highly leveraged as the typical dealer operation, may benefit from similar use of financial futures with the exception of speculating on changes in the shape of the yield curve. Probably the two most prominent of these type of hedges are protecting inventory assets and hedging a government auction.

INVENTORY HEDGES

The trading desk's position in bills and bonds could be subject to deterioration of their marketable value quite suddenly. These positions are being held for trading profits and will not be kept for long periods of time. Some may by leveraged so it is important to protect as much value as possible.

As we have discussed earlier in the chapter on asset hedges, a bond's price deteriorates with increases in interest rates. Shorting futures contracts can make up the difference of marketable value lost. As we will discuss in the next chapter, it is very important that the hedge be appropriately sized to compensate for differences in each coupon's response to market changes. There are conversion factors to determine the appropriate size. In the case of a dealer operation, which may be leveraged, another factor needs to be considered as well. This is the cost of money used to finance the futures margin for the hedge. It plays a much greater role in the true cost and net results when the funds are borrowed. Therefore, a dealer trader would alter his hedge conversion factor to adjust for this additional consideration.

HEDGING A GOVERNMENT AUCTION

If you have a securities dealing operation you are probably heavily involved in the government's regular auctions. The quarterly refunding auctions always bring an amount of uncertainty with them to the money markets. How well these auctions go, as judged by the participants and onlookers as well, can often signal rapid changes in market psychology and its resultant changes in rates and prices.

Many dealers often hedge themselves going into the auction, knowing full well they will be buying bonds; if the auction does not go well they may be at great risk with their new inventory. To protect themselves from rapid price deterioration, they sell into the futures market before the auction, putting on anticipatory hedges. There is usually some consensus expectation of what the auction rate will be. They calculate their hedges based on conversion factors for the expected coupon and sell the appropriate number of futures contracts, working backwards from the expected yield and the price at which the futures were sold. Dealers can then bid in the auction accordingly, minimizing risk and possibly even locking in a bargain.

If the auction does not fare as well as anticipated, they are protected and maybe even have locked in a profit, depending on their accepted bid. If the auction is very well bid (compared to expectations) and prices begin to rally after the results are announced, they can very quickly lift their hedges the next morning and make up the futures loss with subsequent price appreciation and trading profits.

Many times one market or another will temporarily overreact and price discrepancies will occur. By simultaneously buying in one market and selling in the other an almost riskless profit can be obtained. And, depending on how long a period of time the transaction covers, the annualized rate of return can be quite handsome. Locking in profits from price discrepancies between cash instruments and futures contracts, and vice versa, is known as arbitrage, and practitioners of this activity are known as arbitrageurs.

Arbitrageurs know that these opportunities are fleeting and act quickly to take advantage of them. They know that the force of convergence, which we have yet to discuss, will, much like gravity, eventually win out and return the prices to their proper relationship and almost guarantee a profit. Their mad rush to seize these opportunities itself creates a force in the market which puts prices back "in line" quite rapidly. This is a very valuable service for hedgers in general.

An arbitrageur looks for the cheapest cash instrument that meets the futures delivery specifications. For example, if he can purchase a particular bond at 94-00 which he knows he can deliver in two months for 100-00 and for which his financing and transaction costs will be less than his gross return on this transaction, he can lock in his profit by buying it and selling the futures contract. He can then wait and deliver the bond in the futures market during delivery month, or he can offset the position with an opposite transaction in each market when prices have come back into proper relationship. The second choice is the preferable in that it is easier and allows him to then redeploy his funds, including profits, to benefit from another similar situation if he can find one. The faster the turnover the higher the possible profits.

What we have just described is known as cash to futures arbitrage. It is also known as "cash and carry arbitrage." One of the most important factors in determining if it is a profitable transaction is the cost of money to finance the purchase of the cash bond and carry (hold) it until prices come back in line and the transaction can be completed.

IMPLIED REPO RATE

As we mentioned earlier, most dealers and arbitrageurs are highly leveraged and borrow most of the funds to consummate their trades. They generally do this by repurchase agreements. This means that they sell their securities and at the same time agree to repurchase them the next day at slightly higher prices. In effect they have received an overnight loan whose rate one can calculate from the price difference. This loan rate, known as the overnight repo rate, is the financing rate by which potential arbitrage opportunities are screened.

Often in the case of cash to futures arbitrage the dealer borrows the securities and agrees to resell them. This is called a "reverse RP." Most RPs are overnight transactions but sometimes one can arrange a longer period of time for the agreement. In that case it would be called a "term RP."

If the arbitrageur finances his "arb" (the common name for his arbitrage trade) with a term RP, he has a riskless transaction. Since term RPs are rare he is left in most cases to finance his trade with overnight rates. This now opens him up to the risk that his financing rate may change during the time he holds his position waiting for it to come into line. (Risk just seems to keep rearing its ugly head.) Since he doesn't know his exact financing cost, he tries to approximate it by factoring in the holding period, coupon price, and basis relationship. This anticipated rate is called the "implied repo rate" and is one decision screen which is used by arbitrageurs to find arbitrage opportunities.

FINDING ARBITRAGE OPPORTUNITIES

An arbitrageur must consider the credit rating, coupon, maturity, and liquidity of each side of the transaction. Since most cash to futures arbitrage involves Treasury securities, credit and coupon requirements are an easy match. However, maturity and liquidity are important considerations as he wishes to have as close to a riskless transaction as possible and one that may be consummated.

An arb should consist of like securities. An arbitrageur does not "ride" the yield curve to speculate on yield curve changes. He takes advantage of price discrepancies without regard to the direction of rates. Also, there must be enough liquidity in each market to get the positions on at his prices and quickly, as both transactions need to be done simultaneously. Liquidity is not a problem in most futures contracts. Only in some of the far out deferred contract months could liquidity pose a potential problem, especially if he wants to do large quantities.

There are "long arbs" and "short arbs." In the first case the arbitrageur is long the cash instrument and short the futures; in the second the situation is just the opposite. Most cash to futures arbitrages are long arbs. Owning the cash instrument generates coupon income while a futures position pays no interest. Another reason is that it also costs more to finance a short position in the cash market.

An arbitrageur's profit may be expressed by the following equation:

$$\text{Net return} = (P_f - P_c) + I_c - (R_p + T)$$
$$\text{where } P_f = \text{price of futures}$$
$$P_c = \text{price of cash instrument}$$
$$I_c = \text{coupon interest (\$ amount)}$$
$$R_p = \text{financing rate}$$
$$T = \text{transaction cost}$$

As we mentioned earlier, the repo rate implied by the cash and futures prices of any given situation and the arbitrageur's actual financing cost are the key determinants of whether an arbitrage opportunity exists. To discover these opportunities the arbitrageur engages in a series of calculations known as "break-even analysis." These calculations, generally done by computer, find the implied repo rate for all combinations of all deliverable coupons and contract months at given prices. The results form a matrix. (See Table 12.1)

To find the cheapest-to-deliver coupon for a particular contract month look in that contract month's column and find the highest implied repo rate. In Table 12.1 this would be the 10 3/8's of Nov. 2009 for the Dec. 81 contract. An arbitrage opportunity exists if this transaction can be financed at a rate less than the implied repo rate, considering transaction costs as well.

Then, if the arbitrageur was quick enough to transact the positions at the given prices, you can see in Table 12.2 his net profit. The matrix in this figure also shows the results of the other combinations as well. Please note that these calculations did not include his commission costs and his cost of margin money.

This type of analysis can also be useful to hedgers in finding basis relationships that are out of whack and may influence their decisions of whether to place the hedge and in what given contract month to do so. There are two computer software packages available to aid in this analysis. One from Data Resources Inc. is available on a timesharing basis, while the Kidder Trade Evaluator is available for use on an Apple® microcomputer.

We only showed an example of a Treasury bond arbitrage; however, similar opportunities are possible for Treasury notes, GNMAs, and Treasury bills. In the case of T-Bill arbitrage some of the calculations are modified to take into account that they are traded on a discounted yield and that the value of a basis point is higher than that of the futures contract.

It is not within the scope of this introductory chapter to delve deeply into these calculations nor to give hedge size ratio calculations to account for any differences between movements in the cash and the futures markets for arbitrage situations. Calculating the proper hedge size for asset and liability hedging, however, is very much within the scope of this book and very integral to the hedging process. We will now proceed to these important calculations.

TABLE 12.2

Cells Contain Cash & Carry Implied Repo Matrix
Implied Repo Rates For Cheap To Carry Analysis
(Prepared In Conjunction With Data Resources, Inc.)

Cash Issue	Cash Price (32nds)	Dec 1981	T-Bond Futures (32nds) Mar 1982	Jun 1982	Sep 1982	Dec 1982
		58.22	59.07	59.20	60.00	60.11
11.750% Of Feb 2001	81.12	5.03	11.76	13.33	13.96	14.30
13.125% Of May 2001	89.12	5.65	11.83	13.15	13.74	14.01
8.000% Of Aug 2001	60.30	(6.76)	6.31	9.65	11.09	11.90
13.375% Of Aug 2001	90.18	8.52	13.34	14.40	14.79	15.00
8.250% Of May 2005	60.20	8.09	12.70	13.61	14.01	14.17
7.625% Of Feb 2007	57.24	1.46	9.93	12.00	12.86	13.34
7.875% Of Nov 2007	59.22	(2.56)	7.95	10.49	11.64	12.23
8.375% Of Aug 2008	61.24	6.11	12.05	13.41	13.95	14.24
8.750% Of Nov 2008	63.06	12.86	14.85	15.02	15.09	15.05
9.125% Of May 2009	65.16	12.89	14.89	15.06	15.12	15.08
10.375% Of Nov 2009	72.26	15.80	16.22	15.94	15.80	15.65
11.750% Of Feb 2010	82.02	11.31	14.48	15.08	15.25	15.35
10.000% Of May 2010	71.04	12.07	14.53	14.84	14.97	14.97
12.750% Of Nov 2010	88.18	10.82	14.05	14.56	14.78	14.83
13.875% Of May 2011	96.12	7.93	12.78	13.74	14.16	14.34

TABLE 12.1

Table of Treasury Bonds Deliverable
Against the Dec 1981 Chicago Board Bond Future
67 day carry to 12/15/81
Based on $100,000 Face Value
(Prepared In Conjunction With Data Resources, Inc.)

Issue	Purchase Price	Final Proceeds Received	Gross Profit	Gross Rate Of Return (365 Days)	Fin. Cost	Net Profit	Net Rate Of Return (365 Days)
11.750% Of Feb 2001	83,131	83,990	859	5.63	(1,913)	(1,055)	(7.83)
13.125% Of May 2001	94,618	95,693	1,075	6.19	(2,111)	(1,037)	(6.97)
8.000% Of Aug 2001	62,133	61,431	(702)	(6.15)	(1,433)	(2,134)	(21.15)
13.375% Of Aug 2001	92,561	94,109	1,547	9.11	(2,130)	(582)	(3.88)
8.250% Of May 2005	63,921	64,962	1,042	8.88	(1,431)	(390)	(3.37)
7.625% Of Feb 2007	58,890	59,129	240	2.22	(1,358)	(1,118)	(11.69)
7.875% Of Nov 2007	62,833	62,613	(220)	(1.91)	(1,409)	(1,629)	(16.42)
8.375% Of Aug 2008	63,002	63,798	797	6.89	(1,452)	(655)	(6.41)
8.750% Of Nov 2008	66,683	68,358	1,676	13.69	(1,492)	183	1.75
9.125% Of May 2009	69,145	70,883	1,738	13.70	(1,547)	192	1.76
10.375% Of Nov 2009	76,957	79,300	2,343	16.59	(1,720)	624	5.15
11.750% Of Feb 2010	83,819	85,662	1,844	11.98	(1,930)	(86)	(0.63)
10.000% Of May 2010	75,120	76,887	1,767	12.82	(1,680)	87	0.74
12.750% Of Nov 2010	93,656	95,621	1,965	11.43	(2,092)	(127)	(0.86)
13.875% Of May 2011	101,917	103,501	1,584	8.47	(2,276)	(693)	(4.32)

NOTE: 14.00% and 16.00% financing assumed on 90.00% of base cost
and 10.00% of accrued interest, respectively...

Financing rates are quoted on a 360 day year basis
Reinvestment of coupons assumed at a 365 day year rate of 14.00%

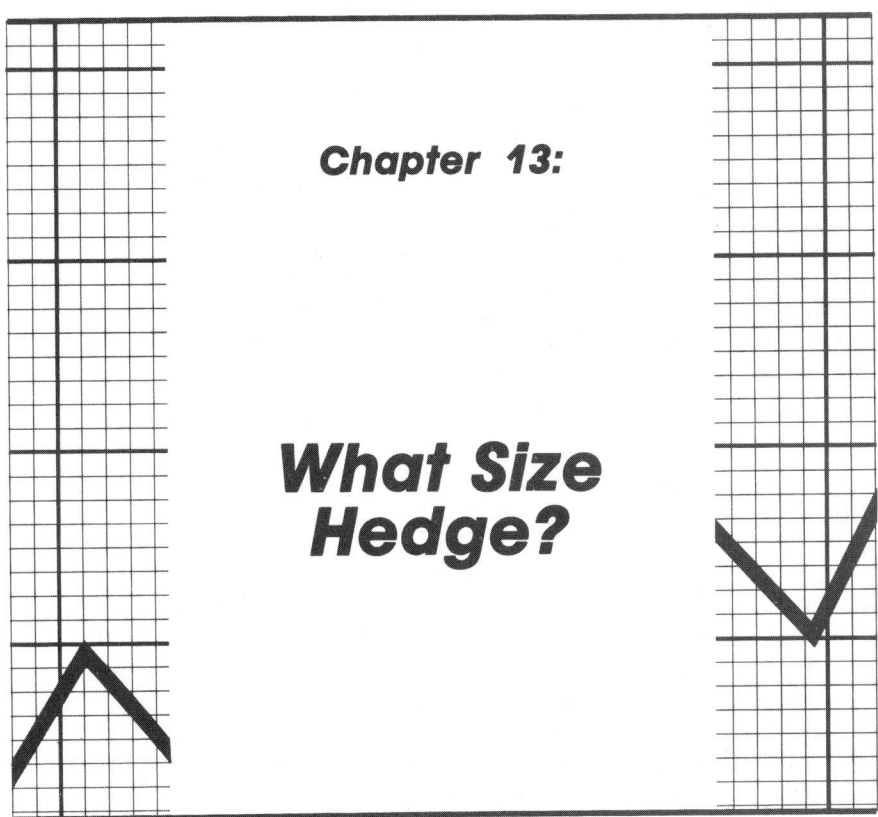

Chapter 13:

What Size Hedge?

ABOUT NOW it is likely that many readers are beginning to wonder about the size of hedge which is appropriate. This is a two-part question which can only be answered sequentially. The first part of the question concerns the percentage of the institution's interest rate risk which it wishes to hedge—do you want to nail down *all* risks by being fully hedged all the time or are you willing to take on some risk in the expectation of making above-average returns? This is not an easy question to answer. There is no questionnaire which can be filled out and fed into a computer to produce an answer. That is probably a good thing, otherwise computers could run the place by themselves. The first part of the chapter focuses on the issues that are relevant to this issue—how to decide how much to be hedged.

The second part of the chapter focuses on the second issue, *which is only relevant when the first question has been answered.* This involves the nuts and bolts of determining how many contracts to use in structuring a hedge. Futures exchanges operate like any other business in that they design products which will appeal to the widest possible customer base. Consequently, there are few financial futures contracts which will perfectly correspond in all respects to specific assets or liabilities that a bank or savings and loan association will want to hedge. And even if there is a contract based on the exact security you want to hedge, there is some slippage between the cash market and the futures market.

Most of the time, therefore, the face amount of futures contracts being used will differ from the amount of assets or liabilities being hedged. Hedging a $1,000,000 Treasury bond may only require $600,000 of bond futures contracts or it may require $1,200,000 of contracts. Using the incorrect amount of futures contracts means you are hedging over or under the amount you decided on. This may or may not be a serious problem depending on the circumstances, but you definitely will not get the results that were planned. These issues are examined in detail in part two of this chapter.

PART ONE: THEORETICAL CONSIDERATIONS

The decision about how much of the institution's interest rate risk should be hedged is not one which can be made quickly or lightly. A great deal is at stake here. In Part I of this book we discussed the identification and measurement of the institution's interest rate risk. We saw that different assets and liabilities have different risk profiles individually and that different combinations of assets and liabilities also project different risk profiles (that is the GAP concept). Before jumping off head first into the process of making a final decision it will be useful to do a lot of homework. This will not only make the decision easier but it will provide you with an enormous amount of useful information which can be used in other ways, not the least of which is a sound basis for changing your strategy later on.

The homework that you have to do is the detailed financial analysis mentioned in Chapter 2. In that chapter we talked about calculating the institution's gap at different points in time. This is only the beginning in terms of deciding how much to hedge. Finding and measuring the institution's gap gives you the starting points for the more detailed analysis necessary at this stage of designing a hedging program. What is now required is a retrospective look at these gaps over time. The amount of time varies by institution, but at least six quarters are recommended in order to be at all useful.

GAP ANALYSIS

The number of time periods over which gaps should be examined varies in the following way: If the institution has at some point in the recent past undergone a radical shift in the structure of its assets and liabilities, there is no point in examining gaps prior to that point. For example, suppose a savings and loan association decided two years ago to stop making mortgages for its own portfolio and began in earnest to transform itself into a mortgage banker, making all loans for sale and with only loan origination and servicing by the association. In that case looking at the gaps the institution experienced three years ago would not be of any value at all since the association is not even in the same business now.

This is quite a bit more subtle than it may appear on the surface. A cut-off point for retrospective gap analysis is suggested by the structure of the institution *only if* there has been a change in structure of such magnitude as to move the institution away from one type of business to another so that its risk profile is affected. That is, suppose a bank decided two years ago to abandon its credit card business and to expand its marketing of checking account overdraft privileges. This is still a consumer credit line of business not materially different from offering credit cards. An even more subtle example would be a bank which decided to stop extending credit to farmers and began to finance inventories of small businesses and to factor accounts receivable. To a great many uninformed people this might appear to be a fundamental shift since agricultural lending is different from inventory financing or factoring. Indeed it is, but in terms of the risk profile of the bank there is not a lot of difference. The only real difference is in the underwriting process—small business risk is small business risk whether it is cotton farming or a hardware store.

Where, then, is the cutoff point if there hasn't been any fundamental shift in the risk profile of the institution in the last eight or 10 quarters? Obviously, arbitrarily picking a point will not prove to be useful in most cases. One very practical solution is to go back in time far enough to capture one entire business cycle since interest rate risk varies over the cycle. This will generally be a 12- to 24-month period. What you want to do is examine the institution's periodic gap at regualr intervals over this time period. The periodicity of gaps that you will want to examine is largely a function of the size of the institution, as outlined in Chapter 2.

Consider now what this information reveals to you about the institution's ability to profit from rising or falling rates. As you are aware a positive gap—rate sensitive assets exceed rate sensitive liabilities—allows the institution to profit from rising rates, and a negative gap—rate sensitive assets are less than rate sensitive liabilities—allows the institution to profit from falling rates. It will probably be useful to plot the size of the institution's gap on a chart like the one shown in Fig. 13.1, which also shows the pattern of interest rate changes over the same period of time.

This information provides the first type of scorecard on the institution's ability to position itself to take advantage of falling or rising interest rates. Anyone involved in management of a financial institution will know that this is not easy to do at any given time and is particularly difficult over a long period of time. What hedging is designed to do is take some of the risk out of the process. In order for hedging to be effective it is necessary to know where the risk is. The analysis that you have just done is designed for that purpose. Now you know when and where things have gone wrong and

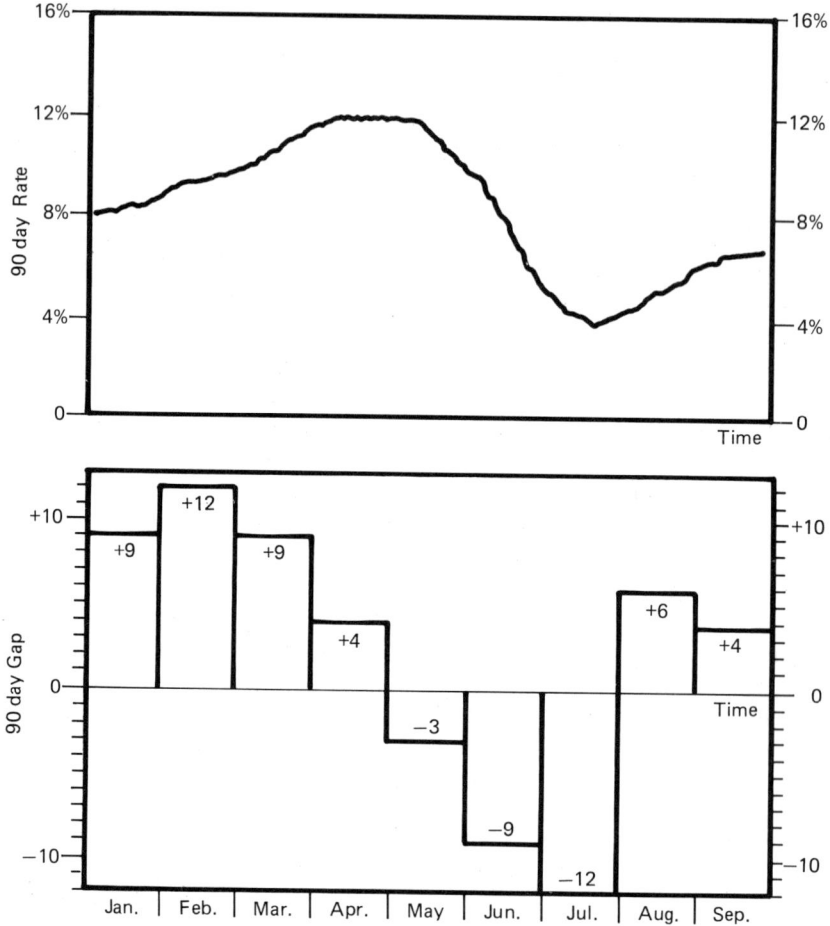

Figure 13.1.

by how much. The main point here is that the percentage of your risk that you may want to hedge depends on how much risk you have and where the risk lies. Again, what we want to do is look at the entire enemy and then divide and conquer as appropriate.

RISKS AND REWARDS

Consider the following example: A bank has $100 million of 90-day commercial loans funded by 180-day certificates of deposit. However, the bank has $10 billion in total assets so that this mismatch represents only 1 percent of its total asset base. The contribution to overall bank profits by this category of assets is, therefore, limited. However, the marginal contribution to profit of this one asset category can be quite important. Why would you not want to maximize the profit on every single asset? You would, of course, but using futures may not be the best way to do it. Match funding the commercial loans with 90-day certificates of deposit would remove the interest rate risk entirely. This is the real issue to be decided: do you want to remove all risk?

From a theoretical standpoint one thing seems clear. Higher risks are rewarded in the marketplace with higher returns or bigger losses. For many years the theoretical literature dealing with financial institutions advocated the perfect matching, or near-perfect matching, of asset and liability maturities to insure stability of returns. That the academic community got a lot of mileage out of this proposition is not of any particular importance. What is of importance, though, is that the regulatory community tried in the past to get mileage out of it. The greatest manifestation of this attempt is in the area of restrictions on the types of liabilities that depository financial institutions could offer and the types of assets that they could hold.

The entire proposition of perfect maturity matching is absolute nonsense because it ignores the trade-off that exists between risk and return, as well as the function of financial intermediation. A bank that perfectly matched asset and liability maturities would be taking almost no risk at all and would, in a competitive market, therefore be entitled to almost no return at all. But that is not banking, it's simply safekeeping of funds. The increasing emphasis by some banks on fee income represents an attempt to avoid most risk and to simply charge customers for these safekeeping or brokerage services. This is an important idea to keep in mind when deciding on the degree to which your institution will hedge its interest rate risk. If you shift all of that risk to customers—which is what maturity matching does in reality—you will lose some of your customers. If you shift it all to speculators in the futures market you will have to pay for that insurance as well. In either case the net return on the institution's capital will be reduced.

Consider again the information that you developed in the gap analysis. That exercise revealed the areas of greatest risk in your portfolio. If you have large positive gaps at 90 days and large negative gaps at 180 days, this is tantamount to a bet that interest rates will increase over the next 90 days but will fall in 180 days. Suppose you have the following:

	90 days	180 days
Rate Sensitive Assets	100	50
Rate Sensitive Liabilities	50	100
GAP	+ 50	− 50

Over the first 90 days the institution is positioned so as to profit from rising rates; in the subsequent 90 days it is positioned so as to profit from falling rates. This particular structure is an implicit forecast that rates will return to their current level 180 days hence. During the first 90 days the institution is loaded up with assets which will increase in yield but has limited its exposure to rising cost liabilities. Over the second 90-day period it does the opposite, locking in high-yield, fixed-rate assets while letting its liability costs float downward. If the forecast were that rates would actually fall below their current level you would want to have an extremely short gap, perhaps even going so far as to eliminate all rate sensitive assets in order to lock in as high a yield as possible, while letting the cost of all liabilities float down with the general fall in rates. If you think this sounds like the interest rate forecasting game all over again, you are absolutely correct. The objective of reading this book, and learning how to hedge your portfolio in the futures market, is to learn how to stop playing that game. Here's the plan.

Structure your portfolio so as to maximize the spread between assets and liabilities based on your best interest rate forecast. Then hedge your largest risks. When you do that, remember to *manage* your hedge. Managing a hedge is a very disciplined process which should be undertaken cautiously only by experienced hedgers. If you just put on a hedge and leave it on all the time you will eliminate losses from unforeseen rate changes that go against you, but you will also eliminate gains from unforeseen rate changes that go with your position. Recall the simple hedging strategy in Chapter 8 in which you hedge the cost of money market certificates. If you leave the hedge on all the time you will lose money on the futures position which will be offset by rolling over the MMCs at a lower rate. This is breaking even. Lifting the hedge will eliminate the loss in the futures market, but the MMCs will still roll over at a lower cost.

For a financial institution the risk is always two sided—if there can be a huge loss there can also be a huge gain. Believe it or not, it is possible to have it both ways. By *selectively* hedging you can take advantage of the potentially high gains which stem from high-risk strategies. This will eliminate the risk of a huge loss but will enable you to capture a large part of the huge gain *if you lift the hedge at the right time.*

HEDGE ANALYSIS

The most effective way to analyze this problem is to employ the simple elements of Game Theory, the so-called "scenario" approach to planning. You've seen this sort of thing for years: the best case, the worst case, and the most likely case. Most of the time it is used in banking applications as an overall forecast of profitability when a number of conditions—interest rates, market share, regulation, etc.—are expected to change. The only necessary step to make use of this technique in futures hedging is to break it down to all component parts—construct scenarios on all categories of assets and liabilities that expose the institution to interest rate risk.

In applying this process to bank asset and liability management, it is important to remember that the key variable is always the interest rate of a specific category of assets or liabilities. Also, remember that in order to construct a set of scenarios on these items it is necessary to do some forecasting. What you are going to do is to construct a set of scenarios for each asset or liability which indicates the best, worst, and most likely course of interest rate *movement* over time. The period of time that is relevant depends on the type of asset or liability, as well as the specific gap period that you wish to analyze. This, of course, is tedious to do manually and will require a great deal of time. However, most computer-based asset and liability management models will accomplish the analysis for you in a matter of seconds. All you need to do is supply the outer bounds in order to define the relevant interest rate spread. That is, is the computer supposed to construct scenarios based on an interest rate range of 10–14 percent or 6–10 percent?

Suppose now that you have input your best guess into the computer and generated the following set of scenarios:

TABLE 13.1
Interest Rate Scenario, 180-Day Gap Analysis
(Amounts in Basis Points)

A/L Item	Worst Case	Most Likely Case	Best Case	Percent
MMC	+ 100	+ 40	− 50	20
MMA	+ 45	+ 15	− 70	40
CD	+ 125	+ 50	− 40	10
T-bills	− 50	+ 40	+ 100	10
Prime Loans	− 50	+ 50	+ 125	60
US Bonds	+ 65	+ 15	− 25	5

A word or two of explanation concerning Table 13.1 is in order before proceeding. The column labelled "Percent" indicates the percent of the institution's assets accounted for by this asset or liability item. The worst case for the rate on MMCs occurs if that rate increases by 100 basis points. At the same time, for Treasury bills the best case is if that rate increases by 100 basis points. Since the rate on T-bills affects both the bank's assets and liabilities due to the link between T-bills and MMCs, the same interest rate change produces opposite scenarios. The same relationship holds between the CD rate and the Prime Loan rate; a jump in the CD rate increases costs but pushes up the Prime Rate, thereby increasing revenues. Notice, though, that this mirror-image symmetry *does not* hold throughout the balance sheet. In the case of U.S. bonds the worst case occurs when rates increase and the best case occurs when rates decrease. This is due to the fact that we are examining a 180-day gap during which time long-term bonds will not mature and be rolled over. The rate increase in the long end of the market during the next 180 days will simply mean that the market value of the bonds falls.

The question now is, where are the largest risks for the institution? From the information in Table 13.1 it should be clear that the institution is positioned for a rise in rates. The most likely scenario and the best case scenario are for rising rates on 70 percent of the institution's assets. On the liability side the largest single deposit account, the MMA, shows a most likely scenario as only a small increase in rate and a best case scenario as a huge rate decline. By inspection alone the institution's gap indicates large risks with MMCs and CDs. How much of this risk should be hedged?

Part of the risk is already internally hedged over the next 180 days. MMCs account for 20 percent of assets, but Treasury bills held account for 10 percent of assets. Since the rate on both will be reset at approximately the same time, the institution is exposed to interest rate risk on only half of its MMCs. There is no point in hedging all of the MMCs when hedging half of them will eliminate the risk. By hedging half of the MMC position the institution positions itself to withstand a greater rate increase without narrowing its spread, since the most likely case is an across-the-board rise in interest rates.

More importantly, the most likely scenario also indicates a rotation in the yield curve as the long-term Treasury bonds are seen as going up by only 15 basis points, but the short-term Treasury bills are seen as rising by 40 basis points. Hedging against this yield curve rotation requires something more than a simple MMC hedge with T-bill futures. A hybrid hedge or a spread is more likely to nail down this risk.

This example underscores the importance and necessity of substantial analytical work prior to putting on a hedge. In the absence of the scenario analysis it is unlikely that all of the institution's risk would have been detected. If undetected it will also go unhedged. Deciding on how much to hedge requires three pieces of information:

1. The amount of risk to which the institution is exposed.
2. The specific nature of that risk.
3. A determination of how much risk is acceptable.

Once these have been determined, the degree to which the institution will want to hedge either its asset or liability portfolio or its overall gap is known. There is one other consideration that is relevant. Since nothing else ever stays the same forever, it is totally unrealistic to assume that your hedging plan will stay the same. Chances are, you will also change policy over time on the degree of risk that is acceptable. Thus, the optimal size hedge for an institution will change right along with its risk exposure. The best way to go about solving the problem of when to change your strategy is to review your previous analysis and your current hedging plan. If the institution is positioned in both the cash and futures markets for rising rates and rates are rising, then no change will be needed. If, however, you are positioned for rising rates and rates are falling, a change will be indicated. Your first indication will be in your futures margin account.

One of the supreme advantages of the futures market is that it is so easy to change directions. If you are positioned for rising rates and rates fall, you can back off your hedge quickly. Experienced traders tend to think it is obvious when and why you should change the size of a hedge. For the inexperienced hedger it is not necessarily obvious. Suppose now that you are hedged against rising rates over the next 180 days and that 30 days into the plan rates actually start a downward trend. If you go back and redo your scenario analysis you will find that the total risk exposure of the institution is lower than it was before. This calls for a smaller proportion of the portfolio to be hedged. Hedgers with moderate to vast experience in the market will not bother to redo the analysis but will simply lift the hedge a small piece at a time proportionate to the reduction in risk that has occurred. This takes a good deal of time to learn. For now, if you are new to futures hedging it will be a good idea to review your analysis of the institution's risk exposure and change the overall size of the hedge; but you should do it *only on the basis of an identifiable reduction in risk* rather than on a subjective "feel of the market." This procedure will not steer you wrong very often or by very much. This also works in the opposite direction; the size of a hedge can be easily increased if necessary.

PART TWO: PRACTICAL APPLICATIONS: HEDGE RATIOS

Once you have made the determination of how much you should hedge, then you must consider how many futures contracts you must put on to properly hedge that amount.

The objective of every hedge is to match the incremental dollar cost of a move in your cash position with an equal dollar value move in your futures position. This is called "dollar equivalency" or the value of an 01. Dollar equivalency involves not only the principal size of your assets or liabilities and the size of a futures contract but also a time factor, sometimes known as the "duration factor." Also involved in the size of a hedge is a volatility factor which is related to "basis risk," the relationship of futures prices to cash prices.

We will discuss these as we proceed, but the first thing to do is to define exactly what is being hedged. What is the maturity of the rate or instrument and how has it performed in the past? Second, select the interest rate futures contract that you will use to offset this risk. See Chapter 6 for what is currently available. But generally, for rates pegged to T-bills use T-bill futures; for BA's use CD futures; for intermediate rates use T-note futures; for mortgage rates use GNMA futures; and for Treasury and municipal bonds use T-bond futures.

Correlation studies have been done to show the price movement relationship between various cash instruments and futures contracts. Linear regression of the two rates or prices and their first differences provides a measure of fit or basis risk. (See Table 13.2)

TABLE 13.2
Correlation Matrix: June 1979 To July 1981

	(0)	(1)	(2)	(3)	(4)	(5)	(6)	(7)	(8)	(9)
0) DOMESTIC CD'S	1.000									
1) BANKERS ACCEPTANCES	0.987	1.000								
2) COMMERCIAL PAPER	0.998	0.988	1.000							
3) EURODOLLAR CD'S	0.995	0.987	0.994	1.000						
4) TREASURY-BILLS	0.978	0.954	0.973	0.967	1.000					
5) PRIME RATE	0.826	0.865	0.822	0.843	0.794	1.000				
6) OVERNIGHT REPO	0.920	0.934	0.924	0.908	0.907	0.874	1.000			
7) 90-DAY REPO RATE	0.982	0.995	0.983	0.981	0.956	0.879	0.939	1.000		
8) TREASURY-BILL FUTURES YIELD	0.915	0.873	0.904	0.906	0.949	0.649	0.771	0.867	1.000	
9) LIBOR	0.986	0.959	0.984	0.985	0.966	0.788	0.879	0.953	0.921	1.000

Correlation Matrix: January 1977 To July 1981

	(0)	(1)	(2)	(3)	(4)	(5)	(6)	(7)
0) DOMESTIC CD'S	1.000							
1) BANKERS ACCEPTANCES	0.997	1.000						
2) COMMERCIAL PAPER	0.999	0.998	1.000					
3) EURODOLLAR CD'S	0.999	0.997	0.998	1.000				
4) TREASURY-BILLS	0.994	0.989	0.993	0.991	1.000			
5) PRIME RATE	0.966	0.973	0.966	0.970	0.962	1.000		
6) OVERNIGHT REPO	0.977	0.979	0.978	0.973	0.975	0.969	1.000	
7) TREASURY-BILL FUTURES YIELD	0.982	0.975	0.981	0.981	0.989	0.935	0.947	1.000

WEEKLY DATA

Source: *Chicago Board of Trade*

BASIS

Simply defined, the basis is the difference in price between the cash instrument and the price of the corresponding futures contract. Generally, this is the rate you are hedging and the nearby futures month. This relative price movement is a key factor in your success as a hedger. By watching the basis relationship you will be able to choose judiciously which contract to use and when not to put on a hedge. Basis trading will be discussed in Chapters 17 & 18, but for now it is important for you to understand that by using an analysis of this relationship you can structure your hedge appropriately. This is especially critical in cross hedging, when you must hedge your exposed rate with a dissimilar futures contract, eg., municipal bonds with T-bond futures. The basis study gives you the relationship of apples to oranges and quantifies it for your further use.

VOLATILITY FACTOR

Related to basis, the third step in your hedge calculation process is to quantify the relative volatility of the percentage change in the futures price to the percentage change in the cash instrument's price. Statistically, it is the mean variance between the two and is a by-product of regression analysis. The result is known as the volatility or "basis factor." As you will soon see, it can greatly affect the size and effectiveness of your hedge. No, George, you are not expected to become a statistician. You can get these studies or results from your broker, the exchanges, or your consultant. For example, bank certificates of deposit have a volatility of approximately 1.25 to 1 when compared to T-bill futures.

DURATION FACTOR

The next step in the process is to determine the duration of the risk. This is not the maturity of the instrument but the time period to which you will be exposed to risk. For example, six-month money market certificates are reset every six months, which means you are exposed for 180 days, while your duration of exposure is only three months while waiting for the next 30-year bond auction at the quarterly refunding. When the duration is divided by the term of the futures contract, you derive the duration factor. In the case of the six-month MMCs it is:

$$\frac{180}{90} = 2$$

and in the refunding example it would be:

$$\frac{90}{90} = 1$$

DOLLAR EQUIVALENCY

As we mentioned at the outset, what we are trying to achieve with our hedge is an equivalent dollar for dollar move in both the cash and the futures. To achieve this dollar equivalency you may have to adjust the number of contracts in the hedge so that a one basis point move yields the same dollar value of a one basis point move in the futures.

The duration factor can be restated in terms of these 01 values as follows:

$$D = \frac{\text{\$ Value of a change in interest rate of one basis point per unit value of asset or liability risk}}{\text{\$ Value of a change in interest rate of one basis point per unit value of the futures contract}}$$

In the case of \$1 million six-month MMCs the value of an 01 is:

$$\$\ 1,000,000 \times .0001 \times \frac{180}{360} = \$50$$

The value of an 01 for a 90-day T-Bill futures contract is:

$$\$\ 1,000,000 \times .0001 \times \frac{90}{360} = \$25$$

Therefore, $D = \frac{50}{25} = 2$, which means that in order to properly hedge these liabilities you need to sell two T-bill futures contracts for each million in MMCs. The longer the time of risk exposure endured, the more dollar principal risk exposure there is in a basis point change in yield.

HEDGE SIZE CALCULATION

You can now calculate your hedge size by using the following formula:

$$N = \frac{Pc}{Pf} \times V \times \frac{Tc}{Tf}$$

where N = number of contracts to be used in the hedge
    Pc = principal of the cash instrument
    Pf = principal of the futures contract
    V = volatility factor*
    Tc = term of cash instrument exposure (in days)
    Tf = term of futures contract used (in days)

Notes: $\dfrac{Tc}{Tf}$ is the duration factor D which was discussed above

*V could be restated as $\dfrac{Bc = \% \text{ change of cash}}{Bf = \% \text{ change of futures}}$ = mean variance be-

tween the two. In the six-month MMC example, for ease of concept introduction we assumed the volatility factor to be 1 when in reality it would be approximately 1.13.

Coupon Conversion Factors & The Compression Ratio

In the case of bonds, notes, and GNMAs, remember before placing your hedges that the futures are based on 8 percent coupons. Different coupons have different dollar value price changes with a given change in yield of the 8 percent coupon. This variation is called "price compression." If you are hedging any coupon other than the 8, you need to compensate in your hedge for this difference by using a conversion factor sometimes known as a "compression ratio."

For example, if you have $1 million of 14 percent coupon Treasury bonds of 2006-11 and hedge them with a sale of 10 T-bond contracts, you could have the following scenario:

	Cash	**Futures**
11/4/82	Have $1 million 14% of 2006-11 Market value: $1,290,937.50	Sell 10 Dec82 T-bonds @7900
12/3/82	Sell $1 million 14% of 2006-11 Market value: $1,260,312.50	Buy 10 Dec82 T-bonds @7707
	LOSS: $30,625.00	GAIN: $17,812.50
	NET LOSS: $12,812.50	

It is quite apparent that you would not have had full coverage in terms of dollar value change.

Since there are quite a number of bonds eligible for delivery under the specifications of the T-bond futures contract (See Table 13.3), the Chicago Board of Trade has devised a series of conversion factors for each eligible issue. For any delivery month all deliverable issues have a specific conversion factor reflecting their value and maturity at any given time. These factors adjust for differences between the particular coupon's interest stream and maturity and that of the eight percent-based futures contract.

TABLE 13.3.
Conversion Factors
Bond and Note Conversion Factors

The tables below show the Treasury bonds and notes eligible for delivery against CBT bond and note contracts. . . and the conversion factors for the listed delivery months. Additional coupons may become eligible as the Government issues new debt. Traders should be aware of these new issues as they become available.

T-Note Conversion Factors

Coupon	*Maturity*	*Dec 82*	*Mar 83*	*Jun 83*	*Sep 83*
14½	July 15, 1989	1.3245			
10¾	Nov. 15, 1989	1.1410	1.1373		
10¾	Aug. 15, 1990	1.1529	1.1488	1.1452	1.1410
13	Nov. 15, 1990	1.2844	1.2780	1.2708	1.2641
14½	May 15, 1991	1.3868	1.3787	1.3698	1.3613
14⅞	Aug. 15, 1991	1.4182	1.4091	1.4005	1.3911
14¼	Nov. 15, 1991	1.3876	1.3802	1.3719	1.3641
14⅝	Feb. 15, 1992	1.4193	1.4109	1.4030	1.3942
13¾	May 15, 1992	1.3705	1.3640	1.3566	1.3498
11⅞	Oct. 15, 1989	1.1988	1.1935		
10½	Nov. 15, 1992	1.1668	1.1642	1.1610	1.1582

T-Bond Conversion Factors

Coupon	*Issue Date*	*Maturity*	*Dec 82*	*Mar 83*	*Jun 83*	*Sep 83*	*Dec 83*	*Mar 84*	*Jun 84*	*Sep 84*	*Dec 84*
8¼	2/15/78	May 15 2000-05	1.0230	1.0230	1.0226	1.0227	1.0223	1.0223	1.0220	1.0220	1.0216
7⅝	2/15/77	Feb 15 2002-07	0.9537	0.9637	0.9641	0.9641	0.9645	0.9646	0.9650	0.9651	0.9655
7⅞	11/15/77	Nov 15 2002-07	0.9875	0.9878	0.9876	0.9879	0.9878	0.9880	0.9879	0.9882	0.9881
		Aug 15									

$8\frac{3}{8}$	8/15/78	2003-06	1.0375	1.0371	1.0371	1.0367	1.0367	1.0363	1.0363	1.0359	1.0359
$8\frac{3}{4}$	11/15/78	Nov 15 2003-08	1.0751	1.0750	1.0744	1.0742	1.0736	1.0734	1.0728	1.0726	1.0720
$9\frac{1}{8}$	5/15/79	May 15 2004-09	1.1138	1.1135	1.1128	1.1125	1.1117	1.1113	1.1105	1.1102	1.1093
$10\frac{3}{8}$	11/15/79	Nov 15 2004-09	1.2427	1.2419	1.2406	1.2397	1.2383	1.2374	1.2360	1.2350	1.2336
$11\frac{3}{4}$	2/15/80	Feb 15 2005-10	1.3853	1.3833	1.3820	1.3799	1.3785	1.3764	1.3749	1.3727	1.3711
10	5/15/80	May 15 2005-10	1.2061	1.2055	1.2044	1.2037	1.2025	1.2019	1.2007	1.1999	1.1987
$12\frac{3}{4}$	11/17/80	Nov 15 2005-10	1.4938	1.4921	1.4898	1.4880	1.4856	1.4838	1.4813	1.4794	1.4768
$11\frac{3}{4}$	1/12/81	Feb 15 2001	1.3545	1.3520	1.3500	1.3473	1.3452	1.3425	1.3403	1.3374	1.3351
$13\frac{1}{8}$	4/2/81	May 15 2001	1.4872	1.4845	1.4811	1.4783	1.4747	1.4718	1.4681	1.4650	1.4612
$13\frac{7}{8}$	5/15/81	May 15 2006-11	1.6155	1.6135	1.6108	1.6087	1.6058	1.6036	1.6007	1.5984	1.5954
$13\frac{3}{8}$	7/2/81	Aug 15 2001	1.5145	1.5110	1.5082	1.5046	1.5016	1.4979	1.4948	1.4910	1.4877
$15\frac{3}{4}$	10/7/81	Nov 15 2001	1.7458	1.7418	1.7369	1.7327	1.7276	1.7233	1.7180	1.7234	1.7080
14	11/16/81	Nov 15 2006-11	1.6333	1.6313	1.6286	1.6265	1.6238	1.6216	1.6187	1.6165	1.6135
$14\frac{1}{4}$	1/16/82	Feb 15 2002	1.6052	1.6014	1.5982	1.5942	1.5909	1.5868	1.5833	1.5790	1.5753
$11\frac{5}{8}$	9/29/82	Nov 15 2002	1.3566	1.3550	1.3527	1.3510	1.3487	1.3470	1.3446	1.3427	1.3402
$10\frac{3}{8}$	11/15/82	Nov 15 2007-12	1.2540	1.2534	1.2523	1.2517	1.2505	1.2499	1.2487	1.2480	1.2468

Source: Chicago Board of Trade

Therefore, if one were ever to deliver against a futures contract, the following equation could be used to determine the delivery invoice price:

$$\text{contract size} \times \frac{\text{futures contract}}{\text{settlement price}} \times \frac{\text{conversion}}{\text{factor}} = \frac{\text{basic invoice}}{\text{amount}}$$

To apply it to the above situation:

$1,000,000 \times 7707 \times 1.6333 = \$1,261,213.80$
Invoice price $= \$1,261,213.80 +$ accrued interest

For GNMAs the calculation is:

$$\frac{\text{Principal balance of GNMA Xs}}{\text{Conversion factor}} = \frac{\text{Equivalent delivery principal}}{\text{balance of GNMA 8's}}$$

Conversion factors for bonds, notes, and GNMAs are available from the Chicago Board of Trade or from Financial Publishing Co., Boston, Mass.

To determine the compensating hedge ratio, or compression ratio, for your fixed-income securities hedges, you need to determine the change in the value of a 32nd of the coupon versus the value of a 32nd for the T-bond future which is $31.25. The resultant bond and note ratio could be stated as:

$$\text{Compression ratio} = \frac{\text{value of 32nd of 8\% coupon}}{\text{value of 32nd of x\% coupon}}$$

There are a number of ways to determine the compression ratio but since this is a practical handbook, you'll find that you can generally use the conversion factor to calculate a good approximation of the hedge ratio. Therefore, plugging the conversion factor into our hedge calculation formula in place of $\frac{T_c}{T_f}$ and considering $V = 1$, we then can calculate the appropriate hedge size for our bond example as follows:

$$N = \frac{\$1,000,000}{\$100,00} \times 1 \times 1.63 = 16$$

That means the appropriate hedge size should have been 16 contracts instead of 10. Let's see the results:

Cash	Futures
Loss: $30,625.00	Gain from 16 contract hedge: $28,500.00

NET LOSS: $2,125.00

The compression ratio improves this hedge's effectiveness quite markedly, almost offsetting all the risk.

For a GNMA hedge the compression ratio calculation would be:

$$CR = \frac{\text{Conversion factor}}{\text{Principal balance of GNMAs Xs}}$$

You would then use CR in place of $\dfrac{T_c}{T_f}$ in the hedge size calculation formula.

Price compression is dependent on the coupon, level of interest rates, and the maturity of the security. As you will see by an examination of the Table 13.3, a larger hedge should be employed when hedging coupons higher than 8 percent and, conversely, a smaller hedge when hedging smaller coupons. Also, the longer the time to maturity of the same coupon requires a larger hedge.

HEDGE SIZE CALCULATION—LOANS

We now come to situations where your risk exposure changes over time. In the case of loans, both fixed and floating rate, as the life of the loan diminishes so does your exposure to the amount of risk. Therefore, your hedge size will need to be altered during the life of the loan.

For example, for a $10 million one-year loan with interest set daily to three-month T-bill rate,

$$N = \frac{10}{1} \times 1 \times \frac{360}{90} = 40 \text{ contracts,}$$

value of 01 = $100.

As time elapses the number of days remaining at risk is only 330. Thirty days into the loan the hedge requirement would only be:

$$N = 10 \times 1 \times \ 330 \ = 36.6 \text{ contracts},$$
$$\text{value of 01} = \$91.67.$$

Since in this case the resets are daily, we have a constant straight-line reduction in the hedge ratio and hedge size. The rate of this reduction is known as a "decay rate." (See Figure 13.2)

Decay Rate and Decay Size

The rate of decay of risk exposure is dependent upon the frequency of rate resets. If we take the above example, changing the rate only quarterly, we would have a different decay picture. Since the rate will be fixed for the last 90 days of the loan, there are only three resets during the life of this one-year loan. The days at risk are only 270. Therefore, the hedge size by our formula is:

$$N = \frac{10}{1} \times 1 \times \frac{270}{90} = 30 \text{ contracts.}$$

After 90 days into the loan the hedge size required would be only:

$$N = \frac{10}{1} \times 1 \times \frac{180}{90} = 20 \text{ contracts.}$$

As you can see, the decay called for a reduction in the hedge size of 10 contracts.

In our previous situation there was a constant decay rate of approximately four days elapsed for each contract no longer needed for risk protection. In our second case, since the rate was reset quarterly, there was a need for hedge size reduction of 10 contracts per 90-day period. But since the resets were not continuous, these contracts should not be lifted at a rate of nine days per contract as the exposure is still there until the actual time of the rate change. Only then should the contract size be reduced by the lump sum of 10 contracts, giving us a stair-step look to our hedge decay picture. (See Figure 13.3)

The decay rate can be expressed by the following formula:

$$\text{Decay Rate} = \frac{T_c}{N} \times \frac{1}{P_r}$$

where T_c = term of remaining days at risk,
N = number of contracts in hedge,
P_r = period of reset in days.

And, more important and useful for you as a hedger is the fact that this may be reformulated to give you an equation for calculating the decay size for the reset period. In English, this means the number of contracts you need to remove ("lift") from your hedge at the time of each reset.

This decay size formula may be stated as:

$$\text{Decay size} = \frac{N}{T_c} \times P_r$$

where T_c = term of remaining days at risk,
N = number of contracts in hedge,
P_r = period of reset in days.

Taking our second example the calculation would look like the following:

$$DS = \frac{30}{270} \times 90 = 10 \text{ contracts every reset period.}$$

Before we leave the subject of hedge size calculation we need to look at a variation of the risk exposure changing over time. In particular, let's examine the case in which you have committed to making the same loan as in our second example, except that the customer will not activate the loan until six months from now. Since his initial rate is fixed at the time it is drawn upon, you will want some additional rate change protection for the waiting period as well. The variation in our hedge size requirement may be graphically represented as an irregular stair-step affair. (See Figure 13.4)

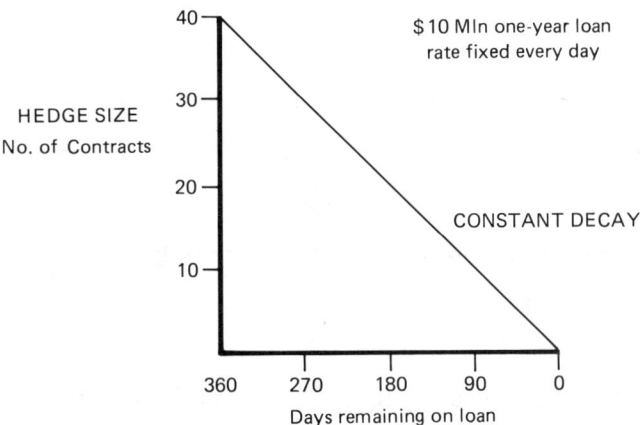

Figure 13.2.

What may be overlooked or misconstrued is that in this case the risk exposure is only 360 days (the term of the loan), not 450 as one might initially think. This is due to the fact that the first rate is not established until the end of the waiting period. This waiting period only adds one additional 90-day rate unknown to our previous position. It is unknown what the rate for the first quarter of the loan will be. If we were looking at this as an isolated situation with only one unknown rate which would expose us to only 90 days of risk, this protection would be calculated as:

$$N = \frac{\$10 \text{ million}}{\$1 \text{ million}} \times 1 \times \frac{90 \text{ days}}{90 \text{ days}} = 10 \text{ contracts}$$

By using our hedge size formula for the whole situation, the total hedge size calculation would look as follows:

$$N = \frac{\$10 \text{ million}}{\$1 \text{ million}} \times 1 \times \frac{360 \text{ days}}{90 \text{ days}} = 40 \text{ contracts},$$

and we then would calculate the decay size for the first reset using the decay size formula:

$$DS = \frac{40}{360} \times 90 = 10 \text{ contracts to be lifted at the first reset.}$$

The decay size for the next reset would be:

$$DS = \frac{30}{270} \times 90 = 10 \text{ contracts},$$

and so on for the remaining period.

SUMMARY OF HEDGE SIZE CALCULATION

Let's review the hedge size calculation process step by step:

1. Define exactly what is being hedged.

2. Select appropriate futures contract for the hedge.

3. Find volatility factor.

4. Determine duration of risk.

5. Calculate hedge size using formula given in this chapter.

Note: A. If you are hedging a fixed-income type security with other than an eight percent coupon, you must find the appropriate conversion factor and use it as $\frac{T_c}{T_f}$, the duration factor.

B. If amount of exposure varies over time, calculate decay rate and decay size with which to decrease the size of the hedge as the risk exposure diminishes.

WEIGHTED V. UNWEIGHTED HEDGES

As you have seen from the above discussion, "weighting" a hedge or "ratio hedging" as it is also known can have a very dramatic impact on the effectiveness of your hedges.

Some of you may wish to simplify your hedge size calculations by leaving out the volatility factor or the compression ratio factor for notes, GNMAs, and bonds, but be aware that while employing an "unweighted" hedge you are only partially offsetting your risk. You may do this initially in your pilot program but when you expand to a larger hedging operation the difference can mean substantial sums unnecessarily unrecovered.

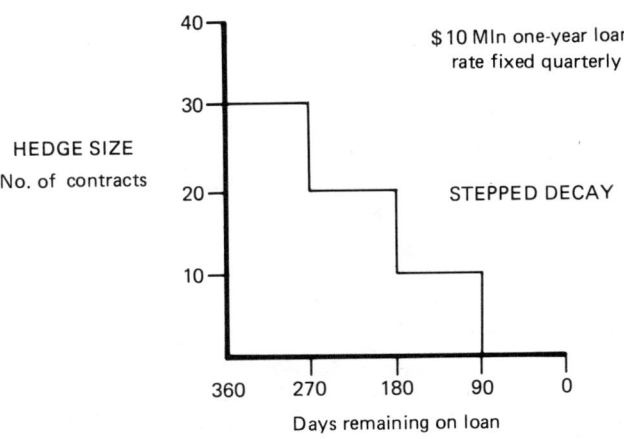

Figure 13.3.

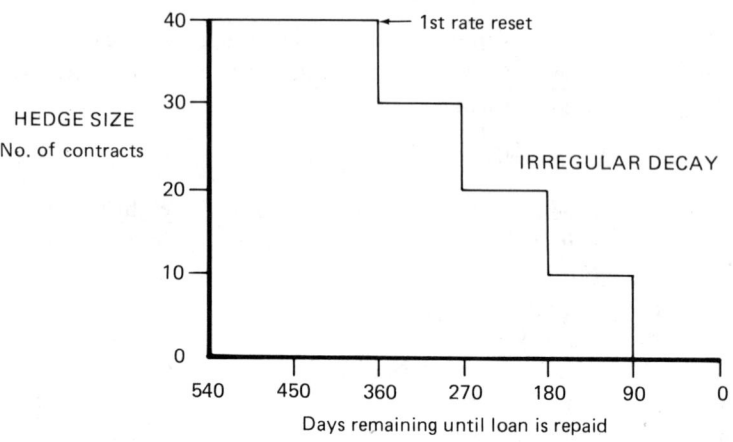

Figure 13.4.

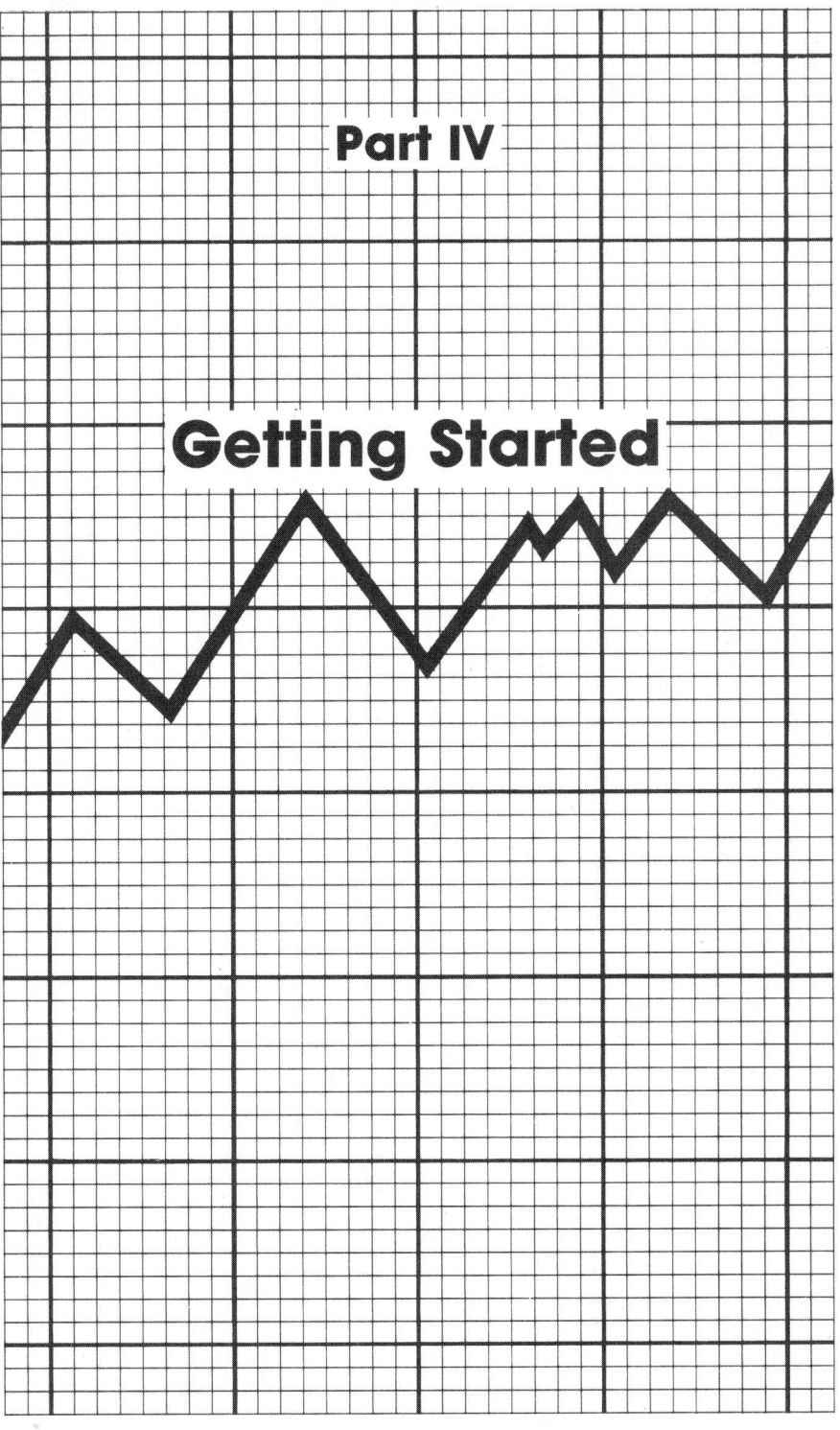

Part IV

Getting Started

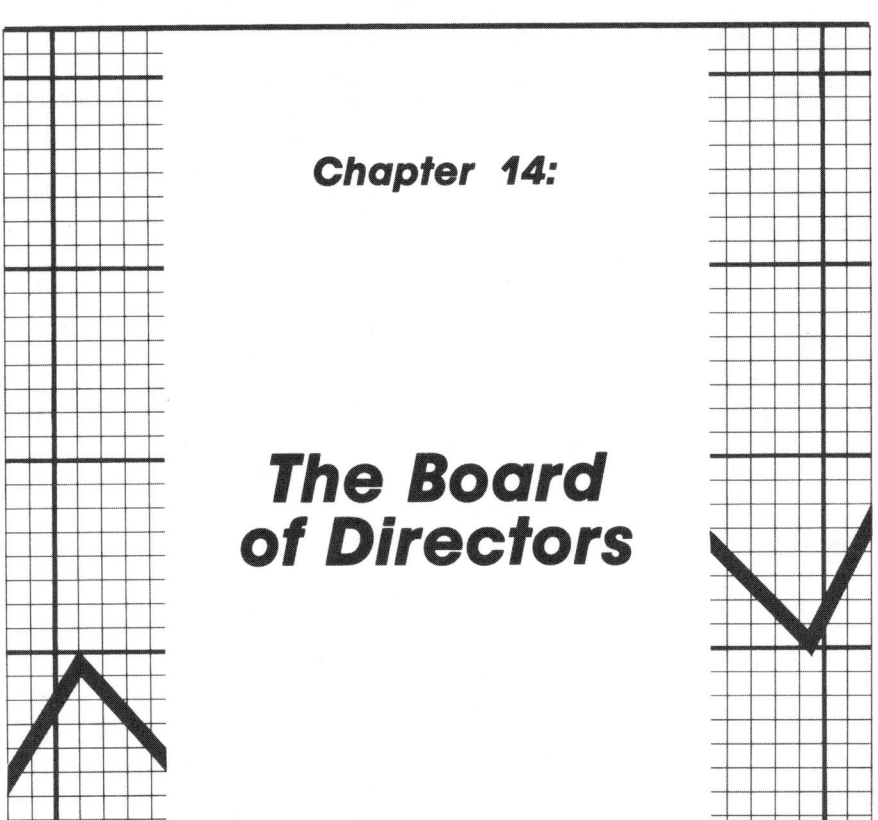

Chapter 14:

The Board of Directors

THE VERY first step in getting started with a hedging program is to get approval from the board of directors. Not only is this required by regulation but commodity brokers will not open an account with your institution until the board has authorized futures trading. It is also just plain good business to get board approval for such an important activity as futures trading.

A resolution authorizing the management of the bank or savings and loan to open a margin account and to trade financial instrument futures will normally suffice for your brokers. They will also want the institution to execute several disclosure notices and releases before they will open an account. More about this in the chapter on brokers.

ESTABLISHING A FUTURES POLICY

Satisfying the regulators and good business practice will take considerably more effort on the part of management. Regulations require the board of directors to establish a corporate policy regarding the trading of financial futures and to monitor continuously the execution of that policy.

This means the board must decide what kind of trades the institution may make, with whom trades can be executed, who can order trades, and up to what limit trading may take place. This may sound simple enough but as you will see it is considerably more complicated. Establishing this policy is simple enough—the board can just vote to authorize all of these things; it's the monitoring of the institution's policy that makes it difficult. In order to monitor management's hedging activities it is essential that the board of directors understands what a hedging program is designed to do, how it is supposed to work, and why it either worked or didn't work according to plan. Management's task at this juncture is to educate the board of directors about a great many things, not just the workings of the futures market. This will require some effort but it will be time well spent.

The institution's board of directors is required to approve a hedging plan; ergo, you must have a plan for them to approve, not just a request to trade financial futures. This phase of the entire futures hedging program may seem to be the most time consuming and possibly the most frustrating. This is not difficult to understand. You have already read most of this book, talked to any number of financial futures professionals, attended seminars and workshops for several months, and worked your way slowly through what is the most complicated financial market in the world. Your directors haven't done any of this and are highly likely to be totally skeptical of the whole idea. Convincing them to approve the idea and your plan will not be easy, but it will have two direct benefits to you. First, if you haven't completely absorbed and assimilated all that you have been exposed to when you start trying to convince the board, you will have by the time you finish. Second, the entire operation of the hedging program will go much more smoothly when the board understands what you are doing and why. They will second guess management less frequently and will not ask why you lost so much money in "that crap game at the Chicago Board of Trade." But be prepared to answer difficult questions over and over again until the directors understand the plan. This won't be fun, but it will pay off handsomely.

The first step in selling the board of directors on the idea of a hedging plan is a rigorous discussion of interest rate volatility and interest rate risk. Over the past several years volatility in interest rates has increased by quantum leaps. That much is obvious to everybody who is involved in finance. What is probably not obvious, though, is that this increased volatility has changed many of the traditional rules under which financial institutions operate. Your board of directors may have an implicit feel for this without having the detailed knowledge necessary to grasp the technicalities of the benefits of futures hedging. This is where the main selling job occurs.

ASSESSING YOUR NEEDS

Before embarking on this task it will be necessary for management to undertake a detailed financial analysis of the institution. Given the multitude of new asset powers and new types of liabilities that have evolved in the past five years, many of the traditional rules of financial intermediation, such as borrow long and lend short or attempt a complete match of asset and liability maturities, are obsolete or simply make no sense. In a world of essentially stable interest rates these rules were workable—when rates rise and fall like a roller coaster, following them can be disastrous. In Chapter 2 we talked about a bank's gap. If rates are rising, the bank with a positive gap will experience a rise in earning, other things being equal. If the rate trend reverses, that bank's earnings will decline *even though it has made no change in its operations.* The bank which successfully switches from a positive gap to a negative gap in this situation will earn higher profits than the bank that does not change its asset and liability strategy. (This is much more easily said than done, of course, but hedging with financial futures will take some, if not most, of the guess work out of the equation.)

Before you can convince the board that you need to hedge with futures, you must convince yourself that you need to hedge with futures. The fact that you find the futures market fascinating or that somebody said you are crazy if you don't use the market is no justification whatever. You need realistic facts to back up your intuition. (Even if you don't think you do, the board of directors will.) The starting point is to identify the institution's gaps and decide if you like what you see. The types of questions that should be asked at this point are: Where have earnings been hurt? Why have they been hurt? Could we have done anything differently that would have changed the outcome? Is futures hedging one of those things? Would an alternative course have made enough of a difference to justify the cost involved? These are not questions with which successful executives are unfamiliar, but they may not look familiar in these surroundings, so please bear with us momentarily.

One of the most dangerous pitfalls to avoid in trying to answer these questions is the "perfect forecast fallacy." Do not fall into the trap of examining alternatives which really depend on perfect forecasting in order to come out as superior alternatives. Similarly, decisions which come out as superior as a matter of luck or just guessing right should be seen in that light. This is not easy to do, to be sure, but should be attempted. Embarking on a futures hedging plan requires planning and discipline. Luck never hurts, but a good plan can be counted on to provide better results more often than luck. Hedging with futures cannot be done with a seat-of-the-pants approach—professional speculators and arbitrageurs will eat your lunch every time.

Now that you have identified the institution's gap—either with your own personnel or with an outside consultant (which may be more cost effective)—and you understand how the futures market works, the question to be answered is whether the futures market is the best way to improve your bottom-line performance. That's how you develop a hedging plan. Before turning to that directly, let's look at the preliminary presentation to the board of directors.

What we have just talked about involves selling yourself and the board of directors on the *idea* of using futures to hedge the institution's interest rate risk. This is likely to take three, four, or more board meetings. At the first meeting a presentation can be made which focuses on the interest rate risk that the institution is facing. This can be done by management alone or with the aid of a consultant who may have done the analysis for you. A simplified presentation on the uses of the financial futures market *to solve the specific problems you have identified* should also be made at the first board meeting. Providing the directors with written material to read before the next board meeting should also be helpful in persuading them to approve a hedging program. This material should deal with specific examples of interest rate changes on various securities and deposit instruments that the bank holds or offers to customers.

A second board meeting should be devoted to answering about 300 questions about the futures market that will be asked by the directors. *This is not a joke!* At this meeting it will usually be helpful to have a futures professional, either one on your staff or an outside expert, at the board meeting. The objective is to have the board approve a hedging plan *in principal* and authorize a "dry run" of the plan to be reported on at a subsequent board meeting. This is where the real work begins.

DEVELOPING A HEDGING PLAN

In order to get the board to approve a plan, whether in principal or in fact, it is necessary to have a plan to discuss. Every financial institution is unique in a number of ways so there are no cut and dried rules for developing a hedging plan for your institution. However, the following guidelines should be useful.

Objectives

As with practically every project ever undertaken, the first thing to do is decide upon the objective—what are we trying to do with our hedging program? This may seem trivial but is absolutely crucial to the development of a good plan. (You must be fully aware of what *can* be accomplished with futures hedging *and* what *cannot* be accomplished.) If the plan sticks to trying to eliminate the interest rate risk the institution faces in the marketplace, it will at least be workable and realistic. If the bank holds a portfolio of underwater mortgages, starting to hedge now will not restore those assets to par; at best you can keep them from sinking further. You must stick to hedging risks that *are hedgeable with futures.*

You must also make a determination of how much of the institution's risk you want to hedge. If there is no risk there is no return, except for spreads which are a reward for assuming credit risk. The question to answer here is how much risk must the institution take on in order to achieve a given return. Alternatively, if a maximum level of risk is chosen, is the return associated with that risk level acceptable? This is not a question that is easily resolved, either by management alone or in consultation with the board of directors. However, it must be resolved at least tentatively or you don't have a hedging plan that can be put into play.

The next major hurdle to overcome is *what* to hedge. Will you hedge only assets, only liabilities, both separately, or both together? This will depend largely on the bank's portfolio. Initially, most financial institutions will choose to hedge a specific liability. The best reason for this is that it is the simplest type of hedge to put on and manage. Asset hedging depends mainly on whether the institution holds assets that are hedgeable with futures. For a bank that holds a large portfolio of marketable securities and acts as a dealer in securities, hedging a trading desk operation may make sense. For a bank which holds short-term marketable securities only to satisfy regulatory liquidity requirements, hedging those assets will most often prove to be far too expensive relative to the gain that can be achieved. Hedging both sides of the balance sheet is the most sophisticated technique and should be attemped only after some experience has been gained with simpler strategies.

You want your hedging plan to be the most cost-effective one you can devise—even though direct costs such as commissions are low, the indirect costs of personnel and management time can be high. The most obvious place on your balance sheet to look for hedgeable items is where the highest risk items are—that's where the biggest payoff comes. Almost universally in today's environment this will be either Treasury-bills or liabilities that are tied to Treasury-bills—the three- or six-month MMCs or the MMA account if it is tied to T-bills. *Cautionary note:* you may achieve fabulous results in containing the costs of these liabilities over time but not affect the bottom line very much unless these items constitute a significant portion of the institution's deposits. Other high risk items are all long-term assets which you may want to sell prior to maturity—mortgages, bonds, GNMAs. But remember, these must hedged when acquired in order to provide maximum risk protection—you can't wait until they're 10 points under book value.

Hedging Instruments

The next step is to decide what to hedge with. The hedging instrument used should be *the most efficient one for this asset or liability*. This may not necessarily be a futures contract but may be an options contract, a forward contract, or some other cash market instrument. You also need to decide what specific type of hedging strategy to use, whether it's a simple hedge, a strip, or a hybrid hedge. (Refer to Section III, "Strategies for Financial Institutions" for more detailed information on this question.)

So far you have decided on the objective of futures hedging, how much you want to hedge, what you want to hedge, and how to hedge it. By now you may be saying, "That's all great, but where is my hedging plan?" *That is your hedging plan!* Once you have made all these decisions (P.S. this will re-quire more than 20 minutes!), you have a hedging plan. You now know what you are trying to achieve with the futures market; you know what contracts you are going to use to hedge what assets or liabilities, or both; you know the position limits for all contracts; and you have a good idea of when to be hedged and when to be unhedged. This last element of the plan is last for an obvious reason—it's the element that is least easily decided in advance. Knowledge of when to lift a hedge is best gained through experience. Learning how to do it is covered in Section V, "Managing a Position."

PRESENTING THE PLAN

Now you have a hedging plan to discuss with the board of directors. Be prepared to answer another 300 or so questions about the plan. At this point you should also give some consideration to what broker(s) you will want to use (see Chapter 15, "Brokers"). This will be necessary for the dry run of the plan, which you are going to do next. You will probably want some type of advice or endorsement from the board for the selection of brokerage firms to handle your account. You must have it anyway, so get that cleared up as soon as the board agrees in principal to futures hedg-ing—you'll have plenty to keep you busy from now on without going back for that later. At this board meeting, probably the third one in most scenarios, you may want to have some brokers that you have talked to previously give a presentation to the board about their firm, the services they will offer, and the prices of those services. The next item for considera-tion by the board is the authorization of a dry run of the plan that has been developed. Suggest it yourself and insist that it be done before you start trading with real money—you won't regret it.

Once the dry run has been authorized, contact one or more brokers who will permit you to make paper trades. This may cost $200 per month but it will be money well spent, for a number of reasons. First, you will get the full flavor of trading futures without actually risking the bank's money. It's all done on a computer so it will appear that you are doing it for real. The broker will send you confirmations of trades, statements of your ac-count, let you know when margin calls are due, and so forth. Second, you will find out how well your plan works. If it doesn't work well you will have a real basis for modifying it. Third, you can have a shakedown cruise for your internal control procedures (see Chapter 16). You may want to con-tinue with the paper trading for a month or two in order to really get the feel of what you're doing and iron out any bugs. Don't worry about missing an opportunity to put on a hedge for real—you are going to do that plenty of times anyway, so don't rush it. After all the time and effort put in to develop the plan, it's worth waiting a little longer to make sure you know what you are doing.

After you have gone on your shakedown cruise, it's time to report back to the board on the results. Do it just as if it were for real—make exactly the type of report that you would if these were actual trades (see Chapter 16). This is another reason for continuing the paper trade for a month or two. The board will probably want to see more than one month's results before they give the final go ahead. Again, don't rush it. If you jump in the water too early and get a cramp, the board probably will not throw you a life preserver.

Once they do give you approval to start real trading you have reached the end of the beginning. Now we show you all of the back office nitty gritty of futures trading.

ADDENDUM A: BOARD OF DIRECTORS' RESOLUTION

The following is a sample board of directors' resolution identical (except for blanks) to those which have been adopted by some financial institutions currently using the futures markets. This resolution form has passed the scrutiny of federal regulatory agencies and should be acceptable for most institutions and regulatory agencies.

Board Resolution

WHEREAS, the management of (bank name) bears responsibility for managing the exposure of the Bank to interest rate volatility; and

WHEREAS, the uncertainty and volatility in present financial markets, combined with rapid changes in commercial bank regulations and increasing competition from other financial intermediaries, have accentuated the interest rate sensitivity of the Bank's balance sheet and have increased the interest rate exposure associated with mismatches in the maturities of assets and liabilities; and

WHEREAS, the Comptroller of the Currency has issued Circular 79 (2d Revision) effective on January 1, 1980, stating that interest rate futures contracts, forward placement contracts, and standby contracts can be used effectively to reduce interest rate risk and that such use is considered to be an activity incidental to banking; and

WHEREAS, the previously approved interest rate risk management tools are inadequate to deal with current trading account activities, volatility and uncertainty in asset/liability management, mortgage banking activities, and management of the investment portfolio of the Bank;

NOW BE IT THEREFORE RESOLVED, that the use of financial instrument futures contracts, including those of United States Treasury bills, United States Treasury notes, United States Treasury bonds, domestic certificates of deposit, Eurodollar time deposits, Government National Mortgage Association ("GNMA") certificates and such other futures contracts as may be allowed by the Comptroller of the Currency for use by national banks ("financial futures"), as well as forward placement contracts and standby contracts with respect to such instruments, be approved, subject to compliance with the policies, set forth on Exhibit A which is attached hereto, the procedural requirements set forth on Exhibit B which is attached hereto, and the accounting requirements set forth on Exhibit C which is attached hereto.

BE IT FURTHER RESOLVED, that the total of all financial futures, forward contract and standby contract positions outstanding at any time shall not exceed the position limits set forth in Exhibit D which is attached hereto, unless approval is obtained in the manner set forth in said Exhibit D.

BE IT FURTHER RESOLVED, that only those individuals specifically designated by resolution of this Board be authorized and permitted to enter into financial futures, forward contract and standby contract transactions on behalf of the Bank, subject to such position limits with respect to each individual as may be determined from time to time by this Board.

BE IT FURTHER RESOLVED, that initially the individuals authorized to effect financial futures, forward contract and standby contract transactions on behalf of the Bank shall be (name of individual) and (name of individual), and that (name) shall have authority to effect transactions up to the maximum position limits set forth on Exhibit D, while (name of individual) and (name of individual) shall be subject to the individual trading limits and procedures set forth on Attachment I to Exhibit D.

BE IT FURTHER RESOLVED, that all commodity brokerage firms, dealer banks and dealers with whom the Bank transacts its financial futures, forward contract and standby contract business be instructed to accept order for such transactions only from those individuals designated by this Board to enter into such transactions on behalf of the Bank.

BE IT FURTHER RESOLVED, that (name), General Vice President of the Portfolio and Funds Management Group of the Bank (or other appropriate title), and his successors in that position, be charged with general responsibility for supervising the use of financial futures, forward contracts and standby contracts by the Bank and with carrying out the purpose and intent of this resolution.

BE IT FURTHER RESOLVED, that (name), Senior Vice President (or other appropriate title), the Bank's internal auditor, and his successors in that position, be charged with responsibility for reviewing all outstanding financial futures, forward contract and standby contract positions on a monthly basis to determine that such positions do not exceed the limits established by this Board, and that he be instructed to submit a written report with respect to such review at each regular monthly meeting of this Board.

BE IT FURTHER RESOLVED, that any use of financial futures, forward contracts and standby contracts undertaken pursuant to this resolution be made in accordance with safe and sound banking practices and with levels of activity reasonably related to the Bank's business needs and its capacity to fulfill its obligations under such contracts.

EXHIBIT A:

Trading Limits for
Financial Futures, Forward Contracts, and
Standby Contracts

The limits for aggregate open futures positions plus outstanding forward contracts and standby contracts held by the Bank at any given time shall be as follows:

Purpose	T-bill	T-note	T-bond	CD	GNMA
Trading Account	xxx	xxx	xxx	xxx	xxx
Asset/Liability Management	xxx	xxx	xxx	xxx	xxx
TOTAL	xxx	xxx	xxx	xxx	xxx

T-bill: One Futures contract on $1,000,000.00 91-day U.S. Treasury bills, or the face amount of a forward or standby on that type instrument divided by $1,000,000.00

T-Note: One Futures contract on $100,000.00 4–6-year U.S. Treasury notes, or the face amount of a forward or standby on that type instrument divided by $1,000,000.00

T-Bond: One Futures contract on $100,000.00 15-year U.S. Treasury bonds, or the face amount of a forward or standby on that type instrument divided by $100,000.00

CD: One Futures contract on $1,000,000.00 91-day bank certificate of deposit, or the face amount of a forward or standby on that type instrument divided by $1,000,000.00

GNMA: One Futures contract on $100,000.00 8% GNMA pass-through certificate, or the face amount of a forward or standby on that type instrument divided by $100,000.00.

In addition to the aggregate limits set forth above, the Board may establish position limits for each of the individuals authorized to effect futures transactions for the Bank. Initially, the individual trading limits shall be as set forth on Attachment I which is attached to this Exhibit D.

The aggregate or individual trader position limits may be exceeded only upon the prior written approval (in the form attached as Attachment II) of the General Vice President of the Portfolio and Funds Management Group (or other appropriate title) of the Bank with the written acknowledgement of the Manager of the Securities Trading Division of the Bank. Such written approval shall set forth the reason for exceeding normal position limits and the expected duration of the positions. A written report regarding any such exception shall be submitted to the Board or the Executive Committee of the Bank at its next regular meeting for ratification.

Certification

This section should contain a certificate by the secretary of the bank or savings and loan association to the effect that the resolution was approved by the Board of Directors on a specific date and that it is in effect.

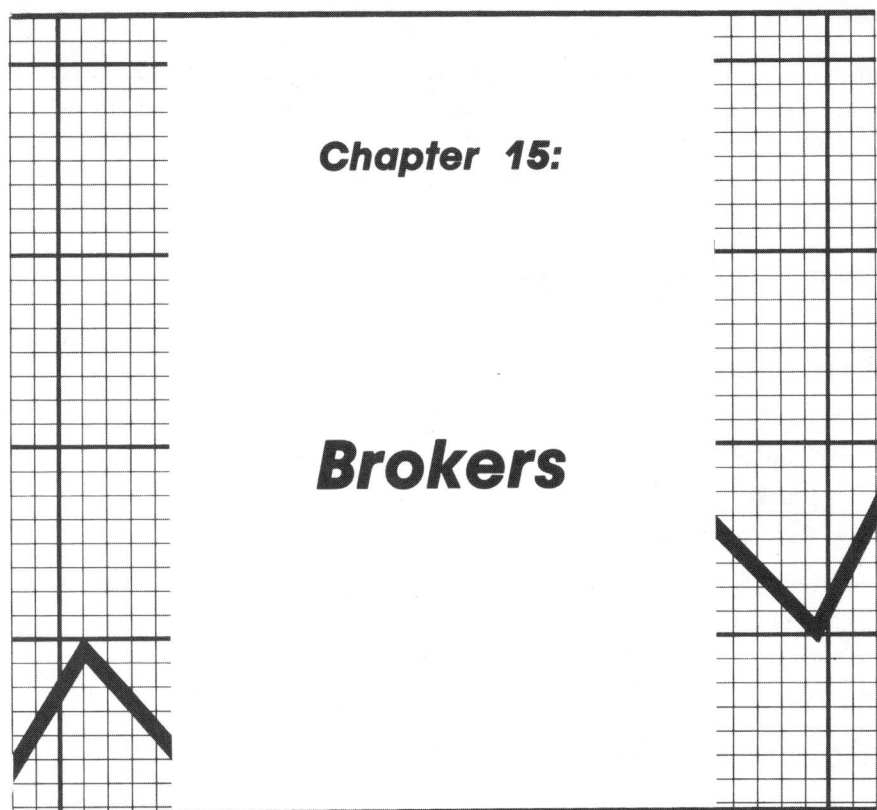

Chapter 15:

Brokers

IN ORDER to access the financial futures markets you will have to go through a broker. Since that term is used several different ways in the industry, let's start with some terminology.

A commodities futures brokerage house is more formally known as an FCM, which stands for Futures Commission Merchant. It is empowered to execute trades for customers on the various exchanges and to charge a fee, known as a commission, for its service. It is subject to the rules of the Commodity Futures Trading Commission (CFTC), a government agency, and the rules of the various exchanges of which it is a member. An FCM can also be what is known as a "clearing member" of an exchange, which means that it owns a certain number of memberships (seats) on that exchange and meets stricter financial requirements than that of an ordinary FCM.

Your orders will be relayed by the FCM to the floor of the exchange to be executed by a floor broker who stands in the pit as a subcontractor of the FCM. The person with whom you will be talking the most is also known as a broker. This person, who is in an office removed from the floor of the exchange, is more formally known as a Registered Commodity Representative of Account Executive of the FCM. He has had to pass an examination required by the CFTC to insure a certain amount of familiarity with the futures market system. From hereon, when we talk about brokers we will be referring, in most cases, to these registered reps and/or the firms they represent.

SERVICES OFFERED BY BROKERS

A good brokerage house will in most instances provide most of the following services:

- Efficient Order Execution
- Floor Access
- Market Information
- Research
- Advice on Hedge Design and Strategies
- Monitoring Assistance
- Accounting/Recordkeeping Services

Let's explore them one by one.

EFFICIENT ORDER EXECUTION

Order execution (filling orders) is the primary service of all FCMs. As in all things in life, some are better than others. You will want a firm that does a large enough volume of financial futures to have a position on the floor close to the pits in which your orders will go. This means that once your order arrives on the floor it will go to the floor broker quickly. Since prices can move quite rapidly at times, this can mean quite a difference in the price at which your order is filled. Also, the firm should have a well-trained staff that takes and handles orders with a minimum of error. Reputation gets around; do some checking.

FLOOR ACCESS

Of all the services offered by brokers, floor access is probably the most misunderstood. In most cases, many financial executives think this means talking directly to the firm's clerk on the floor desk. What it does mean is that your order given to your account executive is transmitted by him or his assistant directly to the floor via the telephone. This is the fastest way to get your order there. Some large national brokerage houses use wire systems which at times are slow and get backed up like bad plumbing. If you do deal with a "wire house" make sure *your* orders are phoned directly to the floor.

In some instances when you may be doing a strip involving contracts in deferred months, floor access in invaluable. Your broker, if he is a good one, will help you by "working the order" to see that you get filled at reasonable prices since liquidity is much thinner out there. You can get "raped" by as much as five ticks on your order if you are not careful. If you are doing very large orders or if you are doing cash to futures arbitrage you may be given authorization by the firm to place your orders directly to a clerk on the floor desk. But remember, you must be aware of the order handling customs and procedures. Futures are transacted verbally at a very rapid pace and floor personnel have neither the time nor the knowledge to help you deliberate on a decision.

MARKET INFORMATION

Futures markets live off information and generate a lot of it themselves. FCMs and brokers will provide you with current price activity, interpretation of news and its impact on the markets, information on what major participants are surmised to be doing in the market, as well as technical chart points and fundamental factors such as economic reports. Also, the financial markets are known to be hotbeds of rumors which do affect people's buy/sell decisions whether the rumors are accurate or not. A good broker will be aware of the major rumors.

RESEARCH

This is the one service provided by FCMs in which you will find the greatest variance and even difference in its meaning. What one firm calls research another might call just market information. A firm with a good financial futures research department will be able to answer questions concerning historical correlations between futures prices and various cash market instruments, as well as issue analyses of recent Fed activity, interpretations of recent economic activity, and the effect of these on interest rate forecasts. In the area of technical analysis, the firm's research department should be able to supply you with moving averages, oscillators, critical chart points, and many of the other technical indicators derived from some of the techniques which we describe in greater detail in Chapter 18.

ADVICE ON HEDGE DESIGN AND STRATEGIES

You can reasonably expect from an FCM that has well-qualified financial account executives (there aren't too many) some assistance in designing hedges to meet your risk reduction goals. This could take the form of helping you to calculate hedge ratios, select the best mix of months for a particular strip, or find appropriate cross-hedging vehicles. It could also take the form of finding undervalued or overvalued contracts either for your hedges or for an arbitrage opportunity. Also, the broker or the firm's research department should be knowledgeable enough to help you adapt or develop strategies for new situations you may encounter, such as creating a synthetic fixed-rate loan or designing a hedge for your best commercial customer.

MONITORING ASSISTANCE

This is a service you will not see mentioned very often, but it is very helpful in keeping you on track with your hedging program. A good financial broker will know what your hedging goals are as well as your institution's policies. He should help you monitor the progress and effectiveness of the hedge, recognize the appropriate instances when to "selectively" lift your hedges, and generally deter you from becoming emotional about market activity.

Also, since regulators are very watchful that you keep good records to document specific hedges, and to keep you from the temptation of speculation, a broker should assist you in these tasks as well. Some have even gone so far as to create their own hedge transaction registers as a guideline for this institutional purpose.

ACCOUNTING/RECORDKEEPING SERVICES

A very important service of the FCM you choose is that of trade documentation. The firm will send you written confirmations of all trades as well as monthly recap sheets which include your current margin balance statement. A firm's "back office" operation is crucial in presenting you with clear and accurate paperwork in a timely fashion. The back office and the margin department are important in keeping track of margin requirements and funds transferred in and out of your account. They will also provide you with the necessary information and assistance in putting your idle funds to work.

Some firms have considerably better internal organization and control systems that provide this service with a minimum of errors. Others are known for mistakes and paperwork bottlenecks. Careful scrutiny in advance could save you hours of checking and double-checking trades and balances.

WHAT A BROKER WILL NOT DO

Do not expect a broker or a broker's research department to be in-depth banking consultants. They will not, nor should they, do the gap analysis of your institution, write your policy manual, set up your internal procedures and control mechanisms, nor intercede with the regulators for you. These are the tasks which you and your staff should do yourselves or you should hire competent consultants to assist you.

Brokers know the futures business well, and a good financial broker knows a fair amount about banking, but he is not a banker and does not know your side of the business as well as you do, or should. Anyway, as we mentioned in an earlier chapter, it is important for you to do your homework really to know your institution so you can readily adapt to a changing market, or regulatory or competitive changes.

Brokers can assist you in finding consultants who are knowledgeable and experienced in financial futures hedging for institutions, and vice versa.

_____ SELECTING A BROKER

Whether you hire a consultant or not, you are left with the difficult task of selecting a broker. The above discussion of services should have given you some insights as to what to look for.

One note of caution: there are brokers and there are brokers. What we mean is that with the rapid growth of the financial futures markets there are not many experienced brokers specializing in financial futures for institutions. With the increased popularity and attention recently being given to financial futures, there are a host of what we call "me-too" brokers; those which have little or no knowledge or experience with interest rate futures contracts except that they know how to buy'em or sell'em just like pork bellies, and, sure they're experts. Watch out. They don't know that if you're a savings and loan you're not allowed to put on a long hedge except in very limited circumstances.

To help you through the maze and onslaught of brokers contacting you, we've made a checklist of things to look for and questions to ask.

_____

Prospective Broker/Firm Checklist

☐ Ask what types of customers the firm services: institutions and corporations or farmers and speculators?

☐ Ask what contracts he trades primarily. If he says everything, politely say goodbye. You want a specialist with extensive knowledge of financial futures. After reading this book you should be able to get an idea of whether or not this is the case.

☐ Test his command of financial terms. Don't expect him to be a banker; he should be familiar with what is going on in the money markets and financial circles.

☐ Examine his views concerning the time frames and constraints involving banks and savings and loans. Does he take a long range view of you as a customer or is he pushing you to ram a program through your board just to get the commission rolling? Does he show an interest and knowledge of your industry and your problems?

☐ Ask him about his prior business experience. Does he have any financial background (preferable) and how long has he traded interest rate futures contracts?

- [ ] Ask what type of equipment he has available to him personally, not somewhere in the firm's Timbuktu office. Does he have a Telerate, financial newswire, Comtrend (electronic charting terminal), or microcomputer?

- [ ] Ask him how he and his firm transmit orders to the floor. Is it done by telephone (floor access) or by wire system?

- [ ] Ask for a financial statement of the firm (FCM) to check its financial stability. Is it a Clearing Member of the major exchanges? If so, it has passed rigorous financial standards.

- [ ] Ask about the firm's research staff. Examine some past and current research reports. Are they geared towards financial institution use?

- [ ] Ask about the firm's "back-office" operation. Is its paperwork essentially error free? Does the firm have its own computer system for this purpose or do they use an outside service?

- [ ] Check what your commission rates will be at various volume levels. Are they competitive? Don't be penny wise and pound foolish.

- [ ] Check around with others concerning the firm's reputation for service, experience, and reliability.

- [ ] This last item is optional, but you may wish to meet your broker-to-be face to face and visit his firm's floor operation.

It is probable that not every broker will fit the above guidelines 100 percent and yet may be right for your needs. You will have to weigh their comparative strengths and weaknesses. What is important is that you select a broker and a firm that offers the mix of services that fit your needs and are delivered to you professionally with a high level of quality and at a reasonable price. Even more important is that you have a good rapport with the individual broker with whom you'll be dealing on a daily basis. With a good mutual understanding, your ability to use the futures markets as an effective banking tool will be greatly enhanced.

_____ DEALING WITH A BROKER—WHAT TO EXPECT

Once you have selected a broker, you are confronted with adapting to and coping with the fast moving world of futures trading. It has its own language, customs, and courtesies. Therefore, we will speak of what to expect right from the start.

The first thing to remember is that a broker is in business to make a profit, just as you are. However, he is compensated solely on the number and size of transactions you make. If he takes a long view of your institution as a viable long-term customer he will spend a fair amount of time with you, giving you information, discussing your goals and the best ways to implement them, monitoring your progress, as well as discussing markets and news affecting the markets. However, do not expect an excessive amount of his time if you are very inactive and are not seriously following a hedging program. If your plan says you should be out of hedges for the moment, he will work with you even if there are no trades for some months. But some institutions will try to "milk" brokers for information without reciprocating with their business when it is time to hedge.

As far as rates go, during your pilot hedging program you will probably be paying the posted retail rates as your volume will not be large enough to warrant a discount. However, once you increase the size of your hedges you can expect your rates to be lowered based on your volume and average activity. You may be able to get a better rate at a discount brokerage firm, but you will not be provided with all the services we have discussed. In the long run, the commission you pay will be worth the services you receive from a good broker and FCM.

Expect to be in fairly close communications with your broker. Depending on your hedging plans and market activity this may vary from hourly to weekly, but in most instances you will be talking daily to him on the phone. The speed of the markets and important developments may make rapid communications vital at critical times. Make yourself available and delegate trading authority for the times when you will be out of the office or generally unavailable. And don't worry about the phone expenses; most brokers have inbound WATS lines.

You will probably discuss general market views, interest rates, and expectations of others with your broker, which can be useful in getting a consensus view of where rates are going. Sometimes your board's view can be bound to your geographic considerations. You may eventually come to factor in your broker's opinion with your own, but do not expect him, just because he is close to the market, to be right all the time. Major economic forecasters are not able to do it, and if your broker could, he would be retired and living in the Bahamas, anyway.

Expect to be faced with margin calls if the futures markets move against your position. More about that in detail in a later chapter. But for now be aware that you will be expected to respond to these on a same day wire transfer basis. As an institution you will probably be on a wire transfer status with the brokerage firm and will only send funds when needed and receive them when you have excess in your futures account. More about this later.

Also, all futures transactions are done verbally and at lightning speed at times. A man's word is his bond, so don't mix up buy and sell. Remember that financial futures are quoted in terms or prices, *not* rates. This is very important. Your broker will always be thinking in terms of prices while you are probably used to thinking in terms of rates. Since financial futures prices are inversely related to rates (prices up—rates down), when your broker says the market is going lower he means higher rates. This difference in perspective is very crucial when placing orders—don't expect the broker to "know what you meant." The futures markets are a high-tension, stressful business. By adapting to their conventions you will avoid costly errors.

ORDERS

Yes, as a senior officer of the institution you're used to giving orders, but in this section we discuss the types of acceptable futures orders and the way to give them to a broker—quite a different matter.

There are more than just two types of orders: buy and sell. There are price orders, market orders, and conditional orders.

A *"price order,"* also known as a "limit order," is an order given either to buy or sell at a given price, e.g., sell 10 September T-bill contracts at 9425. All or as much of your order as possible will be filled at the specified price.

A *"market order"* is a directive to buy or sell at whatever price the market will bear at the moment. It must be executed immediately. In the futures market this order takes precedence over all others and just like a hot potato people in the industry drop everything to get this filled immediately. Brokers put calls on hold, runners scurry, and floor brokers yell and scream. All this is to insure that your order is filled at the best possible price before market conditions change, which sometimes means seconds. Also, there is financial responsibility attached to the timely execution of a market order. If a floor broker and/or FCM is negligent in handling this type of order, he may be required to provide you with a price reasonable to the market based upon the industry's standards of timeliness. On a large order this could be a costly matter. So don't get upset if your broker puts you on hold and comes back and says he had market orders to process. You want this kind of service when it is your order. So does everybody else.

A *"conditional order"* is one which specifies a buy or sell conditional upon certain market activity. The most prevalent conditional orders are MITs, Stops, MOCs, and OCOs.

An *MIT order*, which stands for "Market If Touched," specifies a buy or sell in the market trades at least once at a given price; e.g., sell 10 March T-bills 9200 MIT. This means that once the March T-bills trade at 9200 your order becomes a market order and will be filled at the best possible price at that time. This does not mean that your order will necessarily be filled at 9200 but, in most cases, somewhere near this price. This type of order is one of the favorites of market technicians when prices "bounce" off their lines. Unfortunately, some exchanges (CBT) do not accept them. Your broker will know which ones are accepted by which exchange.

The next type of conditional order is the *"stop,"* which is an order entered either to exit or enter the market once a given price is traded. At that time, the stop order becomes a market (immediately executable) order: Buy 10 March T-bonds 7209 Stop. Stops are often used to protect positions and therefore are sometimes called "Stop-Loss" orders. All of the commodities exchanges accept stop orders.

Locals on the floor try to touch off ("Run") the stops to try to get the market going in their direction. Often this means your order will be filled at a price worse than that at which it was triggered. Such a fill is known as a "skidded stop." To prevent these situations under certain conditions you can place a *"stop limit order."* This is a stop order specifying a limited range of acceptable prices at which the order may be executed; e.g., buy 10 March T-bonds 7809 Stop Limit 7815. If it cannot be filled at any of these prices it will not be executed. Sometimes this is useful but at other times it can mean negating the loss protection usefulness of a stop order, especially if the market keeps on racing against your position.

Another type of conditional order is the *MOC*. This stands for "market on close." This is a market order which is executed only in the last minutes of trading for the day, the time period officially known as "the close." It must be filled during this time period at any price available. Many computer trading systems employ such orders which can result in hectic trading with volatile price movements. A similar order is the "market on open" order for the start of the day. No, for some reason, it's not called a MOO order; that's reserved for cows.

A frequently confusing order, even to brokers, is the *OCO*. This stands for "one cancels the other." Basically, when you place one order in the market above and one below where it is currently trading, one of the orders may be executed. If this occurs you may not want the other order filled. Therefore, each order carries a notation telling of the other order to be cancelled if this one is filled; e.g., sell 10 June T-bills 9150 or 10 June T-bills 9098 Stop OCO. The Chicago Board of Trade does not accept this type of order.

Besides price orders and conditional orders there is also a distinction made on the time period for which an order is valid. Therefore, orders are either day orders or open orders. A *"day order"* is one which is only valid for the day upon which it is placed. It expires at the end of trading if not executed that day. Unless otherwise specified, all orders are assumed to be day orders. An *"open or GTC order"* is one which is left open for a period of time and is Good Till Cancelled, hence the name; e.g., sell 10 June CDs 9700 GTC. A variation of this order is one with a specified ending date; e.g., sell 10 June CDs 9700 good till December 31st.

PLACING ORDERS

Note that in the above examples illustrating orders, each order first specifies the quantity, then the contract month, contract, and the price and/or conditional requirement. To reduce the chance of errors it would be best to follow this format when directing your broker. This is the format to which he is accustomed. Also, use an order-giving tone of voice so as to differentiate between when you are deliberating on whether to place an order or not. This sounds childish but it greatly reduces misunderstandings.

Once you have board approval, your plan set, and have selected a broker and learned about orders, you're almost ready to start. But before you do, you will need to organize your hedging effort, especially in terms of setting up internal control procedures to document your hedging activity. That's where we go next.

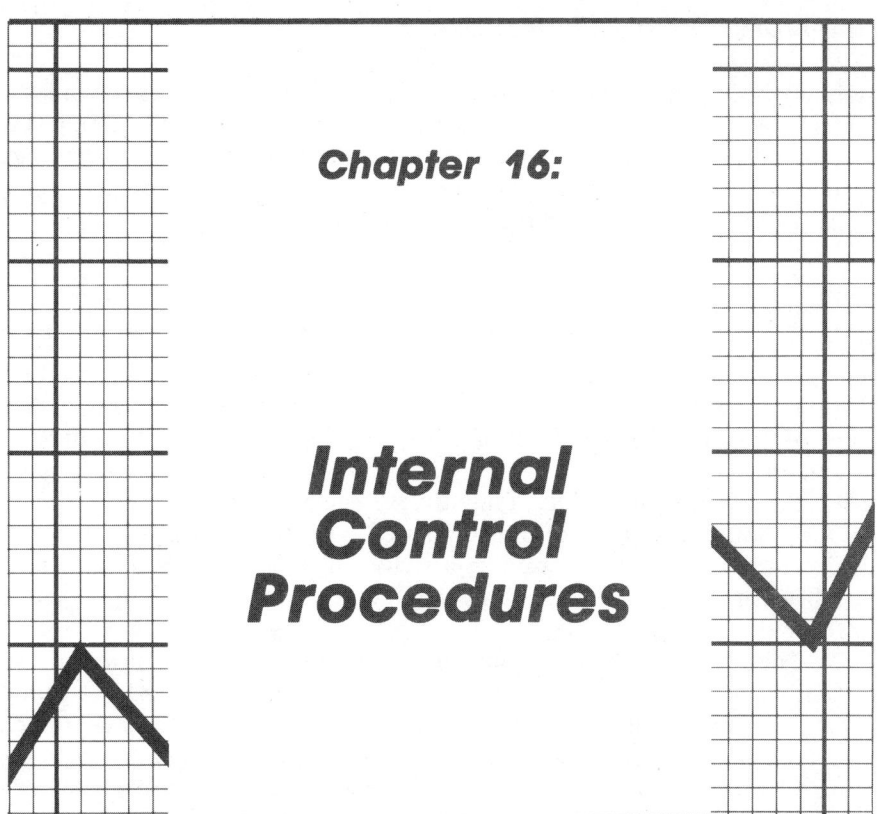

Chapter 16:

Internal Control Procedures

TRADING FUTURES contracts involves large amounts of money and sometimes very short lead times for making decisions about making trades. Common sense, as well as regulations, requires that financial institutions that trade futures contracts have carefully designed internal control procedures for handling the various aspects of futures trading.

This chapter discusses the details of the types of internal control procedures which are workable, feasible, and which will meet with regulatory approval in the majority of cases. Trading futures involves a great deal more than just making a telephone call to order trades. There are regulatory reporting requirements, verification procedures, audit trails to be maintained, reports to be prepared for the board of directors, and a contract register of positions taken and subsequently closed.

A properly designed set of internal control procedures is essential for at least three reasons. First, regulations require them. Second, there is no assurance that errors can be detected and rectified, should they occur, without a strict set of controls on the institution's futures trading activities. Third, in order to evaluate the performance of a hedging program it is absolutely necessary to have a complete record of all transactions which indicates when the decision was made and the time at which the transaction was executed. By employing a detailed set of procedures, the bank or savings and loan association can improve the efficiency of its hedging program over time by referring to its record of prior trading experience.

THE CONTRACT REGISTER

Since regulations are likely to be with us for some time, we will start with the types of controls which are required by regulation. Federal regulation of financial institution futures trading requires that the institution maintain a contract register which will show "at a glance" the open positions that the institution has at any time. Regulations also require a report to the institution's board of directors at each regular meeting of the board which indicates all futures trading activity since the last report. This task can be easily accomplished by designing the contract register to provide this information at a glance.

The contract register should indicate when a futures position was taken, what contract was traded, how many contracts were traded, against what assets or liabilities the hedge was made, when the position was closed, and the net gain or loss that was realized on the position. That much is required by regulators. Additional information, which can be easily included, will prove beneficial to the institution that uses it. Among the additional items worth considering are a notation of the exchange on which the contract was traded, the brokerage firm that handled the transaction, the maturity of the contract, the amount of initial margin and maintenance margin that was required, in what form the margin was put up, as well as all subsequent margin transactions associated with that particular futures position. The contract register should also indicate, along with the information concerning the closing of the position, the commissions that were paid for that hedge.

One cautionary note: Financial institutions are forbidden from taking speculative positions in futures contracts. Therefore, every page of every contract register should conspicuously indicate that these are "hedge" transactions even if the futures contracts are not specifically matched to individual asset or liability positions that the institution holds. When a hedge is placed in order to hedge the overall gap, simply describe the gap being hedged in the space indicating the specific asset or liability being matched. This may seem superfluous but it costs very little and will serve you well in the event that any question arises about your trading activities.

Included at the end of this chapter (Figs. 16.1, 16.2, 16.3) are facsimiles of a contract register that are similar to those being used by a number of financial institutions which hedge with financial futures. All of the items mentioned above are included in the facsimile contract register.

With this and a record of daily futures prices, the person in the institution responsible for trading futures can tell at any moment what the institution's net futures position is, whether it has excess margin that can be wired out of the account, and how well the position is doing relative to the institution's strategy.

Perhaps even more important than the currently open positions, the positions already closed provide an enormous amount of information for analytical purposes if the contract register is organized in this manner. Evaluation of hedge performance requires all the information which would be included in this type of contract register. In the absence of this level of detail it would be extremely difficult to evaluate different hedging strategies, the quality of service provided by the broker, the frequency with which funds should be withdrawn from the margin account, or the advisability of using particular futures contracts instead of other ones. In addition to providing information for subsequent "post mortems," it will be much easier to prepare reports for the institution's board of directors.

MONITORING THE HEDGE PROGRAM

Internal control procedures are also required in order to be sure that the hedging program is being carried out according to plan. In most institutions more than one person will have the responsibility and authority to implement futures trading. If such is the case, and even if it is not, more than one person in the institution should have the responsibility for monitoring trading activity. Independent verification by another person will increase the likelihood that errors will be avoided or detected quickly if they occur. Remember, we are talking potentially in terms of millions of dollars. One small undetected error can mean the difference between an efficient hedging plan and a disaster.

The internal control procedures that are appropriate for your institution will depend for the most part on the existing structure of your institution—there are no universal rules of thumb. Therefore, the following discussion should be viewed as an artist's sketch rather than a blueprint.

THE PERSONNEL

Selecting the personnel in the institution to be responsible for various phases of futures trading activity is very important. The overall strategy of futures hedging will normally be decided by the board of directors. Short- and intermediate-term decisions will normally be made by either the senior management or the asset and liability management committee. While these groups will set the broad picture of hedging for the institution, the person who actually makes the trading decisions will have an enormous impact on the success or failure of that strategy. Most frequently that person will be the vice-president for finance or the chief financial officer, who may be the same person. It is absolutely essential that the person doing the trading be completely familiar with all aspects of the financial structure of the institution. In the absence of detailed and current information about the institution's assets and liabilities, and the likely changes that may take place, it is impossible to implement even the best hedging plan.

The first place to start in designing internal control procedures is with the actual process of ordering a trade through the broker. The person who actually places the telephone call to the broker should also be responsible for maintaining an entry of the transaction in the contract register. This person should also have the authority to order wire transfers into and out of the margin account. It is tempting to think that having another person responsible for ordering wires will provide an internal check on the hedge manager. However, this is very often an incorrect perception, not because it doesn't provide such a check, but rather because it provides too much of a check, creating a bottleneck. A great many opportunities for efficient hedging will be lost if margin money cannot be placed quickly. What happens if a margin call is required and the person who can order wires is out of the office? You can be closed out of a position whether you want to be out or not.

After the transaction is executed the broker will send the customer a verification of the order. This verification, or a copy of it, should go to someone other than the person who ordered the trade. In this way the person who ordered the trade can verify that it was executed properly, and the third party involved can verify that the transaction was properly recorded on the institution's contract register.

In most instances the financial officer, or whoever is responsible for actual trading decisions, will confirm each trade, after it is executed, with the president of the institution or the chairman of the asset and liability committee. Again, this may seem superfluous but it will maintain an orderly process and decrease the likelihood of arbitrary and independent action by the trader manager which may be at variance with the institution's overall plan as adopted by the board of directors. Remember, you made a large effort to convince the board to hedge with futures—you don't want a wheeler-dealer trader wrecking your carefully thought-out plan.

On the other side of the internal control coin, senior management must make an effort to monitor the institution's trading activity. Simply filing reports and trade confirmations won't do. Senior management must take an active role in monitoring the institution's hedged and unhedged positions in much the same way that it monitors the overall asset and liability position. This does not mean the president of the bank has to duplicate all of the efforts of the trader-manager step by step, rather he or she should be familiar enough with the bank's position that a daily report from the trading desk is meaningful and is not just another memo.

The responsibility for reporting to the board of directors should also be shared by the trader-manager and the senior management of the institution. The essence of the reports to the board is to show whether the futures trading undertaken by management is consistent with the policy developed by the board *and* to provide the necessary feedback to the board in order to evaluate that policy and make changes in it, when and where necessary. A report that says "Here's what we did and here are the results" in most cases will simply not be sufficient for the institution which is seriously concerned with decreasing its interest rate risk through the use of financial futures hedging.

REPORTING THE RESULTS

The report to the board should indicate in summary fashion the actual trades that were made. The detail in the report will be most usefully spent on an analysis of the degree to which the institution's interest rate exposure has been altered by trading futures. That is, if the cost of funds has risen, has the hedging program been able to produce trading profits to offset those increased costs? This is what it should do. If hedging has not done so, why hasn't it? When trying to answer this question one consideration that should be kept in mind is the degree to which futures trading can offset changes in costs or the value of assets. If the bank's cost of funds has risen because it aggressively sought higher cost deposits, hedging with futures cannot offset those increases if, in general, interest rates fall. If rates rise over the time frame in question, there should be trading profits to offset some, but not all, of the higher cost. The degree of offsetting profits is subject to basis risk which is discussed in Section V, Managing a Position.

The focus of the report should be on a comparative, what-if basis—what would we look like now if we hadn't used futures to hedge our risk—rather than on the absolute bottom line profit/loss figures. Hedging with futures is designed to shift the institution's risk of unfavorable and unforeseen interest rate changes to somebody else. The futures market cannot protect you from the consequences of embarking on a bad marketing plan or the wrong advertising campaign or making bad loans. This should be made clear to the directors long before they receive the first monthly report of futures trading. It wouldn't hurt to re-emphasize this point occasionally, either.

ADDENDUM: INTERNAL CONTROL DOCUMENTS

The following items are sample documents that are encountered in the internal control procedures that accompany hedging with futures by financial institutions. Those shown here are not the ne plus ultra in this field but are for illustrative purposes only, to indicate the types and nature of control procedures which it is prudent to employ. In almost all cases some modification in the style and substance will be required in order to conform to the existing internal structure of the bank or savings and loan association.

AGREEMENT WITH BROKER

Notwithstanding anything in the Agreement or any related agreement to the contrary, the following provisions shall be binding on both parties:

1. Any purchase or sale by the broker-dealer or any closing of outstanding contracts pursuant to paragraph 4 shall be effected at the settlement price for such security, commodity, or contract, if traded on an exchange, or the fair market value of such items as of the date such action is taken by the broker-dealer. Promptly upon taking any such action, the broker-dealer shall give written notice to (bank name) of the details of such action.

2. Broker-dealer hereby acknowledges that it is aware of the fact that (bank name) will engage in commodity hedging activities as defined and to the extent permitted by the Comptroller of the Currency (or appropriate regulatory agency.)

3. Any margin funds or other funds held by broker-dealer in the account of (bank name) shall be held in Treasury bills or other instruments approved in writing by the (bank name) and any interest income or yield earned on such funds shall be the property of the (bank name).

4. A confirmation of each commodity futures trade caused to be executed by (bank name) shall be promptly sent by first-class mail to (bank name) by the broker-dealer to the attention of Compliance and Control Officer, Investment Operations (or other appropriate title) at (bank address).

5. Broker-dealer shall only effect financial futures, forward contract and standby transactions of (bank name) with (name of individual) and (name of individual). Broker-dealer shall not effect transactions with (name of individual) in excess of the maximum position limits set forth on Exhibit A attached hereto, and shall not effect transactions with (name of individual) or (name of individual) in excess of the individual trading limits set forth on Attachment I to Exhibit A attached hereto. The Bank shall give broker-dealer written notice of any change in the trading authority of the individuals named herein.

AUTHORIZATION TO TRADERS

Please be advised that you are hereby authorized to execute financial futures transactions in connection with Securities Trading Division activities according to the below listed limits, showing number of contracts for the several instruments we expect to use.

T-Bill	T-Note	T-bond	CD
100	100	100	50

It should be understood by each of you that while you are individually authorized to execute transactions up to the maximum listed above, said limits represent the maximum Trading Account Limits. Therefore, to the extent that either of you has executed transactions in some lesser amount, and to the extent that said transactions remain in the Trading Account position, your individual trading limits are reduced accordingly.

You are further authorized upon the condition of my prior approval, to execute financial futures transactions in connection with the (bank name) asset/liability management activities in accordance with the below listed schedule, also indicating number of contracts.

T-bill	T-note	T-bond	CD	GNMA
250	150	150	200	50

Exceptions to these limits will be dealt with in the manner set forth in Exhibit D of the Resolution adopted by the Board of Directors of the (name of corporation) on (date of resolution).

Please acknowledge your understanding of these trading limits by signing and returning the attached copy of this memorandum.

SPECIFIC
HEDGING CASH POSITION OF _____

HEDGE TRANSACTION RECORD

WITH FUTURES ☐ EURO ☐ CD ☐ T-Bill ☐ GNMA ☐ T-BOND ☐ OTHER

AMOUNT $ _____ MATURING DATE ___/___/___ RATE/PRICE ___/___ ECXHANGE _____

Date	B/S	Qty.	Contract Month	Ratio Factor	% Hedged	Price	Settle	Basis	Gain/Loss	Comments

Reissue Rate _____ %

$ Amount Cost Increase $ _____

FINAL EFFECTIVE RATE WITH HEDGE _____ %

$ _____ Total Gain/Loss Futures

_____ % Recapture

Figure 16.1 Specific Hedge Transaction Record (Contract Register)

HEDGE TRANSACTION RECORD

HEDGING OUTSTANDING AMOUNT $ _____   WITH FUTURES   ☐ EURO ☐ CD ☐ T-Bill ☐ GNMA ☐ T-BOND

DESCRIPTION _____   ☐ OTHER _____

FOR PERIOD ____ MONTHS ____ BEGIN DATE __/__/__   END DATE __/__/__   RATE/PRICE __/__   EXCHANGE _____

Date	Trans-Action	Contract Month & Qty.	Prices		Effective Strip Yield	Basis	Gain/Loss	O/T Equity	Total Equity	Comments

Reissue Rate ____ % $ Amount Cost Increase $ _____ $ _____ Total Gain/Loss Futures

% Hedged ____ %

Ratio Factor _____   FINAL EFFECTIVE RATE WITH HEDGE _____ %   _____ % Recapture

If Loan, Decay Rate ____ Days

Figure 16.2 General Hedge Transaction Record (Contract Register)

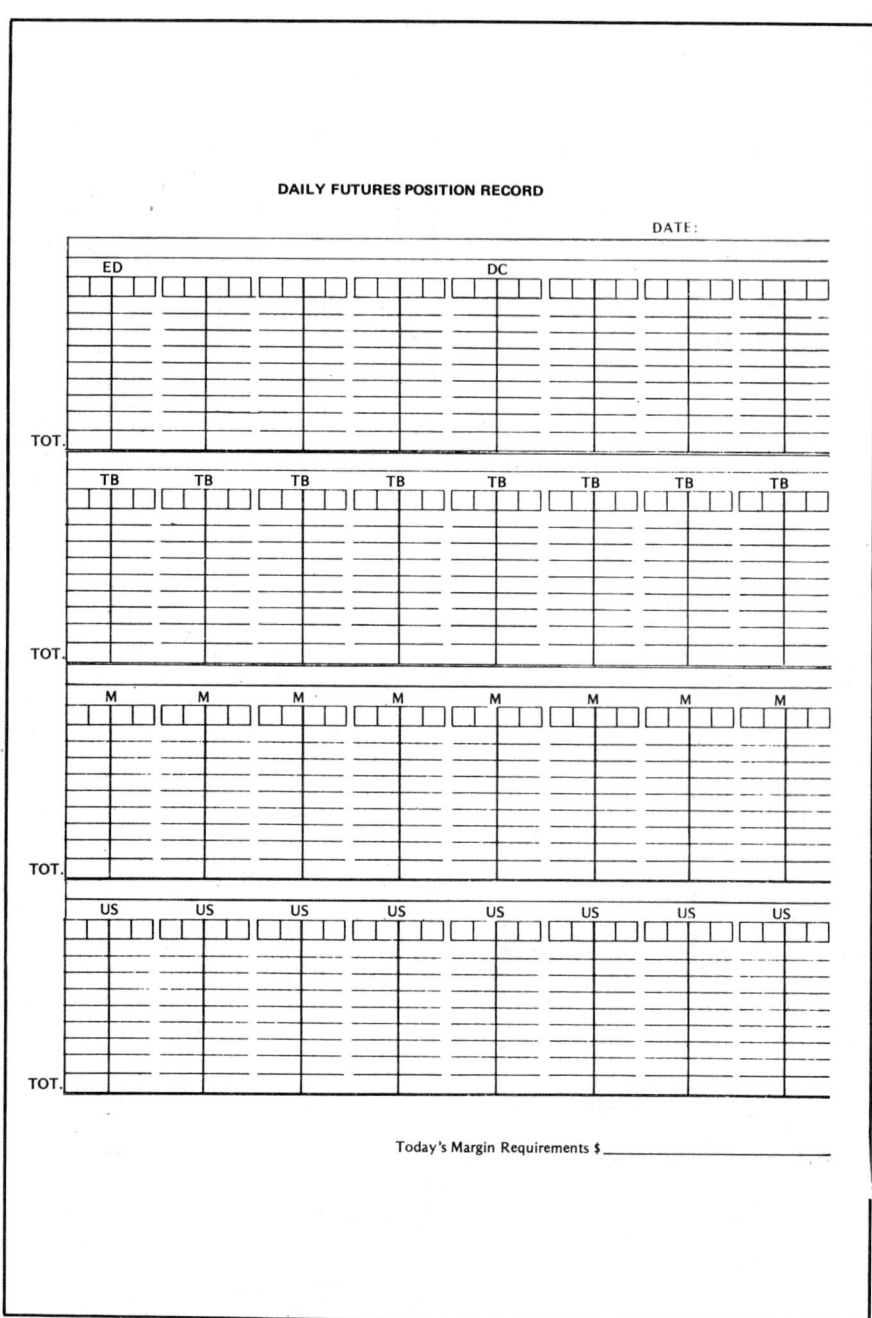

**Figure 16.3 Daily Futures Position Record
(Contract Register)**

IMPORTANT
SEE CONDITIONS
ON REVERSE SIDE

COMBINED COMMODITY STATEMENT

DATE
Aug 17, 1983
ACCOUNT NUMBER
260999

Retain for tax records.

FIRST NATIONAL BANK USA
1234 MAIN ST.
ANYWHERE ST 90909

DATE	BOUGHT	SOLD	COMMODITY/OPTION DESCRIPTION	TRADE PRICE	AMOUNT DEBIT	AMOUNT CREDIT
8/16/83	Account Balance - Segregated Funds					43,765.20
			--- C O N F I R M A T I O N ---			
WE HAVE MADE THIS DAY THE FOLLOWING TRADES FOR YOUR ACCOUNT AND RISK.						
		10	Dec. 83 T-Bills	90.36		
		10	Dec. 83 T-Bills	90.36		
			--- P U R C H A S E & S A L E ---			
5/31/83		10	Dec. 83 T-Bills	90.83		
6/10/83		10	Dec. 83 T-Bills	90.66		
8/17/83	10		Dec. 83 T-Bills	90.36		
8/17/83	10		Dec. 83 T-Bills	90.38		
	20*	20*	P & S			18,750.00
			Commission		1,000.00	
			Fee		36.60	
			Total Commissions & Fees		1,036.60	
			Net Profit on Loss From Trades			17,713.40
CURRENT ACCOUNT BALANCE			SEGREGATED FUNDS			61,478.00
			--- O P E N P O S I T I O N S ---			
6/21/83		10	Dec. 83 T-Bills	90.60		3,500.00
7/05/83		5	Dec. 83 T-Bills	90.42		750.00
7/05/83		5	Dec. 83 T-Bills	90.43		875.00
7/12/83		10	Dec. 83 T-Bills	90.25	2,750.00	
8/03/83		5	Dec. 83 T-Bills	89.93	5,375.00	
8/03/83		5	Dec. 83 T-Bills	90.00	4,500.00	
	40*		OPEN TRADE EQUITY		7,500.00	
			SETTLEMENT	90.36		
			TOTAL FUTURES OPEN TRADE EQUITY		7,500.00	
			TOTAL EQUITY			53,978.60

Grains in 000's
PLEASE REPORT ANY DISCREPANCIES INCURRED. THIS STATEMENT SHALL BE DEEMED ACCURATE UNLESS OBJECTED TO BY TELEPHONE, TELEGRAPH OR LETTER WITHIN 5 BUSINESS DAYS OF ITS DATE.

Figure 16.4. Combined Statement from Brokerage Firm—statement of confirmation of sale, purchase & sale, and open trades

CARGILL INVESTOR SERVICES INC.

141 West Jackson Boulevard, Chicago, Illinois 60604
Telephone (312) 435-8300
Atlanta • Kansas City • Geneva • Miami • Minneapolis
New York • Zurich • London • San Francisco

IMPORTANT
SEE CONDITIONS
ON REVERSE SIDE

MONTHLY COMMODITY STATEMENT
ACTIVITY AND OPEN POSITIONS

PERIOD ENDING
Aug 31,1983
ACCOUNT NUMBER
260999

Retain for tax records

FIRST NATIONAL BANK USA
1234 MAIN ST.
ANYWHERE ST 90909

DATE	BOUGHT LONG	SOLD SHORT	COMMODITY/OPTION DESCRIPTION		PRICE	AMOUNT DEBIT	AMOUNT CREDIT
7-29-83	BALANCE FORWARD						53,390.20
8-02-83	W25468		WIRE SENT		CASH	40,000.00	
8-04-83	W		WIRE RECEIVED		CASH		5,000.00
8-08-83	W25650		WIRE SENT		CASH	20,000.00	
8-16-83	W		WIRE RECEIVED		CASH		45,375.00
8-17-83		20	Dec. 83	T-Bills	P & S		17,713.40
8-18-83	40	40	Dec. 83	T-Bills	P & S	9,423.20	
8-29-83	W		WIRE RECEIVED		CASH		20,000.00
8-31-83	ACCOUNT BALANCE -- SEGREGATED FUNDS		. . . .				72,055.40*
NET REALIZED PROFIT OR LOSS FOR MONTH						8,290.20	

* * * * * * * * * OPEN POSITIONS * * * * * * * * * * * * * OPEN POSITIONS * * * * * * * * * *

DATE	BOUGHT LONG	SOLD SHORT	COMMODITY/OPTION DESCRIPTION		PRICE	AMOUNT DEBIT	AMOUNT CREDIT
8-25-83		30	Dec. 83	T-Bills	90.37		21,750.00
8-29-83	27		Dec. 83	T-Bills	90.12		2,700.00
8-29-83	3		Dec. 83	T-Bills	90.13		375.00
	60*		OPEN TRADE EQUITY		90.08		24,825.00*
			TOTAL OPEN TRADE EQUITY				24,825.00
			TOTAL EQUITY				96,880.40

Grains in 000's
PLEASE REPORT ANY DISCREPANCIES INCURRED. THIS STATEMENT SHALL BE DEEMED ACCURATE UNLESS OBJECTED TO BY TELEPHONE, TELEGRAPH OR LETTER WITHIN 5 BUSINESS DAYS OF ITS DATE.

Figure 16.5. Monthly Activity Statement from Brokerage Firm

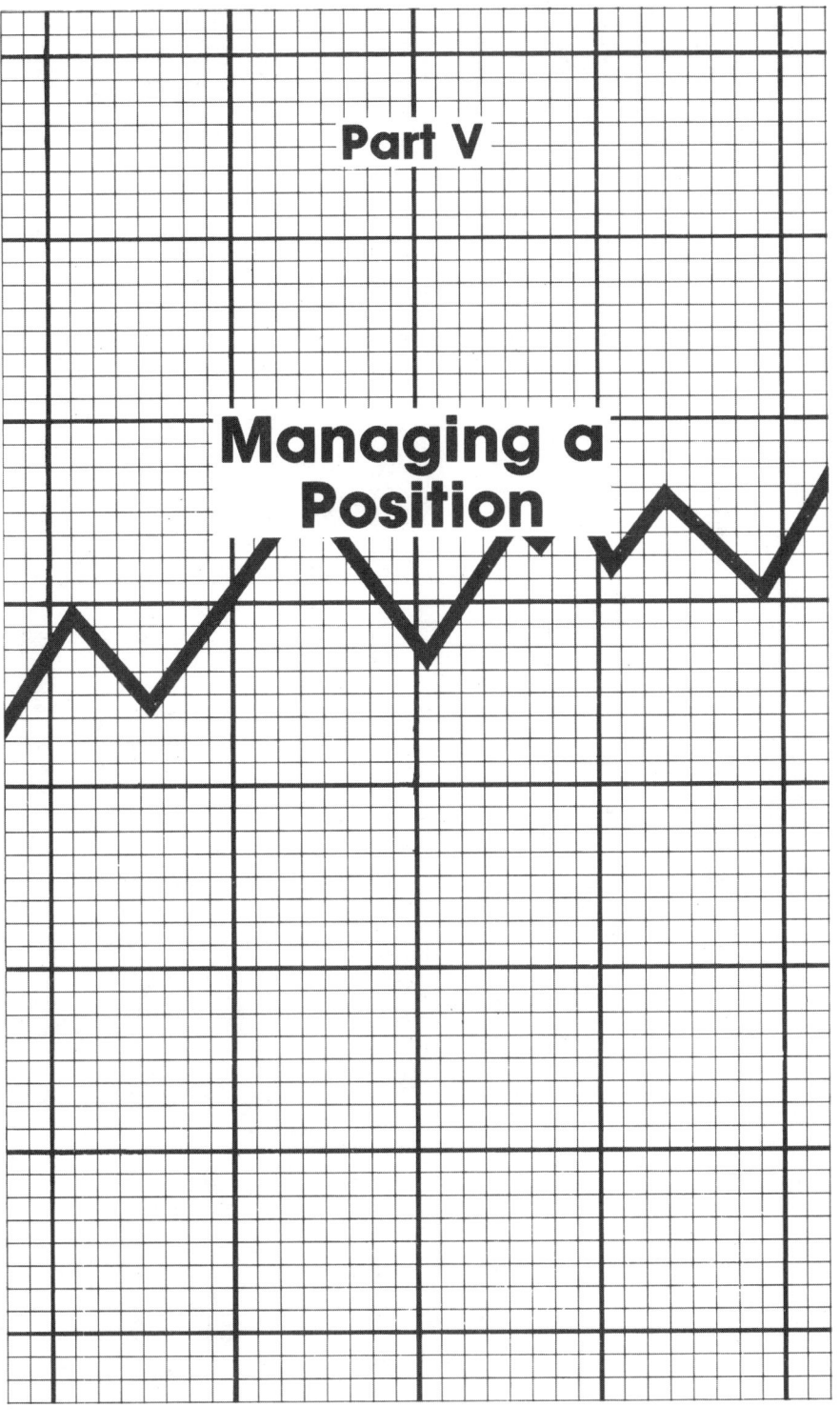

Part V

Managing a Position

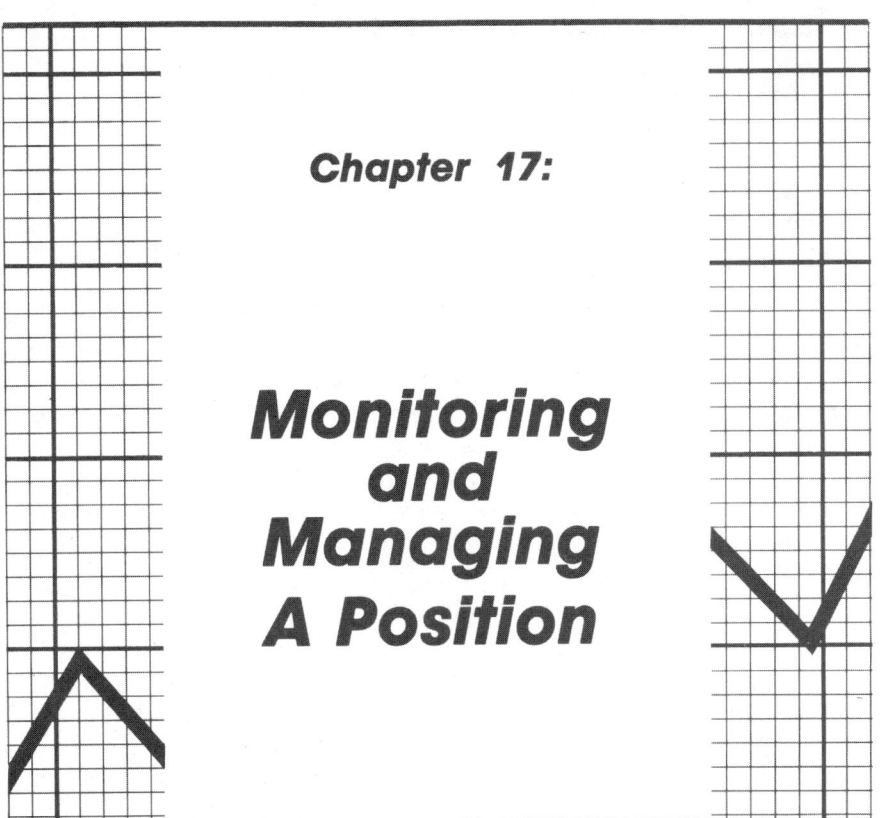

Chapter 17:

Monitoring and Managing A Position

ONCE YOU have your hedges on, you will need to monitor the markets to make sure that they are working properly and to adjust to changing conditions. Managing a position entails more than just watching the movement of rates, it is also watching fundamental economic changes, technical markets indicators, and above all monitoring your cash flow situation on your leveraged futures contract. Also, it involves some decision making concerning managed versus non-managed hedges.

SELECTIVE OR MANAGED HEDGING

Whether you employ "selective" hedging or not is a major decision you should arrive at before you establish your hedges. Simply, selective or "managed hedging," as it is called, means that using some objective guidelines such as technical indicators or major Fed policy changes, you will lift all or part of your hedge during the life of that hedge. Depending on conditions, you may take the hedge off and replace it several times.

The reason for selective hedging is to adjust to market conditions which are working in your favor. Now some may call this speculating, which you definitely are not allowed to do, but it really is just altering your hedging plan while underway—a mid-course correction, if you will. The important point, and this should be followed carefully, is that you do not lift hedges just because you "feel" that the direction of rates has changed, but that objective indications show that this conclusion is highly probable. Only then should you proceed on this course of action. What are these indicators that you will use as your guide? Primarily, they will be major Fed announcements, a radical change in government economic reports, or time-tested technical charting techniques employed by futures professionals. Also, it will be important for you to watch the changing basis relationship of cash to futures. Selective hedging can, at times, greatly increase the effectiveness of your hedging program and, anyway, why would you want to stay hedged in the event that the government came out with a proclamation insuring favorable rates?

PERSONNEL

Before you embark upon your hedging activities, it is important that you delegate or share some of the responsibilities for implementing and managing hedges. Generally, it is best that at least two individuals in the institution have the authority and the knowledge to conduct the hedging operation. This is good for several reasons. As we mentioned in the section on brokers, sometimes it will be important for your broker to contact someone who has trading authority at your institution in the event of major market changes or extremely volatile markets. Also, this provides an effective counterbalance in the decision making process as you each have a sounding board. This will prevent rash decisions, as well as insure that you keep to your hedging plan and guidelines.

Ideally, one of the hedge managers should be a senior executive in the institution with access to the firm's total picture. He is probably a member of the Asset/Liability Committee. Also, ideally the other member of the hedging team should have had some actual trading experience, whether in the cash markets, on your trading desk or portfolio management team, or in the futures markets themselves.

WHAT TO WATCH

Once you have decided upon the hedging team, there are several major things they should watch in monitoring and managing the hedges, the first of which is to see if the hedge is performing as expected. Is the basis changing resulting in the futures not moving in line with cash as much as it was when the hedge was initiated? Have there been major shifts in money supply growth or changes in the targets issued by the Federal Reserve? Has your institution's exposure changed, requiring a change in the size of the hedge? Are technical indicators showing a shift in the trend of interest rates such that it is highly probable that professional traders will come in and move the market against your futures position, causing too large a margin call for your institution?

As you can see, there are quite a number of things to watch. In this chapter we will discuss the basis relationship and fundamental economic factors affecting the financial futures markets. We have already shown you how to watch your institution by using frequent gap analysis. Technical analysis of futures markets could fill a whole book itself, but we will devote the next chapter to introducing briefly its major concepts and their use. And since the bottom line is where it's all at, after all, we will study the consequences of margin calls and the control of cash flow in a separate chapter.

BASIS

Basis, the difference between the price of the cash instrument being hedged and the futures price, is important for you as a hedger to watch, as it is the key to the real world of hedging. By that we mean that up until now you probably have been shown quite a few examples of "perfect" hedges in the materials put out by the exchanges and most of the brokerage houses. These examples assume the basis relationship stays constant for the life of the hedge. The world, as we well know, is not a perfect place and, consequently, most hedges you place will be "imperfect" to an extent varying for the most part with the change in the basis relationship. This means that at times your hedge, even though sized with the proper calculations, could still only partially offset your interest rate exposure if the basis changes.

As you have probably realized by now, by hedging all you are doing is exchanging interest rate risk for basis change risk. You will still be open to some risk, but this will be considerably smaller than the risk incurred when no hedging is employed.

Generally, basis relationships do not change radically over a long period of time because both the cash and the futures are influenced by the same economic conditions. Changes in the basis are usually short-term variations which are eventually put back into line by arbitrageurs. However, in the meantime, they can make a great impact on the efficiency of your hedges.

Therefore, it is of great importance for you and your hedging team to keep track of the basis relationships which would affect any hedges that you would establish. In the section on Technical Charting we will show some examples of basis charts. By paying attention to these relationships you will be better able to judge when it is advantageous or disadvantageous to establish or keep a hedge.

A positive basis (positive carry) exists when the price of the cash instrument exceeds the price of the futures contract. Conversely, a negative basis (negative carry) exists when the futures price exceeds that of the cash instrument.

A strengthening basis refers to a basis that becomes increasingly more positive, that is, the difference by which the cash price exceeds the futures becomes greater. A strengthening basis will be advantageous for a short hedge as the futures price drops faster than the cash price or, in a rising market, the cash price gains faster on the futures price (See Figure 17.1).

A weakening basis refers to a basis that becomes increasingly negative. Opposite of the strengthening basis, this scenario is more advantageous for a long hedger as the futures price increases faster than the cash or, in a falling market, the cash price drops faster than the futures price (See Figure 17.1).

CONVERGENCE

As the time to the expiration of the futures contract nears, cash and futures prices tend to converge. In other words, the basis approaches zero. This happens because the cost of carry decreases as the contracts mature. Therefore, their prices will become closer to those of the related cash (spot) financial instrument.

Convergence has an important implication for hedgers. As we stated earlier, basis can be either positive or negative, reflecting positive or negative "cost of carry," respectively (See Figure 17.1). If you establish a hedge with a basis unfavorable to your position, that is, a weak basis for a long hedge and a strong basis for a short hedge, the force of convergence will work against you. As the contracts mature this "magnetic" force will bring the futures prices closer to the cash price. If you went short futures when they were cheaply priced (undervalued) or went long when they were rich (overvalued) you have little hope of your hedge efficiency improving. Your

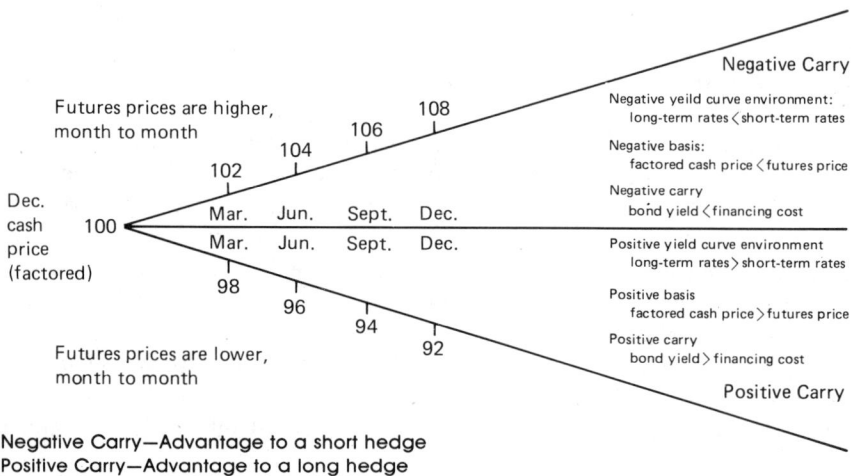

Negative Carry—Advantage to a short hedge
Positive Carry—Advantage to a long hedge

Figure 17.1. Convergence

Source: Chicago Board of Trade

hedges will still be lessened due to the basis loss. A point to remember before establishing a hedge is to look at the basis, whether it is positive or negative and whether it is weakening or strengthening.

FUNDAMENTAL ANALYSIS

Besides watching the basis one should also be aware of the fundamental factors that move the interest rate markets. You are probably already quite familiar with most of these, but we will recap them here nonetheless:

Factors that Move the Market

- Money Supply
- Fed Funds
- Fed Activity—Matched Sales—Repos—Discount Rate Changes
- Treasury Auctions
- Supply of Corporate Bonds
- Retail Demand for Securities
- Loan Demand
- Economic News, such as tax cuts, spending cuts, budget deficits
- Monetary and Fiscal Policy
- Housing Starts and Permits
- CPI and PPI
- Leading Economic Indicators
- Retail Sales Figures
- Unemployment
- Savings Flows in and out of Financial Institutions
- Prime Rate Changes
- Broker Loan Rate Changes
- Status of the Dollar versus Other Currencies
- World Political and Economic Events (defaults, etc.)

Fundamental analysis must be factored into your view of the markets. But, as international bankers have found in the foreign exchange sector, such information is often not as useful as are technical indicators for calling shorter-term moves in the markets.

HOW OFTEN?

These factors, not to mention the technical market indicators we are yet to discuss, are quite a lot to watch. And the question that initially comes to mind is "how often and how close?" After all, you know the maxim about watching water boil.

A crucial factor in the how often question is the type of hedging plan upon which you have decided. What is your horizon for interest rates that affect your plan? Are you selectively hedging?

Generally, for a medium-sized institution ($300 million—$1 billion) you should be watching the government economic reports monthly and the money supply figures weekly with a keen eye to the M2 figure issued monthly. You should also be aware of the monthly decision of the Federal Reserve Open Market Committee Meeting (FOMC). Treasury bill auction results should be monitored weekly and attention should be given to quarterly refunding announcements and their subsequent auctions.

Daily monitoring should be conducted on financial futures prices and their resultant technical indicators. Also, news items or interest rate pronouncements by major economic forecasters should be watched continuously. They have had quite a volatile impact on the money markets in recent years. Also, you should be watching Fed funds and Fed activity every day, as these are widely watched and interpreted by market participants.

TOOLS OF THE TRADE

As a hedger, depending upon the amount of size that you do, you may want to employ a number of modern conveniences to help you in your monitoring procedure. There is quite a lot to watch, and some of these devices can even be programmed to beep when key events occur. In the event that your hedging operation cannot justify the cost of these, your broker will probably have most of these tools and will convey the information to you if something of consequence to your position occurs.

Of the electronic quote screens available with cash market information, Telerate is perhaps the best. Along with pages upon pages of cash quotes you can get additional news and commentary pages, as well as futures price quotes. For news you may have the Reuters or Dow Jones Financial Wire Services. And to round out your electronic menagerie of gadgets, you might add a Comtrend® electronic futures charting terminal and an IBM PC® microcomputer with software already pre-programmed with enough technical study capability to make a market technician think he has died and gone to heaven.

Since this is a practical handbook, you probably should have some good old-fashioned graph paper and triangles to keep daily price charts on the futures markets as part of your daily monitoring regimen (or "homework" as the brokers call it). A chartbook service such as Data Lab Financial Futures or Commodity Perspective will save you a lot of work. All you need to do is keep them current manually.

If you are a subscriber to "Innerline" or a similar computer network, you should be able to retrieve a fair amount of useful information from it, as it has the *American Banker* on it on a real-time basis. Several other services, including an asset/liability planning model and some futures services are also available.

Of course, if you want to spend the money, you can choose from a number of time-sharing services such as Data Resources and Chase Econometrics. Also, there are a number of technical timing services available, but be careful; as we pointed out earlier, if they had the market timed so well they would be retired or you couldn't afford their service.

RECORD KEEPING

Before we move on to the land of the technical elves, as Louis Rukeyser calls it on "Wall $treet Week," let's first discuss some of the records you should keep as part of your hedge monitoring operation.

As we mentioned earlier in the section on internal control procedures, the contract register is an important monitoring document, not only for the sake of the regulators, but also for your own management of the hedges. If you design your paperwork for this journal with a mind to using it as a source of data for hedge monitoring and performance evaluation as well, you will have quite a nice compact reporting system. Some examples of information to include are: basis, hedge ratio factor, percent hedged, percent recapture, and room for comments.

Going back over this register later, along with your futures price charts and a log of whatever technical indicators you choose to follow, will provide you with insight into the performance of futures hedges in varying market conditions. Hopefully, this will result in better hedges in the future, as well as better selective hedging strategies that you will develop over time.

Also, these records are important since you probably will be expected to report the status of the hedging program to your board of directors at each monthly meeting. The directors are responsible for knowing how the program is currently affecting the institution.

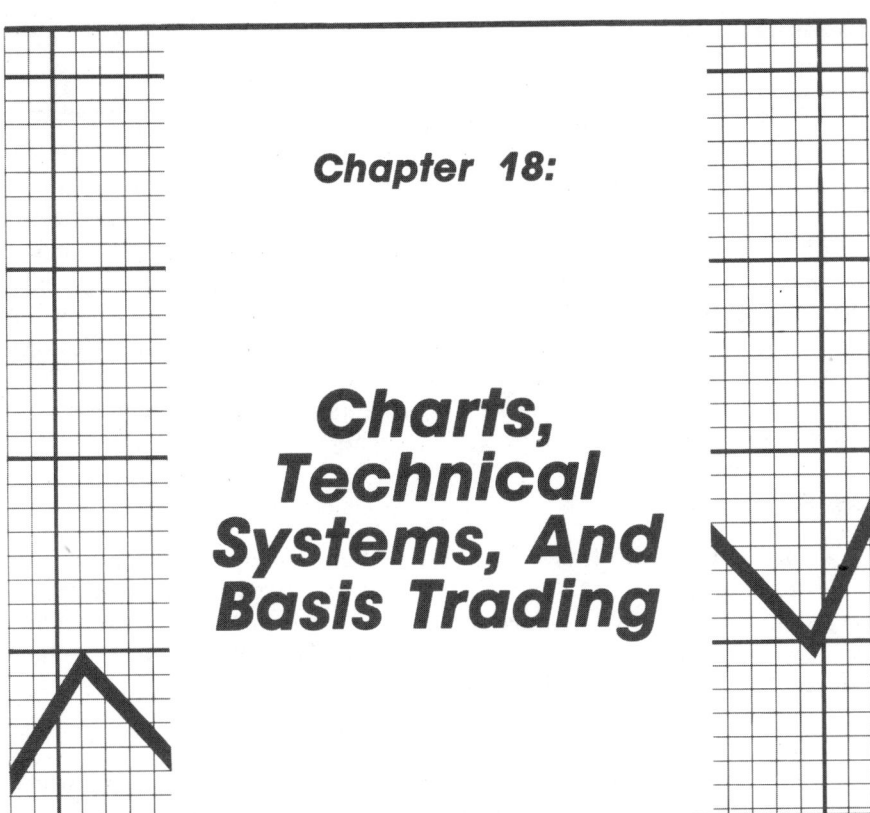

Chapter 18:

Charts, Technical Systems, And Basis Trading

PERHAPS THE most difficult decision to be made in selective or managed hedging is when to place a hedge and when to take it off. There are a multitude of different methods for making these decisions. Some speculators have been known to buy and sell futures by a seat-of-the-pants approach based on their feel of the market. This is inappropriate for a financial institution trying to reduce its risk.

As mentioned earlier, there are a number of technical market indicators used by the more professional futures traders which can be of considerable use to the financial hedger. Most of these technical tools are used to determine the trend of prices, price level objectives, and timing for entry and exit of positions. Since a discussion of the application these techniques could fill books, we will give you only a brief exposure to the more important of them, providing you with an overview of the world of technical analysis.

TECHNICAL ANALYSIS _____

Technical analysis is the futures term for the forecasting of market movements based upon the study of actual market price activity, both past and current. There has been much debate over the underlying causes for its validity and usefulness. Some try to make cases for random-walk theory, yet many professional futures traders find technical indicators, especially charts, most helpful and fairly reliable; enough so to risk their money on them. Whether these market signals are just self-fulfilling prophecies or a fairly simple way of reducing tons of information the market has absorbed, the fact remains that many market participants watch these indications and base many of their decisions upon them. They move the markets.

CHARTING

First and foremost in the world of technical analysis is charting. This is the graphic representation of historical price activity. Futures charts are very similar to the stock market charts you have probably seen decorating the *Wall Street Journal* and other business publications. In fact, much of futures technical analysis has its origins in the stock market.

Bar Charts

The most common form of chart is the bar chart. This is one on which each period's price activity (price range and settlement) is graphed as a vertical line with a crossbar indicating the settlement price. Monthly, weekly, and daily bar charts are used for differing market perspectives (long term vs. short term). Since the futures markets are so active, the most frequently used charts are the daily bar charts. (See Figure 18.1)

Note that weekend days are omitted from the charts. Also, you will find that these charts contain daily information about volume (vertical lines near the bottom) and open interest (continuous line just above volume bars). Each contract month of each futures contract is charted independently.

Basis Charts

Often cash instruments are charted as a line on the bar chart showing the relationship of futures to cash. This relationship, known as the basis, which we have already discussed, is sometimes charted as a separate line chart, similar to a bar chart but plotting only the difference between the daily closing prices of cash and futures. (See Figure 18.2)

These two types of charts are very useful to you as a hedger, to keep abreast of recent market activity and the relative value of particular futures contracts. As we will soon see, the interpretation of daily bar chart patterns can often be very useful in forecasting short-term moves in the futures. There are a number of chartbook services available. Data Lab Financial Futures contains the most detailed information on almost every conceivable financial future and related cash information. Commodity Perspective, however, is easier to update manually on a daily basis.

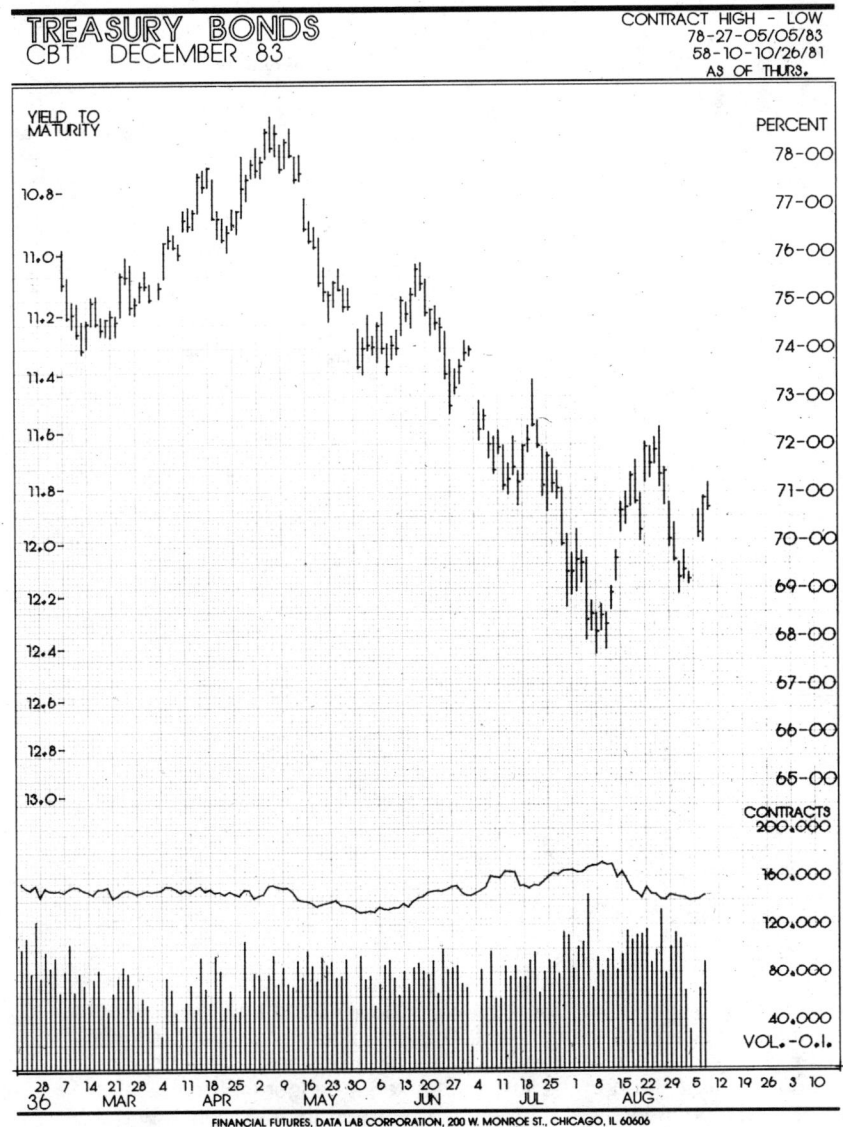

Figure 18.1. Typical Daily Bar Chart

U.S. Treasury Bond 14
With September 82 basis
January 1981-July 1982

32ND OF 100 PCT.

U.S. Treasury Bond 14

September 1982
U.S. Treasury Bond
Futures Contract

$$14 \text{ of } 2006-11 - \frac{US}{SEP. 82} \times 1.6359$$

	32ND OF 100 PCT.
	110-00
	108-00
	106-00
	104-00
	102-00
	100-00
	98-00
	68-00
	66-00
	64-00
	62-00
	60-00
	58-00
	56-00
	4-00
	2-00
	0-00
	-2-00
	-4-00

21 28 4 11 18 25 1 8 15 22 1 8 15 22 29 5 12 19 26 3 10 17 24 31 7 14 21 28 5 12 19 26 2
JAN.   FEB.   MAR.   APR.   MAY.   JUN.   JUL.

Basis chart showing prices for the 14% Treasury bond and the September 1982 Treasury bond futures contract. The third line on the graph shows basis movement. By counterbalancing his cash position with an opposite and equivalent position in the futures market, a hedger limits his risk to that of a change in basis, the difference between the cash price and the futures price. Such fluctuations are less volatile and more predictable than fluctuations in either cash or futures prices. Cash prices for the basis movement line have been divided by the factor of 1.6359 to reflect the same coupon (8%) and maturity as the futures contract on the graph.

Figure 18.2. Basis Chart

Point & Figure Charts

Another favorite chart of technicians is the point & figure chart. Unlike the bar chart it is a non–time-dependent chart. All price activity is shown by a series of x's and o's without reference to time. This type of chart gives one a different perspective from which to view the market. (See Figure 18.3)

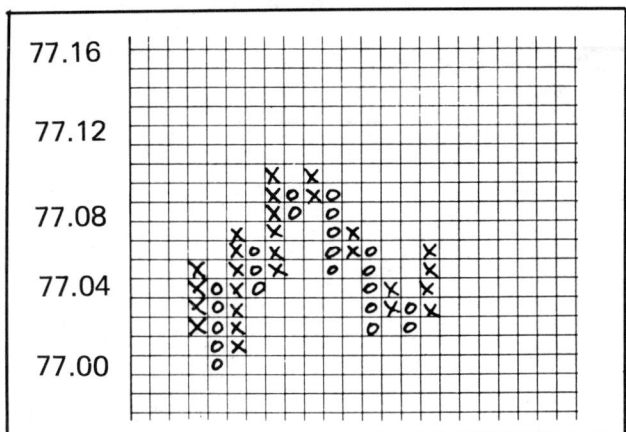

Figure 18.3 Typical Point and Figure Chart

When prices move up, this activity is denoted on a point & figure chart by a column of x's; price movement to the downside by o's. Each box on the graph can be made to represent an 01 or any convenient size of price change. The decision of when x's turn to o's on this chart is based on the reversal size. The most common point & figure charts are based on a 1 point (01) box size and a 3 point reversal and are known as 1 x 3's (one by threes). This means that each time a price moves in an opposite direction to its current direction by 3 points (ticks), that activity is denoted by the opposite marking (x or o) until such time as the price reverses again by 3 ticks. The size of the box and the reversal determine the perspective of the market view and most are multiples of 1 x 3 (e.g., 2 x 6, 3 x 9, 4 x 12, 10 x 30).

INTERPRETING CHARTS

For all their seeming objectivity, the reading and use of charts is more an art than a science; just as navigators have found, sometimes an unknown sandbar or current materializes, temporarily upsetting the best of plans. To guide them through the shoals, market technicians, commonly referred to as "chartists," have identified over the years a number of price patterns which are pretty reliable indicators of market movement.

Trendlines & Channels

The first and most important goal of a market technician in reading his charts is to identify a trend. Are prices generally moving up or down, and at what angle? To do this the chartist connects, if possible, three or more daily lows with a line and three or more daily highs with a line. These resultant parallel trendlines should form a channel in which prices have been moving. If prices move out of the channel it is an indication that the trend may have changed. (See Figure 18.4)

As with most charting principles, what works on a large scale works on a small scale. Therefore, a chartist may have a small downtrend within a

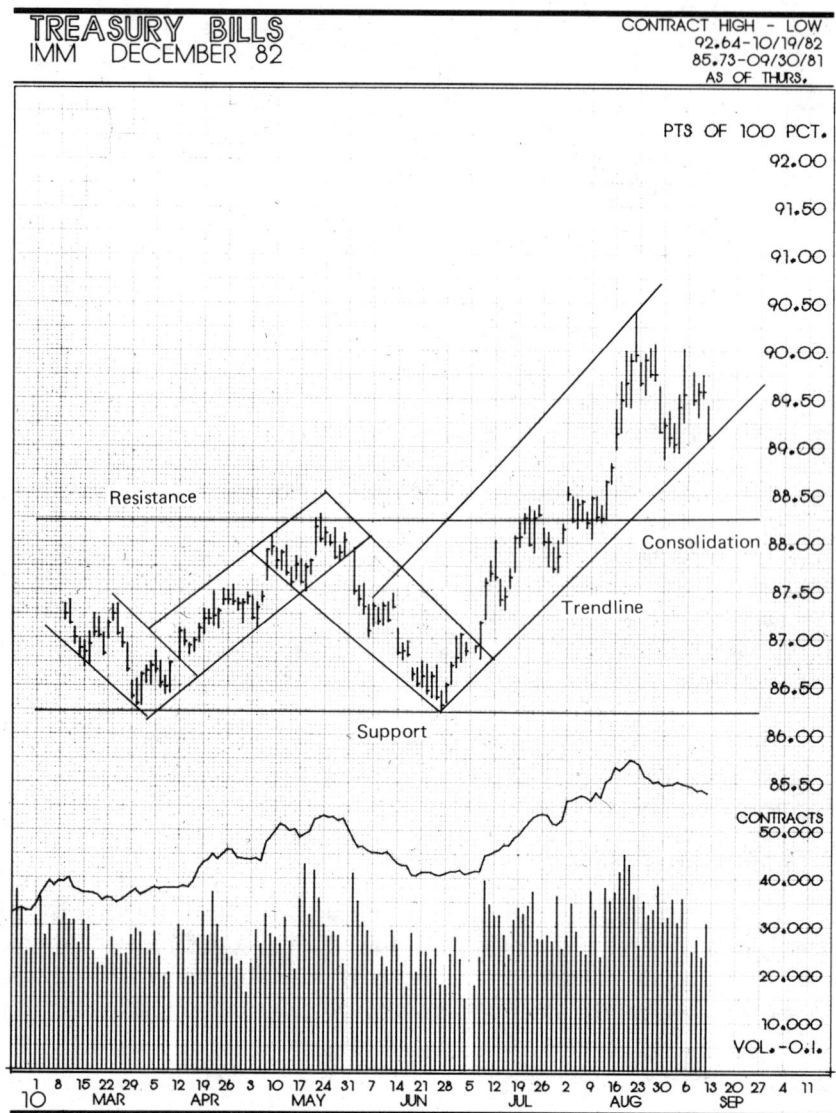

Figure 18.4

larger uptrend. To distinguish the difference he labels them minor and major trends, generally working within a few months' time horizon. For trendlines spanning six months to years the label "long-term trendline" is given.

Chartists often speak in terms of "chart points." These are price points along their trendline for any given day. There is great attention paid to these chart points by traders on the floor and elsewhere, whether or not they are technicians. Many stop orders are placed in the market based on these technical price points.

Support & Resistance

Also important to market technicians are price levels which exhibit "support" and "resistance." Just as water seeks a level, so, too, do market prices tend to certain key price levels. These levels may be determined by market psychology or economic factors. Chartists try to divine these by drawing horizontal lines across market highs or lows, levels at which prices have stopped in the past on the chart. When projected into the future part of the chart they become chart points of potential support and resistance.

When prices move decisively through one of these levels, the former resistance level then becomes a new level of support, your basic one man's ceiling is another man's floor in a high-rise concept. Also of interest are areas of consolidation, which are price levels at which trading seems to be confined for periods of time. These consolidation zones are indicators of support and resistance levels.

By the way, chartist terminology is often peppered with phrases as if the market had a life of its own. In the case of consolidation areas, they talk of the market digesting or getting up steam for its next move.

Market Formations

The next level of chart interpretation is pattern recognition. Technicians eye their charts to identify recurrent formations that historically have indicated market movement accurately. These formations generally fall into two categories, reversal and continuation patterns.

Reversal Patterns—Primary interest in chart pattern recognition is given to finding changes in the market's trend. There are quite a few formations known for signaling significant market tops and bottoms, and these are classified therefore as reversal patterns.

Tops and bottoms come in a number of forms (see Figure 18.5). The most frequent tops are single tops, double tops, and complex tops such as "head and shoulders" and descending triangles. Market bottoms often exhibit similar patterns, except in reverse. Therefore, chartists look for single ("V") bottoms, double bottoms, head and shoulders bottoms, and ascending triangles.

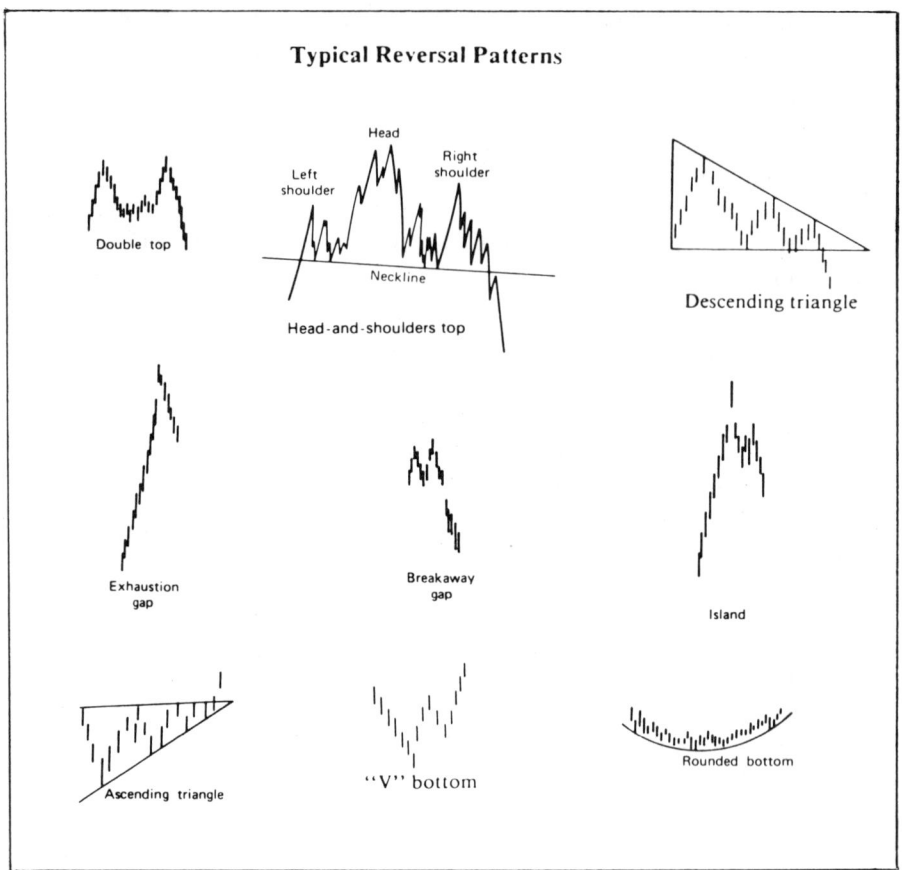

Figure 18.5

Occasionally, one sees "island" tops or bottoms on a chart. These occur when the reversal in trend is so sudden and dramatic that the market does not even trade at the next price level the following day leaving a "gap" in the chart. (You thought you knew all about gaps by now, huh?) The next day the market becomes exhausted and starts correcting for this overbought or oversold condition by gapping in the other direction.

The more common types of gaps, exhaustion and breakaway, also signal significant changes in market direction. Chartists are always watchful for gaps not only as a signal of strong market direction but because they have an old saying, "Gaps are always filled." Consequently, market technicians are vigilant for a temporary setback in prices until the gap price level is traded. Then they look for the new trend to continue.

These reversal patterns are quite useful in that they anticipate prices moving out a given channel well before that occurs. This greatly increases the market technician's market timing for entry or exit of positions and significantly increases the profitability of his trades.

Continuation Patterns—Many futures charts exhibit certain formations which indicate continued movement in prices in the same direction for an extended period of time. The most common of these continuation patterns are flags, pennants, and runaway gaps (see Figure 18.6).

Caused by market activity digesting or consolidating previous gains, these patterns most frequently occur mid-way in a given price move and enable a chartist to set some price objectives for the total move.

Point & Figure Patterns—Many of the formations described above which are found in bar charts also occur, and are used similarly, in point & figure charts. However, due to their uniqueness, point & figure charts also exhibit a number of other patterns which give chartists additional buy and sell indications (see Figure 18.7).

Price Objectives

Market technicians can glean more than just directional indications from a chart. They can also set price objectives for a particular market move based upon its component formations, angle, and duration. The calculation of anticipated price movement has been codified into a series of rules of thumb and measuring procedures. An example of one of these is pictured in Figure 18.8.

There are too many of these price setting techniques to cover here, including rules for flags, pennants, horizontal consolidation, and gaps, to mention a few. One important term to be aware of is "count." When a chartist (maybe your broker) says a contract has made its count, he means that the price has moved sufficiently to fulfill the anticipated price objective as set by common charting rules.

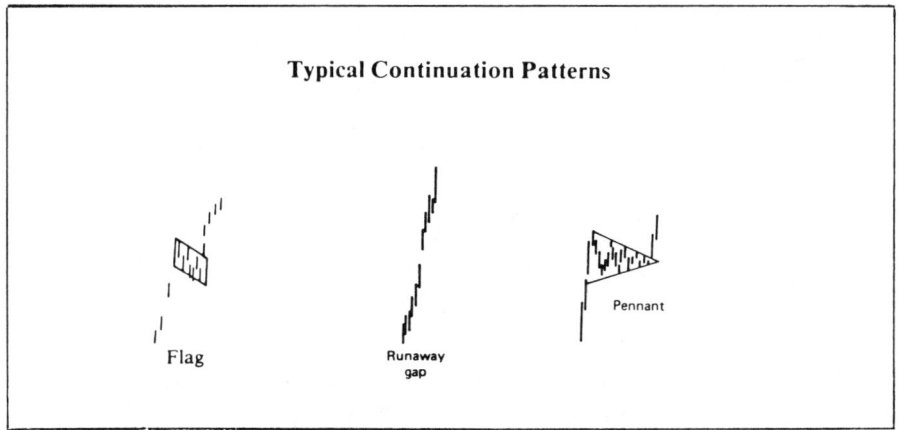

Typical Continuation Patterns

Flag

Runaway gap

Pennant

Figure 18.6

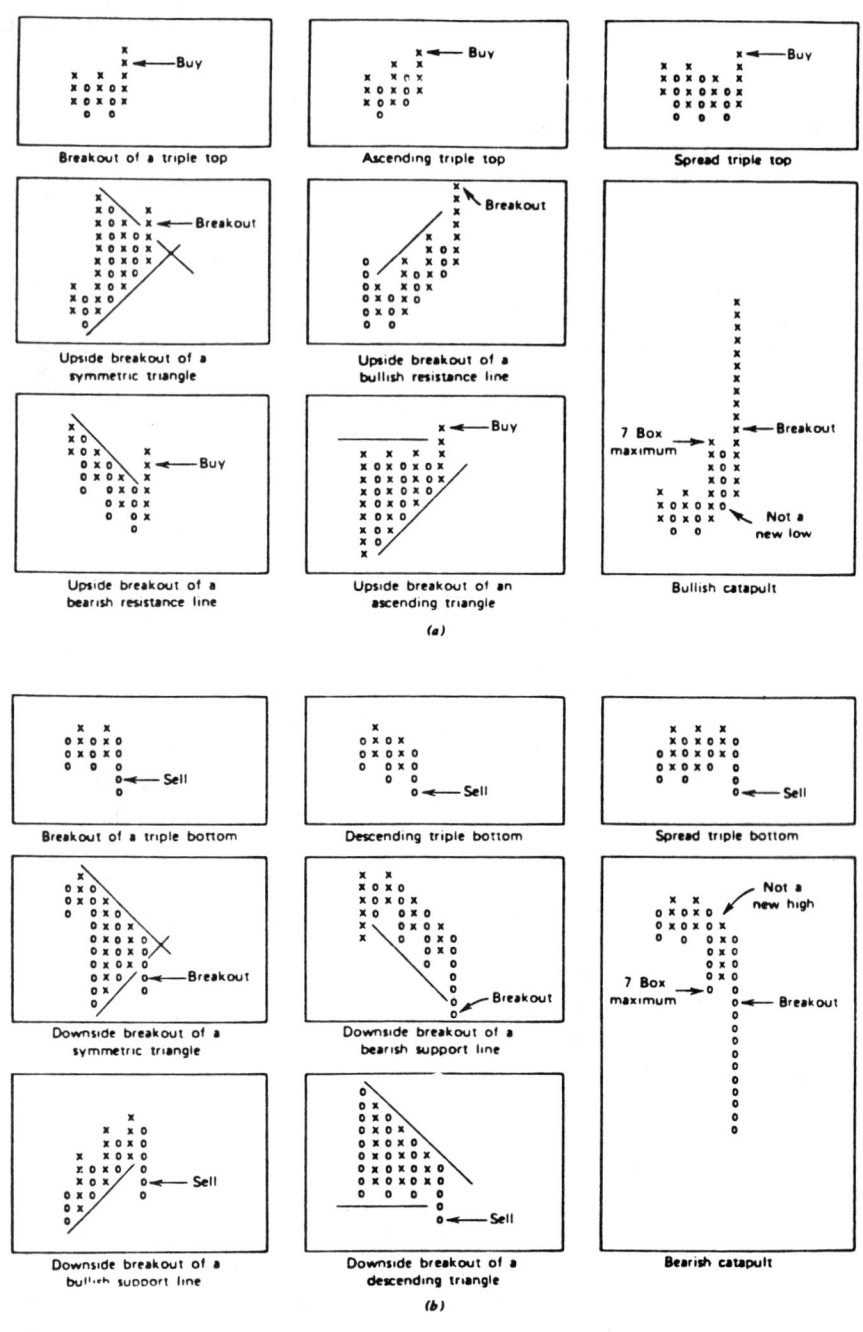

Figure 18.7. (a) Compound point-and-figure buy signals.
(b) Compound point-and-figure sell signals.

Source: Commodity Trading Systems & Methods by P.J. Kaufman

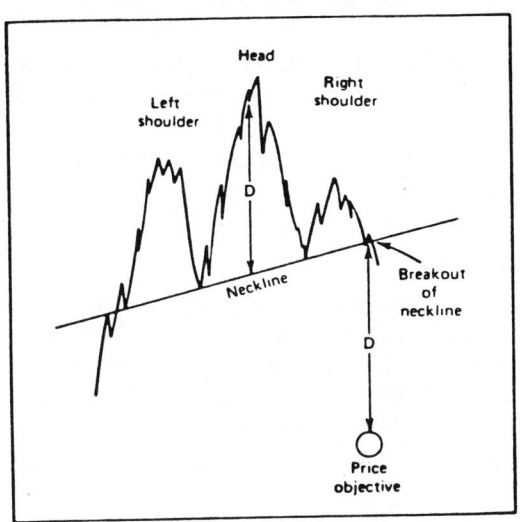

Figure 18.8. Price Objective of Head and Shoulders Formation
Source: Commodity Trading Systems & Methods by P.J. Kaufman

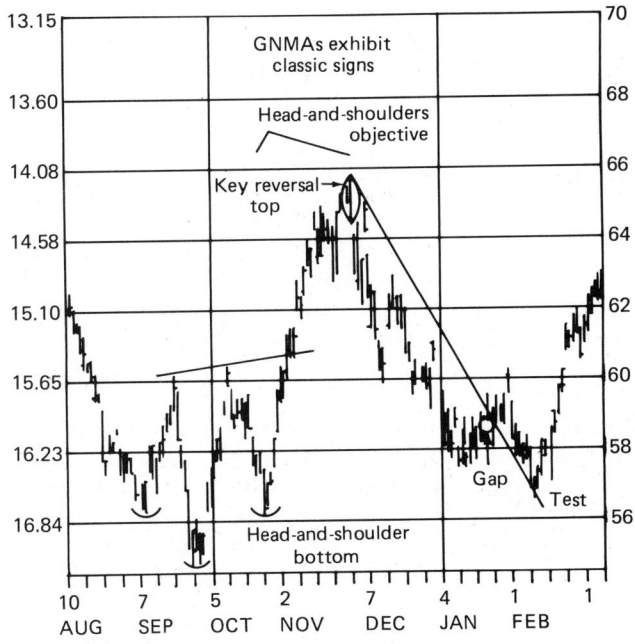

Figure 18.9

215

When trendlines and chart patterns are used in combination with accepted chart measuring techniques, one can get a fairly descriptive interpretation and idea of which direction and to what extent a particular market is currently anticipated to move. See Figure 18.9 for an example of an integrated chart analysis.

VOLUME & OPEN INTEREST

These two pieces of market information are also analyzed in conjunction with market direction on bar charts as an indication of whether a particular chart signal is accurate or short-lived. For example, rising prices on light volume accompanied by declining open interest is generally not considered to be bullish and the move may soon fail.

OTHER TECHNICAL SYSTEMS

Charts are only one part of a market technician's repertoire. There are many more analytical tools available to him which quantify and study market psychology or mathematically "massage" price activity. Using these, a technical elf can move, crossover, oscillate, regress (and sometimes digress) futures prices to his heart's content.

Market psychology can sometimes be assayed by studying commitments of small and large traders and watching the bullish consensus, a type of trader's voting exit poll. A more precise analysis of market potential is accomplished by using the panoply of mathematical techniques available.

MATHEMATICAL TECHNIQUES

Most of the mathematical techniques used in the analysis of futures markets are employed either to find or project a trend. We will only briefly describe some of the most popular ones.

Regression analysis is a curve-fitting routine which, when applied to futures price data, finds short-term trends which can then be projected to forecast prices in the near future.

Moving Averages

Probably the most popular of all the mathematically based market decision making systems is the moving average. It smooths the price movement to give a clearer picture of the true price trend by averaging the past x days' settlement prices. This process could be described mathematically as:

$$MA_n = \frac{P_1 + P_2 + \cdots + P_n}{N}$$

where N = number of days for the average and P = daily price. The following day a new price is averaged in while dropping the oldest price.

The number of days in a moving average can change one's perspective quite a bit, the fewer the days the more sensitive the average is to "noise." Technicians have done and continue to do numerous studies trying to find the optimum moving average for each futures contract to give accurate buy and sell signals. These signals are generated as follows:

> Buy when the price settles over the moving average
> Sell when the price settles under the moving average

Also, in the search for the Holy Grail, moving averages have been weighted and exponentially smoothed in the chance that this may increase their performance.

Another variation of the moving average system is the double moving average crossover system. In it two moving averages of different length (one short, the other longer) are calculated daily, and when they cross they generate buy/sell decisions as follows:

> Buy when the shorter moving average is larger than the longer moving average

> Sell when the shorter moving average is smaller than the longer moving average

This is graphically illustrated in Figure 18.10.

Some of the more popular double moving average systems are the five-and 20-day, four- and nine-, nine- and 18-day. Optimization studies are also run for each contract although each technician has his own combination that he swears by.

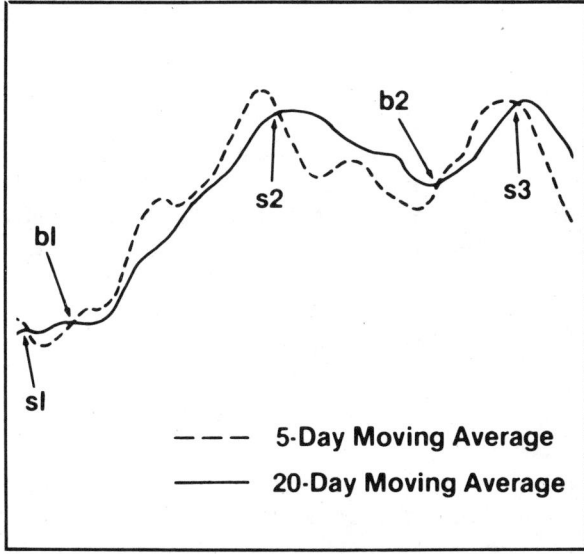

Figure 18.10

Momentum & Oscillators

Not only is the change in price levels studied but also the rate of change in prices as well. This is known as momentum and is calculated in the case of a five-day momentum value as today's price minus the price five days ago. This difference is calculated daily and plotted, giving its own buy and sell signals.

Since momentum fluctuates above and below a certain line, it may be said to oscillate. When technicians speak of oscillators, generally they are referring to the difference between two moving averages as plotted relative to a horizontal zero value line. (See Figure 18.11)

Relative Strength Index

A ratio of moving averages of up days to down days put into index form is known as the "relative strength index" or RSI. Divergence between prices on a bar chart and the corresponding RSI can be an important indicator of a market turning point. The two most common RSI periods are either nine or 14 days.

Cycles

Since futures price data are essentially time series, they can be analyzed for periodicity. Spectral analysis can indicate potential cycles in prices. Many technicians, looking for another market indicator, study both very short-term and very long-term cycles in price activity.

You will find that most cycle work is subject to variations in the periodicity, often as much as a week or two. Consequently, this market indicator can only give general price tendencies and needs to be coupled with other more precise indicators to determine market entry or exit timing.

RULE SYSTEMS

Charts or mathematical calculations are not the only technical indicators used by many market participants. Numerous systems of rules, both simple and complex, have been evolved over the years, claiming strong followings. Some names of the most popular ones are Donchian, Wilder, Gann, Elliott, and FiBonacci. (No, it's not the name of a law firm.) Also, some market technicians have also reached out to more exotic indicators from time to time to include even moon cycles and planetary cycles. If red squirrel population changes accurately forecasted interest rates, they would use it and so would you.

COMPUTER TRADING

A discussion of the world of technically based futures trading would not be complete without mentioning the impact of computers. Computers have great effects on the markets from time to time as large sums of pooled speculative money are guided by decisions generated by computer calculation of the various trend-following systems which we have been viewing.

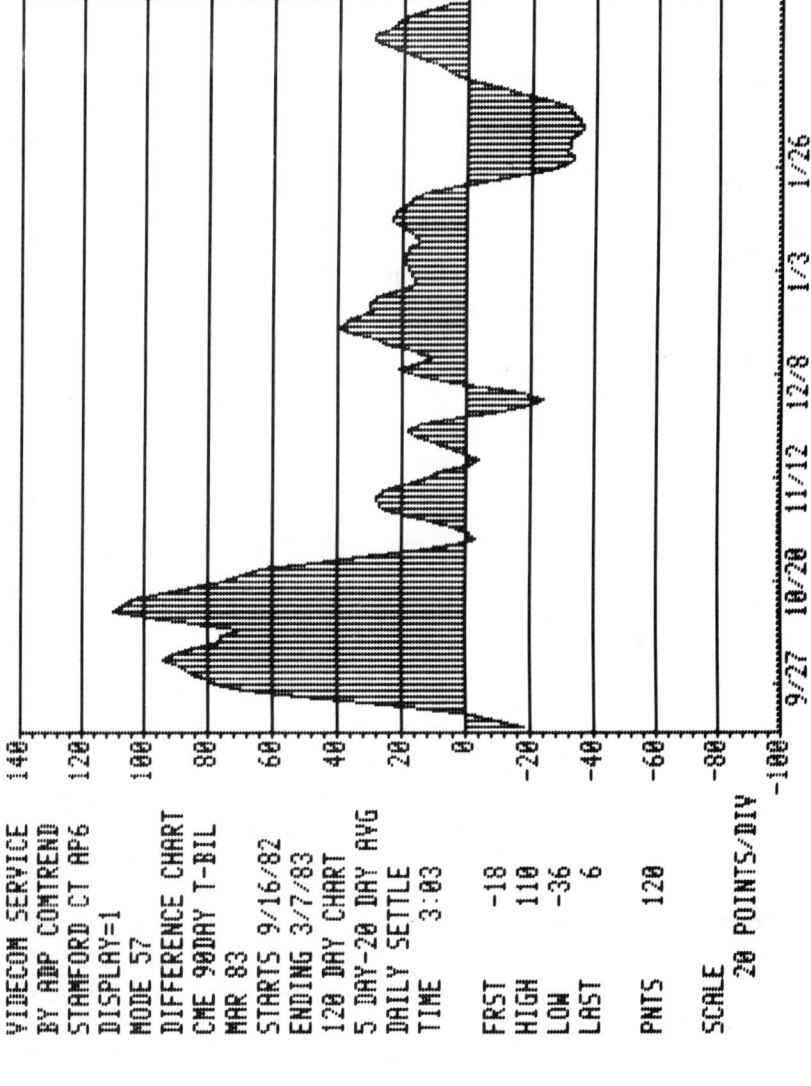

Figure 18.11 Oscillator Chart.

Since most use variations of the double moving average crossover system, they often kick in at the same time, generating what is known on the floor as "massive computer buying" or selling. It is good to be aware of these crucial market points as you may not want to stand in the way of a steam roller or may want to take advantage of an excessive price fluctuation due to this type of activity.

Technical Aids

Speaking of computers, the new micros have found their way into futures trading analysis. They are a natural for keeping track of all this market information and to do all the necessary number crunching. The Computrac software available for the Apple and IBM® PC microcomputer has more technical studies available than you could possibly want. Also computer-based but with a mainframe is the ADP Comtrend technical charting service we mentioned earlier. Besides charting, it also performs moving average, oscillator, and RSI calculations and presents them in tabular and/or graphic form.

If you wish to explore the world of technical analysis in greater detail you may find the following books helpful:

Technical Analysis of Stock Trends by Robert Edwards and John Magee (John Magee Inc., Springfield, Mass.)

Commodity Trading Systems and Methods by P.J. Kaufman (John Wiley & Sons, N.Y.)

BASIS TRADING _____

While crunching numbers and watching markets closely you may be able to take advantage of market opportunities to adjust your hedges for incremental increases in efficiency based on basis changes. This aggressive form of hedge management is known as "basis trading."

By studying historical basis relationships and tracking the current "normal" basis you may be able to use a strengthening or weakening basis to your advantage. You might lift a hedge when the basis starts to go against your position and re-establish it when the basis is more favorable. For example, a short hedger may remove his hedge when the basis strengthens beyond normal parameters and put it back on when the basis weakens. See Chapter 17 for a discussion of changing basis. Here we are concerned with its practical application.

The tools for basis trading are the basis charts which we described earlier and your hedge transaction register. You may have noticed that on the register sheet is a column marked basis. In this column you have the choice of recording the basis as defined earlier or "my basis." The basis is the difference in price or yield between the cash instrument and the futures instrument. "My basis" relates to the difference in price or yield in the futures and your particular coupon issue or the specific rate you are hedging. For example, the T-bond futures contract usually tracks with the longest issue Treasury bond. The basis relationship you and others will be watching in this case is, let's say, the March 83 contract and the 10 3/8 percent of 2007-12. You may actually be hedging the 7 5/8 percent of 2002-07 with the March contract. In this case the difference in that issue's price times the conversion factor .9637, and the March futures price is what you would consider "my basis."

One basis ("the" basis) gives you an indication of how the two markets are currently corresponding while the other ("my" basis) gives you your actual gain or loss on your hedge. If you trade the basis and record your transaction in terms of basis gained or lost, you can then add the results and determine that activity's contribution to overall hedge performance.

Basis trading can be useful when favorable opportunities arise; however, be careful not to lift hedges when the basis is going against your hedges hoping to make it back on the cash side. After all, you are hedging, and doing that defeats the purpose. In basis trading we are describing actions for opportunities that exist, not those that may exist.

With all these visions of charts and numbers dancing in our heads, let's return to the concrete world of the bottom line and see how futures hedging may affect your cash flow.

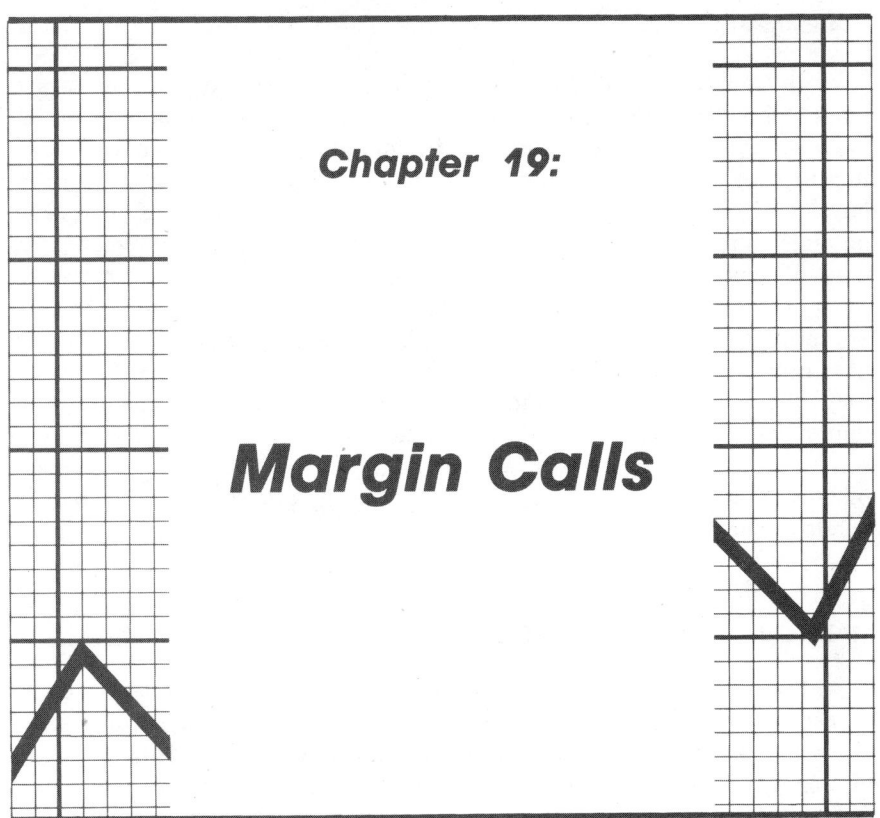

Chapter 19:

Margin Calls

CONGRATULATIONS! YOU have gotten approval from the board of directors to go ahead and start hedging for real. You are equipped with the latest technology in charting and technical trading systems. Your internal control mechanism has been pre-tested with two months of paper trading; your plan seems to work well. You have just sold an 18-month strip of 500 Treasury bill contracts to hedge your total portfolio of money market certificates. The next day someone you have never heard of calls from your brokerage house and tells you that if they don't receive $600,000 in cash by 11:30 a.m. you will be sold out of your position and you will owe the broker an additional $15,000 in commissions. Now what do you do? First, you do not panic, you don't jump out of the window, and you do not ignore this seeming idiot on the phone. You call your broker for confirmation of the margin call. If it's correct you order a wire for $600,000 to the broker. See, it's all very simple and very orderly. It's just that kissing $600,000 goodbye is not a lot of fun. If you think you need to know more about margin calls, you are right. Read on.

In Chapter 4 we discussed briefly the concept of margin in the futures market and its relationship to daily price limits. To reiterate what you already know, margin is a performance bond required of all participants to insure that they will make or take delivery at the maturity of their contracts if they haven't offset their position prior to maturity. There are initial margin requirements for initiating a trade, and maintenance margin requirements that must be kept up as long as a position is open. The margin requirements are set by the exchange for each contract traded on that exchange. These requirements are subject to change as market conditions vary. The exchanges' minimum margin requirements may be increased by individual brokers if they choose. Speculative trading normally imposes higher margin requirements than hedge trading. Now that your memory is refreshed about some of the basics of margin, we will continue with an in-depth discussion of how to manage your margin account, or why you do not jump out the window when you get that $600,000 margin call.

MANAGING THE MARGIN ACCOUNT

The purpose of margin in the futures market goes beyond a performance bond to insure the integrity of trades. The additional function of margin is to support the daily mark-to-market accounting system used by all exchanges. This system is best understood by contrasting a futures contract with a forward contract. Suppose you enter into a forward contract with someone to buy a $100,000 Treasury bond at par 10 days hence. The bond is selling at par now but declines by $100 per day over the 10-day period. Under the terms of the forward contract you are obligated to pay $100,000 for a bond that you could have bought elsewhere for $99,000; you have lost $1000 on the transaction. On the other side of the contract, the seller of the bond has made $1000 by being able to sell you a bond now worth $99,000 for the previously agreed-upon price of $100,000. During the 10-day period of the forward contract the profit and loss continues to accrue but no money actually changes hands. In the futures market it does not work this way. The existence of margin and the daily mark-to-market system insures that the money being lost or gained actually changes hands every day. Taking this same transaction in the futures market, here's what would happen: You go long a Treasury bond contract at a price of 100 and put up an initial margin of $2000. For the next five days $100 is subtracted from your margin account at the end of the day. On the sixth day $100 is subtracted and you have to put up more money. Your account will be down to $1400, which is below the minimum maintenance margin, so it will have to be restored to the initial margin level of $2000. At the end of 10 days when you offset your position with a sale, the money in the margin account is free for any further use including withdrawal by the customer, less the $1000 that you lost; you made total deposits of $2600 and you get back $1600 less commissions.

On the other side of the contract is the person who shorted the Treasury bond. That trader's margin account is increased by $100 every day until the contract matures or the short position is offset. That trader also started with $2000 initial margin. Every day as his account is augmented by $100, he could withdraw that money if he chose to do so. At the end of the 10-day period he has either $3000 in his margin account or $3000 less whatever he has withdrawn during the 10 days.

The chief difference, then, between the forward market and the futures market is that winners take their profits at the end of every day and losers must pay over their losses at the end of every day. The clearing corporation of the exchange keeps track of all the winners and all the losers on open contracts every day and notifies the clearing firms what their net margin position is each day. It is the clearing member that notifies you, the customer, what your net position and account balance is each day. In essence, the clearing corporation calculates the net effect of offsetting each position at the settlement price each day and then re-establishing the position at that same price the next morning. They don't actually do that, of course, but the effect of the daily mark-to-market system is the same. If you want to hedge your portfolio with futures contracts you simply have to play by these rules. However, you need not be hog-tied by them.

Even if you lose money on your position, you may not always have to wire in more money. All margin requirements are determined on a consolidated basis. All gains and losses on all positions are added together to determine the margin account balance. Suppose that you have open positions in several contracts simultaneously. For example, you are short Treasury bills, Treasury bonds, and CDs all at the same time. (You may well have a position like this; it depends on your hedging strategy.) On a given day Treasury bond prices may rise and you lose money on that position. If the prices of T-bills and CDs fell that day, you would make money on those positions. In the consolidated margin system, if the gain on the bills and CDs is equal to or greater than the loss in the bonds, you will not have to add more margin money.

Meeting a margin call involves wiring Fed funds to your broker. Although you can put up the initial margin by depositing a Treasury bill, meeting margin deficiencies must be done in cash, or "good funds." Since the broker must deposit cash with the clearing corporation, he will want cash from you. The broker is required to put up additional margin on the day it is due—he will not wait until the next day to get it from a customer. Should a customer fail to meet a margin call, the broker can reverse the customer's position and then bill him for whatever additional funds are due.

Taking the other side of the coin for a moment, what happens if you have excess margin in your account? Chances are, the broker will *not* call you to let you know that you can take money out. You will have to call him and ask. Most brokerage firms make a large part of their profit by investing their customers' excess margin in Fed funds or Treasury bills overnight if it is not wired out by 4:00 p.m. each day. If you are a large futures trader, *and you insist on it*, the broker should invest your excess margin in Fed funds or Treasury bills to your benefit rather than to the benefit of the brokerage house. If your broker will not do this for you, your options are to wire the money out yourself or find a broker who will do it. When to wire money out, how frequently, and in what amounts is a somewhat complicated topic which we will take up in a moment. For now, though, let's look at an example of how a margin account would fluctuate over a month's trading.

The following example indicates what would have happened to a margin account supporting a short position of 100 March 83 Treasury bill contracts during December 1982. For the example, it was assumed that a hedger sold the 100 contracts on the IMM on December 1st at a price of 92.44, made no other trades during the month, and covered the position on December 31st. The table shows, for each day the position was open, the settlement price for that day, the change in the settlement price from the previous day, the change in equity that occurred that day, the required margin, the equity balance in the margin account, and the amount that that balance is in excess or deficient regarding margin requirements.

Although the results of this trade would have been negative overall, the issue at hand is the management of the margin account. Even though it is possible to withdraw excess funds from the account, it is not always advisable to do so. Frequently, gains made one day will be wiped out by losses in the next day's trading session. The most disconcerting days during December were the 3d, when a $167,500 margin deficiency occurred and the 14th, which racked up a $72,000 margin call. Meeting those margin calls is absolutely essential if you wish to hold onto your position. However, this is not what we mean by managing a margin account.

Managing a margin account is not appreciably different from managing a deposit account. The objective is to make deposits and withdrawals so as to minimize the amount of idle balances. Unlike a checking account you can't wire out a margin account at 4:00 p.m. every day. You can get close to that, though. Referring to Table 19.1, look at the margin balance for December 8. At the end of the day there were excess funds of $80,000. Suppose the hedge wired out the $80,000 excess funds that day. For the next five days the account would have looked like Table 19.2 below:

As it turns out, in this case, withdrawing the excess margin would not have been a good idea since you would then have been left with having to meet two margin calls on the 13th and 14th for a total of $153,000. All well and good, you say, but how do you know when it is the right time to withdraw excess funds and when it is the wrong time? Most of the time you will be better off *not* withdrawing excess funds. It can be seen from just one month's trading that more than 50 percent of the margin account balance

TABLE 19.1:
Margin Account Summary

Contract Position: Short 100 Mar83 T-bills at 91.20 on December 1, 1982; Initial Margin = $250,000, Maintenance Margin = $200,000

Date	Settlement Price	Price Change	Gain or Loss	Equity Balance	Excess or Deficit
12/1	91.19	-.01	2,500	252,500	2,500
12/2	91.40	+.21	-52,500	200,000	0
12/3	91.87	+.47	-117,500	82,500	-167,500
12/6	91.79	-.08	+20,000	270,000	20,000
12/7	91.73	-.06	+15,000	285,000	35,000
12/8	91.55	-.18	+45,000	330,000	80,000
12/9	91.73	+.18	-45,000	285,000	35,000
12/10	91.50	-.23	+57,500	342,500	92,500
12/13	91.76	+.26	-62,000	280,500	30,500
12/14	92.17	+.41	-102,500	178,000	-72,000
12/15	92.23	+.06	-15,000	235,000	0
12/16	92.10	-.13	+32,500	267,500	17,500
12/17	91.98	-.12	+30,000	297,500	47,500
12/20	91.96	-.02	+5,000	302,500	52,500
12/21	92.15	+.19	-47,500	255,000	5,000
12/22	92.06	-.09	+22,500	277,500	27,500
12/23	92.08	+.02	-5,000	272,500	22,500
12/27	92.19	+.11	-27,500	245,000	0
12/28	92.09	-.10	+25,000	270,000	20,000
12/29	91.98	-.11	+27,500	297,500	47,500
12/30	92.10	+.12	-30,000	267,500	17,500
12/31	92.28	+.18	-45,000	222,500	0

TOTAL DEPOSITS: $489,500

FUNDS WITHDRAWN: $222,500

LOSS: $267,000

TABLE 19.2:
Managed Margin Account

$80,000 Withdrawn on December 8

Date	Settlement Price	Price Change	Gain or Loss	Equity Balance	Excess or Deficit
12/8	91.55	−.18	+45,000	250,000	0
12/9	91.73	+.18	−45,000	205,000	0
12/10	91.50	−.23	+57,500	262,500	7,500
12/13	91.76	+.26	−65,000	197,500	− 52,500
12/14	92.17	+.41	−102,500	147,500	−102,500

TABLE 19.3:
Margin Account Summary

Contract Position: Short 100 Mar83 T-bills at 91.20 on December 1, 1982; Initial Margin = $500,000, Maintenance Margin = $200,000

Date	Settlement Price	Price Change	Gain or Loss	Equity Balance
12/1	91.19	− .01	+ 2,500	502,500
12/2	91.40	+ .21	− 52,500	450,000
12/3	91.87	+ .47	− 117,500	332,500
12/6	91.79	− .08	+ 20,000	352,500
12/7	91.73	− .06	+ 15,000	367,500
12/8	91.55	− .18	+ 45,000	412,500
12/9	91.73	+ .18	− 45,000	367,500
12/10	91.50	− .23	+ 57,500	425,000
12/13	91.76	+ .26	− 62,000	363,000
12/14	92.17	+ .41	− 102,500	260,500
12/15	92.23	+ .06	− 15,000	245,500
12/16	92.10	− .13	+ 32,500	278,000
12/17	91.98	− .12	+ 30,000	308,000
12/20	91.96	− .02	+ 5,000	313,000
12/21	92.15	+ .19	− 47,500	265,500
12/22	92.06	− .09	+ 22,500	288,000
12/23	92.08	+ .02	− 5,000	283,000
12/27	92.19	+ .11	− 27,500	255,500
12/28	92.09	− .10	+ 25,000	280,200
12/29	91.98	− .11	+ 27,500	308,000
12/30	92.10	+ .12	− 30,000	278,000
12/31	92.28	+ .18	− 45,000	233,000
TOTAL DEPOSITS:			$500,000	
FUNDS WITHDRAWN:			$233,000	
LOSS:			$267,000	

can be made or lost in one day. This argues strongly for not touching the excess funds—why wire it out today and then have to wire it right back tomorrow? It may even be advisable to open a position with excess funds *on purpose*. Doing so may allow you to avoid having to meet any margin calls at all. Remember, exchange rules specify the *minimum* margin—there is no maximum. If you have the right brokerage firm you will be earning interest on most of the money in your account, so putting up excess funds from the beginning entails no opportunity cost in terms of lost earnings on liquid assets. Consider the example in Table 19.3. In this example the hedge is up *double margin* when the position was opened.

By putting up double margin at the beginning this hedger avoided meeting two margin calls totaling $242,500 and had to meet no margin calls during the month. By holding $500,000 initial margin against a position requiring $250,000 margin, there was an enormous amount of excess margin in the account most of the time. Under the exchange rules a margin account that falls below the required maintenance margin level must be brought back to the level required for initial margin. This never occurred in December, as Table 19.3 indicates. The largest loss in one day, $117,500, left an excess balance in the account of $82,500 so that no additional deposits were required. Since the margin account balance will frequently flip-flop on consecutive days, that extra margin in the account will cushion your position and result in fewer and smaller margin calls. The costs of doing so are nearly zero, *if you have sufficient liquidity to do it*.

The decision to put up excess margin at the beginning, when to wire money out, and how much to wire out are the key decisions to be made in managing an account. These decisions hinge largely on the size of the account and on the type of hedging being conducted. A bank or savings and loan which does a substantial amount of hedging should have a totally different approach to managing a margin account than an institution which does limited hedging. It's a simple proposition, really; the bigger the pie the more opportunities there are for creative slicing.

The first consideration in managing an account is the size of the account. Consider a $1 billion bank that hedges 40 percent of its deposit liabilities, which are distributed as follows:

Deposit Liability	Amount (millions)
Checking/NOW	$200
Passbook savings	120
MMCs	250
MMAs	150
Large CDs	80
TOTAL	$800

As a matter of policy the bank has decided not to try to hedge checking/NOW accounts or passbook savings accounts ($320 million) and only to hedge two-thirds of its other deposits. These accounts—MMCs, MMAs, and CDs—total $480 million, so the bank's maximum open futures position will be $570 million. The bank's MMA is tied to the long-term Treasury yield so it will hedge those accounts with T-bond futures. MMCs are hedged with T-bills (2 for 1 to insure dollar equivalency) and CDs are hedged with CD futures. For a simple hedge the bank would short 1500 T-bonds, 500 T-bills, and 80 CD futures, a total of 2080 contracts. The required initial margin is now $4.45 million; minimum maintenance margin is $4.16 million. If the bank chooses to use a strip hedge, the margin is increased proportionately by the increased number of contracts the strip requires.

This hedge structure allows the hedger more flexibility in managing a margin account than a hedge that consisted of only one type of contract. A basket of futures contracts will seldom exhibit the same price variation of any single contract in the basket. Even though all interest rates, and financial futures prices, do tend to move in the same direction *in the long run*, they frequently move in opposite directions *in the short run*. It is not unusual for bond prices to fall on the same day that bills and CDs rise. Consolidation of margin accounts will offer the bank some insulation from margin calls should this occur. The bank's position in T-bills and CDs may require additional margin *on their own*, but this may be offset by a gain on the 1500 bond contracts. In this example, a drop in the bond price of 2/32ds would offset a six basis point rise in both bills and CDs, leaving the bank's margin account, in fact, slightly over the required initial level (1500 x 2 x $31.25 = $93,750 and 580 x 6 x $25.00 = $87,000).

Actual trading experience with a specific portfolio and a specific hedging strategy will be the best guide in deciding when to wire excess funds out of the account. In general, however, the larger the position and the greater the diversity of contract types, the lower is the risk of withdrawing excess funds. Risk in this context means the possibility of having to meet a margin call the day after excess funds were withdrawn. Funds supporting a large futures position in multiple contracts should be held at the minimum required level during "normal" market sessions. If the futures markets become extremely volatile, additional margin should be held. It will probably be required, anyway, as the exchange doubles or triples margin requirements in an attempt to keep pace with the market's fluctuations.

Consider now a small savings and loan association ($100 million) which has the following deposit structure:

Deposit Liability	Amount ($ millions)
Checking/NOW	$20
Passbooks	12
MMCs	25
MMAs	15
Large CDs	8
TOTAL	$80

The association has decided not to try to hedge its checking/NOW accounts or its passbook savings accounts. It has decided to hedge 100 percent of its other deposit liabilities. This association's MMA is tied to the T-bill rate so it would hedge both MMAs and MMCs with T-bill futures. It hedges its CDs with CD futures. The maximum position the association would have is 80 T-bill contracts and 8 CD contracts, a total of 88 futures contracts at one time. (Again, strip hedges are ignored for now.) The initial margin for this hedge would be $220,000.

In this situation the savings and loan association is not afforded the flexibility in managing its margin account to the extent that the bank had in the previous example. The savings and loan is hedging its liabilities solely with short-term money market instruments. The correlation between three-month CD rates and three-month Treasury bill rates is so high that it is unlikely that one of these futures contracts would go up when the other one went down. If the market moves against the association's position—rates fall and prices rise—it will lose ground on both contracts together and will ultimately have to meet a margin call. There are no other futures positions which might show a gain the same day, thereby forestalling a margin call. However, holding a double initial margin would. This argues for holding excess funds if one's futures position is highly concentrated in one contract or in contracts which have a high price correlation among them.

Consider now the possibility of strip hedging either of these liability portfolios. As you recall, a strip hedge is one in which the hedger shorts several contracts for different delivery months as a way of extending the duration of a hedge out into the future. Suppose that the bank in our example used a 3-6-9 month strip hedge on all of the liabilities that it was hedging. It would now be shorting 750 T-bill contracts against its MMCs—250 contracts in the nearby month, 250 in the next contract month, and 250 contracts in the next delivery month after that. That is, if it began in January it would short 250 March contracts, 250 June, and 250 September contracts. Similarly, it would also short 240 CD contracts against its CDs, and 4500 Treasury bond contracts against its MMAs, all split equally among three delivery months. The initial margin requirement for the 5490 contracts would be $11.475 million, with a minimum maintenance level of $10.98 million.

With this variety of contracts the insulation factor from margin calls is even greater than in the simple hedge example. The bank is actually short nine different types of contracts—three T-bills, three CDs, and three T-bonds. In addition to the difference in variability among contracts for different securities, there is variability among different delivery months for the same type of contracts. The price of March T-bills not only behaves differently from the price of March bonds, it also behaves differently from that of June T-bills and September T-bills. If March bills went up by the same amount that June bills went down, the bank's margin position would be unaffected. To see the logic of this proposition one need only look at the activities of spreaders in the futures market. If the prices of different contract months *did not* vary by different amounts and in different directions, there would be no profit in spreading and therefore no spreaders in the market. This is demonstrably not the case. Introducing strip hedges into the margin account equation simply adds more diversity into one's futures position, which reduces the possibility, somewhat, of having to meet margin calls.

The same premise would hold for the small savings and loan association. Instead of shorting 48 contracts to hedge its MMCs, MMAs, and CDs it would short 144 contracts. Despite the fact that the association would still only be hedged with futures contracts representing the shortest-term securities, it would lower its margin risk by being spread out over three delivery months rather than one. This does not introduce the degree of diversity inherent in the bank's position in different types of contracts but it does help. In short, *greater diversity in one's futures position reduces the need to hold excess funds. In any event, actual experience with a specific portfolio and a specific hedge will always be the best guide to margin account management techniques and strategies*. The principles outlined here represent only the basics of margin account management necessary to get you started. Your own experience, and the experience of your broker or consultant, will more fully round out your strategy.

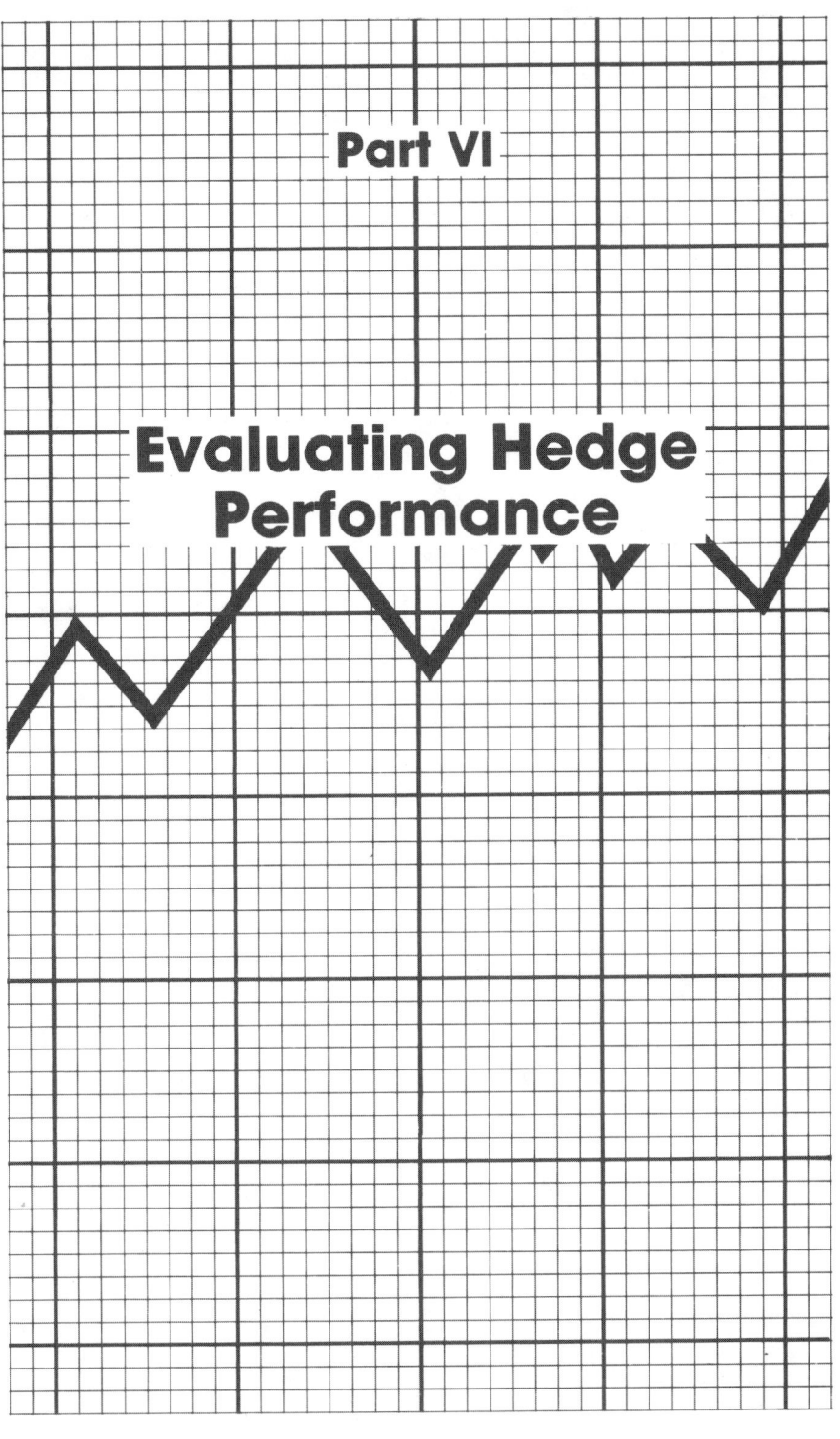

Part VI

Evaluating Hedge Performance

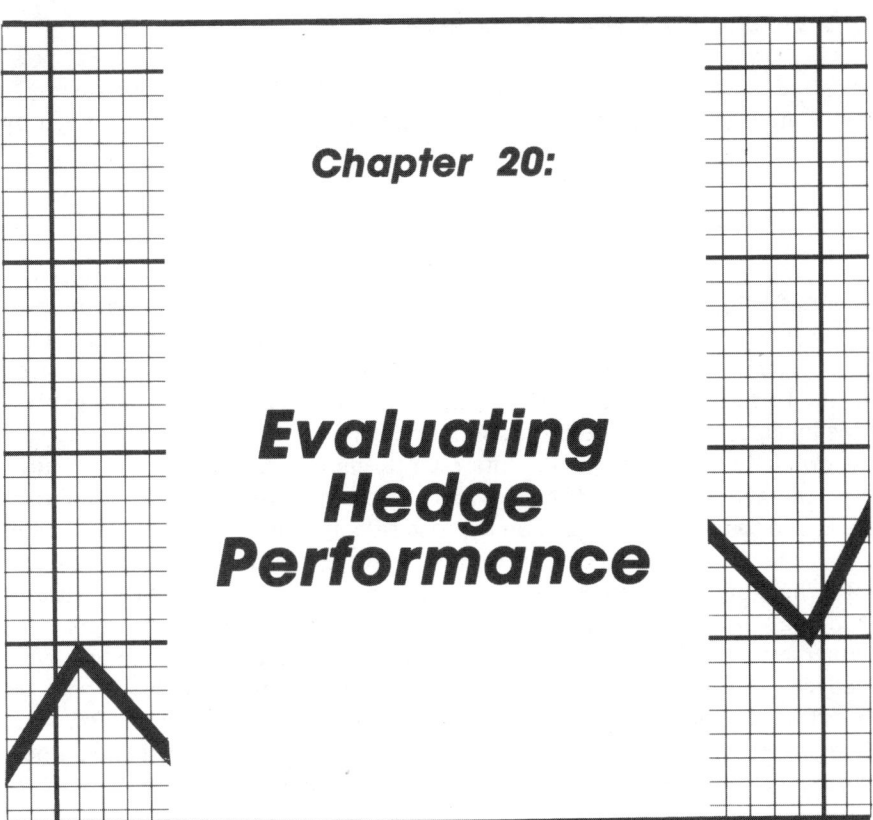

Chapter 20:

Evaluating Hedge Performance

JUST AS with any other program which your institution undertakes, there is the need to measure the success of a futures hedging program. The ultimate consideration is: Is it working and to what extent?

IS IT WORKING?

In order to answer this question you must first review your hedge plan objectives. What percentage of the institution was to be hedged? Did you identify your risk? Were you trying to eliminate a specific gap or hedge only a specific liability? What was a tolerable rate you were trying to lock in? What interest rate forecast scenario were these objectives based upon?

After reviewing your objectives, you need to divide the program into components to be measured and evaluated individually, as well as the net overall effect of the program. This is important as the overall answer to whether you have reduced your risk may be favorable enough, but not indicative of where problems or improvements could be found. This component analysis will not only give you a clearer picture but also will open up avenues for increased hedge efficiency and performance.

MEASUREMENT

Before proceeding with the components we should discuss measurement of hedge performance. If you are going to evaluate your hedging program, what do you measure and against what are you going to compare?

The most logical measurement is how much your risk has been reduced in the form of lower net cost of funds or reduced gap. You could express this by calculating the dollar amount of gain on the futures as a percentage of dollar loss due to adverse interest rate movement. This ratio is called "percentage recapture." If there was a loss on the futures side, it should then be added to the resultant gain on the cash side, giving you a net effective rate.

The most obvious comparison to be made in evaluating the usefulness of a hedging program is: What would your position have been without hedging? Since this is a competitive world (yes, now even for bankers, too) you may want to compare your institution's overall performance, both hedged and unhedged, against a model institution or an index of bank or S & L performance. When you view it in this manner you can see how your hedging program has contributed to an increase in overall institutional performance. Now, let's proceed with the component analysis.

HEDGE POLICY

The first component to examine is your hedging policy. This includes the decision making process on rate forecasting, when to hedge, what to hedge, how much of the institution to hedge, and whether or not to use a selective hedging strategy.

When evaluating your hedge policy the primary factor to look for is whether your strategy is highly dependent upon your ability as a rate forecaster. If it is, you have fairly well defeated much of the use of a hedging program, which is to protect you from adverse moves in interest rates against the way you have positioned the institution.

Also, when reviewing your hedging policy, attention should be given to see how responsive your preset selective hedging parameters were in removing hedges and replacing them versus actual rate changes. Is your plan too slow or hair-trigger sensitive? Did it keep you hedged when there was erratic market activity but questionable direction of rates?

HEDGE DESIGN

The second component for review is how you have structured your hedges. Did you choose contracts with high enough correlation to what you were hedging? Did you accurately calculate the size of the hedge for the time period of the risk? Did you put on enough contracts using a weighting factor to compensate for volatility or price compression?

Also, when structuring your hedges did you elect to use a continuing roll-over type of hedge versus a strip? Did you choose appropriate months with enough liquidity? Did you have to compromise and design your hedge as a hybrid due to the lack of depth of some new contracts? When hedging loans did you properly calculate the period at risk and reduce the size of the hedge when your remaining risk was reduced?

HEDGE IMPLEMENTATION

The third component to evaluate is how well you implemented your hedge plans. Did you place your hedges when your plan and market conditions called for them? Or, did you wait a little to see if things would get better and consequently miss 25 percent of the move and the resultant protection? Was the basis relationship normal to favorable when you placed the hedges? Or, did you place them without any regard to basis and have convergence working against your hedge for the rest of the time?

When you placed your hedges what type of orders did you use? Did you fixate upon a certain price and place limit orders, only to miss placing your hedge by an 02 and then be forced to chase the market or, worse yet, not get your hedge on at the right time? Did you place stop loss orders too close for normal market activity or within a much watched trend channel?

HEDGE MONITORING AND MANAGING

The fourth component to examine is your monitoring and managing of the hedges and hedge process. Was there someone with trading authority always available and aware of market activities? Did you keep in contact with your broker for new developments and to learn of the sentiment of other market participants? Did you keep your technical charts up-to-date including all the major chart points?

If you were selectively hedging, what technical indicators were you using for market decisions? Did they accurately give indications of subsequent market activity? If not, which ones are you considering as replacements?

Also, review your record keeping. Did you log all transactions, pegging each hedge to a specific hedgeable risk? Were you able to determine quickly your total outstanding futures position at any given moment? Is your log adequately annotated to explain unusual activity? Are your internal control procedures adequately double checking all transactions and do they tie in with accounting's figures?

Review the management of your cash flow regarding your hedges. Did you maintain adequate balances at the brokerage firm and meet margin calls promptly? Did you have excess funds wired back to you so they would not sit idle? Were you forced to meet very large margin calls due to the board's inflexibility (or downright stubbornness) about not lifting hedges?

Also regarding the monitoring of your hedges, were the directors regularly and clearly informed about the institution's futures position and its impact on the firm?

BASIS CHANGE

The fifth component of your hedge review is an examination of the basis relationships both when you put on your hedges and during the life of the hedges.

Did the basis change during the life of your hedge? Did this change work to your advantage or disadvantage on your hedges? Could you have better anticipated these basis changes by studying historical relationships? Or, were these changes out of the norm due to unusual market conditions?

What was the amount of basis risk that you exchanged for rate risk? In dollar amounts was this an acceptable amount of risk? If not, what type of alternative hedging strategy would have given you a greater amount of protection?

HEDGE RESULTS

The sixth item to evaluate is not a component but the result of each particular hedge and the net overall effect of all the hedges cumulatively.

For each hedge calculate the dollar amount of cost increase or decrease of the cash side and the dollar amount of gain or loss of the futures side. Expressed as a percentage, how much of the loss was recaptured by using the hedge? What was the net effective rate with the hedge?

Repeat this process, totalling the results of all the hedges to obtain similar cumulative results. Overall, did the hedging program provide you with the amount of protection that you had anticipated? Did you hedge too much or not enough? Did you reduce your gap(s) to the extent desired? Or, did you unwittingly create undesired gaps and therefore more, instead of less, risk? Did you fail to lift hedges at appropriate times thereby creating an opportunity loss?

Stepping back from all these trees, generally did your hedging program result in providing your institution with a measure of stability in a volatile rate environment? And, even more important, compared to your competition, did your hedging program give you a competitive advantage either in the form of lower cost of funds or more attractive loan products?

REVIEW OF THE CONCEPT OF HEDGING

About this time when you are presenting the results of your hedging program (especially if there are "losses" on the futures side of the transactions) you may be confronted with the situation of directors questioning the usefulness of the program. After all, if you hadn't done the futures hedges, look at what your rates could have been. This is the time at which you must go back to square one and refresh their memories about the whole concept of hedging. What would they say if the rate scenario was quite different and you didn't hedge? What would the bottom line of the institution look like then? In fact, would it even be in existence at all?

For some strange reason many financial executives can quite readily accept (but not like) loan losses and lower profitability due to higher cost of funds, but when it comes to futures they somehow equate it with avoidable risk. Perhaps this is due to all the press attention that speculation in futures has received in the past. We hope this will change as they and their peers learn of other institutions using futures and hear of their contribution to the bottom line and financial stability.

In any event, this is the moment of truth regarding your hedging program. It is at this point that you will learn how much the directors understand about true risk in banking and, more important, how to minimize it. Of course, if the futures side of the equation has "gains," you'll be considered a hero and may never know if they truly understand what you are doing.

COULD IT WORK BETTER?

As with most things there is always room for improvement. Without overdoing the "would haves," "could haves," and "should haves," you should review each of the components of your hedging program with an eye to altering it based on your experiences and new developments in the field.

Looking back is easy, but was your hedging program flexible enough to protect you in any number of interest rate scenarios? Or, did you just get lucky? Hedging, as our examples have shown, is not a seat-of-the-pants procedure but requires a fair amount of analytical skills to be applied. Perhaps you should consider adding staff to the operation or seek outside help.

Below is a summary of the components with some key areas in which to seek improvement:

- Hedge Policy–how much and what to hedge
- Hedge Design–size calculations and structure (rollover vs. strip, etc.)
- Hedge Implementation–when-timing, basis, technical indicators
- Monitoring & Managing–internal control procedures and selective hedging indicators
- Basis Changes–historical parameters and influences

Your psychological responses to market and business conditions need to be reviewed for improvement also. Did fear of futures (either yours or the board's) cause you to be overly cautious to the extent that you did not carry out your hedging plan fully or waited too long to put on the hedges? Did you try to second guess interest rates and override your plan as a result? Did all that optimistic talk from the Federal Reserve sway your judgment? Did the prospect of actually having to meet a six-figure margin call prompt you to lift your hedges at just the wrong time?

HOW OFTEN TO EVALUATE?

What is a practical review period for a hedging program? That depends at what stage you are (introductory, intermediate, or advanced) and on how much you are doing.

Initially, you'll want to review the program at the end of the first few hedges. If you start with hedging six-month MMCs you'll probably assess the program's effectiveness after six months along with monthly progress reports to keep you alert to any problems before then.

After you've graduated to an ongoing hedging program, you will probably want to continue with monthly progress reports and do a more thorough hedge effectiveness analysis both quarterly and annually. Of course, if you are hedging very large sums you may want to speed up this timetable, especially for shorter-term hedges which can show results more rapidly, so as to avert any substantial losses caused by a misapplication of hedging techniques.

After you have evaluated your program, you may find that it is working moderately well with room for some minor improvement. In the event that you find that you are "off track," so to speak, you need to back up through the hedging process step by step, re-evaluating each hedge component in reverse order to that presented in this chapter. At the very worst you'll be back to the start, questioning your basic hedging plan and exactly what your risk is. More than likely, however, you will find that you need to re-vamp or optimize your technical indicators for entry or exit of hedges, as well as reassess volatility factors as the interest rate environment changes.

NEXT TIME

We all learn by doing and futures are no exception. In fact you can dry run on paper for a long time but it's not the same as a "live" market. Your perception and responses change when there is real money at stake. The only real way to learn how to do it is by actually going and doing it. You'll be surprised at how quickly you will speed up your learning curve by just testing the water with a one-contract pilot program.

Once you have some experience with market activity you can proceed to a more reasonable test of a hedge strategy. With feedback from your first few hedges you should then have a moderate amount of experience and be comfortable enough to proceed with a full-fledged hedging program.

From then on, you'll be constantly expanding your experience base, trying new strategies, and discovering new techniques and applications of futures hedging to reduce risk.

Appendix A: Futures Trading Regulations for Commercial Banks

The following documents:

Banking Circular 79 (3rd Rev), Office of the Comptroller of the Currency,

Policy Statement Concerning Forward Placement or Delayed Delivery Contracts and Interest Rate Futures Contracts, Federal Reserve Board,

Revised Statement of Policy Concerning Interest Rate Futures Contracts, Forward Contracts, And Standby Contracts, Federal Deposit Insurance Corporation,

represent the most up to date regulations concerning the use of financial futures by commercial banks as of May 1, 1983.

B C-79(3rd Rev.)

BANKING ISSUANCE

Comptroller of the Currency
Administrator of National Banks

Type: Banking Circular	Subject: National Bank Participation in the Financial Futures and Forward Placement Markets

TO: Chief Executive Officers of All National Banks, Deputy
Comptrollers (District) and Regional Administrators

This circular is a revision of Banking Circular 79 (2nd Rev.) issued
on March 19, 1980, which is withdrawn. Banking Circular 79 was
originally issued on November 2, 1976. The circular was amended by
the issuance of Banking Circular 79, Supplement 1, on August 1,
1977. Banking Circular 79 and Supplement 1 were withdrawn on March
19, 1980, and replaced by Banking Circular 79 (2nd Rev.).

This circular considers policies and procedures that should be
initiated by national banks that engage in financial futures
contracts, forward placement contracts or standby contracts in their
commercial banking activities. We view these contracts as neither
inherently prudent nor imprudent. Evidence has shown that they can
be used effectively to reduce interest rate risk. Any use of these
contracts by national banks should be in accordance with safe and
sound banking practices and with levels of activity reasonably
related to the bank's business needs and capacity to fulfill its
obligations under the contracts.

DEFINITIONS

Financial Futures Contracts. These contracts are interest rate
futures, which under Section 2 of the Commodities Exchange Act, as
amended (7 U.S.C. § 2) are commodities contracts traded on and
guaranteed by an exchange. These contracts represent a commitment
to purchase (to take delivery by the "long") or to sell (to make
delivery by the "short") a standardized amount of the deliverable
grade security at a specified price during a specified delivery
month in accordance with the exchange rules regarding delivery
procedures.

Forward Placement Contracts. These contracts are over-the-counter
contracts for delayed delivery of securities in which the buyer
(long) agrees to purchase and the seller (short) agrees to make a

B C-79 (3rd Rev.)

BANKING ISSUANCE

Comptroller of the Currency
Administrator of National Banks

Type: Banking Circular

Subject: National Bank Participation in the Financial Futures and Forward Placement Markets

delivery of a specified security at a specified price for future delivery. Cash market transactions other than "when issued" transactions, specifying delivery (settlement) in excess of thirty (30) days following the trade date shall be deemed to be forward contracts. Forward contracts are not traded on organized exchanges, the terms are not standardized, and the contracts can only be terminated by agreement of both parties to the transaction.

Standby Contracts. These are optional delivery forward placement contracts. The buyer of a standby contract (put option) pays a fee for the right or option to sell (deliver) an agreed upon amount of specified securities to the issuer of the standby contract at a specified price at a specified future date.

GUIDELINES

These contracts are not considered investment securities within the meaning of 12 USC 24(7). However, with the distinctions described below for investment or non-dealer operations, asset-liability management, and dealer-bank trading activities, the use of these contracts is considered to be an activity incidental to banking. The following are minimal guidelines to be followed by national banks that engage in these markets.

1. Distinctions

   a. For investment portfolio or non-dealer operations in fixed-rate assets, banks should evaluate the interest rate risk exposure resulting from their overall investment activities to ensure that the positions they take in futures, forward and standby contract markets will reduce their risk exposure. Short positions in futures and forward contracts should reasonably relate to existing or anticipated cash positions, and should be used to enhance liquidity of the portfolio. Rather than using short hedges against portfolio holdings for purposes of income generation, we would expect, where practicable, that contract gains would

BANKING ISSUANCE

Comptroller of the Currency
Administrator of National Banks

Type:	Banking Circular	Subject:	National Bank Participation in the Financial Futures and Forward Placement Markets

be used to offset losses resulting from the sale of portfolio securities as asset yields are upgraded. Long positions in futures and forwards should reasonably reflect the bank's investment strategy and ability to fulfill its commitments.

b. Asset-liability management involves the matching of fixed-rate and interest-sensitive assets and liabilities in order to maintain liquidity and profitability. Futures and forward contracts may be used as a general hedge against the interest rate exposure associated with undesired mismatches in interest-sensitive assets and liabilities. Long positions in contracts could be used as a hedge against funding interest-sensitive assets with fixed-rate sources of funds; short positions in contracts could be used as a hedge against funding fixed-rate assets with interest-sensitive liabilities.

c. Dealer-bank trading activities that employ futures, forward and standby contracts should be in accordance with safe and sound banking practices reasonably related to the bank's legally permitted trading activities.

2. The Board of Directors should consider any plan to engage in these activities and should endorse specific written policies and procedures in authorizing these activities. Policy objectives should be specific enough to outline permissible contract strategies and their relationships to other banking activities. Recordkeeping systems must be sufficiently detailed to permit internal auditors and examiners to determine whether operating personnel have acted in accordance with authorized objectives. Bank personnel are expected to be able to describe and document in detail how the positions they have taken in futures, forward and standby contracts contribute to attaining the bank's stated objectives.

BANKING ISSUANCE

Comptroller of the Currency
Administrator of National Banks

Type: Banking Circular	Subject: National Bank Participation in the Financial Futures and Forward Placement Markets

3. The Board of Directors should also establish limitations applicable to futures, forward and standby contract positions for each distinct category described in item 1 above. The Board of Directors, a duly authorized committee thereof, or the bank's internal auditors should review all outstanding contract positions at least monthly and ensure that these limits are not exceeded.

4. Underlying security commitments relating to open futures and forwards should not be reported on the balance sheet. The bank should maintain general ledger memorandum accounts and commitment registers to adequately identify and control all commitments to make or take delivery of securities. Such registers and supporting journals ordinarily would include:

   a. The type and amount of each contract;
   b. The maturity date of each contract;
   c. The current market price and cost of each contract; and
   d. The amount of money held in margin accounts.

5. Accounting Requirements

   a. The market value of all open contract positions should be determined at least monthly regardless of whether the bank is required to deposit "margin" or a performance bond in connection with a given contract. Market values for forward and standby contracts should be based on the market value of the underlying security, except where published and widely distributed forward contract price quotations are available. All standby contracts should be marked to the lower of cost or market. However, losses on standby contracts only have to be computed by the issuer (the party committed to purchase under the contract) and only where the market value of the underlying security is below the contract price, reduced by the amount of the deferred fee described in item 7 below. All futures and forward contracts with the exception of contracts described in item

BANKING ISSUANCE

Comptroller of the Currency
Administrator of National Banks

Type: Banking Circular	Subject: National Bank Participation in the Financial Futures and Forward Placement Markets

5b, should be valued by a consistent method of either mark to market or mark to the lower of cost or market. The bank's Board of Directors may choose which method of valuation (either market or lower of cost or market) it prefers and document it in the written policies and procedures described in item 2 above. All losses resulting from monthly contract value determination should be recognized as a current expense item; those banks that choose to value contracts on a mark to market basis would recognize gains as a current income item. For the specific line entries to be made, refer to the call report instructions. Because these contracts are <u>not</u> investment securities, net losses or gains <u>cannot</u> be taken "below the line" as an investment security gain or loss.

b. Futures and forward contracts associated with the hedging of mortgage banking operations, i.e. the origination and purchase of mortgage loans for resale to investors or the issuance of mortgage-backed securities, may be accounted for in accordance with the generally accepted accounting principles applicable to such activity.

6. In the event the above described futures and forward contracts result in the acquisition of securities, such securities should be recorded on an accounting basis consistent with that applied to the contracts (either market or lower of cost or market). Acquisition of securities arising from standby contracts should be recorded on the basis of lower of adjusted cost (see item 7(c)) or market.

7. Fee income received by a bank in connection with the issuance of a standby contract should be deferred at initiation of the contract and accounted for as follows:

a. Upon expiration of an unexcercised contract, the deferred amount should be reported as income;

BANKING ISSUANCE

Comptroller of the Currency
Administrator of National Banks

Type: Banking Circular	Subject: National Bank Participation in the Financial Futures and Forward Placement Markets

b. Upon a negotiated settlement of the contract prior to maturity, the deferred amount should be accounted for as an adjustment to the expense of such settlement, and the net should be transferred to the income account; or

c. Upon exercise of the contract, the deferred amount should be accounted for as an adjustment to the basis of the acquired securities. Such adjusted cost basis should be compared to market value of securities acquired. See item 6.

8. Bank financial reports should disclose in an explanatory note any futures, forward and standby contract activity that materially affects the bank's financial condition.

9. To ensure that banks minimize credit risk associated with forwards and standby contract activity, banks should implement a system for monitoring credit risk exposure associated with various customers and dealers with whom operating personnel are authorized to transact business.

10. To ensure adherence to bank policy and prevent unauthorized trading and other abuses, banks should establish appropriate internal controls including periodic reports to management, segregation of duties, and internal audit programs.

The issuance of long-term standby contracts, i.e., those for 150 days or more, which give the other party to the contract the option to deliver securities to the bank, will ordinarily be viewed as inappropriate. In almost all instances where standby contracts specified settlement in excess of 150 days, regulatory authorities have found that such contracts were related not to the investment or business needs of the institution, but primarily to the earning of fee income or to speculating on future interest rate movements. Accordingly, national banks should not issue standby contracts specifying delivery in excess of 150 days, unless special circumstances warrant.

B C-79(3rd Rev.

BANKING ISSUANCE

Comptroller of the Currency
Administrator of National Banks

Type: Banking Circular	Subject: National Participation in the Financial Futures and Forward Placement Markets

National banks engaging in the futures, forward and standby contract markets must submit a short letter notice stating their intention to the Regional Administrator of National Banks for their region or Deputy Comptroller for their district. We intend to monitor national bank transactions in futures, forward and standby contracts to ensure that any such activity is conducted in accordance with safe and sound banking practices.

The reporting and recordkeeping requirements of this circular carry OMB number 15570094 with an expiration date of March, 1987.

H. Joe Selby
Senior Deputy Comptroller for
Bank Supervision

(Docket No. R-0261)

Policy Statement Concerning Forward Placement or Delayed Delivery Contracts and Interest Rate Futures Contracts

Agency: Board of Governors of the Federal Reserve System.

Action: Policy Statement (Revised).

Summary: The Board of Governors has revised a previously published policy statement (44FR 68033, November 28, 1979) which contains policies and procedures that the Board of Governors believes should be instituted by State member banks that engage in interest rate futures contracts,[1] forward contracts,[2] or standby contracts,[3] on U.S. government and agency securities to insure that such activities are conducted in accordance with safe and sound banking practices. The policies and procedures apply to outstanding contracts as of January 1, 1980 as well as those entered into subsequent to that date. However, the accounting procedures contained in numbered paragraph 5 of the policy statement apply only to those futures and forward contracts entered into, renewed or extended after January 1, 1980.

In response to comments received, the previously published policy statement has been revised (1) to give banks the option to carry futures and forward positions on a market or lower of cost or market basis, (2) to exempt futures and forward contract activities associated with *bona fide* hedging of a mortgage banking operation from the otherwise prescribed accounting treatment with respect to such contracts, and (3) to exempt those futures and forward contracts executed prior to January 1, 1980 from the accounting procedures contained herein. Other technical amendments, including a relaxation of the requirement that a bank's board of directors review contract positions at least monthly, have also been made.

[1]*Futures Contracts:* These are standardized contracts traded on organized exchanges to purchase or sell a specified security on a future date at a specified price. Futures contracts on GNMA mortgage-backed securities and Treasury bills were the first interest rate futures contracts. Several other interest rate futures contracts have been developed, and it is anticipated that new and similar interest rate futures contracts will continue to be proposed and adopted for trading on various exchanges.

[2]*Forward Contracts:* These are over-the-counter contracts for forward placement or delayed delivery of securities in which one party agrees to purchase and another to sell a specified security at a specified price for future delivery. Contracts specifying settlement in excess of 30 days following trade date shall be deemed to be forward contracts. Forward contracts are not traded on organized exchanges, generally have not required margin payments, and can only be terminated by agreement of both parties to the transaction.

[3]*Standby Contracts:* These are optional delivery forward contracts on U.S. government and agency securities arranged between securities dealers and customers and do not currently involve trading on organized exchanges. The buyer of a standby contract (put option) acquires, upon paying a fee, the right to sell securities to the other party at a stated price at a future time. The seller of a standby (the issuer) receives the fee, and must stand ready to buy the securities at the other party's option.

Date: The original policy statement became effective January 1, 1980. The revised policy statement is effective immediately.

For Further Information Contact: Robert S. Plotkin, Assistant Director, or Michael J. Schoenfeld, Senior Securities Regulation Analyst ((202) 4522-2782), Division of Banking Supervision and Regulation, Board of Governors of the Federal Reserve System, Washington, D.C. 20551.

Supplementary Information: In November 1979 the Board of Governors adopted, effective January 1, 1980, a policy statement concerning forward placement or delayed delivery contracts and interest rate futures contracts. At the time of publication, public comment on the policy statement was invited and approximately 55 letters of comment were received. The majority of comments concerned the accounting provisions contained in the policy statement. Other less controversial issues were also raised. Several of the comments questioned the appropriateness of the bank regulatory agencies establishing accounting procedures and suggested that the determination of such procedures should be left to the accounting industry. A letter from the American Institute of Certified Public Accountants stated that it had recently convened a task force to examine the issue of accounting for futures and forward contracts and after the task force completes its deliberations it will submit its advisory conclusions to the Financial Accounting Standards Board for its conclusions and resolution. The letters of comment reveal, however, that there is at present no accepted industry practice and, indeed, there is a difference of opinion in the accounting profession as to what accounting standards should be adopted. As noted

previously, the guidelines prescribed in the policy statement are necessary, in the Board's judgment, to prevent unsafe and unsound banking practices. Accordingly, although the Board stands ready to confer with representatives of the accounting profession and to modify, or even eliminate, the prescribed accounting procedures upon adoption of acceptable accounting standards by the accounting industry, the Board believes that the prescription of accounting standards at this time is within its statutory responsibility to prevent unsafe and unsound banking practices.

A number of commenters noted that the requirement to carry futures contracts at market conflicted with the requirement to enter securities acquired pursuant to futures contracts on the bank's books on the basis of the lower of contract price or market price on settlement date. The revised policy statement specifies that securities acquired pursuant to contracts be recorded on a basis consistent with that applied to contracts. In addition, some commenters stated that it is unfair to make banks recognize forward contract losses but preclude them from recognizing gains. The revised policy statement gives banks the option of carrying forward contracts, as well as futures contracts, at market providing that trading account contracts be carried in a manner consistent with other positions in a trading account.

The revised policy statement also gives banks the option to carry futures positions at the lower of cost or market. This option will permit banks to defer gains resulting from a futures activity but will preclude them from delaying recognition of losses on such activity.

Other comments suggested that the prescribed accounting treatment would be inconsistent with accounting standards that have been prescribed with respect to mortgage banking activities (AICPA Position No. 74-12) and that the new procedures are neither necessary nor appropriate where a bank has a mortgage banking department or conducts mortgage banking activity. Since there were already accounting industry standards for this activity, which the Board believes are appropriate, the revised policy statement excludes futures and forward contract activities associated with *bona fide* hedging of mortgage banking operations from the accounting standards prescribed in the policy statement.

A number of commenters faulted the effective date of the accounting procedures contained in the policy statement. They argued that it is inequitable to change the accounting procedures during the period a contract is held, especially since the decision to enter into a contract was made without knowledge of the subsequent accounting guidelines. Upon reconsideration, the Board has agreed that the accounting procedures contained in numbered paragraph 5 of the policy statement are not required to be applied to futures and forward contracts entered into prior to January 1, 1980. Accordingly, these accounting procedures apply only to futures and forward contracts entered into, renewed or extended after January 1, 1980. No change has been made concerning the effective date of the policy statement with respect to standby contracts.

Finally, many commenters noted that the requirement in the original policy statement that the bank's board of directors review contract positions at least monthly to ascertain conformance with limits previously established by the Board is unduly burdensome and, in some cases,

impractical. Accordingly, the revised policy statement provides that the position review may be carried out by the board, a duly authorized committee of the board or the bank's internal auditors.

Acting pursuant to its supervisory authority over State member banks contained in Section 9 (12 U.S.C. 321 *et seq.*) and Section 11 (12 U.S.C. 248) of the Federal Reserve Act and the Financial Institutions Supervisory Act of 1966 (12 U.S.C. 1818(b)) and related provisions of law, the Board of Governors has amended its previously published policy statement which, as revised, is hereinafter set forth in its entirety.

Statement of Policy Concerning Forward Contracts and Futures Contracts

The following is a Board policy statement relating to State member bank participation in the futures and forward contract markets to purchase and sell U.S. government and agency securities. Information contained below is applicable specifically to commercial banking activities. An additional statement of policy applicable to trust department activities of State member banks may be issued at a later time.

The staff of the Treasury Department and the Board of Governors of the Federal Reserve System recently completed a study of the markets for Treasury futures. In part, the study notes that there is evidence that financial futures can be used by banks effectively to hedge portions of their portfolios against interest rate risk. However, the study also cautions that improper use of interest rate futures contracts will increase interest rate risk—rather than decrease such risk. In addition, various participants have advised that certain salespersons are attempting to suggest inappropriate futures transactions for banks, such as taking futures positions to speculate on future interest rate movements. Furthermore, some banks and other financial institutions have recently issued standby contracts (giving the contra party the option to deliver securities to the bank at a predetermined price) that were extremely large given their ability to absorb interest rate risk. In so doing, these institutions have been exposed to potentially large losses that could (and sometimes did) significantly affect their financial condition.

Banks that engage in futures, forward and standby contract activities should only do so in accordance with safe and sound banking practices with levels of activity reasonably related to the bank's business needs and capacity to fulfill its obligations under these contracts. In managing their assets and liabilities, banks should evaluate the interest rate risk exposure resulting from their overall activities to insure that the positions they take in futures, forward and standby contract markets will reduce their risk exposure; and policy objectives should be formulated in light of the bank's entire asset and liability mix. The following are minimal guidelines to be followed by banks authorized under State law to participate in these markets.

1. Prior to engaging in these transactions, a bank should obtain an opinion of counsel or its State banking authority concerning the legality of its activities under State law.

2. The board of directors should consider any plan to engage in these activities and should endorse specific written policies in authorizing these activities. Policy objectives must be specific enough to outline permissible contract strategies and their relationship to other banking activities, and record keeping systems must be sufficiently detailed to permit internal auditors and examiners to determine whether operating personnel have acted in accordance with authorized objectives. Bank personnel are expected to be able to describe and document in detail how the positions they have taken in futures, forward and standby contracts contribute to the attainment of the bank's stated objectives.

3. The board of directors should establish limitations applicable to futures, forward and standby contract positions; and the board of directors, a duly authorized committee thereof, or the bank's internal auditors should review periodically (at least monthly) contract positions to ascertain conformance with such limits.

4. The bank should maintain general ledger memorandum accounts or commitment registers to adequately identify and control all commitments to make or take delivery of securities. Such registers and supporting journals should at a minimum include:

(a) the type and amount of each contract,

(b) the maturity date of each contract,

(c) the current market price and cost of each contract, and

(d) the amount of money held in margin accounts.

5. With the exception of contracts described in item 6, all open positions should be reviewed and market values determined at least monthly (or more often, depending on volume and magnitude of positions), regardless of whether the bank is required to deposit

margin in connection with a given contract.[4] All futures and forward contracts should be valued on the basis of either market or the lower of cost or market, at the option of the bank.[5] Standby contracts should be valued on the basis of lower of cost or market.[6] Market basis for forward and standby contracts should be based on the market value of the underlying security, except where publicly quoted forward contract price quotations are available. All losses resulting from monthly contract value determination should be recognized as a current expense item; those banks that value contracts on a market basis would recognize gains as a current income item. In the event the above described futures and forward contracts result in the acquisition of securities, such securities should be recorded on a basis consistent with that applied to the contracts (either market or lower of cost or market). Acquisition of securities arising from standby contracts should be recorded on the basis of lower of adjusted cost (see Item 7(c)) or market.

6. Futures or forward contracts associated with *bona fide* hedging of mortgage banking operations, i.e., the origination and purchase of mortgage loans for resale to investors or the issuance of mortgage-backed securities, may be accounted for in accordance with generally accepted accounting principles applicable to such activity.

7. Fee income received by a bank in connection with a standby contract should be deferred at initiation of the contract and accounted for as follows:

a. upon expiration of an unexercised contract the deferred amount should be reported as income;

b. upon a negotiated settlement of the contract prior to maturity, the deferred amount should be accounted for as an adjustment to the expense of such settlement, and the net amount should be transferred to the income account; or

c. upon exercise of the contract, the deferred amount should be accounted for as an adjustment to the basis of the acquired securities. Such adjusted cost basis should be compared to market value of securities acquired. See item 5.

8. Bank financial reports should disclose in an explanatory note any futures, forward and standby contract activity that materially affects the bank's financial condition.

9. To insure that banks minimize credit risk associated with forward and standby contract activity, banks should implement a system for monitoring credit risk exposure associated with various customers and dealers with whom operating personnel are authorized to transact business.

---

[4]Underlying security commitments relating to open futures and forward contracts should not be reported on the balance sheet. Margin deposits and any unrealized losses (and in certain instances, unrealized gains) are usually the only entries to be recorded on the books. See "General Instructions" to the Reports of Condition and Income for additional details.

[5]Futures and forward contracts executed for trading account purposes should be valued on a basis consistent with other trading positions.

[6]Losses on standby contracts need be computed only in the case of the party committed to purchase under the contract, and only where the market value of the security is below the contract price adjusted for deferred fee income.

10. To assure adherence to bank policy and prevent unauthorized trading and other abuses, banks should establish other internal controls including periodic reports to management, segregation of duties, and internal audit programs.

The issuance of long-term standby contracts, i.e., those for 150 days or more which give the other party to the contract the option to deliver securities to the bank will ordinarily be viewed as an inappropriate practice. In almost all instances where standby contracts specified settlement in excess of 150 days, supervisory authorities have found that such contracts were related not to the investment or business needs of the institution, but primarily to the earning of fee income or to speculating on future interest rate movements. Accordingly, the Board concludes that State member banks should not issue standby contracts specifying delivery in excess of 150 days, unless special circumstances warrant.

The Board intends to monitor closely State member bank transactions in futures, forward and standby contracts to ensure that any such activity is conducted in accordance with safe and sound banking practices. In light of that continuing review, it may be found desirable to establish position limits applicable to State member banks. Supervisory action in individual cases under the Financial Institutions Supervisory Act (12 U.S.C. 1818(b)) may also be instituted if necessary.

By order of the Board of Governors of the Federal Reserve System, March 12, 1980.

Theodore E. Allison,
Secretary of the Board.

Revised Statement of Policy Concerning Interest Rate Futures Contracts, Forward Contracts and Standby Contracts

Agency: Federal Deposit Insurance Corporation.

Action: Revised Policy Statement Concerning Interest Rate Futures Contracts, Forward Contracts and Standby Contracts.

Summary: On November 13, 1979, the Board of Directors of the Federal Deposit Insurance Corporation approved a policy statement outlining policies and procedures governing participation by State nonmember banks in interest rate futures, forward and standby contracts on U.S. Government and agency securities. The policy statement was developed jointly with the Board of Governors of the Federal Reserve System and the Comptroller of the Currency and became effective January 1, 1980 for contracts outstanding at that time and for those entered into subsequently. Interested parties were invited to submit comments on the statement by December 15, 1979. The Federal Deposit Insurance Corporation has considered the comments received and has determined that the statement will not apply to those contracts outstanding as of January 1, 1980. The Corporation is also revising certain guidelines of the policy statement. The revisions provide for an exception to the mark to market requirements for futures and forward contracts that relate to mortgage banking activities and also give banks the option of carrying futures and mandatory forward contracts at either market or lower of costs or market.

Effective Date: Immediately.

For Further Information Contact: Ms. Sally Y. King, Chief, Securities Analysis Section, or Mr. Paul L. Sachtleben, Projects and Planning Specialist, Projects and Planning Branch, Federal Deposit Insurance Corporation, 550 17th Street, N.W., Washington, D.C. 20129 (202-389-1906 or 202-389-4141).

Supplementary Information: Following are the revisions to the policy statement concerning futures, forward and standby contracts along with discussions of those revisions:

Revised Statement re Applicability of the Policy Statement:

These policies and procedures will apply to contracts entered into after January 1, 1980.

Discussion

The policies and procedures included in the original policy statement applied to contracts outstanding as of January 1, 1980 as well as to those entered into thereafter. Commentators from savings banks objected very strongly to the application of the statement to open contracts as of January 1, 1980. They stated that the retroactive feature was unfair and that they had relied upon what they believed to be appropriate accounting for such contracts. In view of these objections and the complexity of the accounting issues involved, the policy statement will be prospective from the effective date of the original statement.

Revised Guideline 3

3. The board of directors should establish limitations applicable to futures, forward and standby contract positions; and the board of directors, a duly authorized committee thereof, or the bank's internal auditors should review periodically (at least monthly) contract positions to ascertain conformance with such limits.

Discussion

Several commentators objected to original guideline 3 which requires the bank's board of directors to establish limitations on contract positions and review monthly the conformance with such limits. They stated that these requirements were inappropriate because they require the board to become directly involved in a management function. The Federal Deposit Insurance Corporation feels that it is extremely important that the bank's board of directors establish the position limitations and will continue that requirement. However, we would agree that the review function could be delegated to a duly authorized committee of the board of directors or the bank's internal auditors, and accordingly have revised guideline 3.

Revised Guideline 5

5. With the exception of contracts described in guideline 6, all open positions should be reviewed and market values determined at least monthly (or more often, depending on volume and magnitude of positions), regardless of whether the bank is required to deposit margin in connection with a given contract.[4] All futures and forward contracts should be valued on the basis of either market or the lower of cost or market, at the

---

[4]Underlying security commitments relating to open futures and forward contracts should not be reported on the balance sheet. Margin deposits and any unrealized losses (and in certain instances, unrealized gains) are usually the only entries to be recorded on the books. See "General Instructions" to the Reports of Condition and Income for additional details.

option of the bank.[5] Standby contracts should be valued on the basis of the lower of cost or market.[6] Market basis for forward and standby contracts should be based on the market value of the underlying security, except where publicly quoted forward contract price quotations are available. All losses resulting from monthly contract valuation should be recognized as a current expense item; those banks that value contracts on a market basis would recognize gains as current income items. In the event the above described futures and forward contracts result in the acquisition of securities, such securities should be recorded on a basis consistent with that applied to the contracts (market or lower of cost or market). Acquisition of securities arising from standby contracts should be recorded on the basis of lower of adjusted cost (see item 7(c)) or market.

Discussion

The policy statement, as originally adopted, requires futures contracts to be valued at market and forward contracts to be valued at lower of cost or market. Several of the written comments received by the agencies stated that the different methods of reflecting market risk for futures contracts and forward contracts were inconsistent. Revised guideline 5 removes this inconsistency by giving the bank the option of valuing all futures and forward contracts (other than those relating to mortgage banking activity) at either market or lower of cost or market.

Revised Guideline 6

6. Futures or forward contracts associated with bona fide hedging of mortgage banking operations, i.e., the origination and purchase of mortgage loans for resale to investors or the issuance of mortgage-backed securities, may be accounted for in accordance with generally accepted accounting principles applicable to such activity.

Discussion

This issue was not addressed previously in the policy statement. Revised guideline 6 exempts those futures or forward contracts from the mark to market requirements that are specifically identified with mortgage banking operations. Generally accepted accounting principles specifically address mortgage banking activities by requiring that mortgages held in inventory (for resale) be revalued on the basis of lower of cost or market. The futures or forward contract associated with this mortgage banking activity is a commitment to sell the inventory of mortgages. As the inventory of mortgage loans is already required to be marked to the lower of cost or market, it is inappropriate to also require that the related futures and forward contracts be similarly marked.

Certain Language Changes

The Federal Deposit Insurance Corporation has made certain language changes to improve the clarity and readability of the policy statement. These changes do not significantly alter the intent of the original statement.

---

[5]Futures and forward contracts executed for trading account purposes should be valued on a basis consistent with other trading positions.

[6]Losses on standby contracts need be computed only in the case of the party committed to purchase under the contract, and only where the market value of the security is below the contract price adjusted for deferred fee income.

Revised Policy Statement

Revised Statement of Policy Concerning Interest Rate Futures Contracts, Forward Contracts and Standby Contracts

The following is a Board of Directors policy statement relating to insured State nonmember bank participation in the futures and forward contract markets to purchase and sell U.S. government and agency securities. Information contained below is applicable specifically to activities of commercial and mutual savings banks. An additional statement of policy applicable to trust department activities of State nonmember banks may be issued at a later time.

The staff of the Treasury Department and the Board of Governors of the Federal Reserve System recently completed a study of the markets for Treasury futures. In part, the study notes that there is evidence that financial futures can be used by banks effectively to hedge portions of their portfolios against interest rate risk. However, the study also cautions that improper use of interest rate futures contracts will increase rather than decrease interest rate risk. In addition, various participants have advised that certain salespersons are attempting to suggest inappropriate futures transactions for banks, such as taking futures positions to speculate on futures interest rate movements. Furthermore, some banks and other financial institutions have recently issued standby contracts (giving the contra party the option to deliver securities to the bank at a predetermined price) that were extremely large given their ability to absorb interest rate risk. In so doing, these institutions have been exposed to potentially large losses that could (and sometimes did) significantly affect their financial condition.

Banks that engage in futures,[1] forward[2] and standby[3] contracts should only do so in accordance with safe and sound banking practices. Levels of activity should be reasonably related to the bank's business needs and capacity

---

[1]*Futures Contracts*: These are standardized contracts traded on organized exchanges to purchase or sell a specified security on a future date at a specified price. Futures contracts on GNMA mortgage-backed securities and Treasury bills were the first interest rate futures contracts. Several other interest rate futures contracts have been developed and it is anticipated that new and similar interest rate futures contracts will continue to be proposed and adopted for trading on various exchanges.

[2]*Forward Contracts*: These are over-the-counter contracts for forward placement or delayed delivery of securities in which one party agrees to purchase and another to sell a specified security at a specified price for future delivery. Contracts specifying settlement in excess of 30 days following trade date shall be deemed to be forward contracts. Forward contracts are not traded on organized exchanges, generally have no required margin payments, and can only be terminated by agreement of both parties to the transaction.

[3]*Standby Contracts*: These are optional delivery forward contracts on U.S. government and agency securities arranged between securities dealers and customers and do not currently involve trading on organized exchanges. The buyer of a standby contract (put option) acquires, upon paying a fee, the right to sell securities to the other party at a stated price at a future time. The seller of a standby (the issuer) receives the fee, and must stand ready to buy the securities at the other party's option.

to fulfill its obligations under these contracts. In managing their investment portfolios, banks should evaluate the interest rate risk exposure resulting from their overall activities to ensure that the positions they take in futures, forward and standby contract markets will reduce their risk exposure and policy objectives should be formulated in light of the bank's entire asset and liability mix. The following are minimal guidelines to be followed by banks eligible under State law to participate in these markets.

1. Prior to engaging in these transactions, a bank should consult its State banking authority or obtain an opinion of bank counsel concerning the legality of these activities under State law.

2. The board of directors should consider any plan to engage in these activities and should endorse specific written policies in authorizing these activities. Policy objectives must be specific enough to outline permissible contract strategies and their relationship to other banking activities. Record keeping systems must be sufficiently detailed to permit internal auditors and examiners to determine whether operating personnel have acted in accordance with authorized objectives. Bank personnel are expected to be able to describe and document in detail how the positions they have taken in futures, forward and standby contracts contribute to the attainment of the bank's stated objectives.

3. The board of directors should establish limitations applicable to futures, forward and standby contract positions; and the board of directors, a duly authorized committee thereof, or the bank's internal auditors should review periodically (at least monthly) contract positions to ascertain conformance with such limits.

4. The bank should maintain general ledger memorandum accounts or commitment registers to adequately identify and control all commitments to make or take delivery of securities. Such registers and supporting journals should at a minimum include:

(a) The type, nature of position (long or short) and amount of each contract,

(b) The maturity date of each contract,

(c) The current market price and cost of each contract, and

(d) The amount of money held in margin accounts.

5. With the exception of contracts described in guideline 6, all open positions should be reviewed and market values determined at least monthly (or more often, depending on volume and magnitude of positions), regardless of whether the bank is required to deposit margin in connection with a given contract.[4] All futures and forward contracts should be valued on the basis of either market or the lower of cost or market, at the

---

[4]Underlying security commitments relating to open futures and forward contracts should not be reported on the balance sheet. Margin deposits and any unrealized losses (and in certain instances, unrealized gains) are usually the only entries to be recorded on the books. See "General Instructions" to the Reports of Condition and Income for additional details.

option of the bank.[5] Standby contracts should be valued on the basis of the lower of cost or market.[6] Market basis for forward and standby contracts should be based on the market value of the underlying security, except where publicly quoted forward contract price quotations are available. All losses resulting from monthly contract valuation should be recognized as a current expense item; those banks that value contracts on a market basis would recognize gains as current income items. In the event the above described futures and forward contracts result in the acquisition of securities, such securities should be recorded on a basis consistent with that applied to the contracts (market or lower of cost or market). Acquisition of securities arising from standby contracts should be recorded on the basis of lower of adjusted cost (see item 7(c)) or market.

6. Futures or forward contracts associated with bonafide hedging of mortgage banking operations, i.e., the origination and purchase of mortgage loans for resale to investors or the issuance of mortgage-backed securities, may be accounted for in accordance with generally accepted accounting principles applicable to such activity.

7. Fee income received by a bank in connection with a standby contract should be deferred at initiation of the contract and accounted for as follows:

(a) Upon expiration of an unexercised contract, the deferred amount should be reported as income;

(b) Upon a negotiated settlement of the contract prior to maturity, the deferred amount should be accounted for as an adjustment to the expense of such settlement, and the net amount should be transferred to the income account; or

(c) Upon exercise of the contract, the deferred amount should be accounted for as an adjustment to the basis of the acquired securities. Such adjusted cost basis should be compared to market value of securities acquired. See guideline 5.

8. Bank financial reports should disclose in an explanatory note any futures, forward and standby contract activity that materially affects the bank's financial condition.

9. To ensure that banks minimize credit risk associated with forward and standby contract activity, banks should implement a system for monitoring credit risk exposure associated with the customers and dealers with whom operating personnel are authorized to transact business.

10. To assure adherence to bank policy and prevent unauthorized trading and other abuses, banks should establish other internal controls including periodic reports to management, segregation of duties, and internal audit programs.

The issuance of long-term standby contracts, i.e., those in excess of 150 days, which give the other party to the contract the option to deliver securities to the bank will ordinarily be viewed as

---

[5]Futures and forward contracts executed for trading account purposes should be valued on a basis consistent with other trading positions.

[6]Losses on standby contracts need be computed only in the case of the party committed to purchase under the contract, and only where the market value of the security is below the contract price adjusted for deferred fee income.

an inappropriate practice. In almost all instances where standby contracts specified settlement in excess of 150 days, regulatory authorities have found that such contracts were related not to the investment or business needs of the institution, but primarily to the earning of fee income or to speculating on future interest rate movements. Accordingly, the Board of Directors concludes that insured State nonmember banks should not issue standby contracts specifying delivery in excess of 150 days, unless special circumstances warrant.

The Board of Directors intends to monitor closely insured State nonmember bank transactions in futures, forward and standby contracts to ensure that any such activity is conducted in accordance with safe and sound banking practices. In light of that continuing review, it may be found desirable to establish position limits applicable to insured State nonmember banks. This policy statement is issued pursuant to the Financial Institutions Supervisory Act, 12 U.S.C. 1818, and the supervisory authority of the Federal Deposit Insurance Corporation with respect to nonmember insured banks.

By order of the Board of Directors, March 12, 1980.

Federal Deposit Insurance Corporation.

Hoyle L. Robinson,

Executive Secretary.

(FR Doc. 80-8493 Filed 3-19-80, 8:45 a.m.)

BILLING CODE 6714-01-M

Appendix B:
Futures Trading Regulations for Savings and Loan Associations

The following regulations:

12 CFR Parts 545, 563 and 571,

govern the trading of financial futures and financial futures options by savings and loan associations. The first set of regulations apply to all federally insured associations; the options trading regulations apply to federally chartered associations.

12 CFR Parts 545, 563 and 571

Futures Transactions

Agency: Federal Home Loan Bank
Board.
Action: Final rule.

Summary: The Board is amending its regulation and policy statement governing use of interest-rate futures markets by institutions the accounts of which are insured by the Federal Savings and Loan Insurance Corporation, so that institutions more effectively may protect their operations against interest-rate risks. Major changes include permitting use of any futures contract designated by the Commodity Futures Trading Commission and based upon a security in which the institution has authority to invest, permitting institutions to engage in futures transactions that reduce their net interest-rate risk exposure, eliminating eligibility requirements for engaging in futures transactions, eliminating the regulatory position limit on futures transactions, extending coverage of the regulation governing futures transactions to State-chartered institutions as well as Federal associations, and providing general principles governing accounting for gains and losses on futures contracts.

Effective Date: July 10, 1981.

For Further Information Contact: Susan Kelsey, Office of Policy and Economic Research (202-377-6914), Robert Losey, Office of Federal Savings and Loan Insurance Corporation (202-377-6620), or Peter Barnett, Office of General Counsel (202-377-6445), Federal Home Loan Bank Board, 1700 G Street, N.W., Washington, D.C. 20552.

Supplementary Information:

Proposed Amendments

On April 23, 1981, the Board proposed amendments to its regulation (12 CFR 545.29) and policy statement (12 CFR 571.12) governing use of interest-rate futures markets by institutions the accounts of which are insured by the Federal Savings and Loan Insurance Corporation. *See*, Board Resolution No. 81–207; 46 FR 24579 (May 1, 1981). The Board's proposal was intended to give institutions greater flexibility in using interest-rate futures than was permitted under existing regulatory guidelines, taking into account developments in the expanding interest-rate futures markets, the deregulation of the liabilities of insured institutions and the increased volatility of interest rates.

The Board received approximately 75 comment letters from the Federal Home Loan Banks, savings and loan association trade groups, insured institutions, commodity futures exchanges, commodity futures brokers and dealers, accounting firms and other interested persons. Almost all commenters supported the liberalization of regulatory guidelines for interest-rate futures transactions; however, some commenters suggested modification of particular aspects of the Board's proposal as discussed below.

Authorized Transactions

The Board proposed to revise existing limits on the types of interest-rate futures transactions authorized for insured institutions. The existing regulations provide that institutions may engage only in GNMA futures transactions (interest-rate futures transactions based on mortgaged-backed securities guaranteed by the Government National Mortgage Association) and limit permissible transactions to those which can be matched directly against: (1) Firm commitments, which are defined as commitments to make, purchase, issue or deliver mortgage loans or mortgage-related securities; or (2) anticipated reinvestments in mortgages and mortgage-related securites of expected mortgage repayments over the forthcoming 12-month period.

The proposal would have eliminated the restriction that the only futures positions permitted were those matched directly against firm commitments or against anticipated reinvestment of mortgage repayments. Instead, insured institutions would have been permitted to engage in interest-rate futures transactions to hedge operations against the risk of unanticipated changes in interest rates. Hedging would have included interest-rate futures transactions intended as temporary substitutes for, or as opposite positions to, cash market transactions or positions, except that long positions would not have been permitted unless they were used to offset short positions.

Commenters supported liberalizing the restrictions of the existing regulations on the types of interest-rate futures transactions permitted for institutions; however, many commenters suggested that the Board permit institutions to engage in transactions that would have been prohibited under the proposal. In particular, most commenters suggested that the Board permit institutions to take various long positions.

In undertaking to amend its regulations governing interest-rate futures transactions by insured institutions, it is the intent of the Board to permit institutions to engage in futures transactions that reduce the net interest-rate risk exposure arising from an institution's asset and liability structure. Net interest-rate risk exposure is the volatility in an institution's earnings that can arise from the mismatching of the effective maturities of assets and liabilities. At the same time, the Board desires to prohibit institutions from engaging in transactions which would increase their net interest-rate risk exposure.

Upon consideration, the Board has determined not to define permitted transactions in terms of whether they "hedge" specific aspects of an institution's operations against unanticipated changes in interest rates. The matching of futures market positions and cash market positions does not, by itself, ensure that the net interest-rate risk exposure of an institution will be reduced. In addition, even though they do not lower a firm's overall risk exposure, many transactions not permitted under the final regulation are sometimes referred to as "hedges" by futures market participants. Therefore, the final regulation permits insured institutions to engage in interest-rate futures transactions that reduce the net interest-rate risk exposure of the institution. These include, but are not limited to, short futures positions used:

(i) To protect against the risk resulting from forward commitments to originate or purchase mortgages or mortgage-related securities;

(ii) To protect the value of mortgage loans or other investments held in portfolio;

(iii) To fix liability costs; and

(iv) To protect against other risks resulting from a maturity imbalance between assets and liabilities.

With regard to long positions, the Board continues to believe that the risk inherent in the typical savings and loan association's asset and liability structure would not be lessened, and most probably would be increased, by long positions in the futures market. Because the asset and liability structure of the typical insured institution exposes the institution to losses when interest rates rise unexpectedly, and because long futures positions pose similar risks, long positions normally should be viewed as compounding the interest-rate risk inherent to the savings and loan industry. However, those institutions which engage in mortgage banking operations may find it desirable to use long positions when they have contracted to sell mortgages not yet originated or to issue mortgage-related securities to be based upon mortgages not yet originated. Although the asset and liability structure of the typical insured institution reduces the risk associated with this type of mortgage banking activity, this risk reduction may not be sufficient either because of the extent of the mortgage banking activities, or because the benefits from the risk reduction may be spread over several accounting periods while the effects on earnings of the mortgage banking activity may be concentrated in one period.

Accordingly, the Board has decided to permit long futures positions to be taken in connection with forward commitments to sell mortgages not yet originated or to issue mortgage-related securities to be based upon mortgages not yet originated. However, these long futures positions are permitted and may be maintained only to the extent that an institution's short forward commitments exceed 10 percent of long-term assets. Long-term assets are those fixed interest rate assets having remaining terms to maturity in excess of five years. The 10 percent threshhold requirement is set at a level at which changes in the earnings from an institution's long-term asset portfolio approximately will offset losses on the 10 percent of short commitments which are not permitted to be covered by long futures positions under this regulation.

Many commenters who suggested that long positions be permitted did so in the context of "spreading." Spreading is the simultaneous purchase and sale of futures contracts, covering different interest-bearing securities or having different delivery dates, with the expectation that price and yield relationships between the two positions will change so as to result in a profit when the two positions are subsequently offset. The Board has determined that spreading does not come within the context of the futures activities that are being authorized under this regulation. Spreading is undertaken primarily in the expectation of a profit; it is not generally intended to reduce, and may increase, net interest-rate risk exposure. While some spreading techniques may reduce net interest-rate risk exposure, these techniques are substitutes for the short positions permitted by the Board, and institutions may achieve the same effective risk reduction without spreading under the final regulation.

The Board notes that the provisions of this regulation arise in large part from the current asset and liability structure of the savings and loan industry. It recognizes that many institutions will be changing their operating methods and restructuring their balance sheets in the coming years, and that futures transactions not now authorized, including the use of spreading techniques, may well be appropriate in the future. The Board will monitor changes in the industry and how futures transactions can be used in connection with those changes, and will review its regulation accordingly.

Eligibility Requirement

The Board proposed to eliminate the threshhold eligibility requirements of the existing regulations which provide that an institution meet the following, unless waived by the Board, before it may engage in interest-rate futures transactions:

(1) The net-worth requirements of 12 CFR 563.13(b);

(2) A ratio of scheduled items to assets not exceeding 2.5 percent; and

(3) Appraised losses offset by specific loss reserves to the extent required under 12 CFR 563.17–2.

Commenters supported elimination of eligibility requirements, and in this respect the final regulation is adopted as proposed.

Eligibility requirements were imposed at a time when the futures market in interest rates has been recently established, and the consequences of participation by insured institutions were uncertain. The Board has determined that it is not necessary to specify these requirements as a prerequisite to engaging in futures transactions that reduce an institution's net interest-rate risk exposure. Limiting futures transactions to those appropriate for savings and loans for this purpose provides the assurance of safe and sound operations intended by the eligibility requirements and is in keeping with the current deregulation evidenced by the Depository Institutions Deregulation and Monetary Control Act of 1980, Pub. L. No. 96–221, 94 Stat. 132, and recent Board actions. Moreover, institutions most in need of the interest-rate risk protection afforded by the futures market could have been precluded from engaging in futures transactions if the eligibility requirements of the existing regulation had been retained.

Authorized Contracts

The Board proposed to permit insured institutions to use U.S. Department of the Treasury ("Treasury") bills, notes and bond

futures contracts in addition to GNMA futures contracts. In response to the Board's solicitation of comments on the appropriateness of the proposed contracts and whether transactions in additional interest-rate futures contracts should be authorized, many commenters suggested that the Board not specify the particular contracts in which institutions could trade. Some commenters suggested that the Board permit futures transactions in any contract designated for trading by the Commodity Futures Trading Commission ("CFTC") to take into account newly designated contracts without amendment of the regulation. The Board agrees that the regulation should be flexible enough to avoid the need for amendment as the CFTC designates new contracts. Therefore, the final regulation permits institutions to engage in interest-rate futures transactions using any interest-rate futures contract that is designated by the CFTC and is based upon a security in which the institution is authorized to invest.

Position Limit

The existing regulations limit an institution's gross futures position to an amount equal to its net worth. To permit greater flexibility in using the interest-rate futures markets to reduce net interest-rate risk from operations, the Board proposed to permit institutions to maintain open futures positions up to an amount equal to 85 percent of assets. The Board solicited comments on alternative means of imposing position limits or whether any position limit should be imposed. While few commenters thought that a limit equal to 85 percent of assets was overly-restrictive, several commenters pointed out that hedge ratios between cash market positions and standardized futures contracts would reduce the effective futures position available under the limit in certain circumstances.

Upon consideration, the Board has decided to eliminate the position limit from the final regulation. The Board intended the position limit to be a generous check against superfluous futures transactions. However, because the final regulation limits futures transactions to those which reduce the net interest-rate exposure of institutions, and the position limit raises technical questions that, if taken into account, would complicate the regulation unnecessarily, this check has been deleted. Further, the Board believes that the extent of an institution's use of futures transactions is unique to the needs of the institution and is properly left with management as a business, rather than regulatory, decision.

Board of Directors' Authorization

The proposed regulation required specific authorization from its board of directors before an institution could engage in futures transactions. The proposal would have required the adoption of written policies and internal control procedures with respect to futures transactions and specification of the personnel authorized to engage in futures trading, along with their duties, responsibilities and position limits.

The Board continues to believe that it is essential for institutions to formulate a strategy for futures trading that relates such activity to the legitimate business of the institution and for the board of directors to endorse the strategy. The final amendments, therefore, are adopted essentially as proposed, but require additionally that the board of directors set a position limit for the institution's futures activity. In addition, the final regulation clarifies the Board's intent with respect to an institution's internal control mechanisms and requires that the board of directors review the position limit, all outstanding contract positions and unrealized gains and losses on outstanding contracts, at each regular meeting.

Recordkeeping Requirements

In a manner similar to existing regulations, the proposal specified the recordkeeping requirements for an insured institution engaging in interest-rate futures transactions. These included: (1) a register of all outstanding futures contracts; (2) for each futures contract outstanding, the purpose for which the contract was entered into and the cash market transaction(s) or position(s) matched; and (3) retention of the records specified in (1) and (2) for all closed-out futures transactions for a period of two years.

Because meaningful records are necessary to provide examiners with a basis for evaluating futures transactions, the Board is adopting this aspect of the final regulation essentially as proposed. Consistent with other changes in the final regulation, the manner in which corresponding cash and futures market records must be kept has been clarified. These clarifications are intended to assure that an institution's records document the net interest-rate risk to which the institution is exposed and how the futures positions taken reduce this risk. The records must include a schedule of the assets and liabilities for which the institution is reducing the net interest-rate risk exposure.

Accounting

The Board proposed to allow institutions to utilize hedge, sometimes referred to as deferral, accounting for their futures transactions. This was supported by most commenters who discussed accounting. As was the case when the proposal was made, neither the American Institute of Certified Public Accountants nor the Financial Accounting Standards Board is expected to adopt guidelines in this area in the near future. Therefore, because of the need for an accounting treatment consistent with the purpose of the futures transactions permitted by the final regulations, the Board is adopting the principle of hedge accounting as proposed. The final regulations make certain clarifying amendments in the proposed accounting provisions and provide greater technical detail in stating the rules.

The purpose of the futures transactions permitted by the final regulation is to reduce the net interest-rate risk associated with an institution's cash market transactions. Hedge accounting recognizes and reflects this basic intent by relating the accounting for futures transactions to the cash market position with which it is matched. For interest-rate futures contracts matched with assets or liabilities carried at cost, gains or losses on the futures contracts shall be deferred and amortized over the expected life of the corresponding assets or liabilities rather than recognized immediately. It should be understood, and the regulation has been amended to so provide, that futures contracts matched with assets carried at the lower of cost or market are to be accounted for in the same manner as the corresponding asset, that is, the gains or losses on the futures contract are to be considered in the periodic adjustment to the carrying value of the asset. The Board intends to issue further clarification and detail with respect to accounting for futures transactions as necessary.

The Board specifically requested comment on whether an institution should be permitted to choose between a market value accounting method or hedge accounting with respect to its futures transactions. Most commenters who responded recommended not permitting this choice because of the potential for abuse. Accordingly, the final regulation requires the use of hedge accounting and does not permit the institution to choose its accounting method.

The Board intends to monitor the development by the accounting profession of accounting rules for futures contracts and will review the accounting provisions of the regulation once generally accepted accounting principles have been established.

Application to all Insured Institutions

As a result of the potential growth in the volume of interest-rate futures transactions by insured institutions, the expansion of the types of instruments traded, and the increased interest-rate risk faced by all insured institutions, the Board proposed to apply the regulation governing interest-rate futures transactions directly to all insured institutions. The Board's existing regulation governing mortgage-futures transactions (12 CFR 545.29) applies only to Federal associations. By a separate policy statement (12 CFR 571.12), the Board has urged all insured institutions to comply with the requirements applicable to Federal associations. While the legal authority of State-chartered institutions to engage in interest-rate futures transactions may be derived from State law, the Board, through the Federal Savings and Loan Insurance Corporation, has the authority to promulgate rules and regulations for insured institutions to assure that all insured institutions have safe financial policies and management. Speculative activity in interest-rate futures can pose a serious threat to the safety and soundness of insured institutions. Therefore, the final amendments apply to interest-rate futures transactions of all insured institutions to assure that such transactions are used to reduce the net interest-rate risk exposure and to provide uniformity in examination and enforcement for all insured institutions.

"Grandfathering" of Existing Positions and Transition Period

When the Board proposed to amend the regulations governing interest-rate futures transactions, it intended that the amended regulations would apply prospectively only. Two commenters suggested that the Board expressly state how outstanding positions not permitted under the amended regulation will be treated. The Board agrees with this suggestion and, in addition, desires to provide for a transition period between existing regulatory requirements and the amendments adopted today. Accordingly, the final regulation provides that until August 3, 1981, institutions may continue to engage in interest-rate futures transactions as authorized immediately prior to the effective date of the final regulation. Institutions holding interest-rate futures contracts entered into before August 3, 1981, that would not be permitted pursuant to the final regulation will be permitted to continue to hold those contracts, provided that the contracts were authorized when entered into and are not renewed.

Service Corporations

On April 23, 1981, the Board adopted final regulations governing the service corporation investments of Federal savings and loan associations. *See*, Board Resolution No. 81–208; 46 FR 24526 (May 1, 1981). These amendments clarified the authority of service corporations to engage in futures transactions without prior Board approval by expressly referencing 12 CFR 545.29 governing futures transactions by Federal associations and exempting service corporations from the eligibility and notice requirements applicable to Federal associations. Consistent with the final regulation adopted today, the Board amends 12 CFR 545.9–1 to reference expressly 12 CFR 563.17–4 and to exempt service corporations from notice requirements. The Board notes, however, that service corporations may apply to the Board for broader approval to engage in futures transactions on a case-by-case basis.

Options

A few commenters recommended that the Board include in the futures regulation authority for associations to trade on the GNMA options market currently being developed by the Chicago Board Options Exchange. While the Board agrees that options trading by insured institutions is an activity that should be considered, the Board believes that options trading would be addressed more appropriately in a separate regulation.

Final Regulatory Flexibility Analysis

Pursuant to Section 3 of the Regulatory Flexibility Act, Pub. L. No. 96–354, 94 Stat. 1164 (September 19, 1980), the Board is providing the following final regulatory flexibility analysis.

1. *Reasons and objectives underlying the rule.* These elements have been incorporated elsewhere into the supplementary information regarding the proposal.

2. *Issues raised by comments on the Initial Regulatory Flexibility Analysis.* The Board did not receive any comments on the Initial Regulatory Flexibility Analysis.

3. *Alternatives to the rule.* The basic regulatory requirements included in the rule are limitations on the types of futures transactions permitted; a written policy endorsed by the institution's board of directors; maintenance of records of futures transactions, including the corresponding cash market positions and the purpose of the interest-rate futures transactions; establishment of internal control mechanisms; periodic review by the board of directors of the position limit and all outstanding contract positions; and providing monthly notice to the District Director-Examinations. These requirements, together with monitoring by the supervisory staff, are minimally necessary requirements to ensure that futures trading is undertaken in a safe and sound manner. It would not be possible to eliminate or modify these requirements for smaller entities and still expect them to engage in futures trading in a reasonable manner.

Information requirements contained in this regulation have been approved by the Office of Management and Budget under OMB Number 3066-0031.

Because there is a present need to afford institutions greater protection against volatile interest rates and because the proposal generally reduces regulatory burdens and relieves existing restrictions, the Board is making the final regulations effective on July 10, 1981.

Accordingly, the Federal Home Loan Bank Board hereby amends Parts 545, 563 and 571, Subchapters C and D, Chapter V of Title 12, *Code of Federal Regulations*, as set forth below.

SUBCHAPTER C—FEDERAL SAVINGS AND LOAN SYSTEM

PART 545—OPERATIONS

1. Revise paragraph (c)(20) of § 545.9-1 to read as follows:

§ 545.9-1 Service corporations.

•   •   •   •

(c) *Permitted activities.* A service corporation in which a Federal association may invest is permitted to engage in the following activities:

•   •   •   •

(20) Engaging in interest-rate futures transactions subject to the provisions of § 563.17-4 of this Chapter, but not subject to any notification requirements thereof;

•   •   •   •

2. Revise § 545.29 to read as follows:
§ 545.29 Interest-rate futures transactions.

A Federal association may engage in interest-rate futures transactions in compliance with § 563.17-4 of this Chapter.

SUBCHAPTER D—FEDERAL SAVINGS AND LOAN INSURANCE CORPORATION

PART 563—OPERATIONS

3. Add a new § 563.17–4, to read as follows:

§ 563.17–4 Futures transactions.

(a) *Definitions*. As used in this section, the following definitions apply unless the context otherwise requires:

(1) *Interest-rate futures contract*. A transferable agreement to make or take delivery of a standardized amount of an interest-bearing security, of standardized minimum quality grade, during a month specified in the agreement, under terms and conditions established by an exchange designated and regulated by the Commodity Futures Trading Commission.

(2) *Interest-rate futures transaction*. Purchase or sale of an interest-rate futures contract.

(3) *Long position*. The holding of an interest-rate futures contract to take delivery of securities.

(4) *Mortgage-related securities*. Securities based on and backed by mortgages, including mortgage-backed securities guaranteed by the Government National Mortgage Association ("GNMAs"), Mortgage Participation Certificates of the Federal Home Loan Mortgage Corporation, and similar obligations issued by the insured institution or in which the institution is authorized to invest.

(5) *Offset*. To cancel an obligation to make or take delivery of securities under an interest-rate futures contract. A futures contract to purchase securities is offset by a futures contract to sell securities of the same type for the same delivery month. A futures contract to sell securities is offset by a futures contract to purchase securities of the same type for the same delivery month.

(6) *Short position*. The holding of an interest-rate futures contract to make delivery of securities.

(b) *Permitted transactions*. To the extent that it has legal power to do so, an insured institution may engage in interest-rate futures transactions to reduce its net interest-rate risk exposure as provided in this paragraph (b). For purposes of this section, net interest-rate risk exposure is the volatility in an institution's earnings that can arise from the mismatching of the effective maturities of assets and liabilities. An insured institution may enter into short positions that are appropriate for reducing its net interest-rate risk exposure. An insured institution may enter into long positions, other than those that offset short positions, only under the following conditions:

(1) The futures position must be matched against a firm forward commitment to sell mortgages not yet originated or to issue mortgage-related securities to be based on mortgages not yet originated. For purposes of this paragraph (b), a firm forward commitment is a written commitment obligating the seller to make delivery, and the buyer to take delivery, of mortgage loans not yet originated or mortgage-related securities to be based on mortgages not yet originated, at a price and on or before a date specified in the commitment; and

(2) The futures position may be entered into and maintained only to the extent that the institution's firm forward commitments exceed 10 percent of long-term assets with fixed interest rates. For purposes of this section, long-term assets are those having remaining terms to maturity in excess of five years.

Until August 3, 1981, insured institutions may continue to engage in interest-rate futures transactions as authorized immediately prior to July 10, 1981. Institutions with interest-rate futures positions entered into before August 3, 1981, that are not permitted under this paragraph (b), will be permitted to continue to hold those futures contracts: *Provided*, That the interest-rate futures transactions were authorized when entered into and the contracts are not renewed.

(c) *Authorized contracts.* An insured institution may engage in interest-rate futures transactions using any interest-rate futures contracts designated by the Commodity Futures Trading Commission and based upon a security in which the institution has authority to invest.

(d) *Board of directors' authorization.* Prior to engaging in interest-rate futures transactions, an institution's board of directors must authorize such activity. In authorizing futures trading, the board of directors shall consider any plan to engage in interest-rate futures transactions, shall endorse specific written policies, and shall require the establishment of internal control procedures. Policy objectives must be specific enough to outline permissible contract strategies, taking into account price and yield correlations between assets or liabilities and the interest-rate futures contracts with which they are matched; the relationship of the strategies to the institution's operations; and how such strategies reduce the institution's net interest-rate risk exposure. Internal control procedures shall include, at a minimum, periodic reports to management, segregation of duties and internal review procedures. In addition, the minutes of the meeting of the board of directors shall set forth limits applicable to futures transactions, identify personnel authorized to engage in futures transactions, and set forth the duties, responsibilities and limits of authority of such personnel. The board of directors shall review the position

limit, all outstanding contract positions, and the unrealized gains or losses on those positions at each regular meeting of the board.

(e) *Notification.* An institution engaging in interest-rate futures transactions shall notify the District Director-Examinations of the Federal Home Loan Bank District in which it is located that it is engaging in such transactions. The institution shall report its gross outstanding long and short interest-rate futures positions on the Federal Home Loan Bank Board Monthly Report.

(f) *Recordkeeping requirements.* An institution engaging in interest-rate futures transactions shall maintain records of such transactions sufficient to document how the transactions reduce the net interest-rate risk exposure of the institution in accordance with the following requirements:

(1) *Contract register.* The institution shall maintain a contract register adequate to identify and control all interest-rate futures contracts and including, at a minimum, the type and amount of each contract, the maturity date of each contract, the cost of each contract, the dollar amount and description of the asset or liability with which the futures contract is matched, and the date and manner in which a contract is closed out. Such register shall be prepared in a manner sufficient to indicate at any time the institution's total outstanding long and short interest-rate futures positions.

(2) *Other documentation.* The institution shall maintain, as part of the documentation of its interest-rate futures strategy, a schedule of the assets and the liabilities for which net interest-rate risk exposure is being reduced and the purpose of each contract entered into.

(3) *Maintenance of records.* The records designated in this paragraph (f) shall be maintained for all futures transactions closed-out during the preceding two years.

(g) *Accounting* (1) *Purchase or sale.* Upon the initial purchase or sale of an interest-rate futures contract, a memorandum entry of the information specified in subparagraph (f) (1) of this section shall be made and appropriate margin accounts shall be established.

(2) *Gains and losses.* Gains and losses on interest-rate futures contracts shall be accounted for as follows:

(i) Gains and losses on futures contracts that are matched with assets or liabilities to be carried at cost shall be deferred and included in measurement of the dollar basis of the asset acquired or the liability incurred and amortized over the estimated life of the asset or liability as an adjustment to interest income or interest expense.

(ii) Gains and losses on futures contracts that are matched with existing assets or liabilities carried at cost shall be deferred and included in measurement of the dollar basis of the asset or liability and amortized over the estimated remaining life of the asset or liability as an adjustment to interest income or interest expense. If the asset or liability is sold or otherwise disposed of, the unamortized gain or loss shall be recognized in income.

(iii) Gains and losses on futures contracts that are matched with existing asset positions carried at the lower of cost or market shall be deferred and recognized in determining the lower of cost or market adjustment of the corresponding asset at the end of each reporting period, or upon sale or disposition of the corresponding asset.

No. 82-557

Date: August 11, 1982

FEDERAL HOME LOAN BANK BOARD

12 CFR PARTS 545, 563

FINANCIAL OPTIONS TRADING

Agency: Federal Home Loan Bank Board

Action: Final rule

Summary: The Board is adopting regulations: (1) authorizing federal savings and loan associations to trade financial options on domestic exchanges, (2) governing the extent to which institutions the accounts of which are insured by the Federal Savings and Loan Insurance Corporation (FSLIC) are permitted to trade financial options, and (3) making conforming amendments in the regulations governing the extent to which insured institutions may engage in forward commitment activities. The regulations permit institutions to buy options and to write call options without regulatory position limits and to write put options subject to limitations on outstanding positions.

The regulations require authorization by the institution's board of directors, notification of Board supervisory personnel, and recordkeeping similar to existing requirements for interest-rate futures contracts and forward commitments, and specify the regulatory accounting treatment for options transactions. The regulations also restructure the regulatory position limit for forward commitments and aggregate forward commitments and short put options for purposes of those limits. The regulations will provide insured institutions with a means to reduce their interest-rate risk exposure.

Effective Date: September 13, 1982

For Further Information, Please Contact: Peter M. Barnett ((202) 377-6445), Associate General Counsel, Michael S. Joseph ((202) 377-6994), Office of Examinations and Supervision, or Jerry Hartzog ((202) 377-6782), Office of Policy and Economic Research, Federal Home Loan Bank Board, 1700 G Street, N.W., Washington, D.C. 20552.

Supplementary Information:

Proposed Amendments

On February 25, 1982, the Board proposed regulations authorizing federal associations to trade financial options on domestic exchanges, governing the extent to which all insured institutions may trade financial options, and making conforming amendments in the regulations governing the extent to which insured institutions may engage in forward commitment activities. Board Resolution No. 82-135; 47 FR 9472 (1982). The Board received a total of 40 comment letters in response to its proposal. Comments were submitted by insured institutions, savings and loan trade groups, commodity brokers, commodity trading advisers, and accounting firms. Almost all of the comment letters supported Board action to permit insured institutions to trade financial options, however, several suggested amendments to the proposal. Many commenters also suggested amendment of existing interest-rate futures regulations. These suggestions are included in the discussion of the issues to which they relate.

Background

In February of 1981, the Securities and Exchange Commission (SEC) authorized the Chicago Board Options Exchange (CBOE) to establish a market in options on Government National Mortgage Association (GNMA) securities. In April of last year, the Chicago Board of Trade (CBOT) filed a petition in the United States Court of Appeals for the Seventh Circuit challenging the authority of the SEC to authorize the CBOE to establish a GNMA options market. The Commodity Futures Trading Commission

(CFTC) joined the lawsuit disputing the jurisdiction of the SEC. On March 24, 1982, the Seventh Circuit issued an opinion holding that the GNMA options contract proposed by the CBOE was within the exclusive regulatory jurisdiction of the CFTC and that the SEC has no jurisdiction to authorize trading in GNMA options. *Board of Trade of the City of Chicago v. SEC*, No. 81–1660 (March 24, 1982). Legislation currently moving through Congress, however, would resolve the jurisdictional dispute between the SEC and CFTC. The legislation is expected to be enacted during the current Congress.

In November of 1981, the CFTC adopted final regulations authorizing the trading of options on futures contracts on domestic commodity exchanges, including options on GNMA and other interest-rate futures contracts. 46 FR 54570 (1981). The CFTC currently is considering applications by a number of exchanges filed pursuant to those rules for designation as contract markets for options on futures contracts. In June of this year, the CFTC proposed rules to expand the pilot options program to permit and govern the trading of options on commodities (physicals) on domestic exchanges. 47 FR 28401 (1982).

The Board believes that these developments portend the opening of options trading on domestic exchanges in the near future. As stated in the preamble to its proposal, the Board believes that its regulations should be timely and flexible enough to permit insured institutions to participate in the development of these markets. While trading of options has not yet commenced on domestic exchanges, the Board believes that the structure for trading is sufficiently established to adopt final regulations.

Authorized Contracts

The Board proposed to permit institutions to trade any option contracts approved by the SEC or designated by the CFTC for trading on domestic exchanges and based upon a security in which the institution is authorized to invest. This authorization was intended to include options on physicals as well as options on futures contracts. One commenter, however, suggested that the use of GNMA options in the examples discussed in the supplementary information and the language of the proposed regulation could be construed to limit the authority to options on certain physicals. In response, the Board notes that the examples in the supplementary information of its proposal were intended to be educational in nature and not to limit the proposal. Since insured institutions already are familiar with GNMA options traded over-the-counter and the CBOE GNMA option was the only contract for which trading had been authorized on a domestic exchange at the time of the proposal, its use in the examples was appropriate. The final regulation clarifies that the contracts permitted for trading include options on any financial instrument in which the institution is authorized to invest or to issue and options on interest-rate futures contracts. The limitations of Insurance Regulation § 563.17–4 on institutions entering into long futures positions should not be construed to suggest any restriction on the trading of financial options based on long futures positions. Institutions with long call options on futures positions, however, must offset those positions rather than take delivery of the underlying long futures contract unless the long position is in conformity with the requirements of § 563.17–4. For institutions with short put options on futures positions, the institution shall, in the event of the exercise of the option, immediately offset the delivered long futures position unless the long position is in conformity with the requirements of § 563.17–4.

Authorized Transactions and Position Limits

As discussed in the proposal, savings and loans often grant discretionary contract terms to customers as part of their ordinary business practices and would be able to reduce the risk inherent in those discretionary contracts by holding option contracts of an offsetting nature. For instance, insured institutions may benefit from the use of long put options to reduce the interest-rate risk exposure of their forward commitments to advance funds in the cash markets. Similarly, institutions could use long call options to reduce the risk associated with forward commitments to sell investments or with loan prepayments. On the basis that the costs of purchasing options will discourage superfluous use of long options, the Board proposed to permit options transactions without a regulatory position limit for long puts and long calls. The comment letters uniformly supported this aspect of the proposal, and it is adopted in the final regulation.

Short call options also can be used to reduce the profit volatility inherent in the asset and liabiliy maturity structure of savings and loans by substituting a steady fee income for potential gains in market value when matched against investments of an institution. The Board proposed to permit institutions to enter into short call positions without a regulatory position limit. This would parallel the treatment of forward commitments to sell securities, which are not limited by Board regulations. The Board expressly solicited comments on this aspect of the proposal, and commenters generally agreed that margin requirements imposed by the exchanges and monitoring by an institution's board of directors should discourage excessive call writing. Consistent with the proposal, the Board has determined that a regulatory position limit on short call options is not necessary, and the final regulations permit short call options subject only to board of director-imposed position limits.

Since, on the other hand, short put options tend to have adverse effects on savings and loan profit volatility in most circumstances, the Board proposed a strict regulatory position limit on such contracts. Moreover, because short put options and forward commitments to purchase securities have similar effects on profitability, the Board proposed to impose a limit on the aggregate amount of these positions. Many commenters suggested that the proposed limit on short put options was too low. A few commenters noted that the effect of combining short put options and forward commitments to purchase securities would subject forward commitments to purchase securities to stricter limits than currently applicable. No commenter, however, was able to demonstrate how short put options could be used to lessen the interest-rate risk exposure of insured institutions.

The Board continues to believe that short put options should be subject to a regulatory position limit. In addition, because short put options are substitutes for forward commitments to purchase securities, the Board believes that subjecting both types of transactions to the same limitation is appropriate. Accordingly, the limitations on short put options and forward commitments contained in the proposal are included in the final regulation. As suggested by one commenter, however, the final regulation clarifies that the limitation only applies to new positions, so that positions permitted when entered into would not be affected by subsequent changes in net worth. Accordingly, the final regulations permit institutions to write put options and to issue forward commitments to purchase securities so long as the aggregate outstanding positions do not exceed five percent of assets if net worth is less than three percent of assets, 10 percent of assets if net worth is three percent to less than five percent of assets, and 15 percent of assets if net worth is five percent or more of assets.

Board of Directors' Authorization

The Board believes that it is essential for an institution to formulate a strategy that relates the trading of financial options contracts to the business activities of the institution and for the board of directors to endorse the strategy. Therefore, the final regulation adopts the requirements of the proposal regarding board-of-director approval. The regulation requires specific authorization from the board of directors before an institution may engage in options trading, and adoption of written policies and internal control procedures with respect to options trading. Internal control procedures include specification of the personnel authorized to engage in options trading, along with their duties, responsibilities and position limits. The board of directors also is required to establish an institutional position limit and to review all outstanding contract positions and unrealized gains and losses on outstanding contracts at each regular meeting.

Notification

The final regulation adopts the notification requirement of the proposal to ensure adequate supervision of options trading activities. Thus, before engaging in financial options trading an institution must notify the District Director—Examinations of the Federal Home Loan Bank District in which it is located that it intends to trade options. In addition, an institution is required to report its outstanding positions and its unrealized gains and losses on those positions in its monthly report to the Board. In response to a few commenters, the final regulation clarifies that notification is necessary only when an institution's board of directors first authorizes options trading.

Recordkeeping Requirements

The Board believes that adequate records are essential for both the Board and an institution's board of directors to monitor options trading, and the final regulations retain the proposed recordkeeping requirements. Thus, an insured institution engaging in financial options trading must: (1) maintain a register of all outstanding options contracts; (2) maintain a record of each options contract outstanding, the purpose for which the contract was entered into, and any cash market transaction(s) or position(s) against which it is matched; and (3) retain the records specified in (1) and (2) for all closed-out options transactions for a period of two years.

Accounting

As discussed in the proposal, there is currently no single recognized accounting treatment for financial options transactions. While accounting guidelines for options transactions likely will be considered by the Financial Accounting Standards Board ("FASB"), it is unlikely that a definitive statement will be forthcoming in the near future. In light of the options trading proposed to be authorized and the importance of the manner in which options transactions are accounted for in terms of their impact on an institution's profitability, the Board believes that it is necessary to establish its own accounting rules to be used by insured institutions engaging in options transactions. Accordingly, certain basic principles were included in the proposed regulation.

The accounting treatment proposed was a combination of mark-to-market and hedge accounting techniques. In addition, the proposal would have required the total option premium to be divided into two components: the option commitment fee and the immediate exercise value of the option. A few comment letters suggested that the proposed accounting treatment was overly complicated. These commenters suggested that division of the total option premium into two components and the determination of an immediate exercise value is imprecise and burdensome. Upon consideration of these comments, however, the Board continues to believe that the proposed accounting treatment best reflects the economic circumstances surrounding the payment of an option premium. The computation of an immediate exercise value will be necessary only where an option is "in-the-money." Since hedge transactions in options ordinarily will involve "out-of-the-money" options with no immediate exercise value, the entire option price could be treated as the option commitment fee. Only in the unusual case of an in-the-money option will calculation of an immediate exercise value be necessary. Therefore, the final regulations adopt the accounting treatment originally proposed.

Accordingly, insured institutions are required to use hedge accounting for recognizing gains and losses on long and short call, and long put, option positions properly matched against cash or forward market positions. Hedge accounting treats the gain or loss from an option position as an adjustment to the carrying amount of the cash or forward market position against which the option is matched. Unmatched long and short call positions, unmatched long put positions and any short put positions must be accounted for on a marked-to-market basis.

For all financial options transactions subject to hedge accounting, the regulation requires that the transactions be matched properly against cash or forward market positions and that the options transactions reduce the interest-rate risk of those corresponding transactions. Proper matching necessitates the pairing of an option and an existing asset, liability, or written commitment, whether firm or standby. Matching options against anticipated cash flow is *not* acceptable matching. Cross hedging and direct hedging of cash or forward market positions are permitted. Matching does not have to be on a dollar-per-dollar basis; however, an institution is required to set forth the rationale for its hedge ratios in its written options strategy. Institutions may use two or more option positions simultaneously as a hedge of a single cash or forward market position.

The regulation also requires the total option premium to be divided into two components: the option commitment fee and the immediate exercise value of the option. The commitment fee is recognized as an expense or revenue item over the term of the option. Changes in the immediate exercise value of the option are treated as gains and losses and are subject to hedge accounting treatment. The immediate exercise value of an option is computed by comparing the adjusted or effective exercise price of the lowest cost financial instrument that is currently deliverable with the cash market price of that same coupon security.

The Board restates its belief that anticipated cash flows are not an acceptable matching for purposes of hedge accounting. Given the asset and liability structure of insured institutions, anticipatory "hedges" increase the term of an institution's assets and the interest-rate risk exposure of the institution. Lastly, the Board reiterates that the accounting treatment adopted will be reexamined at the time accounting rules for financial options are issued by FASB.

Application to All Insured Institutions

Because the trading of options on organized exchanges will affect the interest-rate risk exposure of all insured institutions, the Board proposed to apply the regulations governing financial options to all insured institutions. In order to ensure that options are used in a manner consistent with safe financial policies and management and to provide uniformity in examination and enforcement, the final regulations adopt this position. State-chartered institutions should note, however, that their legal authority to trade option contracts derives from state law, although the extent to which they may exercise that authority is limited by the regulation adopted today.

Financial Futures Transactions

In connection with the proposed regulations permitting institutions to trade options contracts, the Board solicited comments on the regulation governing the use of interest-rate futures transactions (46 FR 36829 (1981), to be codified at 12 CFR 563.17–4). The Board solicited comments on whether and to what extent existing limits on long futures positions should be modified. Commenters were asked to discuss how expanded use of long futures positions could reduce the net interest-rate risk exposure of an insured institution and to present specific examples of techniques for using long positions.

The regulation governing interest-rate futures trading by insured institutions permits the use of long futures positions only in connection with forward commitments to sell mortgages not yet originated or the issuance of mortgage-related securities to be based on mortgages not yet originated. Long futures positions are permitted only to the extent that an institution's forward commitments exceed 10 percent of long-term assets. Almost all commenters suggested that these limits were overly restrictive, but only a few commenters were able to give examples of how long futures positions could be used to reduce net-interest-rate risk exposure. These examples either involved hedge transactions that could be achieved by other means within the current regulation (*i.e.,* the equivalent of T-bond spreads can be achieved with T-bill strips) or would apply to interest-rate risks experienced by only a very small number of institutions (*i.e.,* locking-in the rate for reinvestment of maturing assets reduces risk only for institutions that are net short in the cash market).

On the basis of the comment responses and other available information, the Board continues to believe that the use of long futures positions is generally not appropriate for insured institutions. This is because the asset and liability structure of savings and loans generally exposes them to risk when interst rates rise unexpectedly, similar to the risk in long futures positions. Thus, an institution's interest-rate risk exposure typically is increased, rather than lessened, by long futures positions. For these reasons the final regulations do not permit increased use of long futures positions. The final regulations, however, do make certain technical amendments to §§ 545.29 and 563.17–4 to conform its terminology to that used in the new options regulations.

Forward Commitment Limitations

The proposal also would have amended the current limitations on forward commitment activities of insured institutions contained in § 563.17–3 of the Insurance Regulations. 12 CFR 563.17–3 (1981). As discussed above, these amendments are adopted as proposed. Newly-authorized transactions in short put options and currently-authorized forward commitments to purchase securities are subject, in the aggregate, to the position limits set forth in § 563.17–3. The regulations also limit the combined activities of an institution in forward commitments and short put options based on its net-worth-to-assets ratio. The regulations establish a three-tiered structure to allow an institution with a relatively low net worth to engage in the newly-authorized transactions subject to a lower percentage-of-assets limitation.

The Board also solicited comments on the proper accounting treatment for forward commitments of insured institutions. In particular, the Board was interested in comments on whether and under what circumstances mark-to-market accounting should be required for forward commitments and whether the accounting for forward commitments should parallel the proposed accounting for options transactions. The comment letters did not produce evidence that the current accounting treatment should be amended, and the final regulations do not change these rules.

Final Regulatory Flexibility Analysis

Pursuant to section 3 of the Regulatory Flexibility Act, Pub. L. No. 96–354, Stat. 1164 (September 19, 1980), the Board is providing the following regulatory flexibility analysis.

1. *Reasons, objectives, and legal basis underlying the regulations.* These elements have been incorporated elsewhere into the supplementary information regarding the regulations.

2. *Small entities to which the regulations will apply.* The regulations will apply only to institutions the accounts of which are insured by the Federal Savings and Loan Insurance Corporation.

3. *Impact of the regulations on small institutions.* The regulations permit institutions to engage in options trading activities regardless of size and impose reporting, recordkeeping and other regulatory requirements uniformly based upon the extent of trading activity. To the extent that small institutions effectively reduce interest-rate risk by using options market transactions, the regulations would benefit their operations. There is no disproportionate effect on small institutions.

4. *Overlapping or conflicting federal rules.* There are no known federal rules that may duplicate, overlap or conflict with the regulations.

5. *Alternatives to the regulations.* The basic requirements included in the regulations are limitations on the types of options transactions permitted, a written policy endorsed by the institution's board of directors, maintenance of a register documenting options transactions and their purpose, establishment of internal control mechanisms, and providing quarterly notice to the District Director-Examinations. A limitation on transactions, internal control procedures and monitoring by the supervisory staff are minimally necessary

requirements to ensure that options trading is undertaken in a safe and sound manner and that losses which an institution might incur are limited. It would not be possible to eliminate or modify these requirements for smaller entities and still expect them to engage in options trading in a reasonable manner.

List of Subjects in 12 CFR Parts 545 and 563

Federal Home Loan Bank Board
Savings and loan associations

Accordingly, the Federal Home Loan Bank Board hereby amends Parts 545 and 563, Subchapters C and D, Chapter V of Title 12, *Code of Federal Regulations*, as set forth below.

Subchapter C—Federal Savings and Loan System

Part 545—Operations

1. Amend § 545.29 to read as follows:

§ 545.29 *Financial futures transactions.*

A Federal association may engage in financial futures transactions in compliance with § 563.17–4 of this Chapter.

2. Add a new § 545.29–1 to read as follows:

§ 545.29–1 *Financial options transactions.*

A Federal association may engage in financial options transactions in compliance with § 563.17–5 of this Chapter.

Subchapter D—Federal Savings and Loan Insurance Corporation

Part 563—Operations

3. Amend § 563.17–3 by revising paragraphs (a)(2) and (c)(2) to read as follows:

§ 563.17–3 *Forward commitments.*

(a) *Definitions.*

   *   *   *   *   *

(2) *Securities*: assets in which the insured institution is authorized to invest (except financial futures or financial options contracts entered into pursuant to §§ 563.17–4 or 563.17–5 of this Part).

   *   *   *   *   *

(c) *Limitations.*

   *   *   *   *   *

(2) *Percent of assets.* An insured institution's outstanding forward commitments to purchase securities plus short put options entered into pursuant to § 563.17-5 of this Part may not exceed an amount equal to five percent of its assets if net worth is three percent or less of assets, 10 percent of its assets if net worth is over three percent but less than five percent of assets, or 15 percent of its assets if net worth is five percent or more of assets.

* * * * *

4. Amend § 563.17-4 by: (i) substituting the term "financial instrument" for the term "security" in subparagraph (1) of paragraph (a); (ii) substituting the term "a financial instrument" for the term "securities" each time it appears in subparagraphs (3), (5) and (6) of paragraph (a); (iii) substituting the term "financial futures" for the term "interest-rate futures" each time it appears; and (iv) revising the subtitle and text of paragraph (c) to read as follows:

§ 563.17-4 *Financial futures transactions.*

* * * * *

(c) *Authorized contracts.* An insured institution may engage in financial futures transactions using any financial futures contracts designated by the Commodity Futures Trading Commission and based upon a financial instrument that the institution has authority to invest in or to issue.

* * * * *

5. Add a new § 563.17-5 to read as follows:

§ 563.17-5 *Financial options transactions.*

(a) *Definitions.* As used in this section, the following definitions apply unless the context otherwise requires:

(1) *Call.* An option which gives the holder the right to purchase a financial instrument at a price and on or before the expiration date specified in the option contract.

(2) *Deliverable instrument.* A financial instrument whose terms satisfy the requirements for fulfilling delivery obligations of an option.

(3) *Effective exercise price.* The yield equivalent price of an instrument whose coupon rate differs from the standard instrument specified in the option.

(4) *Financial options contract.* An agreement to make or take delivery of a standardized financial instrument upon demand by the holder of the contract at any time prior to the expiration date specified in the agreement, under terms and conditions established by an exchange designated or regulated by the Commodity Futures Trading Commission or the Securities Exchange Commission.

(5) *Financial options transaction.* Purchase or sale of a financial options contract.

(6) *Immediate exercise value.* The market value gained by exercising an option with the lowest cost deliverable instrument at its effective exercise price compared to purchasing (or selling) an identical instrument with the same coupon rate in the cash market.

(7) *Long position.* The holding of a financial options contract with the option to make or take delivery of a financial instrument.

(8) *Option commitment fee.* The option premium minus the immediate exercise value of the option.

(9) *Option premium.* The price paid or received for establishing an option position.

(10) *Put.* An option which gives the holder the right to sell a financial instrument at a price and on or before the expiration date specified in the financial options contract.

(11) *Short position.* A commitment through a financial options contract to stand ready during the term of the contract to make or take delivery of a financial instrument.

(b) *Permitted transactions.* To the extent that it has legal power to do so, an insured institution may engage in financial options transactions as provided in this paragraph (b).

(1) *Long positions.* An insured institution may enter into long positions without numerical limit.

(2) *Short positions.* An insured institution may enter into short call positions without numerical limit. An institution may enter into short put options to the extent that the aggregate amount of its short put options and forward commitments to purchase securities does not exceed the limitations set forth in § 563.17–3(c)(2) of this Part.

(c) *Authorized contracts.* An insured institution may engage in financial options transactions using any financial options contracts designated by the Commodity Futures Trading Commission or approved by the Securities and Exchange Commission, and based upon a financial instrument that the institution has authority to invest in or to issue, or based upon a financial futures contract.

(d) *Board of directors' authorization.* Prior to engaging in financial options transactions, an institution's board of directors must authorize such activity. In authorizing options, the board of directors shall consider any plan to engage in writing or purchasing financial options contracts, shall endorse specific written policies, and shall require the establishment of internal control procedures. For options positions that will be matched with cash or forward market positions, policy objectives must be specific enough to outline permissible options contract strategies, taking into account price and yield correlations between assets or liabilities and the financial options contracts;

the relationship of the strategies to the institution's operations; the rationale for the ratio of the value of options positions to the value of the matched cash market positions; and how the options strategy reduces the institution's interest-rate risk exposure. For unmatched option positions, policy objectives must specify the relationship of the strategy to the institution's operations. Prudent business judgment shall be exercised by participating institutions engaging in financial options transactions in order to maintain a safe and sound financial position. Internal control procedures shall include, at a minimum, periodic reports to management, segregation of duties and internal review procedures. In addition, the minutes of the meeting of the board of directors shall set forth limits applicable to financial options transactions, identify personnel authorized to engage in financial options transactions, and set forth the duties, responsibilities and limits of authority of such personnel. The board of directors shall review the position limit, all outstanding options contract positions, and the unrealized gains or losses on those positions at each regular meeting of the board.

(e) *Notification and reporting.* An institution shall notify the District Director-Examinations of the Federal Home Loan Bank District in which it is located immediately following authorization of its board of directors to engage in financial options transactions. The institution shall report its outstanding positions together with the total unrealized gain or loss from such positions on the Federal Home Loan Bank Board Monthly Report.

(f) *Recordkeeping requirements.* An institution engaging in financial options transactions shall maintain records of such transactions in accordance with the following requirements:

(1) *Contract register.* The institution shall maintain a contract register adequate to identify and control all financial options contracts and sufficient to indicate at any time the amounts of financial options contracts required to be reported on its monthly report. At a minimum, the register shall list the type, amount, expiration date and the cost of or income from each contract.

(2) *Other documentation.* The institution shall maintain as part of the documentation of its financial options strategy a schedule of any cash market or forward commitment position with which the option is matched and the purpose of each contract.

(3) *Maintenance of records.* The records designated in this paragraph (f) shall be maintained for all financial options closed-out during the preceding two years.

(g) *Accounting.*

(1) *Purchase or sale.* Upon initial purchase or sale of a financial options contract, a memorandum entry of the information specified in subparagraph (1) of paragraph (f) of this section shall be made and appropriate margin accounts shall be established.

(2) Option commitment fee. The option commitment fee paid or received shall be amortized to income or expense over the term of the option, except as provided in subparagraph (3)(ii) of this paragraph (g).

(3) *Options contracts.* (i) Gains or losses on options contracts that are matched with assets or liabilities carried at the lower of cost or market value or carried at market value shall be considered in determining the market value of the asset or liability.

(ii) Options positions that are matched with assets or liabilities carried at cost or to be carried at cost shall be accounted for as follows:

(*a*) if a commitment fee will be or has been received with respect to the matched asset, the option commitment fee shall be treated as an adjustment of such fee. The adjusted commitment fee shall then be treated as a fee paid or received in connection with the matched asset;

(*b*) if a commitment fee has not been received with respect to a matched asset, the option commitment fee shall be amortized to income or expense over the commitment period by the straight-line method;

(*c*) any resulting gain or loss from an option position shall be treated as a discount or premium on the matched asset or liability;

(*d*) in the event that the cash market or forward commitment position with which an option is matched is sold or will not occur, the option shall be marked-to-market.

(iii) The immediate exercise value of short puts and other unmatched option positions shall be carried at their current market value.

(Sec. 409, 94 Stat. 160. Secs. 402, 403, 407, 48 Stat. 1256, 1257, 1260, as amended (12 U.S.C. §§ 1725, 1726, 1730). Sec. 5A, 47 Stat. 727, as amended by sec. 1, 64 Stat. 256, as amended; sec. 17, 47 Stat. 736, as amended (12 U.S.C. § 1464). Reorg. Plan No. 3 of 1947, 12 F.R. 4891, 3 CFR, 1943–48 Comp., p. 1071)

By the Federal Home Loan Bank Board

Gregory B. Smith
Acting Secretary

Appendix C: Futures Accounting

At the time of publication of this book final rules for futures accounting had not been issued by the Financial Accounting Standards Board. An exposure draft of proposed regulations for futures accounting was issued July 14, 1983. The essence of these rules is reprinted below.

FEDERAL ACCOUNTING STANDARDS BOARD
(FASB)

PROPOSED STATEMENT OF FINANCIAL ACCOUNTING STANDARDS

ACCOUNTING FOR FUTURES CONTRACTS

(Exposure Draft)

NOTE

This exposure document published by FASB will not necessarily be the final rule on futures accounting. However, it does cover the entire gamut of issues that are relevant for financial institutions. Most importantly, the FASB ruling, as it stood at publication, would generally rule out macro hedges since it requires specific identification of hedged assets, liabilities, or commitments.

Summary

The provisions of this proposed statement would apply to general purpose financial statements of all enterprises that enter into futures contracts (other then foreign currency futures) that are traded on exchanges. This project was undertaken in response to requests to address the issues in two AICPA Issues Papers that concerned futures contracts and because the board is aware of diversity in practice in accounting for futures contracts.

Initial cash margin payments would be recognized as assets at the inception of the contract. A change in the value of an open futures contract would be recognized as a gain or loss in the period of the change unless (a) the contract qualifies as a hedge of a present exposure or (b) the contract relates to a qualifying anticipated transaction. To qualify in either case, a futures contract would have to be matched with identifiable assets, liabilities, firm commitments, or anticipated transactions.

To the extent a futures contract is effective as a hedge, changes in its market value would be reported as adjustments of the carrying amount of the hedged item. That accounting method would not apply, however, if the futures contract is intended to hedge an item that is reported at fair value (which frequently will be the case for futures contracts used as hedges by investment companies, pension plans, and broker-dealers). A change in the market value of such futures contracts would be recognized immediately in income. The cumulative change in the market value of a contract that relates to a qualifying anticipated transaction generally would be included in the measurement of that transaction when it occurs.

This proposed Statement would be applied for future contracts entered into after December 31, 1983, with earlier application encouraged in annual financial statements that have not been previously issued.

Proposed Statement of Financial Accounting Standards
Accounting for Futures Contracts
July 14, 1983

Introduction

1. The FASB is aware that there is diversity in practice in the accounting for futures contracts. The basic issue involves when changes in the market value of those contracts should be recognized in income. Current practices are to recognize such changes as gains or losses in the periods in which they occur, to recognize some changes in income currently and defer others depending on the reason for entering into the contract, to recognize a decline in value in income currently and defer recognition of a net increase in value until the contract is closed out, or to defer recognition in income of all changes in value until the contract is closed out.

Scope

2. This Statement establishes standards of financial accounting and reporting for futures contracts, except foreign currency futures.[1]

Standards of Financial Accounting and Reporting

3. An initial margin deposit made upon entering into a futures contract shall be recognized as an amount due from the broker that has acted as the enterprise's agent in acquiring the futures position. During the period the contract is outstanding, that asset shall be increased or decreased for changes in the market value of the futures contract.[2]

4. A change in the market value of a futures contract shall be recognized according to the circumstances under which the contract is entered into and the enterprise's method of accounting for related transactions and events. The presumption is that enterprises shall recognize a change in the market value of a futures contract as a gain or loss in the period of the change. That presumption may be overcome, however, if the contract is an economic hedge of an existing exposure or if it relates to certain probable future transactions. In the circumstances specified in paragraphs 5–9, the accounting for changes in the market value of a futures contract shall be related to the accounting for the associated assets, liabilities or transactions.

Hedges

5. A futures contract may be a hedge of an enterprise's (a) asset, (b) liability,[3] or (c) firm commitment to purchase or sell a commodity or financial instrument at a fixed price. A contract may also hedge identifiable groups of like items (for example, loans that have similar terms). A change in the market value of a

---

[1] The provisions of FASB Statement No. 52, *Foreign Currency Translation,* apply to accounting for foreign currency futures.

[2] For purposes of this Statement, the change in the market value of a futures contract means the change in the quoted market price of the contract times the contract size. For example, the change in market value of a $100,000 U.S. Treasury Bond futures contract whose quoted price moves from 80-00 to 78-00 is $2000.

[3] Liability hedges covered by this paragraph are long futures positions that relate to presently outstanding fixed-rate obligations. The accounting for short futures positions that relate to the repricing of variable-rate obligations or anticipated issuances of fixed-rate obligations is covered in paragraphs 7 and 8.

futures contract that qualifies as a hedge of an asset or liability shall be reported as an adjustment of the carrying amount of the hedged item. A change in the market value of a futures contract that qualifies as a hedge of a firm fixed-price commitment shall be included in the measurement of the transaction that satisfies the commitment. However, gain or loss shall be recognized to the extent the futures contract has not been effective as a hedge.[4] A futures contract shall qualify as hedge for purposes of this statment if all of the following conditions are met:

a. *The item to be hedged exposes the enterprise to price risk.* In the absence of the futures contract, the enterprise is exposed to the risk of price or interest rate changes because of owning the asset, owing the liability, or having the firm commitment. The nature of the enterprise's business: current operating conditions; and other assets, liabilities, commitments, and transactions shall be considered in determining whether there is an exposure. For example, ownership of inventory (or having a firm commitment to acquire inventory at a fixed price) would not be considered an exposure if subsequent changes in the fair value of the commodity will have little or no effect on the price at which it, or a product made from the item, can be sold. Also, an investment in fixed-rate interest bearing financial instruments by a financial institution would not be a exposure if that investment, in effect, is funded by fixed-rate obligations of comparable maturities.

b. *The futures contract reduces the exposure to price risk and is designated as a hedge.* It is probable that changes in (1) the market value of the asset, liability, or firm commitment and (2) the market value of the futures contract(s) will be highly correlated. The item that underlies the futures contract may differ from the item to be hedged only if it is not practicable for the enterprise to enter into a futures contract for the identical commodity or financial instrument.

c. *Unrealized changes in the fair value of the hedged item are not included, or are included only in certain circumstances, in the determination of income.* Examples of items that meet this condition are investments carried at cost, liabilities carried at historical proceeds, and inventory carried at the lower of cost or market. If an item does not meet this condition (for example, bonds carried at market by a investment company would

---

[4]The effectiveness of the futures contract(s) as a hedge may be assessed by comparing the change in the market value of the contract(s) and the unrecognized changes in the fair value of the hedged item (asset, liability, or commitment) since the inception of the hedge.

not meet the condition), a change in the market value of a futures contract that is intended to be a hedge of that item shall be recognized as a gain or loss when the change occurs. The required accounting shall commence when the futures contract is designated as a hedge of the asset, liability, firm commitment, or identifiable group of like items.

6. The disposition of the adjustments of carrying amount of assets and liabilities required by paragraph 5 shall be the same as other components of the carrying amounts of those assets or liabilities. Adjustments of the carrying amount of a hedged interest-bearing financial instrument that is otherwise reported at amortized cost shall be recognized as interest income or interest expense over the remaining life of the instrument. That amortization shall commence on the date the hedge is terminated.

Futures Contracts Related to Certain Anticipated Transactions

7. Some futures contracts that do not relate to existing assets, liabilities, or firm commitments may relate to transactions an enterprise expects, but is not legally obligated, to carry out. A change in the market value of such contracts shall be included in the measurement of the related subsequent transaction (subject to the limitations in paragraph 8) when it occurs if *all* of the following conditions are met:

a. *The significant terms of the anticipated transaction are identified.* The significant terms would include the expected date of the transaction, the commodity or type of financial instrument involved, and the quantity to be purchased or sold. Enterprises sometimes may be unable to identify a single transaction because two or more similar transactions are possible. For example, a financial institution that plans to issue short-term obligations at a particular future date may have the choice of issuing various types of such obligations in domestic markets or foreign markets. Identification of more than one possible transaction does not preclude use of the accounting method in this paragraph as long as conditions b, c and d are met for each possible transaction.

b. *It is probable that the subsequent transaction will occur because, in the normal course of business, the enterprise has little discretion to do otherwise.* Considerations in assessing the likelihood that a transaction will occur include: the frequency of similar transactions in the past; the financial and operational ability of the enterprise to carry out the transaction; irreversible commitments of resources to a particular activity (for example, a planted field or a manufacturing facility that can be used in the short run only to process a particular type of commodity); and the time to the anticipated transaction date. If it is likely that failure to make the identified transaction(s) would result in little cost or disruption of operations, condition b generally would not be met.

c. *Consummation of the anticipated transaction at a price substantially different from the current price will have a direct impact on the enterprise's profitability.* Whether this condition is met primarily depends on the relationship of the buying and selling prices (price includes interest rates) faced by the enterprise. For example, for competitive or other reasons, some processors may market their finished products at prices that are relatively stable in the short run. In such circumstances, it may be unlikely that unexpectedly higher prices for important raw material inputs would be recoverable through higher selling prices. Other enterprises—because of contracts, market conditions, or other factors—may be able to adjust sales prices to cover additional raw material costs. In the latter case, condition c usually would not be met.

d. *It is probable that changes in the market value of the futures contract(s) will offset changes in the price at which the transactions can be consummated.* Refer to paragraph 5b.

8. The accounting for a futures contract that relates to a qualifying planned transaction shall be consistent with the enterprise's method of accounting for the related assets or liabilities. For example, a decline in the value of a futures contract that relates to a planned inventory purchase would be recognized as a loss if there is evidence that the amount will not be recovered through sales. Also, a gain or loss would be recognized on a futures contract if unrealized changes in the fair value of the asset or liability subsequent to acquisition or issuance will be recognized in income. If the futures contract is closed before the date of the anticipated transaction, the accumulated change in value of the contract shall continue to be carried forward (subject to the other considerations in this paragraph) and included in the measurement of the related transaction. A pro rata portion of the market value changes that would otherwise be included in the measurement of the transaction shall be recognized as a gain or loss when it become probable that the quantity of the anticipated transaction will be less than originally identified.

DISCLOSURE

9. Enterprises that apply the accounting specified in paragraphs 5-8 of this statement shall disclose: (a) the nature of the items that are hedged with futures contracts or the anticipated transactions to which futures contracts relate and (b) the method(s) of accounting for the futures contracts. The disclosure of the method(s) shall include a description of the events or transactions that result in recognition in income of the changes in value of the futures contracts."

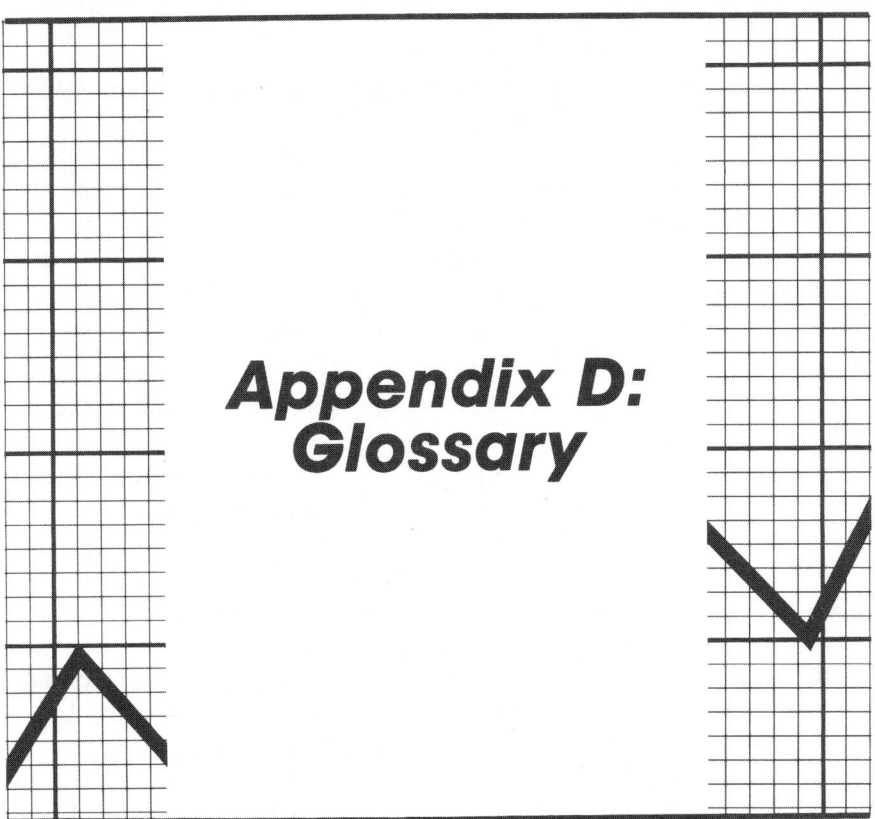

Appendix D: Glossary

Arbitrage: a transaction which involves buying a commodity in one market and simultaneously selling it in another market in order to profit from a disparity in prices between two markets; it is a riskless transaction. In the futures market arbitrage usually refers to a transaction in which one sells futures and buys cash, or vice versa, in order to profit from an unusually large or small basis.

Asset and Liability Management: a strategy to limit interest rate risk, generally an attempt to match the maturities of assets and liabilities; more than simple matching, asset and liability management introduces the concept of planning horizons of different lengths, e.g., categories of assets are maturity matched within categories of liabilities. **(See Gap.)**

Bar Charts: charts graphically illustrating price activity of the market. The bar is a vertical line drawn on a graph between the high and low price with a small horizontal mark depicting the settlement price. The most common bar charts graph daily price activity.

Basis: the difference in price between a futures contract and its underlying cash instrument.

Basis Risk: the risk that the price of a futures contract and the price of the cash instrument will not move by the same degree. This risk is usually considerably less than interest rate risk.

Broker: a person or firm registered with the Commodities Futures Trading Commission (CFTC) to execute trades on commodity exchanges for customers; generally an individual employed by a brokerage firm or FCM.

Call: an option contract which gives the holder the right to purchase a specified futures contract at a known price on or before the expiration date of the option.

Car: colloquial term for a futures contract originating from the term boxcar as the size of some agricultural contracts are determined by rail car capacity.

Carry: also known as cost of money—the amount of money or rate it takes to finance the ownership of an instrument for a given time period.

Cash Market: the market for immediate payment and delivery of securities or commodities, as opposed to the futures market which calls for payment and delivery at a future date. Also known as spot market.

CDR: Collateralized Depository Receipt, the instrument used as a delivery vehicle against the GNMA contract on the Chicago Board of Trade; a CDR is a receipt for actual GNMA certificates held in trust by the originator of the certificate.

CFTC: Commodity Futures Trading Commission—the governmental agency that regulates futures trading.

Chartists: market technicians that make buy or sell decisions based on technical analysis, e.g., bar and point & figure, charts.

Cheap: an instrument selling for a price lower than that for which all normal pricing factors call; e.g., at times a futures contract may be "cheap" relative to its underlying cash instrument.

Cheaper to Deliver: since futures contracts often allow for a number of instruments to vary within certain parameters to be deliverable, one of them will be cheapest to deliver.

Clearing Corporation: a corporation which is part of a futures exchange and clears trades between members, handles margin accounts, arranges delivery of commodities when required; assures the financial security of the exchange.

Clearing Member: a member firm of an exchange conforming to rigorous financial requirements. It is an integral part of the clearing corporation. Clearing membership provides the financial clout for the clearing corporation.

Commissions: the fees that a broker charges a customer for executing a trade; all commission rates are negotiable. The larger the account in terms of trading volume, the smaller is the commission per trade. All futures commissions are for a roundtrip and are paid when a position is closed.

Convergence: the coming together of cash and futures prices as the maturity date of the futures contract is approached.

Conversion Factor: a factor used to determine the amount of Treasury bonds or GNMAs of a nonstandard coupon which will satisfy delivery requirements; $100,000 face value of eight percent coupon bonds is required for delivery, but an equivalent value of other coupons may be delivered—the conversion factor indicates the acceptable amount.

Conversion: an arbitrage spread consisting of a long futures contract and a short synthetic future (short a call, long a put); also known as a forward conversion.

Correlation Coefficient: a statistical measure of the joint variation of two variables; coefficient varies between -1 and $+1$; a positive correlation coefficient means the two variables usually both increase and decrease together; a negative coefficient means they move in opposite directions; a zero coefficient indicates no relationship between the variables. For hedging purposes the closer the coefficient is to $+1.00$ the better.

Covered Writing: writing (selling) option contracts against cash securities currently held; opposite of naked writing in which an option is sold and the seller does not own or anticipate owning the securities.

Cross Hedge: hedging a commodity with a futures contract based on a different underlying commodity, e.g. hedging municipal bonds with Treasury bond futures contracts. Cross hedges are normally put on when there is no futures contract based on the commodity being hedged.

Daily Limit: The maximum amount a futures contract price may change in one day. It is set by each exchange and subject to change.

Day Trader: a trader who has no open positions at the end of the day. Day traders add a great amount of liquidity to the futures market.

Delivery Month: the month in which a futures contract matures and delivery must be made or taken on any open contracts.

Delta: the change in the theoretical value of an option expressed as a percentage of the change in the futures price.

Disintermediation: the act of withdrawing funds from a financial institution and investing directly in money market instruments or money market funds; usually occurs when deposit rate ceilings become effective.

Dollar Equivalency: a hedge designed so that a change in price of the cash instrument is matched dollar for dollar by the change in price of the futures position.

Dressed Writing: writing (selling) an option against an opposite futures position currently held.

FCM: Futures Commission Merchant; a commodity brokerage firm that deals with the public for profit, charges commission, and handles margin accounts. FCMs must be registered with the CFTC.

Fees: charges in addition to commissions which are transactions costs on futures trades. They are imposed on a per contract basis for the support of the exchanges and the National Futures Association, a regulatory body.

Financial Futures: a futures contract based on financial instruments or indices.

Floor Broker: a trader in the pit who executes trades for public customers of brokerage firms. A firm may use more than one floor broker and one floor broker may handle orders for many different firms.

Forward Contract: a nonstandardized contract with calls for sale or purchase of some item at some future date. Forward contracts are privately negotiated between the contracting parties and may be written in any mutually agreeable fashion.

Fundamental Analysis: analysis of the underlying supply and demand for the commodity behind the futures contract; complement to Technical Analysis or Charting.

Futures Contract: a contract traded on a registered futures exchange which calls for delivery of a standardized quantity and quality of a commodity at a specific location on a specific date in the future for a price agreed upon in the present.

Futures Exchange: an exchange registered with and licensed by the CFTC to trade futures contracts.

Gap: the imbalance between the asset and liability maturity of a financial institution; a measure of that imbalance. Gap refers to a specific time interval, such as a 30-day gap, which is the degree to which assets maturing within 30 days exceed or fall short of liabilities maturing in 30 days.

GNMA: Government National Mortgage Association; also, a mortgage pass-through security of which the interest and principal payments are guaranteed by the Government National Mortgage Association; also, a futures contract based on and calling for delivery of GNMA pass-through securities.

Hedge: a transaction in which one attempts to shift risk to someone else; in a hedge transaction the hedger deals in a futures contract for a commodity that is used in the hedger's normal course of business.

Initial Margin: the amount of margin that must be deposited in order to initiate a futures position; the amount varies from contract to contract and exchange to exchange but is normally in the $700–$4000 range.

Intermarket Spread: the simultaneous purchase and sale of futures contracts in different markets; e.g., bonds and GNMAs.

Intramarket Spread: the simultaneous purchase and sale of different contract months of the same futures contract; e.g., March and June T-bills.

Limit Move: a change in a futures contract price equal to the amount of the daily limit.

Limit Order: also known as price order; an order which specifies a buy or a sell at a given price.

Liquidity: degree of ease with which an asset can be turned into cash; in futures markets, liquidity indicates the ease of taking or closing a position—markets with large volume and large open interest have the highest liquidity.

Local: an independent trader on a commodity exchange floor who trades for his own account; he is a speculator who hopes to profit from fluctuations in prices.

Long: a futures position in which the trader buys a futures contract; a trader who takes a long position.

Long Bond: the 30-year U.S. Treasury bond, used by market participants as a "bellwether" of trends in the market.

Long Hedge: a hedge in which the trader takes a long position in futures, i.e., buys futures contracts; a long hedge insures against the risk of interest rate declines.

Maintenance Margin: the amount of margin that must be kept on deposit while a futures position is open. This varies from contract to contract and exchange to exchange but is in the range of $500–$3000.

Margin Call: a call from a broker to a customer indicating that the amount in the margin account is deficient and additional margin money must be deposited within 24 hours. In extreme market conditions it could be demanded immediately.

Market Order: an order to buy or sell commodities at the best obtainable price in the market at the present time. It must be executed immediately.

Mark-To-Market: accounting system used in the futures market; at the end of every day all contract positions are valued to reflect gains or losses that would have been made that day if the position were closed at the end of the day.

MIT Order: Market If Touched order calling for the order to become a market (immediately executable) order upon anyone trading the specified price; e.g., "buy 10 USH 68-01 MIT." Note: some exchanges (CBT) will not accept this type of order.

Momentum: a tool of technical market analysis relating to the acceleration and deceleration of prices. It is usually done by taking the difference between today's price and the price at a fixed interval in the past, e.g., 20 days. This procedure is repeated daily.

Moving Average: an average value of the price of something over a specific period of time that is continuously updated; a 12-day moving average of the value of a futures contract over the last 12 days, dropping the oldest value when a new one becomes available. Moving averages are popular in a number of technical trading systems.

Naked Writing: writing (selling) option contracts against cash rather than securities currently held; speculating in options.

Nearby: the next available delivery month for a futures contract; in February the nearby month is March if the delivery months for the contract are March, June, September, December.

Offset: to close an open futures position; i.e., sell after having previously purchased or buy after having previously sold.

Open Interest: the number of outstanding positions in a contract that have not been offset; the number reported is half the number of traders with positions since there is a long and a short for each open position.

Open Position: an outstanding position in a futures contract, one which has not been offset; if not covered prior to maturity, the trader is liable for taking or making delivery of the underlying commodities.

Option: a right (but not an obligation) to buy or sell a futures contract on or before a certain date in the future at an agreed-upon price.

Oscillators: used to represent a momentum index often revealing "overbought" and "oversold" market conditions; another tool in the technician's toolkit. There are several ways to calculate oscillators.

PCs: Participation Certificates, securities issued by the Federal Home Loan Mortgage Corporation which represent an undivided interest in a pool of mortgages held by the Corporation.

Pits: the area on the trading floor where futures contracts are traded, so called because they are tiered and resemble a pit.

Point & Figure Chart: a non-time dependent chart of price activity consisting of x's for upward movement and o's for downward movement; one of the tools of technical analysis.

Position: having a position in a futures contract means to have bought or sold the contract; same as **Open Position.**

Premium: the price paid by the buyer of an option contract.

Put: an option contract which gives the holder the right (but not the obligation) to sell a futures contract at a known price on or before a certain date.

Rate Sensitive Asset: an asset, held by a financial institution, which will experience a change in its yield over a certain time period; a new three-month T-bill is a rate sensitive asset in a six-month planning horizon but not in a one-month planning horizon.

Rate Sensitive Liability: a financial institution's liability which will experience a change in its cost over some specific time period; a newly issued six-month Money Market Certificate is rate sensitive in a one-year planning horizon but not in a one-month planning horizon.

Ratio Hedge: a hedge using a greater number of contracts to compensate for an imperfect correlation between the futures contract used in the hedge and the underlying instrument being hedged; used especially in cross hedges.

Reverse: to take a futures position opposite one previously held, e.g. a short position of 10 contracts is reversed by buying 20 contracts, leaving a long position of 10 contracts.

Reverse Conversion: an arbitrage spread consisting of a short futures contract and a long synthetic future (long a call, short a put).

Rich: an instrument selling for a price higher than that for which all normal pricing factors call; opposite of cheap.

RSA: see Rate Sensitive Asset

RSI: Relative Strength Index, a technician's indicator of up averages divided by down averages over a given period of time put into index form which, at times, may indicate market turning points.

RSL: see Rate Sensitive Liability

Scalper: a local trader on the floor of the exchange who buys and sells more or less continuously in order to profit from small moves in futures prices.

Secondary Market: the market for reselling outstanding securities, opposite of primary market in which newly created securities are sold.

Sensitivity Analysis: another term for Gap analysis; an evaluation of an institution's make-up, revealing the areas in which it is exposed to the risk of changing interest rates.

Short: to sell a futures contract; a trader who has short position in a commodity.

Short Hedge: a hedge transaction in which futures contracts are sold first and then purchased; a short hedge protects the hedger against interest rate rises, the major risk faced by financial institutions.

Spread: the simultaneous purchase of one futures contract and sale of another, either of different contract months or underlying instruments. One does this to try to profit from differing rates of change in different contract months or contracts, often due to changing market factors, i.e., rising or falling rate, shifts in yield curves, etc.

Standbys: non-binding commitments to make or take delivery of securities, commonly used in the mortgage market when dealing with the Federal National Mortgage Association (FNMA).

Stop: an order entered either to exit or to enter a market once a given price is traded. At that time the stop order becomes a market (immediately executable) order. Stops are often used to protect positions and are sometimes therefore called "stop loss" orders.

Stop Limit: a stop order entered specifying a limited range of acceptable prices between which the order may be executed; e.g., "68-01 stop limit 68-05." If it cannot be filled at any of these prices, it will not be executed.

Strike Price: the price at which an option contract may be exercised; also known as the exercise price.

Strip: a hedge transaction which involves selling or buying the same futures contract across several delivery months, e.g., selling T-bills for June, September, and December all at the same time. The objective is to lengthen the effective hedging period.

Technical Analysis: the evaluation of markets based upon mathematical and graphical (charting) analysis of price activity, volume, and open interest. Adherents of technical analysis are sometimes also known as chartists.

Variation Margin: see Maintenance Margin.

Volume: the number of futures contracts that were traded during one day's trading session; high volume indicates an active and liquid market.

Yield Curve: a graphical representation of the relationship between yield and maturity of securities in the market, sometimes thought to be an indication of market expectations of future interest rates.

Index